SILVER

Also by Mihir Bose

History and Biography
The Lost Hero: A Biography of Subhas Bose
The Aga Khans
Bollywood—A History
The Memons
False Messiah: The Life and Times of Terry Venables
Michael Grade: Screening the Image
From Midnight to Glorious Morning?

Business
How to Invest in a Bear Market
Fraud—the Growth Industry of the 1980s (co-author)
The Crash: the 1987–88 World Market Slump
Crash! A New Money Crisis: a Children's Guide to Money
Insurance: Are You Covered?
William Hill: The Man and The Business (co-author)

General Sports
The Spirit of the Game
Sports Babylon
Sporting Colours: Sport and Politics in South Africa
The Sporting Alien

Cricket
A History of Indian Cricket (Winner of the 1990 Cricket Society Literary Award)
A Maidan View—The Magic of Indian Cricket
Cricket Voices
All in a Day: Great Moments in Cup Cricket
Keith Miller: A Cricketing Biography

Football
Manchester Unlimited: The Rise and Rise of the World's Premier Football Club
Manchester DisUnited: Trouble and Takeover at the World's Richest Football Club
The World Cup: All You Need to Know
Behind Closed Doors: Dreams and Nightmares at Spurs
The Game Changer

SILVER

The Spy Who Fooled the Nazis

THE MOST REMARKABLE AGENT
OF THE SECOND WORLD WAR

MIHIR BOSE

FONTHILL

Fonthill Media Language Policy

Fonthill Media publishes in the international English language market. One language edition is published worldwide. As there are minor differences in spelling and presentation, especially with regard to American English and British English, a policy is necessary to define which form of English to use. The Fonthill Policy is to use the form of English native to the author. Mihir Bose was born in Kolkata and educated in Bombay and now lives in London; therefore British English has been adopted in this publication.

Fonthill Media Limited
Fonthill Media LLC
www.fonthillmedia.com
office@fonthillmedia.com

First published in the United Kingdom
and the United States of America 2016

British Library Cataloguing in Publication Data:
A catalogue record for this book is available from the British Library

ISBN 978-1-78155-371-8

Typeset in 10pt on 13pt Sabon
Printed and bound by CPI Group (UK) Ltd, Croydon, CR0 4YY

To Caroline and Indira, for everything.

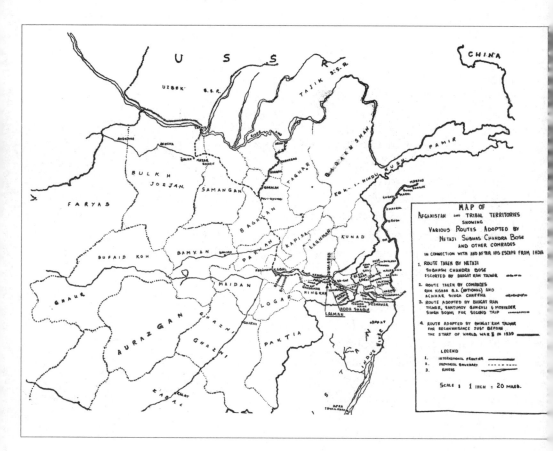

The various routes through hostile tribal areas Silver, and some of his colleagues, took during the war when they journeyed between India and Kabul. This rough map with very poor legibility is taken from Silver's (Bhagat Ram Talwar's) own book from 1976, *The Talwars of Pathan Land and Subhas Chandra's Great Escape*.

Preface

I first became aware of Silver back in the mid-1970s when I was researching *The Lost Hero*, my biography of Subhas Bose, the Indian revolutionary. We share the same surname but are not related. At that stage a comprehensive full length biography of Bose had not been written, my book was the first using recently released British and Indian documents. The material available included the story of how Silver had helped Bose escape India during the war to secure foreign help to free India. I corresponded with him but the way he told his story made me wonder if it was quite the whole truth. Was he only a spy for the Axis powers? Or had he spied for the British and the Russians as well? Indeed had the British and the Russians collaborated in running his spy operation? My questioning of senior Indian communist party officials, who had advised Silver, increased my doubts and I raised some of them in the first edition of *The Lost Hero*.

How, I wondered, was it possible that by 1942 all Silver's associates had been arrested by the British but he was free to carry on with his spying. I concluded that, 'even when we have allowed for [his] extraordinary brilliance at deception we are left with some doubts.... The record is so murky that a clear answer is impossible'.

It was while my book was with the printers that the truth began to emerge through Milan Hauner. For my book I had read Milan's Cambridge thesis on India in Axis strategy during the war. This was largely based on German sources covering the years 1939–1942 and was the first truly historical look at this fascinating and little known story of the war. As I finished by book Milan decided to convert his thesis into a book taking it up to 1945 but had to cope with the fact that under the thirty year rule it was difficult to get access to British records. Then one day, while working in the old British Public Records Office in Chancery Lane, and looking at files relating to the tribal areas on the North-West frontier of what was British India he stumbled across a carbon copy of Silver's confession to the Lahore police in November 1942.

A document concerning the Punjab police should not have been in that file. It might have got there by mistake, or maybe, because the events concerned the tribal areas. It was an amazing discovery revealing all his secrets which until then Silver had so successfully concealed. However, when Milan mentioned the find to his friend Hugh Toye, a wartime British intelligence officer who had interrogated those who fought in the army Subhas Bose organised to fight the British during the war, and written an excellent book on Bose, Toye's reaction surprised Hauner. 'Hugh got very nervous. He put gentle pressure on me not to write about it. He felt Silver had made a deal with the British about his spying and it would be wrong to breach that. Indeed he contacted the PRO and tried to close the file. I, as an independent historian, could not accept that, but I decided I would not sensationalise the story.' Hauner combined his fresh discovery with the German material he had and other material treating the subject of Silver's war-time activities with due care. When he came to write his book the Silver story formed one, fairly small, part of his 750 page book, *India in Axis Strategy*. The book has many strands and remains the most authoritative study on India's relationship with the Axis powers during the war.

I cannot thank Milan enough for his pioneering work and the help and encouragement he has continued to give me. This has included supplying me with research by the Russian historian Iurii Tikhomirov on Silver, in particular a fascinating document that Kim Philby sent to his Moscow controllers and also other significant discoveries in British archives by Eunan O'Halpin.

Many years after Hauner's find the historian Patrick French succeeded in getting the Indian Political Intelligence files open to the public. Patrick kindly directed me to the IPI files called The Bose Conspiracy which had further fascinating material on Silver and his associates; so my thanks to him.

In my revised edition of *The Lost Hero* published in 2004 I did use some of this material with a chapter devoted to 'The Man called Silver', using the code name the British had given him. But the idea of writing a full length biography of Silver came from Professor Tapan Raychaudhuri. In his foreword to my revised edition he wrote, 'This prince among spies surely deserves a biography in his own right and perhaps even a film. Hats off to a man who deceived everybody and survived the War without being hanged'. The idea this sparked led to an initial standalone article on Silver, 'Everyone's Man in Kabul', in *History Today* in 2009 and I am indebted to the encouragement that Paul Lay, the editor, gave me when I suggested it to him.

The decision to write the biography meant a further trawl through the secret documents of the SOE and other branches of the British Government now in the National Archives in Kew and also research in other archives round the world. As with all my other books during the course of research I have met some wonderful people and on this occasion it has been my pleasure to get to know Dr Sayed Wiqar Ali Shah, a great scholar on the North West Frontier Province and a man who hails from the same part of the world as Silver and knew some of the men who worked with Silver.

Richard Heller was, as ever, a wonderful sounding board and the assistance of Graham Coster and Brian Oliver was very valuable. Sharmila Chandra, who has been such a wonderful editor for two of my books dealing with India, kindly arranged for her husband to gather some valuable information from the National Archives of India in Delhi. Swapan Dasgupta opened the doors of the impenetrable Nehru Memorial Museum Library, gaining me access to the oral recording Silver gave to the library and I cannot thank him enough. I am grateful to Devi Leena Bose for persistently knocking on the doors of the NMML. I am grateful to many who responded to my requests in particular, Thaddeus Holt and Bernard O'Connor. I would also like to thank the staff at the National Archives at Kew for their help, the India Office Library and Records housed in the British Library, the Imperial War Museum, the Special Collections Service at the Museum of English Rural Life, University of Reading, the Italian Diplomatic Archives at Farnesina in Rome, the United States National Archives, Washington and College Park, the United States Navy Operations Archives, Washington Navy Yard and the Hoover Institution Library and Archives in Stanford, California. Gaetano Petraglia diligently unearthed interesting Italian material and translated them as did Jennifer Radice.

Two libraries deserve special mention. The London Library continues to be a treasure trove of many books and material and the staff are always very helpful. And so is Simon Blundell the librarian of my London club, the Reform.

Alan Sutton has been a wonderful publisher, both supportive and patient. Rose Chisholm has been a very diligent researcher and extremely inventive in suggesting solutions to many problems. I am grateful to my dear friend Susanna Majendie for introducing me to her godson, Freddie Michel, who took time off from his studies in Russia to translate some valuable material in Russian on Silver.

As ever I am indebted to my wife Caroline for the marvellous way in which she sustains my spirit, combines encouragement with a sharp awareness of what works and what is needed to reach the stated goal.

But, as always, for all the help I have received I remain responsible for the errors and omissions that may still remain.

Mihir Bose
London

October 2016

Contents

	Preface	7
	Introduction—From Cook to Spy	13
1	The Remarkable Pathan	27
2	A Rebel is Born	44
3	Learning Politics from a Bullock	57
4	The Stagehand Becomes the Main Actor	63
5	Searching the Road to Kabul	75
6	Seeking Stalin Finding Hitler	89
7	The Italian Job	101
8	Hitler, the Faqir and the Nazi Intrigues	114
9	The Phantom Italian Spy	127
10	Moscow Calling	140
11	Taking the Nazis for a Ride	153
12	More Nazi Loot in Kabul	165
13	Russia's Gift to Britain	179
14	Silver's Moscow Centre	200
15	Britain's Man	206
16	A Very Special Sahib	217
17	The Problem with Mary and Oliver	226
18	Silver and the new Great Game	240
19	Now We Have Five	257
20	Back to the Beginning	276
	Epilogue—The Unsolved Mystery	295
	Appendices:	
1	Chronology	305
2	Money given to Silver by the Axis powers	319
3	British Guide to Good Mullahs	321
4	Main Characters	323
5	Codes used in the Silver Operation by the British	329
	Endnotes	331
	Bibliography	344

Introduction
From Cook to Spy

On the afternoon of 22 February 1941, a small, clean-shaven, nondescript man, whom one British official described as 'unattractive of appearance', walked down an alleyway in Kabul and knocked on the back door of the Italian Embassy. Afghanistan was a neutral country, the war far away from its borders and, despite having started 17 months earlier, it was not quite a world war yet. The Nazis were supreme in Europe, with only Britain holding out. Hitler and Stalin, having parcelled out Poland between them, were still allies. Japan had a very fraught peace with the United States where, five weeks previously, Franklin Roosevelt had been sworn in as President for his third term, having promised 'the mothers and fathers of America' that 'your boys are not going to be sent into any foreign wars'.

The Afghan employees of the Embassy who were gathered round the back entrance having a smoke had little reason to doubt that the man seeking entrance was anything other than a local. Like many Afghans he wore the Karakuli Afghan cap, a long shirt that came down below his knees, and flowing, loose-fitting trousers. The man's mission was to see the Italian ambassador. But, aware he could not just turn up and ask to see him, he told the guards he was a cook who had been sent to work for him. The guards showed him into a high-ceilinged room where the ambassador was sitting behind a large desk framed by the Italian flag and a huge picture of the Italian dictator, Benito Mussolini.

The ambassador, who was in the middle of talking to one of his Afghan employees, was more than a little upset at seeing the man. For a start he was not in a good mood. Two weeks earlier, Hitler had sent Rommel to Libya to rescue the Italians, who had been forced to flee by Wavell's forces despite having five times more troops than the British. Like all the foreign diplomats in Kabul he dreaded unannounced visits from local Afghans, unsure whether they were spies of the government or of other embassies. He could not be sure whether this man was a spy. His mood was not improved when the man told him he had been sent by Herr Thomas, the German who ran Siemens' Kabul office. 'What for?' roared the Italian. But instead of being cowed the man replied in a very firm and determined voice, 'I don't know. I have just been asked to see you.'

There was something in the man's voice that made the Italian think this was no ordinary Afghan. He now had a good look at the man: he was small, but had a strong, wiry frame. The Ambassador picked up the phone and rang Thomas. For a few minutes the Italian and the German spoke, the Italian listening attentively to what the German was saying and, occasionally, murmuring. They spoke in German, which the ambassador, who was half German, knew well. The visitor, not knowing the language, could not understand a word, but because of the way the ambassador nodded, he sensed the conversation was serious. A few minutes later the Italian put down the phone, and asked his Afghan assistant, and the servant who had brought the man to his office, to leave. As they did so the ambassador closed the door behind them, offered a seat to his visitor and, speaking slowly in English, said, 'My name is Pietro Quaroni and I am the Ambassador of the Italian Legation in Kabul.'

The man then told Quaroni his name was Rahmat Khan, although, as we shall see, that was not his real name. He was more honest when he told the Italian that he was not an Afghan but an Indian who had arrived from India on 27 January, having made the near-200-mile journey from Peshawar to Kabul on foot, through tribal territory that separated Afghanistan from British India. Khan then explained that he had not travelled alone but had acted as guide and escort to the charismatic Indian revolutionary, Subhas Bose, who had escaped from India and now wanted to go to Berlin to seek German help to free India from British rule. Khan and Bose had established contact with the German Embassy in Kabul some weeks earlier, which is how they had been put in touch with Herr Thomas. But, despite several meetings, no firm arrangement had been made to get Bose out of Kabul. The pair were worried that the longer they stayed in Kabul the more they were exposing themselves to great danger. They had entered Afghanistan illegally, had no passport or any other papers, and had just managed to avoid being arrested by bribing an Afghan policeman. They were convinced they could not hold out much longer and feared that if they were arrested by the Afghan police they would immediately be handed over to the British. Khan's call on Quaroni was the last throw of the dice to make sure Bose secured travel documents which would help him cross the Afghan–Russian border and then, via the Soviet Union, make his way to Hitler's Germany.

Unlike the Germans, who appeared to be stalling, Quaroni proved very willing. After several meetings over the next three weeks Bose, given the passport of an Italian diplomat, was escorted over the Afghan border and put on a train to Moscow, from where he took the overnight sleeper to Berlin.

There he plotted ways to free his country, met Hitler, and eventually travelled to Japan to raise an army to fight the British. He died in a plane crash days after Japan's surrender. In India he remains a hugely controversial figure worshipped by many, some of whom still refuse to believe he died in the crash.[1] But in many ways it was what happened to the man he left behind in Kabul, Rahmat Khan, that is an even more extraordinary story. And one that has not yet been fully told.

Within days of Bose's departure for Europe, Khan the escort was converted into Khan the spy for the Italians. Since the start of the war Quaroni had been trying to find a weapon with which to strike at the British in India. Having diligently followed events in the country he was convinced India was Britain's weak link, and a blow against the jewel of the British crown would have a tremendous impact. So when Bose nominated Khan as his agent to work with the Italians, Quaroni seized the opportunity. A few months later Khan was taken over by Italy's Axis partner, Germany. But while Khan took money from both the Italians and the Germans he was no fascist, in fact a communist, and from the beginning was deceiving both countries. While initially this deception game was virtually a freelance effort, once Hitler had unleashed Operation *Barbarossa*, his invasion of the Soviet Union, Khan worked with the Russians to continue to fool the Nazis. Later still he worked for the British, who gave him the name Silver. This was a sort of British joke as there was a real Mr Silver, who was a high official based in London and involved in supervising undercover work in India.

The Germans rated him so highly that they awarded him the Iron Cross, Germany's highest military decoration, for his services to the Reich, and gave him a transmitter which he used to broadcast directly to the headquarters of Abwehr, Hitler's secret service, in Berlin. He also swindled the Axis of £2.5 million in today's money (See Appendix 2: Money given to Silver by the Axis powers). The Germans never for one moment suspected these broadcasts were fictitious military information concocted by the British in the garden of Delhi's Viceregal Palace. Before the war had ended he also deceived the Japanese, making him a quintuple agent, the only one of the war.

There were many remarkable spies in the war. The Spaniard, Juan Pujol, had 27 names, the most legendary of which was Garbo: he helped the Allies deceive the Germans on where the D-Day landings would take place, thus playing a crucial role in the success of the Allied offensive. Richard Sorge proved himself to be the Soviet Union's greatest spy, providing them with many intelligence scoops, including the fact that Hitler was about to invade Russia, although the paranoid Stalin refused to believe Sorge. Cicero, Elyesa Banza, the valet of the British ambassador to Turkey, proved to be one of Hitler's most successful spies. He provided Germans with details of British and Allied policies both on the diplomatic and military front.

What puts Silver on an altogether different level from any other Second World War spy, and makes him very special indeed, was the unique theatre in which he operated during the length of the war. Unlike Garbo, Sorge and Cicero, who essentially operated from one base—Garbo in London, Sorge in Tokyo, Cicero in Istanbul—Silver was constantly shuttling back and forth between Kabul and India. This meant dodging British and Afghan border guards and travelling through tribal territories. This is where towards the end of the nineteenth century Winston Churchill fought his first war and established his reputation as a writer of note. More than a century later the region saw more drama. Then in the aftermath of 9/11 Mullah Mohammed Omar, the Taliban leader, having refused to hand over Bin Laden to the Americans, took refuge there after being forced to flee Afghanistan by the American-led coalition that had invaded his country. Today, this area, although part of Pakistan [known as the Federally Administered Tribal Area], is essentially the domain of the Taliban and murderous Muslim Jihadis plotting the destruction of the unbelievers. In the period we are talking about, the area nominally under the control of the British was also where the British fought a relentless and often brutal campaign to supress rebellious tribes.

The Second World War is widely seen as a great fight for freedom with the British and their Allies liberating countries from Nazi occupation. But on the North West Frontier of India it was the British who were seen as the occupiers, denying freedom to tribes who had never accepted any master. The tribes generally had no political or even religious agenda. They fought the British Empire largely to assert their right to their traditional occupations of raiding and looting, or in pursuit of clan quarrels which were generations old. The British paid bribes to keep the tribes sweet and, a year after the war in the west had begun, a secret British report showed that up to 31 December 1940, the bribes paid in Waziristan, one of the tribal areas, amounted to a total of Indian rupees (INR) 248,845 with some of these allowances dating back to the 1920s and 1930s.[2] But even such bribes could not stop the tribes waging war against the British.

We shall hear more about one of these rebels, a Faqir of Ipi, of his intrigues with the Nazis and how Silver got involved. But just to provide a flavour of the terrain that Silver repeatedly crossed on foot during the war consider this fact. At the start of the Second World War a third of the Indian army was stationed at the frontier between India and Afghanistan trying to control rebellious tribes who, as the Viceroy, Lord Linlithgow, put it in October 1939, were 'not only fanatical but armed to the teeth'.[3] It cost the Government more than 15 million rupees a year to try to keep some semblance of order; at times they required both the Royal Air Force and Royal Indian Air Force to bomb villages, in addition to machine-gunning the inhabitants from armoured vehicles. However in keeping with the British sense of fair play, white and red warning leaflets, a version of football's yellow and red cards, were dropped before the bombs rained down on the villages. For Silver journeying back and forth from India to Kabul was no sport. He always had to make sure he was nowhere near the areas of the white and red leaflets.

Throughout the war Silver also operated in an area where Mullahs ruled, whom the British monitored carefully. In December 1941, 10 months after Quaroni recruited Silver to spy for the Italians, C. E. Joyce, Deputy Director of Government Intelligence at Peshawar, grading the most influential Mullahs from hostile through to friendly, produced a report that made gloomy reading for the British.[4]

The Silver story is also framed against another dimension that makes it very different to any of the other more famous spies of the war. While he shared certain characteristics with Garbo, Cicero and Sorge, there was one crucial difference. All three hailed from free countries able to shape their own destinies. Garbo and Cicero were citizens of Spain and Turkey, both of which remained neutral during the war. Sorge was a German communist, who saw his higher loyalty as helping defeat the evil regime of his country and preserve the Soviet Union. Silver was a citizen not of a free country but one ruled by the British, who at that stage had no plans to relinquish control over their jewel in the crown.

At its historic meeting in August, 1917 the British War Cabinet, presided over by Lloyd George, had estimated that it would take 500 years for Indians to learn to rule themselves. Even then, Arthur Balfour, the Foreign Secretary, told his cabinet colleagues that parliamentary democracy on the Westminster model, as adopted by Australia and other white dominions, would be too specialised for the Indians as they were not of the same race as the British.[5] Lord Birkenhead, who was Secretary of State for India in the 1920s, a crucial period that shaped what led to 1947 and the eventual partition of India, had in a book forecasting what the world would look like in 2030, expressed his firm conviction that even then Britain would have to rule India.

British rule in India was, of course, always a curious phenomenon. For a start there was not one but two Indias; British India and Princely India. Princely India was a third of the Indian land mass, contained nearly 40 per cent of the country's population, and under the internal control of the Indian princes. British laws did not apply and the railways the British had introduced did not extend there. By contrast, in British India only a few thousand sahibs, the term for white men in India, ruled millions of Indians. In 1931, when Silver was 23 years old and already active in politics, the British undertook their last full-scale census of India and it emerged that out of a total Indian population of almost 353 million, the number of British citizens was 155,555, less than half a per cent of the population. And this 155,555 was also a very small proportion of the then total British population back home, more than

46 million. So around 99 per cent of the UK population in 1931 had no first-hand experience of India; it held little interest for most people in Britain, and no serving British Prime Minister visited India during British rule. Clement Attlee, then a backbench MP, was reluctantly persuaded to go to India in 1928, but came back to find he had been forgotten by the Commons staff. After his first speech in the House on his return, Hansard misspelled his name.

That such small numbers of whites could rule such a huge brown country much impressed foreign rulers, particularly the two foremost dictators, Stalin and Hitler. In 1939, after the Nazi–Soviet pact was signed, Stalin told Hitler's Foreign Ambassador, Joachim von Ribbentrop, that 'it was ridiculous that a few hundred Englishmen should dominate India'. For Ribbentrop's master, this was a source of great admiration as it demonstrated the power of the white races. In November, 1937 Hitler had told Lord Halifax that his favourite film was *The Lives of a Bengal Lancer*, a film featuring Gary Cooper and set in the North West Frontier. 'I like this film,' the Führer told the British Foreign Secretary, 'because it depicted a handful of Britons holding a continent in thrall. That is how a superior race must behave and the film is a compulsory viewing for the SS.'

The British knew they ruled India because millions of Indians collaborated with British rule. More Indian sepoys, soldiers, had died securing Clive's victory in Plassey that launched the empire than British. The British could never have held on to India during the revolt of 1857 but for the support of their Indian collaborators. But, sensitive to the use of the word 'collaboration', the British always described these Indians as 'loyalists'. In this way the occupation by a foreign power was made to look like a natural state of affairs. Interestingly, Indians now describe them as 'camp followers' of the British as if to classify them as collaborators, even in independent India, is a step too far. Silver wrestled with this issue of loyalty, becoming a spy of the British having seen the inside of a British jail for his participation in the Indian freedom movement, and his beloved older brother executed after a botched attempt to assassinate the British Governor of Punjab.

However the British, aware that many Indians were also hostile to their rule, had built up sophisticated intelligence organisations, both in India and in Britain to snuff out any threat to its rule. In London there was the Indian Political Intelligence, set up just before the outbreak of the First World War, to monitor Indian anarchist activities in England directed against the Raj. Staffed by British police officers it was located in the same Whitehall buildings as MI5 and after Indian independence subsumed into MI5. Its head, Philip Vickery, signed himself as IPI just as the head of MI5 was 'K' and that of MI6 'C'. Vickery, who had served in the Indian police and had protected the King Emperor's cream 'bedroom tent' every night during the Durbar held in Delhi in 1911 for King George V, also had a connection with Silver. During the

First World War Vickery had foiled an attempt by Indian exiles in Canada to destabilise the Raj, winning an OBE and later promotion to head of IPI. Many years later the Indian movement that had organised this failed attempt against the Raj went on to create the political party that Silver joined.

The historian Patrick French writes:

Indian Political Intelligence occupied the unique position of operating from London, a privilege denied to any other imperial or dominion intelligence agency. Its financial resources were supplied 'from secret service funds appropriated for that purpose from Indian revenues', which meant that Indian taxpayers paid for their own surveillance.

It had powers to ban books considered subversive from entering India. IPI's definition of subversive material was surprisingly broad, so that many unremarkable works of literature could only enter India by being smuggled through French or Portuguese colonial territories.[6]

This was the organisation that the real Mr Silver worked for and, as we shall see, he had to assess what Silver, the spy, was doing. Throughout British rule many of those who worked in the Special Branch, MI5 and SIS had served in India and had often begun their careers there. In some ways India was a sort of training ground for intelligence work in Britain. Silver in India came under the overall control of IPI's counterpart the Indian Intelligence Bureau, known by its acronym IB. By the time Silver appeared IB was well established, working under the auspices of the Viceroy and the Home Department of the Government of India, and headed by Sir Denys Pilditch. It was Pilditch who made the unflattering comments on Silver's looks which we have quoted but was later so impressed by his work that he even tried to claim that IB had recruited Silver to work as a spy, a palpable falsehood.

But if Silver was not a Pilditch creation his organisation did control a vast network of spies and informers in India who kept detailed files on anyone considered potentially hostile to British rule. IB agents had penetrated all the important Indian political organisations and regularly intercepted and opened the mail of anyone considered a suspect. The IB files were considered so sensitive that they were destroyed just before the British left India.

The war made the need for security all the more important. Gandhi's call for the British to 'Quit India' sparked such a major revolt that on 20 March, 1943, Major General Rob Lockhart, Military Secretary in the India Office, wrote in a secret note: 'For the duration of the War, and probably for some time after, India must be considered as an occupied and hostile country'. Linlithgow reported to Churchill that it was 'by far the most serious rebellion since that of 1857, the gravity of which we have so far concealed from the world for reasons of military security'.[7] To add to British problems the war brought the Americans and Chinese to India and the British, always sensitive to any foreign presence in their crown jewel, set up intelligence operations to monitor the activities of their allies. This included intercepting all items of mail addressed to American consulates in India, sometimes censoring them, and planting bugs in their offices. In August 1944 the American consul wrote to his government that 'representatives of the United States government in India should bear in mind at all times that they are functioning in a police state'. The British had allowed the OSS [Office of Strategic Services], the Americans' wartime secret service that later became the CIA, to operate in India, but one American OSS officer observed: 'We had been warned in Delhi that the British were past masters at intrigue and had planted spies in all American agencies to piece together information'.[8] In order to counter this, in February 1944, the OSS established its own counter-espionage unit, X-2 Branch, in India. To keep a check on what the Chinese were doing the government of India set up a 'Chinese intelligence wing', headed by a man who had been a medical missionary in Sinkiang in the 1930s. This unit intercepted mail between the United States and China.

This was not all that made the background of Silver's spy career very different to that of Garbo in London, Cicero in Istanbul, Sorge in Tokyo or any other spy of the war. Silver also had to cope with how the war impacted on India. The only fighting India saw was in 1944, when Japan invaded. Yet during the war three and a half million Indian civilians died. (The comparable figure for UK civilian deaths is 67,200). This was during the Great Bengal famine. Famines were hardly unknown in India, and during British rule there had been many. But this one, in the summer of 1943, was the worst in twentieth-century south Asia history. It was caused not by lack of food, but by dreadful incompetence on the part of British Raj officials and the local Bengal government, which was run by Indians. With Japan at the gates of India, the British feared a Japanese invasion and instituted a scorched earth policy in Bengal where boats, the primary form of transport in a land crisscrossed with rivers, were destroyed. There was also a 'rice denial' policy, which involved throwing thousands of tons of rice into the rivers and soldiers being ordered to set fire to stacks of rice.[9] The indifference of the British to the famine was exemplified by Linlithgow, who could find no time to visit Bengal during the famine. Yet in April 1943, with corpses mounting in the streets of Calcutta, he found time to hunt tigers in the Himalayan resort of Dehra Dun, near Delhi, while riding an elephant. The whole thing was worsened by a reluctance by the British War Cabinet to divert shipping to take food to India.

Here, the influence of Lord Cherwell, a close Churchill adviser, played a huge part. As the historian Lawrence James has put it, Cherwell 'held all non-white people in contempt'. He had once been to India, but was by so horrified at the prospect of being touched by blacks that he took along his English valet.

Cherwell, according to historians Christopher Bayly and Tim Harper, 'seems to have thought that the Bengalis were a weak race and that overbreeding and eugenic unfitness were the basic reasons for scarcity'. Cherwell's influence on Churchill was demonstrated at the War Cabinet meeting of 10 November 1943. Leo Amery, Secretary of State for India recorded:

> Winston, after a preliminary flourish on Indians breeding like rabbits and being paid a million a day by us for doing nothing about the war, asked Leathers [Lord Frederick Leathers, Minister of War Transport] for his view.[10]

This view was transport could not be diverted. It is interesting to note how Guy Liddell, MI5's Director of Counter Espionage during the war, saw the famine from London. His diary entry of 19 August 1943 reads:

> The distribution of food is not good and the situation is aggravated by the fact that the Indians would sooner lie down and die of starvation than eat anything that they are not accustomed to. Many have died, and we of course get the blame.[11]

At that very moment people were dying in their hundreds on the streets of Calcutta and were so desperate for food that they begged not so much for rice, but *fana*, the water in which it was cooked and which has some nutritional value. Liddell could only have formed his impression of what was happening in Calcutta because he had a set, preconceived, stereotypical notion about Indians. Important as it is to resist the temptation to view the past from today's perspective, Liddell's view of the famine does not sound very different to how a Nazi might have reacted to Jewish suffering. Yet Liddell knew all about Silver and was a great admirer of his work. However, that a man like Liddell, who was held in wide esteem, could come to such a conclusion about Silver's fellow Indians gives us a flavour of the times and frames the background against which Silver operated. Silver during his spying career had to cope with the consequences of the famine and we shall see how he reacted when his German paymasters asked him to capitalise on the British responsibility for this tragedy.

Silver's story also challenges the widely accepted version of the Second World War being a straightforward story of the good Allies versus the evil Nazis. While the Allies had every right to claim the moral high ground in the war, in much of Asia they also had skeletons in their cupboards. To ignore that, as George Orwell pointed out in his brilliant essay of the same name, is a case of 'Not Counting Niggers'. Orwell, writing two months before the war began, pointed out that all references to Britain and France as democracies ignored the fact that they also had huge colonial empires:

... The unspoken clause is always 'not counting Niggers'... What we always forget is the overwhelming bulk of the British proletariat does not live in Britain, but in Asia and Africa. It is not in Hitler's power, for instance, to make a penny an hour a normal industrial wage: it is perfectly normal in India and we are at great pains to keep it so. One gets some idea of the real relationship of England and India when one reflects that the per capita income in England is something over £80 and in India about £7. It is quite common for an Indian coolie's legs to be thinner than the average Englishman's arms. And there is nothing racial in this, for well-fed members of the same race are of normal physique; it is due to simple starvation. This is the system we all live on and which we denounce when there seems to be no danger of it being altered.[12]

As the historian, E. H. Carr, writing in September 1939, pointed out, the idea that all human beings should have the same rights was a novel, untested, notion:

It is only in recent time that there has begun to even be a presumption that all inhabitants of a territory are members of the community. Jews in Germany and the coloured inhabitants of the Union of South Africa are today not regarded as members of the community. In the United States, most white Southerners would hesitate to admit that the Negroes are members of the community in the same sense as they are themselves.[13]

Yet even for Carr this was not very significant, as it merited no more than a footnote in his book.

All the European democracies ruling over their vast colonial empires went to war making it clear the much advertised fight for freedom from Nazi tyranny did not extend to their non-white colonies. During the war Churchill told the House of Commons that he was not going to preside over the dissolution of the Empire. That was not a British war goal. Australia said its White Australia policy was sacrosanct, and De Gaulle, leading the free French, summed up the view of many in France that at the end of the war France would resume, indeed strengthen, its prewar colonial rule. The Dutch and the Belgians took the same view and the Portuguese held on to their empire until the 1970s. When, in 1960, India sent in its army to liberate Goa the Portuguese turned to its oldest ally Britain to help stop 'the invasion' of a territory it regarded as part of metropolitan Portugal. Even the United States, founded on a hatred of empires, had a colony, the Philippines. And while it had promised freedom to the Philippines, it had also brutally put down a Filipino freedom movement, reference to which formed part of Donald Trump's Presidential campaign in 2016. To complicate matters there was a huge contradiction in America's China policy.

After Pearl Harbor the US Congress praised China for its 'gallant resistance' against the Japanese. But the Chinese themselves were not welcome in the US, so much so that even Chinese seamen taking shore leave in the US were arrested for fear they may settle in the country. Between 1882 and 1913, 15 laws, or parts of US law, had mentioned the Chinese as undesirable immigrants. The war did lead to a nationwide debate about these racist laws and in 1943 the US allowed a maximum of 105 Chinese to enter the country every year, and those Asians already there were now eligible for naturalisation, something that had not been allowed since 1790. Even then Congress had to overcome protests from the American Legion, the Veterans of Foreign Wars, and the American Federation of Labor. And while Roosevelt championed Indian freedom, much to Churchill's fury, he was Commander-in-Chief of an army that was racially segregated: white American troops refused to mix with the 'Negro' soldiers both in Britain and in India when they were stationed there.

This background is important in Silver's case because, despite the fact that the Second World War was truly global like no other, the great majority of wartime histories reflect the white view of the world: whether they are western Europeans, eastern Europeans, Russians or Americans. Despite the fact that a million Indians fought for the British—the largest volunteer force in the war— you will not find the name of an Indian commander in these histories. The simple reason is that, while many Indian soldiers fought with great bravery in many fields and won honours, there was no Indian commander. The highest ranking Indian officer, and that towards the end of the war, was Kodandera Madappa Cariappa, a Temporary Lieutenant-Colonel. It was only after Indian independence that he became the first Indian commander-in-chief.

The Second World War did give Indians more chances in the Army, but that is because the First World War gave none. During the 1914–1919 war there was no King's Commissioned Officer for, as Lord Roberts, who had been commander-in-chief in India, had put it:

> Native officers can never take the place of British officers ... Eastern races, however brave and accustomed to war, do not possess the qualities that go to make good leaders of men ... I have known many natives whose gallantry and devotion could not be surpassed, but I have never known one who would not have looked to the youngest British officer for support in time of difficulty and danger.[14]

In the inter-war years Indians were finally admitted to Sandhurst, the officer training centre in Surrey. But this caused much anguish, with Sir Henry Rawlinson, who helped to plan the Battle of the Somme, noting in his diary: 'People are frightened, old officers say they won't send their sons to serve under natives'. All this meant that on 1 October 1939, there were 396 Indian officers in the Indian army in comparison with nearly 4,000 British officers, a ratio of 10.1:1. By 1 September 1945 British officers still vastly outnumbered Indians but the ratio of British to Indian was now 4.1:1.

It was one thing having Indian officers, but another for these officers to command British troops. In 1942 when Wavell, Commander-in-Chief in India, requested that the few Indians who commanded British troops should be allowed to discipline them it provoked a furious response from Churchill about 'the poor, much harassed British soldier having to face the extra humiliation of being ordered about by a brown man'. The British War Cabinet meeting of 27 July recorded that a War Office representative agreed, saying that the 'face of the white man in the East is low enough and this is not the time to do it'.[15] With Gandhi planning to call for the British to leave—his Quit India movement was launched within weeks—the official went on to say that this was not the time to enhance the power of Indian officers.

Here again we have an interesting Silver connection. Wavell recruited Peter Fleming to head intelligence in India; Fleming controlled Silver and Wavell himself often briefed Silver. While Fleming met Churchill and once, on a return visit to Britain, had lunch with him there is no evidence he mentioned Silver to him. Had he done so it would have been fascinating to know what Churchill, who was keen on intelligence, made of this particular brown man? Would he have considered him an exception to his general distrust for brown people?

The war produced many stories of Indian officers constantly having to break down ceilings, such as being able to share a swimming pool in a local club with the memsahibs, the wives of their white colleagues. In one amusing incident, after an Indian officer found that an English woman splashed to the edge of the pool whenever an Indian entered the water as if she had seen a shark, they decided to band together and play a game. 'When an English girl went in, we went in. And when she got out, we got out. So after a while she got tired of all this going in and coming out and there was no problem'.[16]

Hard as it is to imagine such a world today, that was the wartime world for many Indians who had anything to do with whites. In his spy career, Silver interacted not only with the white rulers of his country, but also with whites from many nationalities. He not only coped with them but carved out a spying career during which he was never seen as inferior to a white man or woman. Indeed he did so well that Michael Howard, the doyen of British historians of wartime intelligence work, wrote:

> India had a figure comparable with Garbo himself; comparable if not in inventiveness, then certainly in intelligence, personality and the dominance he established over his control ... [he was] a kind of Lawrence of Arabia, a master of disguise, held in numinous respect by the hill tribes of the north-west frontier.[17]

This praise for Silver cannot be over-emphasised, for in the histories of the Second World War no other Indian on the Allied side is so singled out for praise. Silver parleyed with the British, Italians, Germans, and Russians confident in his own ability and never doubting he was their equal. The fact that he was a brown man from a country held in colonial subjugation by a white country made no difference to him. He could deceive anyone and often did, even, at times, the Russians and the British whites he worked for. Yet before the war had started he had never even met a white man. So from where did he get the confidence to think of himself as the equal of a white man and, what is more, go on to prove himself to be so? Given that as Liddell had said 'India [was] a second-class war area and had to wait for everything'[18] it is truly extraordinary that Silver emerged as such an outstanding spy.

Some commentators, in order to explain this Silver riddle, have described him as educated. In fact he was not. He was a Matriculate, which can only very charitably be described as the equivalent of passing a few English GCSEs. English was not his first language, he spoke broken English, and he knew no other European tongue. Nor did he have distinguished looks. When, during the war, Major Peter Thorne of the Grenadier Guards first set eyes on Silver he was struck by the fact that he was short and lean.[19] He came from a small, remote village of about 1,000 people, which gave no hint of having been touched by modern, western civilisation and progress. There were none of the comforts of life that his white contemporaries took for granted. But then, almost everything in Silver's life was astonishing, starting with his most unusual upbringing. For a start the name he gave Quaroni, Rahmat Khan, had suggested to the Italian that he was Muslim. He was not.

Silver the spy proved the great deceiver of the Second World War. And in many ways his upbringing, and where he grew up, was the starting point of this deception.

The Remarkable Pathan

Silver, whose real name was Bhagat Ram Talwar, always insisted that his upbringing was like no other. He was brought up to oppose the oppression of both the rich landlords and the British conquerors of his country and, if necessary, use violence to free his land. Yet his family were well-off landowners and his own father, who instilled in him the desire to see India liberated, worked both with other landlords and the British, indeed was even commended by the British. By the time Silver came to write about his life and times, at the age of 68, with India about to celebrate 30 years as an independent country, he clearly felt the need for a great deal of embellishment.

The starting point of Silver's distinctiveness was that he was born and brought up a Hindu in the north-west region of the subcontinent, bordering Afghanistan, where the overwhelming majority were Muslims, Sunnis of the Hanafi school of Islam. While the region has generated copious writing, with British writers fascinated by both the place and the people, almost nothing has been written about the Hindus who lived there. So much so that the very word Pathan, as the people of this region are called, has come to denote a Muslim. [The inhabitants of this area can also be called Pakhtuns or Pashtuns, the terms now used in Afghanistan and Pakistan, with Indians still using Pathan. Silver found these names interchangeable. He titled his autobiography *The Talwars of Pathan Land* but the very first chapter is called, 'The Pakhtun Land and Her People'. In this book I have stuck with Pathan.] Reading the voluminous British literature set in the region, a Hindu Pathan, which is how Silver saw himself, seems an absurd invention.

So consider the writings of two great Englishmen, both of whom were Nobel laureates in literature and had first-hand knowledge of the area: Rudyard Kipling and Winston Churchill. Some of Kipling's best writing was inspired by the land of the Pathans, including his famous narrative poem, 'The Ballad of East and West' and his memorable story 'The Man Who Would Be King', which was later made into a gripping film. Kipling rarely missed anything.

His sharp journalistic eye, combined with his ability to convert life in British India into wonderful fiction, deservedly gives him the reputation as the best writer in the English language to have emerged during the British rule of the subcontinent; yet Hindus do not feature in either his journalism or in much of his fiction set in the land of the Pathans. And even when the odd Hindu pops up in this part of the world Kipling makes it quite clear he does not belong.

His story 'The Head of the District' is about a Hindu, Grish Chunder Dé, transferred from Bengal in the east to take over a district in the North West Frontier, running away at the first sign of trouble with the tribes. The result is that an Englishman has to take over from the cowardly Hindu to help restore order. Kipling admired Muslims, and found the Hindu religion incomprehensible. He contemptuously dismissed the great Hindu epics *Ramayana* and *Mahabharata*, calling the latter 'hopeless, aimless diffuse drivel [tempered with puerile obscenity]',[1] books that Silver, like all Hindu children, knew well. He would have judged Silver's claims to be a Pathan as yet another Hindu fantasy, something for which, or so Kipling believed, Hindus had a great propensity.

Like Kipling, Winston Churchill, for whom Silver worked during the war, would also have been horrified by the thought that he was a Hindu. In 1945, after his return from Yalta, where Churchill, Franklin Roosevelt and Joseph Stalin decided the post-war future of the world, the British Prime Minister had dinner with his Downing Street secretary, John Colville, and Arthur Harris, head of Bomber Command. Colville's diary entry of 23 February 1945 records Churchill's thoughts about the Hindus:

> The PM said the Hindus were a foul race 'protected by their mere pullulation from the doom that is their due' and he wished Bert Harris could send some of his surplus bombers to destroy them.[2]

Three years earlier Churchill had told Ivan Mikhailovich Maisky, the Soviet ambassador in London, that, should the British be forced to leave India:

> Eventually, the Moslems will become master, because they are warriors, while the Hindus are windbags. Yes, windbags! Oh, of course, when it comes to fine speeches, skilfully balanced resolutions and legalistic castles in the air, the Hindus are real experts! They're in their element! When it comes to business, when something must be decided on quickly, implemented, executed—here the Hindus say 'pass'. Here they immediately reveal their internal flabbiness.[3]

Had Churchill ever met Silver it is hard to see how he could ever have accepted he was really a Hindu.

Churchill's contrasting views of the Hindus and Muslims had been formed half a century before when he had fought his first war not far from where Silver was born. Churchill had taken part in what was called 'a frontier war' with the British, putting down a rebellion by Pathans in the Swat Valley, now part of Pakistan. The war formed the subject of the first of his many books: *The Story of the Malakand Field Force*. The Hindus do not feature in the book and while Churchill is critical of the Muslims he admired their courage. The book provides graphic details of the 'fanaticism' of the 'Mad Mullah' ready to kill the 'infidels', presenting the British as the forces of good against what we would now call Islamic fundamentalism. The war was brutal and the British burned rebel Pathan villages, which Churchill had no problems justifying:

> ... I invite the reader to examine the question of the legitimacy of village-burning for himself. A camp of a British brigade, moving at the order of the Indian government and under the acquiescence of the people of the United Kingdom, is attacked at night. Several valuable and expensive officers, soldiers and animals are killed and wounded. The assailants retire to the hills. Thither it is impossible to follow them. They cannot be caught. They cannot be punished. Only one remedy remains—their property must be destroyed. Their villages are made hostages for their good behaviour. They are fully aware of this, and when they make an attack on a camp or convoy they do it because they have considered the cost and think it worthwhile. Of course, it is cruel and barbarous, as is much else in war, but it is only an unphilosophic mind that will hold it legitimate to take a man's life and illegitimate to destroy his property.[4]

Despite this, as he gazed down on the destroyed Mohmand villages and their trampled crops, he found much to admire in the Muslims:

> ... it would be unjust and ungenerous to deny to the people of the Mamund [the spelling then used] Valley, that reputation for courage, tactical skill and marksmen which they have so well deserved. During an indefinite period they had brawled and fought, in the unpenetrated gloom of barbarism. At length they struck a blow at civilisation, and civilisation will yet ungrudgingly admit that they are a brave and warlike race.[5]

As we shall see during the war Silver walked through the tribal territories of the Mohmands on 12 occasions between 1941 and 1945 while making the journey from Peshawar to Kabul, and each time deceived the tribals into believing that, far from being a Hindu 'windbag' full of 'internal flabbiness', he was actually very much a member of the 'brave and warlike race' of Muslims.

Churchill's sentiments regarding the brave Muslims were universally shared by British officials who got to know the region. Mountstuart Elphinstone, a classical scholar who led the first serious mission to Afghanistan in 1808, made no secret he preferred the Islamic faith over that of the superstitious Hindus and wrote, 'They have also a degree of curiosity which is a relief habituated to the apathy of the Indian." He went on to say, "I know of no people in Asia who have fewer vices or are less voluptuous or debauched." For all the talk of the great civilising mission of imperial rule British officials were happy that none of this 'brave and warlike race' wanted to be 'civilised' or have anything to do with British education, let alone western values and ideas. Four years after Silver's birth Beatrice Webb and her husband, Sidney Webb, visited Peshawar and recorded how the British officials saw the uneducated Muslim Pathans:

We are amused at the universal praise of the wild Pathans (Afridis and Afghans) of these parts. Everyone says they are fine fellows, far superior to the Hindoos! [then a common spelling for the Hindu]. We learn on cross-examination they are cruel and treacherous, shockingly addicted to unnatural vice and habitually given to stealing each other's wives; that murder and robbery are so common as noted as not to be deemed crimes; that the men do little work, leaving the agriculture and the care of their goats mostly to the women and boys; and that the only occupation considered worthy of manhood is the promiscuous shooting at each other, taken unawares, which they call war. When we ask why a people is admired which breaks nearly every Commandment, and is apparently of no earthly use in the universe, we are told they are fine manly fellows, 'good sportsmen', with a sense of humour! Verily our English standards are peculiar. The fact is the British officer likes them because (1) they admire and respect him and his special qualities; (2) they make good soldiers under him; and (3) they in no way compete with him or 'claim equality' or excel in directions in which he feels himself deficient. When we ask a thoughtful Civilian whether he sees any reason to believe that even in a couple of centuries, the Pathan will have developed into anything like a civilized people, or into anything else of use in the world, he is bound to admit there is no sign of any such a possibility.[6]

It is clear from Webb's journal that the British who administered that area did not tell them that there were any Hindus there. Olaf Caroe, the renowned British administrator, who like so many Britons fell in love with the Pathans and wrote what is still considered the classic history of the Pathans, briefly mentions the Hindus, but merely as people who had many centuries earlier been part of the region but had then been conquered by the invading forces of Islam and either killed or converted to the faith of their conqueror. In the

1930s Silver, as we shall see, played a part in helping a secular party get power in the North West Frontier, the first time and only time a secular party has ever exercised control in that part of the world. It was allied to the Congress, the main nationalist party in India. The Congress, though secular, was Hindu-dominated, not surprising since India is predominantly a Hindu country. And a bewildered Caroe wrote: 'It is hard to see how the Pathan tradition could reconcile itself for so long to the Hindu leadership, by so many regarded as smooth-faced, pharisaical and double-dealing'.[7]

But, unnoticed by the British, a small group of these 'smooth-faced, pharisaical, double-dealing' Hindus had survived in the region for centuries. They were Silver's ancestors and for the most part they had also lived in harmony with the Muslims and often controlled the trade in many of the small villages and towns of the province. Indeed the Hindus and Muslims even combined against oppressive Muslim landlords. There were, of course, limits to how close the two communities could become. So there was little or no intermarriage, reflecting the fact that, in the subcontinent, living together nearly always stops at the threshold of the bedroom.

This, then, was the wider background of the land where Silver was born in November, 1908. This made him 17 months younger than Peter Fleming, his eventual spymaster. The contrast in the lives of these two men, who went on to form such a remarkable partnership during the Second World War, could not have been greater. We know everything about the birth of the Englishman. He was born at 10 minutes to midnight on 31 May 1907 in Green Street, off Park Lane in London's Mayfair, to rich parents who had two other properties, including a large Oxfordshire estate. We do not even know the date in November when Silver emerged into the world. 'Sometime' was the best he could remember years later. Fleming was born at the heart of the capital of then the greatest empire in the world; Silver's birthplace, Ghalla Dher, was a little-known outpost of the empire, and Silver's parents did not register his birth. That was simply not done then in that part of the world, so there is no birth certificate to confirm the details of his birth, merely what has been passed down verbally by family members. However, Silver and Fleming had one thing in common: their mothers both produced boys in quick succession. Almost exactly a year after Peter came Ian, the creator of James Bond, and by 1913 Eve Fleming had produced two more sons. Eve Fleming was universally described as 'strikingly beautiful'; Winston Churchill called her a 'flamingo' and Augustus John painted her repeatedly, though Fleming's biographer feels he always showed her eyes having 'a most disconcerting look of calculation'.[8]

There was never any question of any painter sitting down in front of an easel to paint Silver's mother, Mathura Devi, and we do not know how she looked in her youth. The only picture we have of her is of a shrivelled old woman, tight-lipped, perhaps to conceal the fact she has lost all her teeth, and looking both surprised and vacant as she stood before the camera. But, compared to Eve, she was a child-producing factory: nine sons and two daughters, almost at nine-monthly intervals.

Ghalla Dher is a small village, a dozen miles from Nowshera, the nearest town, and 35 miles from Peshawar, the capital of what the Pakistanis now call the Khyber Pakhtunkhwa, Land of the Pashtuns of the Khyber. In 1908 the area was known as the North West Frontier Province [NWFP], a new province created four years before Silver's birth by the then Viceroy, Lord Curzon, by taking a chunk of land from the Punjab. This was part of Curzon's great plan to deal with Afghanistan and also the tribal territories that separated Afghanistan from British India. By the time Silver was born the British, who during their rule fought three unsuccessful and very costly wars to subdue and conquer the country, had given up all hopes of conquering Afghanistan. Their main concern was to maintain the peace between the tribal areas and the newly created NWFP. These areas were populated by tribes who had historically raided the plains of India and they saw no reason to stop just because the British now ruled India. The result, as Beatrice Webb put it, was that the British had 'settled down to a policy of mingled bribery and reprisals',[9] paying tribesmen to maintain order within the tribal areas, with British troops withdrawn from the areas but stationed close by and ready to go in at short notice to maintain order. So at Nowshera the British had a big military cantonment, a huge army camp of Indian soldiers commanded by British officers.

The wars the British fought with the tribes were known as the frontier wars and in 1897, eleven years before Silver's birth, Churchill, then a second lieutenant in the 4th Hussars, had come to Nowshera to fight his own 'frontier war'. Churchill thought Nowshera sounded more than a passable imitation of 'nowhere' and describes how the Malakand Field Force travelled from Nowshera to the Malakand Pass in *tongas*, small pony-driven carts. During his journey to the front he saw 'much beating of galled and dilapidated ponies'. By the time Silver was born Nowshera was not quite nowhere; planes had arrived and Risalpur, four miles from Nowshera, would soon become one of the largest British air bases in the area. Along with this show of military force the British had also brought the railways and for some of the journey from Nowshera to Ghalla Dher there was a train. But at Raskhail, five miles north of Risalpur, the line stopped and the only way to reach Ghalla Dher from there was on foot or by cart, very similar to the one Churchill had travelled on.[10] By the early years of the twentieth century the British had been ruling India for almost 150 years but a visitor to Ghalla Dher would have struggled to find any evidence of western civilisation. The 700 homes were what Indians called *kutcha*—mud houses—with only a couple of brick-and-mortar houses. Time had stood still and this was a village where poor peasants tilled the land, which was all owned by the Nawab of Toru, the local ruler.[11] However, unlike the other villagers Silver's family had not always lived there and were what we would call economic migrants, Silver's great, great grandfather, Sardar Jassa Singh, having migrated to the village from the family's original home in Bhera-Miani in neighbouring Punjab. Though this was a 500-mile-long westward trek Jassa Singh had shrewdly judged that Ghalla Dher would provide him a very good living.

He was a farmer and a good shot. The Muslim ruler of the area, the Nawab Qader Khan of Toru, needed men who could subdue the 'dacoits', armed gangs of marauders and outlaws who infested his small kingdom. Khan's choice of a Hindu might seem impossible to us but it demonstrated how back in the nineteenth century Muslim rulers found Hindus useful, and also that not all Hindus were traders. Jassa Singh did so well he was given land and became a rich landowner. It is possible that it was Jassa Singh's success in acting as the military arm of the Nawab that gave Silver his family name of Talwar, as the word in Urdu, and other Indian languages, means sword. In his memoir Silver, the dedicated communist, did not denounce his great grandfather's wealth instead saying:

> ... due to his honesty and sociable nature [Jassa Singh] was widely popular among the people of the area. Even the poor tenants of the Nawab would sometimes come to him with their complaints and take from him medicines about which, it seems, he had some knowledge.[12]

Jassa Singh's son, Diwan Chand, built on his father's fortunes, but his growing wealth did not please Qader Khan the Nawab, or his two brothers Mohabat and Karim. He was, says Silver, a 'notorious bully', using the protection provided by the British to terrorise and plunder. However, he had to wait until Qader's death and Mohabat taking over before showing his hand. The word Mohabat in Urdu means love and, while the new ruler ostensibly lived up to his name, one evening in the dead of the night Karim and his gang arrived at Diwan Chand's house. As Silver tells the story what followed was a Pathan version of a classic Western. A gang member lured Diwan Chand out of his house on the pretext that his father was ill and needed urgent medical attention. When he emerged he was brutally assaulted and the gang raided the house, seeking his two-and-a-half-year-old son, Gurudasmal, Silver's father. Fortunately his mother, Laxmi Devi, had divined the killers' intentions and hid her son under a heap of cotton clothes in the corner of the room. She then told Karim Khan that Gurudasmal had been taken by her sister to the next village. The gang, which by then had discovered the vast hoard of jewellery and ornaments Diwan Chand had accumulated, did not look hard for the child and never bothered to lift up the mound of cotton garments. Diwan

Chand was still alive when they left and Laxmi Devi, helped by members of her family, managed to get him to the hospital in Mardan. But he died three days later. And while saving Gurudasmal's life was a consolation, Laxmi Devi was now faced with the delicate problem of bringing him up in a society where life for a widow was never a happy one.

Fortunately for Gurudasmal his sister and brother-in-law stepped in to take charge of his upbringing. They also managed Diwan Chand's still considerable estate and, when Gurudasmal came to maturity, happily handed it over to him. Gurudasmal grew up as a strict disciplinarian with a high moral sense of right and wrong, and one of Silver's most painful childhood memories was of stealing flowers from a neighbour's field. His father severely admonished him not only for stealing but also for spoiling a beautiful garden. Silver does not tell us whether this also involved a beating, something that would have been quite common then. But even had there been physical punishment it did nothing to dim Silver's love for his father:

> He had a strong and impressive personality and played a dominant role in moulding the characters of his sons. His personality, strength of character and stature in society would never allow them to stray from the right path. He kept a sharp eye on them to ensure that they grew up as useful and honest citizens of the country and kept them under strict discipline.[13]

Like his father, Gurudasmal had to deal with dacoits, though these were not brothers of the Nawab but local gangs. His answer was to form a sort of unofficial police force with his Muslim friend, Mohammad Azam Khan. This Hindu–Muslim alliance proved so successful that several dacoits, all of them Muslims, were caught. That in the early years of the twentieth century Khan had no problems joining forces with a Hindu to fight fellow Muslims to bring peace to the area shows how different was the world Silver grew up in to the one we know. A century later the area is dominated by the Taliban and a byword for Muslim jihadists who could never imagine forming such an alliance with the *kaffir*, infidel, Hindu. What is also interesting is that, just as his grandfather Jassa Singh had worked with the local ruler, Gurudasmal had no problems engaging with the overall ruler of India, the British. So the dacoits apprehended by Gurudasmal were handed over to the police force that the British had set up and it was the British-established courts that sentenced these men to long years of imprisonment. 'The government', writes Silver, 'highly appreciated the services of Gurudasmal in helping to rid the locality of this scourge of dacoity and issued him licences for keeping fire-arms'.[14]

The British appreciation also took the form of giving Gurudasmal certificates recording his contribution to maintain the Raj. Gurudasmal was so proud of them that they were prominently displayed at his home. However, within a decade, when charged with anti-British activities he explained why his views had changed:

> These certificates were given to me ten years ago when we were not very conscious and did not fully realise the humiliation that people enslaved by foreign rulers have to suffer. We know now how you have occupied our country. It is our moral duty to free our nation and people from your clutches.[15]

So what had happened to make Gurudasmal the proud collaborator into a rebel? The answer lies in the changes that took place in India in the early years of the twentieth century, changes that affected not only Gurudasmal but all of India and would have a profound impact on Silver's life.

Gurudasmal's journey from collaborator to rebel had started just before the First World War, when Silver was still a young boy. An educated man, he had begun to subscribe to *Kesari*, the publication of Tilak, an Indian freedom fighter who had declared, 'Freedom is my birth right.' Seen by the British as a supporter of terrorism, though this was never proved, Tilak was jailed in Mandalay in Burma, a place often used by the British for housing difficult political opponents as it was far away from India. But at this stage Gurudasmal could still reconcile his growing sense of Indian nationalism with his support for the British, as Indians were not seeking complete freedom and the British were considered fair, just rulers. This belief was shattered when Silver was about 11 years old as a result of what happened in Amritsar on a spring day in 1919.

India had responded magnificently in the First World War: £150 million in money, 1.1 million troops in all theatres of the war of whom 138,000 fought on the battlefields of Europe. More than 800,000 Indians fought to extend the British Empire into Mesopotamia, Persia and the Trans-Caspian and Caucasian regions south of Russia. They helped the British conquer Iraq, where for a time the Indian rupee was the currency of the country, and Allenby's victory over the Turks in Palestine was largely due to an army of which two-thirds of the infantry and one-third of the cavalry were Indians. Gandhi won the Kaiser-e-Hind for 'loyally' getting Indians to enlist. More than 60,000 Indian soldiers died, in addition to many lascars, and seamen, serving on naval ships.

While India did not see any fighting the influenza epidemic that swept the world after the war killed an estimated 17 million Indians, 5 per cent of the population. One reason for the high death toll in India was that the war had denuded the country of many doctors and nursing staff.

But instead of thanks the British responded with the rod. The Indians had expected the British to give them some form of home rule, broadly similar to the one the white dominions of Australia, Canada, New Zealand and South Africa had long enjoyed. Ireland, after a long struggle, was soon to be set free but in India the end of the war saw the British retain, under a new name, all the repressive provisions of the Defence of India Act: press censorship, power to ban meetings, arrest without warrant, even jail without trial for up to a year, which could be further renewed. A person carrying a seditious pamphlet could be arrested and denied a lawyer.

The Indians dubbed it 'na dalil, na vakil, na appeal': no argument, no lawyer, no appeal. Gandhi changed from a loyalist to a rebel, launching an agitation against the repressive laws. In Amritsar, 250 miles from Ghalla Dher, on 13 April 1919, the British committed the worst atrocity during their near-200-year rule of the subcontinent. Following protests, Amritsar was handed over to Brigadier General Reginald Dyer, Commander of the Jullunder Brigade, whose military career featured many a frontier war against rebellious tribes. He immediately imposed martial law and on hearing a crowd had gathered at Jallianwala Bagh, a large open space with a single, very narrow entrance, he hurried there. Around 20,000 were listening on that spring day, as contentedly as they would in any Indian political meeting, to their leaders. How many of the 20,000 were there for the politics is debatable. The date marked Baisakhi, a joyous spring celebration that marked New Year's Day in that part of India. It also made little or no impression on Dyer that the crowd was unarmed and contained many women and children. So mixed was the gathering that at some stage that afternoon a funeral procession had wound its way through the Bagh. Dyer found the entrance too narrow for his armoured cars, so he abandoned them there, ordered his troops to block the entrance and, without any warning, ordered his Gurkha soldiers to open fire. By the time his men ran out of ammunition 337 men, 41 women and a baby of seven weeks had been killed, and 1,500 people injured. The Congress would later assert that more than 1,000 had been killed.

Dyer went on to inflict some remarkable punishments: Indian suspects were flogged, and Indians passing through a certain street, where an English woman had been very nearly beaten to death, were made to crawl on their hands and knees in what became known as the crawling order. In the British Library there is a photograph of soldiers of London 25th Regiment prodding a crawling Indian with a bayonet. An Indian who was made to crawl would later recall:

> I had to lie with my belly on the ground and move on my shoulders with the arms bent like a grasshopper's. The street is very long and it is very difficult and painful to crawl like that … If anybody raised his buttocks he was kicked by the *goras* [whites] who patrolled the street.[16]

What made it worse for the Indians was that although Dyer was made to leave the Army, he was not subjected to any disciplinary proceedings, and was allowed to retire and receive his pension. Indeed he was accorded something like a state funeral when he died. Even this fairly minor punishment generated such hostility among many MPs that 129 members in the Commons voted against the government when the issue was discussed. In the Lords a motion deploring the Government's action against Dyer was passed by 129 to 86. Many British, both in India and Britain, saw Dyer as a hero, the man who had saved the Raj, and some British writers still find justification for what he did. A fund was raised for him to which Kipling, who clearly saw nothing wrong in 300 unarmed Indians being gunned down, contributed.

The British for a time tried to stop the news about the massacre spreading across India but Gurudasmal, being in the neighbouring province, heard about it fairly soon and followed the events in Amritsar closely. Dyer's actions convinced him that for all the talk of British fair play, when it came to Britain versus India the British would always support their fellow countrymen. With Tilak now a spent force—he died a few months after Dyer's outrage— Gurudasmal decided he must become a follower of the new prophet of India, Gandhi, who had described British rule as satanic. In 1921 he took Mathura Devi to the Congress session in Ahmedabad. On his return to Ghalla Dher Gurudasmal pulled down the certificates of merit the British had given him and, in their place, hung pictures of Gandhi and started distributing Congress literature in his area. In the years to come he never missed a Congress session. This change in his father's political thinking could not have come at a more crucial time for Silver. As a child he had little memory of his father the collaborator; now, as a teenager, he could see his father as a rebel, and he quickly imbibed the nationalism that Gurudasmal now preached.

But while Gurudasmal wanted India free of the British he wanted to make sure his children acquired some of the education the conquerors had brought with them. However, finding a school in India for your child then was not easy. Although it was almost 80 years since Macaulay had come to India and decided that Indians should be taught in English, universal school education had never been on the British agenda, a classic case of concentrating on the cream on top of the education cake, with no attention paid to developing the cake of primary education itself. By 1947, as the British left India after nearly 200 years of rule, only 18 per cent of Indians were literate, and four-fifths of Indians had never seen the inside of a classroom.

In 1917, when Silver was nine years old, even fewer Indians went to school. That year, of an Indian population of 315 million, 295 million could not read or write in any language. So, after nearly 160 years of British rule, only 6.3 per cent of the Indian population was literate. And while English was the language of government, fewer than 1.75 million, a mere 0.56 per cent of Indians, had any knowledge of English. If all this made it very difficult for Indian parents anywhere in British India to get their children educated, Gurudasmal faced an almost insurmountable problem in NWFP. With an overwhelming Muslim population, primary education for most Muslims meant attending *maktabs*, schools attached to mosques where they were taught the alphabet, sat crossed-legged on the floor, rocking back and forth as they learnt the Koran by heart in Arabic, and other Muslim religious observances and prayers.

The British were happy that the Muslims were not keen to acquire western learning and, in any case, with a high proportion of British administrators being military officers, education had a very low priority in Silver's province. What mattered to them was keeping the peace, not educating young Indians. Beatrice Webb, during her visit to Peshawar, had found that in a city of well over 100,000 there were only three reasonable schools. There was a school for the ruler of Afghanistan and other 'distinguished Oriental visitors', the municipal school where the headmaster was an Anglicised German, and the Hindoo High School, which did not get any grants from the government and was privately funded.[17] The young headmaster, who was keen to push his students hard, was a member of the Arya Samaj, a Hindu sect that campaigned against caste discrimination and idol worship, and sought to project Hinduism as a religion that was in no way inferior to Christianity and Islam. While implicitly accepting the widely-held British view that Hinduism was a dreadfully flawed religion Arya Samajists believed Hinduism could be revived and purified by going back to the Vedas, the oldest of Aryan scriptures. In Arya Samaj thinking the Vedas had solutions to all of mankind's problems. Silver, the adult, would later reject such ideas but as a young boy he did not question Gurudasmal's view that the Arya Samaj philosophy had great merit.

Initially, Gurudasmal chose the Hindoo High School for his children. And while it meant a 70-mile daily round trip from Ghalla Dher to Peshawar, with no schools in Ghalla Dher he had no other option. But for Silver he clearly felt Hindoo High School did not fit the bill and, still believing in Arya Samaj education, he was prepared to look much further afield to find the right school. His choice was Har Bhagawan Memorial High School in Ferozepur in the Punjab, a 280-mile journey from Ghalla Der. In many ways it was not all that different to Hindoo High School. It was also an Arya Samaj school, all the subjects were taught in Urdu and pupils learnt English as a second language only when they went to the sixth standard at the age of twelve. But what probably made it attractive was the fact that the school prepared its students for the Higher Cambridge examination, which meant Silver's overall education would have much more of an English imprint. Gurudasmal may have been committed to removing the British from India but clearly felt it would be useful for Silver to emerge from school with a better grasp of the modern ways of the conquerors of his land.

While Urdu remained Silver's natural tongue and many years later when he came to record his memoirs for the Oral History Project of the Nehru

Memorial Museum Library, he did so in Urdu, unlike his brothers who went to Hindoo High School he could both speak and read English. Admittedly this was, as the Englishmen he met during the war put it, 'broken' English, but many of his siblings could not even manage that. One of his brothers left school unable to even read English and this, as we shall see, would have very dramatic consequences both for him and for Silver.

Today much has changed in Silver's school. It has a different name, teaches not 200 children as in Silver's days but 1,000, and while Silver's fellow students were all boys now it is co-educational. But it still retains its Arya Samaj links and, as in Silver's days, English is taught only when pupils reach the age of 12. When early In 2016 I spoke to its Principal, Prem Shankar Joshi, he did not want to speak in English but preferred Hindi, the sister language to Urdu.

Gurudasmal's choice of school would have an important impact on Silver's life. While he left Ghalla Dher not having seen the inside of a class room he clearly did not feel the sense of alienation and fear little boys feel when they first go to school as he was by now a teenager. And while he had to live away from home for the first time, very likely with distant relatives in fairly cramped surroundings, it meant from his early teens he had the freedom to chart his own course without any parental control. And this late start to his school education, because of the lack of primary education in his own province, also had one other consequence. It meant that by the time he had passed his Higher Cambridge, which was equivalent to O-levels, and returned to Ghalla Dher in March, 1930 he was a few months short of his 22nd birthday.[18] If we consider that by the time Fleming reached his 22nd birthday he had graduated from Oxford, Har Bhagawan for Silver, in effect, doubled up as a school and a university. And right from the beginning he made the most of the chance given to him, impressing his schoolmates and teachers with his 'active habits and interest in social work'.

Silver first demonstrated his ability to make friends and exercise influence when he stood for election as secretary to the Arya Kumar Sabha. He won by a huge majority, securing votes from all age groups, including older boys. This put him in charge of the school library and he made the most of it, devouring the newspapers and periodicals there. The papers were full of political news and he was particularly fascinated by the power struggle then going on in Afghanistan. A feature of life in that country through much of the 1920s, it ended in 1929 with the dethroning of King Amanullah. A Kemal Ataturk-style moderniser, who believed in education and women's rights, he was distrusted by the mullahs and the British and eventually forced to flee. Sitting in his school library Silver read how Amanullah drove away from Kabul in his Rolls Royce, accompanied by his wife Suriya, a beautiful Queen who had refused to veil herself, and a pet canary. Little did Silver know then that, about a decade later, as he went back and forth from Kabul to India, he would have to consider the knock-on effect on his spying career of some Afghans plotting a return of Amanullah and the ruler, then in exile in Italy, being courted by the Axis powers.

But just reading about political events was never going to be enough for Silver and by the time Amanullah fled in his Rolls, Silver was an active member of the Naujawan Bharat Sabha, the Young Indian Association, founded by Bhagat Singh, a socialist much influenced by anarchist thinking. Today in India he is one of the great heroes of the Indian freedom movement with stamps issued in his name. He is the alternative to Gandhi, who did not subscribe to non-violence but preferred Irish-style violence directed at individual British officers and paid for his beliefs by being hanged by the British. Bhagat Singh was 12 when he heard of the Amritsar massacre and the day after had gone to Jallianwala Bagh and, collecting the mud from the ground, told his sister, 'This is the blood of our people killed by the British. Salute it.' By the time Silver started at Har Bhagawan, Bhagat Singh was convinced that only violence could force the British out, seeing it as the first step to the creation of a socialist society modelled on the Soviet Union. Silver was attracted by Singh's ideas and, outside his school hours, devoted much time working for the Sabha. This required him, as per Sabha rules, to pledge that the interests of the country would always come before one's own community. To break down the many barriers that divided Indian society, the Sabha laid down that Halal and Jhatka [a method of slaughter of animals preferred by Hindus, Sikhs] meat was cooked together and eaten by Hindus, Muslims and Sikhs alike. Silver had no problems following this order. Soon Bhagat Singh's actions to secure Indian freedom also made Silver think of taking to the gun.

The drama unfolded in 1928 with the British refusal to give into demands that India should have the same sort of dominion status the British had given the white colonies nearly two decades earlier. With Lord Birkenhead, the Secretary of State for India, convinced that even in 2030 the British would rule India and everything should be done to encourage Hindu–Muslim disunity so the British could play the part, as he put it, of 'composers', a commission was sent to determine how far the Indians had come in learning to govern themselves. To add insult to injury this was an all-white parliamentary delegation which also included Clement Attlee, then a backbench Labour MP. Indians took to the streets in their thousands and during one protest march in Lahore a 63-year-old Indian leader, Lala Lajpat Rai, was assaulted by the police and died a few days later. Silver read the news in the school library and says: 'The death of Lala Lajpat Rai in 1928 at Lahore, consequent to the brutal lathi [Indian baton] charge on him by the police … had a great impact on us'.

Although the actual lathi charge was by Indian policemen, they had, as always, acted under British orders and Bhagat Singh and his friends decided to take revenge by targeting J. A. Scott, the Superintendent of Police who had ordered the lathi charge. But on the day selected, 17 December 1928, Scott did not attend the police station, his assistant J. P. Saunders did, and as Saunders was leaving the station, a colleague of Bhagat Singh, mistaking him for Scott, shot him dead. Bhagat Singh knew it was not Scott but, realising the man was dead, pumped further bullets into the body. Bhagat Singh posted handwritten posters in and around Lahore proclaiming: 'J. P. Saunders is dead, Lalaji is avenged'. Silver, reading the news of Saunders' shooting, could not contain his joy. '... the great revolutionary work of Bhagat Singh and his comrades in taking prompt reprisal by shooting down Saunders thrilled our young heart'.[19] Ten months later Silver was cheering his hero even more.

The killing of Saunders had not, as Bhagat Singh hoped, made the British panic and leave India. His response was, in effect, to put on a show of revolutionary violence which would not kill anyone but demonstrate how willing the Indians were to take up the gun to free their country. He and his colleagues made two bombs which were carefully prepared so as 'not [to] cause any fatal or even serious injury'.[20] It was decided these bombs would be thrown in the chamber of the Legislative Assembly Hall in Delhi, a monumental edifice built by the architect Herbert Baker and seen by the British as teaching Indians the rudiments of parliamentary democracy. For Bhagat Singh this was a puppet chamber filled with 'yes' men and, as the chamber voted for a measure which would allow the government to detain people without trial, Bhagat Singh and his colleague threw the bombs. No one was killed but four or five were slightly injured. Then, as if to demonstrate how different their idea of violence was to that of other revolutionaries, Bhagat Singh and his colleague, who could have escaped, remained in the empty hall and, when the police finally arrived, threw away their revolvers and surrendered. Bhagat Singh was initially sentenced to transportation for life, but when the British discovered he had killed Saunders he was hanged. Bhagat Singh's activities, says Silver:

> ... aroused my keen interest in the field of revolutionary activities in our country. I felt a strong urge in me for such work. With some colleagues from different schools we indeed started revolutionary work in our own way. Our idea of such work was at that time to beat up, and, if possible, even murder British officials at the first opportunity. Once I with one of my friends, Ajit Singh, had actually gone out with the intention of murdering the then deputy commissioner of Ferozepur, Mr Harren, at the dead of the night. We were armed only with daggers. Before going there we had collected some details about the bungalow where the deputy commissioner used to live through Ajit Singh's father who was a carpenter sometimes working for the deputy commissioner at his bungalow. It was summer and the deputy commissioner

used to sleep outside in the open. When we approached his bed with the mosquito net wrapped around it in the courtyard, we found, to our great disappointment, that the bed was empty. Later on we learnt that he was out of station that night.[21]

However, with no established revolutionary organisation in Ferozepur, Silver decided to join the Congress. It may seem strange that a man who had been thwarted from killing a British official merely because he happened not to be at home that night should join the Congress. But this reflected the fact that while the Congress accepted the Gandhian principle of non-violence, and Gandhi had condemned Bhagat Singh, the party was essentially a broad church. It accommodated people who, unlike Gandhi, saw non-violence as a tactic not a principle, and did not rule out violence to remove the British. It also showed how Silver even at a young age was a pragmatist who followed a course that best suited him, a trait he would demonstrate often during his spying career.

Silver had joined the Congress at the right time for, in December, 1929 the organisation was to hold its annual session in Lahore, the Punjabi capital a mere 45 miles from Ferozepur. Silver, accompanied by Ajit Singh, journeyed there and watched history being made. With the British refusing to give dominion status the Congress decided living within the empire was impossible and for the first time set complete independence as its goal with Gandhi himself moving the resolution.

At the midnight hour on 31 December Silver stood along with a mammoth crowd on the banks of the Ravi. As the clock chimed 12, marking the start of the 1930s, he watched Jawaharlal Nehru unfurl the tricolour which would, 17 years later at another midnight hour, become the flag of free India.

Exciting as all this was, Silver was still a student at Har Bhagawan. Indeed, on his return to Ferozepur he had to prepare for his Higher Cambridge matriculation examination, the results of which determined whether the student would gain admission to a college for further education. The examination clearly made few demands on Silver, for he still found time to take part in protest marches and help to organise hartals, a very Indian form of street protest where an entire city is forced to shut down. This meant going round Ferozepur to make sure that on the day chosen all the shops closed and no public transport was available. However, Silver's activities did not go unnoticed by the British authorities:

When I came back to my village after my matriculation examination in March 1930 three CID men used to follow me as Ferozepur police suspected that I had connections with [an] underground revolutionary movement at Ferozepur. Only a day after my arrival at the village the police from Mardan came to me and warned me against taking part in political activities. I told them [that] if I needed any advice from them I would certainly ask them for it; meanwhile I preferred to do just as I pleased. So they went back but posted one of their men to keep watch over my activities.[22]

The response shows that Silver, even at 22, was going to take no nonsense from the authorities and his experiences in Ferozepur had so shaped Silver that he was already very different to his siblings. His brothers, on their return to the village after finishing their education, had helped Gurudasmal look after the vast family estate. His eldest brother, Jamuna Das, even abandoned his studies at DAV College to help his father. But with the speeches in the Lahore Congress and cries for independence still ringing in his ears, Silver could think of nothing but politics. It helped that in Lahore Silver had met some Congress volunteers from his province, and within a month there was dramatic news, what Gandhi's American biographer, the journalist Louis Fischer, called *Drama at the Seashore*. On an April morning in 1930 Gandhi marched to the sea at Dandi on the west coast of India and picked up a pinch of salt to illustrate the iniquity of British rule, as the British imposed a tax on Indians for making salt, something humans had done since time immemorial. By this simple but highly significant act, Gandhi launched the second, and most successful, of his four epic civil disobedience campaigns to free his country. The British response led to 90,000 being jailed, considerable use of lathis by the police on protesters, and some firing on unarmed crowds. This included shooting at an unarmed crowd of Pathans in the Qissa Khwani Bazar of Peshawar, killing many. However, the Raj struggled to contain this India-wide agitation, and the repressive measures did not reassure the British officials and businessmen in India, many of whom would later recollect with anger 'the reprehensible administrative breakdown'. Gandhi's campaign persuaded many Indians to give up their jobs, leave schools and colleges and even their homes to join the liberation struggle. Silver did not for the very good reason that he did not have to.

In what must be considered one of the most remarkable, totally unexpected, political development ever to have taken place in the subcontinent, Silver's province had found its own Gandhi. Immortalised as the land of the brave Pathan, whose only response to injustice and oppression was the sword and the gun, a Pathan leader had emerged who did not believe violence was the only solution for political problems. For Silver this was so electrifying that, despite the presence of the police in Ghalla Dher keeping watch on him, he quickly became a member of this new Gandhi's movement. And only a few weeks after his return from Ferozepur, despite having been away for almost a decade and enjoying the home comforts Mathura Devi provided, he bade goodbye to his family. His destination was the village of Utmanzai, where his own Pathan Gandhi lived.

A Rebel is Born

Silver's Gandhi was a Pathan called Khan Abdul Ghaffar Khan, who was also known as Bacha, an affectionate term in his region for a Pathan, or Badshah, Emperor Khan. Today he is not well-known and there was much surprise when, in the summer of 2013, the Pakistani teenager Malala Yousafzai mentioned his name in her speech to the United Nations. Malala, who was shot by the Taliban for promoting girls' education, explained that her belief in non-violence was inspired by Badshah Khan, bracketing him along with Gandhi and Mother Theresa. But for three decades in the North West Frontier Province he was a pioneer of non-violence who, a devout Muslim, became a dedicated follower of Gandhi. Like Silver, Ghaffar Khan also came from the well-off land-owning class. His movement was called Khudai Khidmatgar, the servants of God, and started as an organisation campaigning against prostitution, but was soon involved in wider social work, including the welfare of farmers and the youth of the province. Ghaffar Khan even started a magazine, Pakhtun, in which he tried to persuade his fellow Pathans to take to education and eliminate just those practices that had horrified the Webbs, such as blood feuds—something British officials had told the Webbs could not be done and should not even be attempted.

Ghaffar Khan always retained a strong faith in Islam. He tried to build a mosque but to his anger was thwarted by the British. He could easily have been co-opted by the British to sustain their rule; indeed that is just what his father, a willing collaborator, wanted. Khan joined the Frontier Guides, a British-created force of Pathans to help them govern the area. But one day, walking in Peshawar with a friend who was also a Guide, a British officer reprimanded his friend for not wearing the customary Pathan turban and parting his hair like an Englishman. There and then, Khan decided to leave the Scouts: 'I had flattered myself that I was specially fitted to look like and enjoy an equal footing with Englishmen. But Allah willed otherwise'.[1] On his road from collaborator to rebel he often found the British hostile even to his attempts to educate his fellow Pathans, with one British officer saying of his plan to set up a school like the missionary school he had himself attended, 'This is not service but rebellion.'[2] By the time Silver went to see him, Khan had done the impossible. In this supposedly archetypal Muslim province of the Islamic warrior, Koran in one hand and the sword in another, whom the British claimed preferred their rule, Khan had organised a Muslim party that believed in non-violence, and wanted an India free of the British and a secular, united, republic. With Ghaffar Khan seeing Gandhi as a soul mate, his party, in effect, became the North West Frontier branch of the Congress.

Given the way religious and Muslim politics in particular were developing in the subcontinent, the rise of Ghaffar Khan would have made him an exceptional leader anywhere in India. But that he emerged in the North West Frontier with a movement which at its height had 100,000 volunteers was truly remarkable. As the historian Anatol Lieven has put it:

> No more unlikely product of Pathan culture can easily be imagined.... So deeply did most Pathans loathe British rule that they were prepared to ally with the main Indian force struggling against that rule, the Congress. They opposed Mohammed Ali Jinnah's Muslim League, which, though made up of Muslims, was regarded quite rightly as doing deals with the British in order to safeguard Muslim interests than in seeking to expel the hated alien rulers.[3]

The British, for all their knowledge of the Pathans, just could not come to terms with this totally unexpected development. How, they wondered, could a people who not only embraced violence but celebrated it as a way of life, accept Ghaffar Khan? For many British the non-violent Pathan seemed something of a fantasy, and they would seek all sorts of explanations for his rise. Even Lord Wavell, who in contrast to his peers understood India much better, could not abide the man, dismissing him as 'stupid but obstinate'. Whether this was due to Khan sometimes sitting before him wearing rough khadi, which he wrapped over his head, is not clear. Mohammad Ali Jinnah, the creator of Pakistan, was even more contemptuous of his fellow Muslim, saying to the British politician Woodrow Wyatt that Khan was 'like another bearer who comes with a chit saying he speaks perfect English, but when you talk to him he doesn't understand a word'. Wavell would later echo this in his letter to George VI, when he wrote of 'Abdul Ghaffar Khan ... whose intelligence and grasp of English are both limited'.[4]

Khan's movement has long passed into history. But it remains a great indictment of the British rule in India that, instead of trying to build bridges with Khan, they impeded him at every turn, portraying his movement as something that ran counter to the fundamental culture of the Pathans the

British knew and loved. Today, almost a century later, we can see how the British, in trying to shore up the control of their crown jewel, missed the larger picture and helped to create a much bigger problem in this part of the world. Silver's homeland is so much the home of the Taliban that in December 2014 Taliban militants killed 141 people, 132 of them children, in an attack on an army-run school in Peshawar. They even justified killing children who had reached the age of puberty in the name of Islam.

People in the subcontinent like to give their leaders names, and with the original Gandhi called Mahatma, the Great Souled One, Silver's Gandhi soon earned the title of the 'Frontier Gandhi'. Gandhi had made his followers discard cotton from the mills of Lancashire for khaddar, white hand-spun cloth, and a boat-shaped white cap dubbed the Gandhi cap, making it the uniform of the Congress party. Ghaffar Khan also had his own distinctive uniform. Originally his followers wore white shirts, but they would soon get dirty as they went round the villages so some of them had the shirts dyed red at a local tannery. This brick-red colour caught on and his organisation was soon known as the Red Shirt Movement. By the time Silver had returned to Ghalla Dher after his O-levels he found that anyone wearing a red shirt was a follower of Ghaffar Khan, and he wasted no time in donning one.

Silver's decision to wear the red shirt did not mean he had abandoned his belief that, when necessary, the gun should be used to secure political objectives. But he now began to understand the art of non-violent street protest. He learned how to organise and demonstrate and, if necessary, collaborate with people who did not share all his views but with whom he could work in a common cause and a very defined objective. In many ways Silver was honing the skills a spy required. Over time he would discard the red shirt, but the political education the movement gave him proved invaluable when he finally took to spying.

Silver's first meeting with the Red Shirts, at a huge conference in Utmanzai, was significant for providing him with both political education and contacts. These would prove very useful when he returned to Ghalla Dher and immediately set about organising public meetings, parades and, above all, demonstrations which formed the bedrock of the campaign. He was well aware what the British response would be and in May 1930 he was arrested. But after two weeks in a jail in Mardan, the same town where his great grandfather had died, he was released. It was as if the British wanted to give him a taste of what was to come should he persist in opposing their rule. Far from dimming his enthusiasm it spurred him on, and soon he was attending an even bigger conference of Red Shirt workers and leaders in Nowshera.

The British had, by now, arrested both Mahatma and Frontier Gandhi, and most of the activists of the civil disobedience campaign. In NWFP this had virtually decimated the top leadership of the Red Shirts. So the Nowshera meeting was attended by essentially the lower ranks of the movement who were still free, their most urgent task being to chalk out a plan that would make sure the campaign did not peter out. This suited Silver very well, for it was an early chance for him to show how he could improvise. By June he had become such a nuisance that it was not just the lone policeman in Ghalla Dher who was monitoring his activity. That month he was again arrested, and this time brought before a magistrate and, after a brief court hearing, was sentenced to one and a half years of 'rigorous imprisonment'. Initially taken to the same Mardan jail in which he had been incarcerated in May, he was soon transferred to the larger Peshawar central jail. This was also the jail to which, two decades earlier, the criminals his father had helped to arrest had been sent. As a political prisoner Silver expected to be treated differently, but soon discovered that he was mistaken:

> In those days conditions inside jail were very bad. A large number of prisoners were herded together and kept in the same barrack. There was resentment against this kind of treatment to political prisoners who raised the slogan of 'Inquilab Zindabad' [Long Live the Revolution]. As punishment young political prisoners were often flogged. I was also once earmarked for this punishment but because of my tender age was spared at the last moment. The jails were then jam-packed with political prisoners. Even the judicial lock-ups were sometimes emptied to accommodate them.[5]

Silver's experience was hardly unique. Jails in British India were segregated along racial lines. Europeans did not share cells with Indians, their cells were better maintained and they had better food and more daily-use items than the Indians. In contrast the Indians were often denied bare necessities, and warders would stand at the cell door and throw bread into the cells much as they might feed animals in zoos. 'To be fair', recalled Silver in his memoir, 'this was the common experience of most Indians then in prison.' But, as Silver tried his best to cope with jail, unknown to him his brother, Hari Kishan, had decided on a course of action which would have a dramatic effect on Silver and his entire family.

Ten months older than Silver, Hari Kishan had also joined the Red Shirt movement and been jailed. The two brothers were close and had much in common, except for one crucial difference. Unlike his sibling, he had not spent enough time at school to become acquainted with English. So when he left school early to help his father manage the family estate he could neither read nor write the language of his conquerors. This was to have a tremendous impact when, soon after his arrest, he was asked to sign a declaration written in English. With the British running out of prisons to house the Indian rebels they decided to release those who were prepared to promise that they would not again violate the law. Such an undertaking ran counter to everything both the Frontier Gandhi and the Mahatma preached. Silver had refused to sign the document but Hari Kishan, unable to read the petition, did not realise what he was signing and readily agreed. On his return to Ghalla Dher, his father berated him, emphasising that his younger brother was still in jail, and refused to accept Hari Kishan's plea that he had been 'tricked' by the British:

> Hari Kishan was deeply hurt by his father's admonitions which, indeed, proved to be a turning point in his life. For though he was, in fact, tricked into signing the apology, he now blamed himself for it and decided to atone for what he had done even though inadvertently. He decided therefore to redeem his honour by making the supreme sacrifice for the liberation of his motherland. He read over and over again the following lines of a poem published in *Pakhtun*:

> > When my friends find me freshly laid in grave,
> > They may curse me all if I have entered it as a slave.
> > If I am not bathed in my blood, as per my pledge,
> > With my unholy touch do not desecrate the mosque's edge.
> > If I am not torn apart by British bullets as I have sworn
> > With what face, dear mother, for me will you mourn?[6]

The poem so moved Hari Kishan that he was convinced he had to abandon non-violence and take to the gun. It is possible that also wanted to emulate what other young Indians in various parts of the country had been doing. They had decided to treat Gandhi's campaign as an irrelevant side show and model themselves on Irish-style violence to free India. Within weeks of Gandhi picking up a pinch of salt revolutionaries had, in what the government called 'an amazing coup', very nearly succeeded in liberating one of British India's most important towns: Chittagong in Bengal. There on Good Friday night, 18 April 1930, 62 young Indians seized the police and auxiliary forces' armouries and set up a provisional revolutionary government. As R. E. A. Ray, Special Superintendent of IB, CID Bengal put it:

> The Chittagong revolutionaries had done what had never been attempted before—what must have seemed to be an unrealizable dream. Bengali youths had attacked and actually captured and held in their possession for a few hours, the armouries of the police and Auxiliary Force in a district.[7]

India's equivalent of the Irish Easter Rising marked the start of a remarkable wave of revolutionary violence. No police officer, whether Indian or British, was immune to attack. Bombs exploded in government offices and on 8

December 1930, three men coolly entered the Writers' Building in Calcutta, where Clive had established the headquarters of the Raj a century and a half earlier, and which was always the greatest symbol of British power, and shot dead the Inspector-General of Police.

Hari Kishan's response was to work on an assassination plot with a relation, Chaman Lal Kapoor. Another member of the Naujawan Bharat Sabha, Kapoor had worked closely with Bhagat Singh and also with Philip Spratt, who had been sent by the British communist party to help the Indians organise their own. He had devised a plan to kill Sir Geoffrey de Montmorency, the 54-year-old Irish-born Governor of the Punjab and one of the Raj's highest officials, having been secretary to the Viceroy, Lord Reading, and also secretary to the Prince of Wales when he visited India in the winter of 1921. Kapoor and his friends had decided that Hari Kishan would be the ideal man to pull the trigger, and in the weeks after his release Chaman Lal often came to Ghalla Dher to meet Hari Kishan and plan the assassination. Gurudasmal soon rumbled what was going on and, despite the fact that he was a follower of Gandhi and prominently displayed the Mahatma's picture in his house, he had no problems about his son taking to the gun. His only concern was whether his son might at the last moment flinch, as he had done when getting out of jail, and thus 'bring shame not only him alone but on the Talwar [Silver] family as a whole'. Once Hari Kishan assured his father that he was a true Pathan who would never again betray his family Gurudasmal readily became part of the conspiracy. When Chaman Lal mentioned they did not have guns, he travelled to Toru to obtain one from a friend. Then the man who had honed his shooting skills while helping the British catch criminals, now took his son to the first storey of their house and spent several hours each day training him so that when he aimed at the British Governor he would not miss. On 19 December 1930 he escorted his son and Chaman Lal to Nowshera station where the pair boarded the Bombay Express for Lahore. Just before the train left Gurudasmal embraced his son and told him:

> All human beings have to die one day or the other. But those who die for their country become immortal. I know you will not falter or stray from the path you have chosen for yourself. I am certain that you will not tarnish the good name of the Talwars.[8]

Gurudasmal knew if Hari Kishan succeeded he would be hanged and as the train left the station he could not restrain his tears.

De Montmorency was to preside over the convocation of Punjab University, of which he was Chancellor, and the plan was to shoot him in the Senate House during the ceremony. However, on arriving at Lahore Hari Kishan found his fellow conspirators were not happy with the arrangements and wanted to abandon the plan. But, aware that if he returned to Ghalla Dher without carrying out his task his father would never forgive him, Hari Kishan insisted on going ahead.

On the day Hari Kishan took his seat among the graduates, conveniently located near the entrance to the hall. He was there well before de Montmorency entered at the head of a number of dignitaries, having decided that just as the Governor took his seat on the dais he would get up and shoot him. However, as he gazed at the assembled company he suddenly decided this was not the right time and would wait until the ceremony was over. He never explained why he made this late change. It is possible he was overawed by the setting. Although he had been arrested and seen the inside of a British jail, both the police and the jail warders were Indians and he had never met a white man before. Now he was in a hall that reeked of British power in India and was confronted with more white men and women then he had ever seen before in one setting. Whatever made the 22-year-old change his plan, it resulted in a huge problem for him.

Not knowing English, he could not follow a word of what was happening and did not realise when the ceremony was over. He only became aware that it had come to an end when de Montmorency and the others on the dais got up and started to leave. It was then that Hari Kishan quickly got on a chair and started shooting. His first bullet hit the Governor's upper left arm. The second grazed his back and, although he was injured, after first aid at the university and then treatment at the hospital he was home later that day. It was Hari Kishan's third bullet that killed: Chanan Singh, an Indian sub-inspector of police. His fourth injured an Indian CID inspector, Budh Singh Wadhawan, and the fifth Miss Dermitt, a British doctor. By this time, with the convocation hall in pandemonium, Hari Kishan had come out to the verandah and fired his last bullet at the opposite wall. Soon he was overpowered and taken away. [Hari Kishan's failure to kill de Montmorency puzzled Gurudasmal who, when he met his son in jail, asked, 'But tell me, how could that giant of a man escape? I had worked so hard in training you.' Hari Kishan could provide no explanation and, when Silver came to write the story forty-six years later in his memoir, he tried hard to prove that this was not because his brother was not a good shot or had panicked. Instead he missed because he did not accidentally want to injure the prominent Indian standing near de Montmorency: Dr Sarvepalli Radhakrishnan, who had given the convocation address and would later become President of the Indian Republic. This may or may not be the truth, but it helped Silver present his brother as a man a world removed from most other terrorists, let alone the jihadi fanatics of our time who kill so indiscriminately.]

In his jail cell Silver had no inkling of what Hari Kishan was up to. As the drama had unfolded that December day in Lahore Silver had followed his by now established jail routine. He had read the paper that someone always smuggled in. Much of the day was spent talking to fellow political prisoners on how the movement against the British was going and how to deal with the warders. Then, after a rudimentary meal of paratha, dal, vegetables, a few pieces of meat, he had slept. Things took a turn only in the small hours of the morning of 24 December. Then a warder came into Silver's cell, shook him violently and without a word of explanation frogmarched him to the office of the jail superintendent. Sitting behind a large teak desk with a Union Jack hanging on the wall behind him, the superintendent, whom Silver had never met before, began to bombard him with questions about Hari Kishan. What were Hari Kishan's politics? Who were his friends? How did he spend his time? Which family members was he really close to? What were their links with various political groups?

Silver could not work out why they should want to ask these questions, and particularly, at such an unearthly hour. Still full of sleep, he answered them in a fairly frank manner, and after an hour the superintendent motioned to the warder that Silver could now be taken back to his cell. Suspecting nothing, he was soon fast asleep. It was only the next day, when reading the paper, he realised why he had been summoned in the middle of the night:

> Then it dawned on me that the police had interrogated me ... because they wanted information from me about Hari Kishan, his colleagues and his possible accomplices in this case and also about relations who might have given him help.[9]

The British originally jailed Hari Kishan in the prison nearest to the university where, says Silver, his brother 'was beaten and tortured', and more was to follow when a few days later he was moved to Lahore Fort, built by the Mughal Emperor Akbar but now one of the main British detention centres in north India. Here Hari Kishan:

> ... was tied hand and foot and made to stand naked round the clock continuously for days together without food so that he might not get a wink of sleep. In the severe cold of Lahore winter he was made to lie down naked on ice slabs and they covered his body with ice slabs also. He was forced to sit on a chair with spikes on the seat. Notorious police officers like K. B. Sheikh and Abdul Hamid who had previously tortured the prisoners of the Lahore Conspiracy Case [the one that involved Bhagat Singh] gave him needle pricks on the back of his hands which bled profusely and forced the nails out of his fingers, which caused intense pain. And a doctor was all the time in attendance so that as soon as he lost consciousness as a result of all this, he could be immediately revived with an injection.[10]

Twelve years later Silver himself would be brought here, but that, as we shall see, was in very different circumstances: he was treated with great care as if a prized treasure.

The British investigations extended to the entire Silver clan and amounted, says Silver, to 'Persecution of the Talwar family', the title of a chapter in his memoir. The Silver family home in Ghalla Dher was 'raided … as if they were storming a fortress occupied by the enemy'. During the raid Silver's mother, aunt and young brothers were turfed out of the house, 'into the bitter cold of a December night and [the police] took possession of the house as if they had captured an enemy fortress'.[11] The raids yielded little except photographs of Gandhi and Nehru that Gurudasmal had collected. Gurudasmal, who on the day of the shooting had been visiting Silver, was arrested and there was some thought of charging father and son, but this was abandoned. Silver's eldest brother, Jamuna Das, who by now was a well-established government official in the Punjab, was also arrested, along with his younger brother, Ishwar Das, who went to a local school and was then staying with him. Jamuna Das's wife and child were forced to vacate their government quarters, and he was told by the superintendent of police that his family were 'traitors' who had betrayed the 'benevolent and civilised' British rule. Despite this he was not immediately sacked: that came well after the case against Hari Kishan had been concluded.

Justice in India can often be very slow, but the Government was keen to have Hari Kishan tried as quickly as possible, and less than a month later, 21 January, a jury had been sworn in at Lahore's sessions court for his trial. The defence failed to get more time to prepare the case or to get the jury changed on the grounds that six of the nine worked for the government. As was standard in such trials under British rule, Europeans, as the British called themselves in India, were well represented, with the foreman and three others being Europeans. The jury reached its verdict only five days later, on 26 January 1931, unanimously finding Hari Kishan guilty but recommending that due to his age, 22, he should be given a life sentence. However, the district and sessions judge, Mr A. H. B. Anderson, overturned their verdict and sentenced Hari Kishan to death for the wilful murder of Chanan Singh. As Hari Kishan was led away neither Anderson nor anybody else in court, could have imagined that exactly 19 years later, on 26 January 1950, the Indian Republic would be proclaimed.

In an attempt to save Hari Kishan the family hired an expensive lawyer from Delhi, a prominent Muslim Congress leader, and the appeal went all the way to the Privy Council in London, where it finally failed.

By now Silver should have been out of jail to become part of his brother's defence team. On the very day Hari Kishan was sentenced Gandhi was released, his civil disobedience campaign having forced the British to the negotiating table. Soon the 'half-naked Fakir' was 'nauseating' Churchill by striding up the steps of the recently constructed Viceregal Palace in Delhi to meet Lord Irwin, the Viceroy, and agree the Gandhi–Irwin Pact by which all political prisoners were released. But this did not include Silver because, 'being the younger brother of Hari Kishan', he 'continued to be detained in jail'.

However, Silver was allowed to see Hari Kishan for a last time before he was hanged and on 7 June 1931 Silver, in handcuffs and under police escort, was taken from Peshawar to Mainwali jail where Hari Kishan was. Much to his surprise Silver found that Gurudasmal and other members of his family were also on the train, having also been given permission to see Hari Kishan. The train arrived in Mainwali the next morning and Silver was immediately taken to the jail to see him. With just 10 months separating them the two were more like twins, 'brothers, friends and comrades rolled into one. We had grown up together and always confided to each other', and Silver had hoped he would be allowed to sit one last time with his brother. But the prison authorities would not allow Hari Kishan out of his cell and all Silver could do was wave his handcuffed wrists in his direction. Having heard how his brother had been tortured in Lahore Fort, Silver expected to see a wreck. But:

> I was very much surprised at my first glimpse of Hari Kishan because of the pink of health I found him in. There was, indeed, a glow on his face which seemed amazing. I had never seen him in such good health ever in my life.[12]

Hari Kishan had also put on 13 lbs since he had been transferred to Mainwali jail after his sentencing. Given that just six months earlier he had been so badly tortured by the police that Gurudasmal had found his whole body blue and swollen and blood clots on his face, Silver does not explain how his brother's health was so transformed. It is possible that after his 'torture' the authorities made sure when he appeared in public for his trial he did not bear any marks. What also surprised him was that Hari Kishan was not morose but 'jovial'. Twenty-four hours before being hanged, he told Silver:

> I am anxiously awaiting the day when I will put the hangman's noose round my neck … I want to get it over with as early as possible so that I may be born again and repeat my action. I am very happy that very soon I will join my mentors like Bhagat Singh [who had been hanged two months previously] and his comrades.

Silver was surprised with his 'self-possession and strength of character at such a moment'. As the police escort told Silver his time was up and led him away, 'In my heart I found his stature had meanwhile grown immeasurably'.[13]

By the time he bade goodbye to Hari Kishan, the last train to Peshawar had gone, so Silver spent a night in Mianwali jail. It was worse than anything he had experienced in Peshawar:

My cell was a small dark room infested with bugs and mosquitoes. As the latrine was also inside the cell the stink was unbearable. Mianwali is known for scorching heat in this month of June. I could neither eat nor sleep.[14]

The next morning at around 6 a.m. Silver heard shouts of 'Inquilab Zindabad' [Long Live the Revolution], 'Bharat Mata Zindabad' [Long Live Mother India], 'Bhagat Singh Zindabad' [Long Live Bhagat Singh], followed by silence. 'I understood what had happened. And there was now a sudden hush in the entire jail for a long time'.[15]

However, what Silver did not learn for a long time was what the British had done with his dead brother's body.

Gurudasmal and the family had been gathered outside the jail since the early hours of the morning but they were not given access to the gallows. They watched as the body was taken on a stretcher, placed in a van and driven to the cremation site with a large police escort. They were unable to follow, and it was a day before they found out where Hari Kishan had been cremated. The family wanted to take back the ashes to Ghalla Dher, hoping to build a little shrine in the village. But this was just what the British authorities did not want, lest the cremation become a focal point for anti-British agitation. So Hari Kishan's body was taken from jail and cremated in an isolated place some distance from Mianwali. Jamuna Das discovered where the site was but as he, along with some family members and friends, walked towards the cremation site the next day they saw the police sprinkle water on the ashes, put them in bags and immerse the bags in the middle of the river. Silver had no doubt this was to 'ensure that not a piece of bone of the martyr might, per chance, be picked up by anybody'.[16]

Despite the secrecy imposed by the British there were protests against the hanging of Hari Kishan, leading to the imposition of Section 144 [a provision in the criminal code used to suppress agitation] prohibiting demonstrations and meetings. Those who violated the order were soon jailed, with some of them taken to the same cell as Silver in Peshawar. Among them was a man with a long, flowing beard called Ghulam Murtaza. He described himself as a Mullah and Silver had no reason to doubt he was a genuine Muslim cleric. One day Ghulam Murtaza asked Silver to shave his beard, and then disclosed that he was not a Muslim preacher but a Hindu called Ram Kishan, who had at one time been President of the Punjab Provincial Naujawan Bharat Sabha and been arrested on the frontier. He asked Silver to make sure his friends and contacts knew where he was. Silver was eager to help, and such was the bond that developed between the two that they spent much time together over the next three months discussing politics. Silver was quickly made aware that this was a man of some standing, a graduate; his name was always written down as Ram Kishan B.A. (National), and the young man was so impressed by the older man's knowledge and experience of politics that '[he] learnt a good deal about political struggles and attained some ideological maturity. I still consider him my ideological guru'.[17]

While no other political prisoner played quite such a role in Silver's life as Ram Kishan there were also other contacts he developed, and they would come in very useful when he did become a spy. This included Haji Mohammed Amin of the Shinwari, a tribe close to the Khyber Pass who the British had often to subdue by razing their villages and shooting the male inhabitants. Silver also met Sanobar Hussain, and both Amin and Hussain were to prove very useful when Silver started shuttling between Peshawar and Kabul during the war.

The Silver family were now rebels in British eyes and Gurudasmal and several of his family members, including Jamuna Das, were arrested. Silver himself was released in September when he had served his sentence but was then immediately rearrested under the Frontier Crimes Regulation Act. After a few days in jail he was taken to a magistrates court where he was asked to provide a bond of Rs 5,000 or face another three years in jail. With Gurudasmal still a fairly well-off landowner this was not difficult to do, and for the first time since Gandhi's civil disobedience campaign had begun the previous spring, Silver was a free man. At this time, with Gandhi in London taking part in the Round Table negotiations, there was some hope that a settlement with the British might be reached.

But Gandhi returned empty-handed and was immediately arrested. In June 1932 Silver was back in Mardan jail. This time it took five months before a trial was held, and he was sentenced to one year's rigorous imprisonment and taken to Haripur central jail, which also housed Jamuna Das and Ishwar Das. So far, in various prison cells there was one thing that was constant: all the political prisoners were united. But in Haripur the Superintendent had reduced the workload of some prisoners, with the result that not all the political prisoners considered themselves equal. Silver decided on a clever ploy: a demand that the jail provide prisoners with footwear. 'This movement caught on ... and demand for footwear now reunited the ranks and brought in militancy and sense of unity amongst them'.[18]

Silver does not tell us whether the Superintendent provided the footwear, but in any event he was soon out, having served a mere three months in jail. However, the Raj had no intention of allowing him to wander free. He was served with a notice that he could not leave his village except every afternoon at four when he had to report to Mardan police station, a six-mile walk. This was popularly called internment and it was not until the end of 1936 that this order was lifted. Jamuna Das and Ishwar Das, both of whom had spent some time in jail, were also released and similarly 'interned' in Ghalla Dher. With three Silver brothers to look after, Mardan police decided the lone officer who had kept an eye on Silver could no longer do the job, and now three CID officials were stationed in the village. But while these officers could make sure Silver never left his village, they could do nothing to stop him moving around within the village.

Most of the villagers were illiterate and had never read a newspaper in their lives, but the age-old word-of-mouth form of Indian twitter had kept them informed. They knew what had happened to the Silver family, the hanging of Hari Kishan and Silver's various spells in jail. While a few of the villagers had joined the Red Shirt movement most of them were too busy eking out a living from the harsh land to have given any thought to whether the British should leave India. Despite this Silver was not seen as a rebel who had to be shunned. For many he was a 'hero', the word used to denote a man of prominence whose activities had made Ghalla Dher's name famous round the province and even in faraway Lahore. The fact that he was the son of one of the richest men in the village was not held against him. And while the British had stopped the family building a shrine to Hari Kishan in the village, his brother's 'martyrdom' had cast a halo over Silver. He was seen as someone who knew the ways of the world and could be turned to when a villager was in trouble. Not long after his return, even as three CID officers made sure he did not leave the village, a local who felt he had been wronged came to him for help. This proved to be the first chapter in what developed into a long story ending with Silver becoming a communist and an uncritical admirer of Stalin's Soviet Union.

Learning Politics from a Bullock

There is an old Indian saying that goes: which is more powerful, intelligence, or the bullock? Answer: the bullock. Silver was made very aware that this was no joke. For his road to communism began with a bullock. It belonged to Gulzada, a poor tenant farmer who tilled land that belonged to the Nawab of Toru, as did many villagers in Ghalla Der. One day his bullock strayed into a neighbouring field of another tenant farmer. This farmer complained to the Nawab's son, Karim Khan, who fined Gulzada Rs 40, an enormous sum then. When Gulzada, who could barely feed himself and his family, failed to pay, Karim Khan seized his bullock and sold it. With the bullock his only property, Gulzada was now destitute. He turned to Silver, whose advice to the farmer was to prove dramatic.

Karim Khan had just planted a new orchard, and Silver told Gulzada to uproot it. Gulzada eagerly accepted the advice, destroying the orchard in the middle of the night and throwing all the plants in the river. Although Karim soon learnt Gulzada had done it he decided to punish the entire village. Until now Karim's seizure of Gulzada's bullock and the latter's reaction had meant little to the villagers, apart from generating much gossip. But Karim's decision to fine the entire village took the dispute to a new level and resulted in such resentment that Silver knew he could now use this to organise the villagers. For Silver this was the Nawab's 'zoolum', tyranny, which could be met only if the entire village stood united and refused to pay. In order to encourage the villagers he decided to set an example:

I was also asked to pay a share of this collective fine. I told the Nawab's son that he had no authority to impose such a fine and challenged him to collect it. This started off the agitation of the peasants against the Nawab and his sons, which became a wide movement for land reforms in the area. It had a big impact on the surrounding villages also where the peasants were undergoing similar hardships. I organised the peasants into a sold phalanx for action against the *zoolum* of the Nawab for land reforms. They got together in meetings, processions and made representations to the government and district authorities. The movement spread to the neighbouring villages also.[1]

But while the movement was supposed to be non-violent a 'few misguided and overenthusiastic young men' murdered one of the Nawab's most hated agents, Dalel Khan:

> This gave a handle to the government and the Nawab, who let loose a reign of terror and tried to supress the movement. Many peasants were put behind bars but they did not yield and somehow continued to keep possession of their land.[2]

Silver, as the son of a well-off landowner, had benefited from the property ownership laws the British had introduced. But now, acting on behalf of the poor peasants, he started agitating against it, considerably widening the remit of the movement. Before the British had arrived the land was collectively owned. The British had introduced the landlord system to create a class that would support their rule, and over the years the landlords had instituted repressive feudal measures. This meant that after the harvest the crops were divided into two parts: one for the landlord, one for the peasant, with the agents of the Nawab often demanding more than their fair share. In addition the Nawab could demand *malba*, requiring the peasant to pay for the guests of the Nawab and their cattle. The most feudal tax was *tora*, which a bride and bridegroom had to pay at the time of their wedding, and then there was *begar*, forced labour without any wages. Worse still, when the peasants decided to sell their own produce they found middlemen in the markets who used weights which were faulty and made all sorts of deductions to defraud the peasants.

Silver found these feudal arrangements intolerable. However he also had a dilemma for just then, for the first time in the history of the province, a sort of western-style democracy had arrived and Silver was keen to become an active participant. While convinced that India, unlike the white dominions, could not be given dominion status, let alone freedom, the British were keen to educate Indians on how to rule themselves. In 1937 there were elections to the provincial assemblies in British India [the elections did not extend to the princely states where the rulers continued to exercise absolute internal power]. That year people in the North West Frontier went to the ballot box for the first time in their history. However, this was only just under 14 per cent of the population, as others were barred by lack of property and education qualifications. Apart from Silver, his relations and a few others, nobody else in Ghalla Dher could vote as they could neither read nor write, did not own any property or paid an annual tax of more than Rs 100. And even then the election was not one we would comprehend. The electorate was divided on the basis of race, religion, sex and occupation. Some Indian provinces had as many as 12 separate electorates: a small general franchise, depressed Hindu castes, Muslims, Europeans, Anglo-Indians, meaning the mixed race, Indian Christians, representatives of commerce and industry, labour, landowners, universities, women in general, Muslim women, Anglo-Indian women. In Silver's province nine of the 50 seats were general seats, which anyone entitled to vote could contest. However, 36 seats were reserved for Muslims, where only Muslims could vote for Muslim candidates; similarly Sikhs had three reserved seats and landowners two. However, there were no reserved seats for Muslim women, presumably because NWFP Muslim women were not considered eligible for such a privilege. And the general seats were further divided between rural and urban.

With Jamuna Das deciding to contest one of the general rural seats in the area around Mardan and Peshawar, Silver decided to take charge of the campaign, and so well did he marshal the Red Shirt movement, of which he was now such a vital part, that Jamuna Das won a thumping majority.

The elections showed how secular and non-sectarian this province then was, with a Congress ministry headed by Khan Sahib, older brother of Ghaffar Khan (who was banned from the province and not contesting the election), taking office. Despite the fact that this was a predominantly Muslim province Jinnah's Muslim League failed to even win a seat. Khan Sahib could not have been a better example of a Muslim who, while retaining his faith, showed how well he had taken to western learning and ideas. A qualified medical doctor, he had been educated both in India and at St Thomas' Hospital in London, where he met his English wife, Mary, the daughter of a Yorkshire famer. Today such an election result would be hailed for demonstrating that, even in an area overwhelmingly Muslim, religion played no part in politics. However, far from welcoming this development, the British administrators of the province were appalled. Gerald Curtis, the British deputy commissioner of Hazara district, was deeply unhappy that Khan Sahib:

> ... was bent on promoting a more egalitarian society. The British had relied on the landowning class, Pathan country gentlemen known generically as 'the Khans', very similar in taste and outlook to the country gentleman who in effect governed England before the Reform Act of 1832. To Dr Khan Sahib and his brother, although they belonged to that class, such elitism was all wrong ... Dr Khan Sahib was genuinely concerned to side with the have-nots against the haves of Pathan society, and to harry corrupt officials and oppressive landowners.[3]

Silver also had a problem with the new Government. This was that Khan Sahib's reforms were not going far enough or quickly enough, and he decided that there was no alternative but to carry on with the agitation in Ghalla Dher. He helped form a war council of leaders and began to use the same tactics of non-violence campaigning and boycott of courts that Gandhi had used against the British, but directed this time at the very Khan Sahib ministry Silver had helped to elect. So intense did the agitation become that Khan Sahib was forced to make an impromptu visit to Ghalla Dher where Silver, along with two colleagues nominated by the peasants, met him to negotiate on their behalf. At the meeting Silver, confronting the leader of the party he nominally supported, made it very clear that to restore peace there must be a ban on *Begar* and the Nawab's right to evict tenants, withdrawal of *Tora*, and also the abolition of *Malba*. He could not forget what had happened with Gulzada's bullock, and wanted complete restriction on the right to impose such illegal fines, in addition to the end of physical harassment of the peasants and forcing them to act as sweepers if they did not follow the Nawab's orders.

The meeting proved tense and did not resolve matters. Silver found that despite being president of a ward Congress committee in Mardan he was not supported by all his fellow Congressmen—some of them were landlords—and he felt increasingly restive that Khan Sahib's government might not be really committed to bringing about the reforms he wanted. In that sense he was like some of the modern Labour left-wingers who, while remaining in the Labour party, opposed Tony Blair's Government. Soon Silver was organising protests and was arrested when leading a procession through the streets of Mardan.

For Silver this was almost like revisiting the agitation against the British. The Khan government now imposed Section 144 in the Mardan district, prohibiting political gatherings and meetings. And when Silver and his colleagues refused to provide security they were sentenced to rigorous imprisonment from six months to two years. Silver watched from jail as the agitation in his village grew, with about a hundred female relatives of the arrested tenants, carrying a red flag in their hands and the Koran on their heads, resisting the forceful takeover of the land by the Nawab's men. As the police moved to arrest them some of them threw themselves in front of the cattle-plough, causing a stampede which resulted in some women and a child being injured. It was not until November 1938, at the initiative of Gandhi, that Silver and his colleagues were released and the government was forced to agree to the reforms Silver and his colleagues were demanding. Sayed Wiqar Ali Shah, a historian of the region, has written:

> The Ghalla Dher movement remains an important episode in the history of the NWFP ... the prominent leaders came from various sections of Pashtoon society. Along with the poor masses, this movement included members from the Pashtoon intelligentsia, and some very important religious figures. Irrespective of their belonging to various religious or social groups they

supported the cause of the poor peasants of Ghalla Dher against the Nawab and his accomplices.

As for Silver Shah has no doubts he was:

> ... one of the most prominent leaders of the movement and was given a central position in the organising committee ... The leaders of the movement focused on the unity of the peasants because they knew that once united the peasants could force the ministry to accept their demands. The provincial government which earlier paid no heed to the demands of the peasants was compelled under the circumstances to take steps to protect the rights of the Ghalla Dheris. All illegal taxes were abolished and the tillers were promised due share in the produce of the land. Further, the forcible eviction of the peasants came to an end. The Ghalla Dher peasants thus gained substantially from their joint struggle and this created more confidence among them ... Lastly, another noteworthy feature of the Ghalla Dher movement was that most of the Ulema [Muslim scholars and theologians] ... also supported the peasant movement and used Islamic and Pashtoon symbols, without making it a communal [religious] issue, unlike what was happening in contemporary Bengal.[4]

In his memoirs Silver would claim, with some justification, that:

> The outstanding achievement of this movement was that the tradition of 'Begar' [working without pay], collection of collective or individual fines, and other such feudal practices were abolished for good.[5]

Silver's involvement in the Ghalla Dher struggle had further enhanced his political skills and seen him form links with the Congress left wing, in particular the Congress Socialist Party, and this soon brought him in contact with a man who was to play a decisive part in his life and ensure that he became a spy.

This man was Subhas Bose, the Indian revolutionary, who had been described as an 'implacable foe' of British rule in a secret British memo in 1933. The British saw Bose and Jawaharlal Nehru as the two main young leaders they should worry about. Unlike Nehru, however, Bose was seen by the British as a man who was not really wedded to the use only of Gandhian non-violence to free India. But, unable to prove any links with the gun men, the British were forced to imprison Bose without trial, using obscure laws such as Regulation III of 1818, which had been designed to deal with Indian princes fighting against the East India Company as it sought to conquer India. Even when Bose was released, often because he had fallen ill in jail, it was done on the condition that he agreed to leave India. On one occasion he was not released until the ship had actually left Indian waters, with the British threatening him with arrest even if he returned to see his dying father. By the time he returned his father was dead.

When Silver met Bose he was a free man, almost as prominent a leader as Nehru, particularly among the young. He travelled up and down the country arguing that a free India must be a socialist country. Bose, however, was not much liked by Gandhi, who agreed with the British that Bose was not committed to non-violence. The Mahatma preferred Nehru, with whom he felt a soul bond, promoting him as his heir. There was a brief rapprochement between Bose and Gandhi when, in 1938, Gandhi agreed Bose could become President of the Congress, an honour that also led to his appearance on the cover of *Time* magazine. But the deep differences between the two could not be concealed and Bose, worried that the Congress was not socialist enough and might compromise with the British, decided to stand again for election as President in 1939, challenging a nominee of Gandhi and sensationally defeating him. Gandhi, who for all his professed saintly qualities could be a ruthless political operator, soon vanquished Bose and forced him to leave the Congress and form his own party, the Forward Bloc.[6]

Silver decided to follow Bose and became the NWFP propaganda secretary of the party. In India at that time the word 'propaganda' was seen in a positive light and Silver gloried in the title. He soon had a chance to prove his worth, for in June 1939 Bose came to Peshawar. Bose had always had a fair amount of support, but his falling-out with Gandhi seemed to have increased his popularity, particularly with the young, and Silver worked hard to ensure that all the potential supporters knew of the visit. The result was that a huge crowd turned up at Peshawar railway station to greet Bose and, as is common in India, Bose, at the head of this crowd, made his way through the city's streets. During the march news came that Khan Sahib's son had died. Bose decided to go to his residence to pay his respects, and Silver helped by stopping the procession so Bose could make the visit. That evening Bose addressed a public meeting to explain why he had left the Congress and, watching the huge crowd that had gathered to listen, Silver felt very pleased with the way he had organised the 'propaganda' for the visit.

However, on this visit Bose and Silver did not meet, and Silver could not have imagined how just over a year later he would meet Bose. This would be in great secrecy in a house in Peshawar, both men trying hard not to be recognised at a meeting that would change the lives of them both. By then war had been declared, and Silver suddenly found himself transported from the world of publicity and street demonstrations into the shadowy world of spying.

The Stagehand Becomes Main Actor

A decision Silver took just before the war began meant he would spend the war years as a spy, shuttling between Afghanistan and India. Sometime in 1939, possibly soon after he had helped to publicise Bose's trip to Peshawar, he decided to join the Kirti Kisan (Workers and Peasants) Party, having become increasingly doubtful about how radical the Congress could be, given its many wealthy supporters. Kirti, a regional communist party based in the Punjab, maintained its distance from the nationwide Communist Party of India (CPI). It had Hindu members, like Silver, and also Muslims, but its leadership was largely Sikh, and it was the Indian counterpart of the Ghadar Party set up by the Sikhs in San Francisco.

These Sikhs, who had migrated to North America around the turn of the twentieth century, had sought to use Canada as a launch pad to free India, with their most spectacular effort coming during the First World War. That had failed thanks to Vickery but, despite this, the drive to eject the British from India remained a goal and in 1929 the Ghadarites helped to set up the Kirti party in the Punjab. It was inspired by communist ideals, with independence seen as the first step to a workers' and peasants' state, and the destruction of the Indian capitalist class.

Silver knew life as a communist could never be easy. For a start it was lonely. In December 1928, when the CPI had been established in India, there were only 78 members all over this vast country. Even in 1942, almost 15 years later, by which time there had been much help from the British communists who sent members to guide Indians on the ideas of Marx and Lenin, there were only some 5,000 members. The authorities in India had always harried the communists, with three well-publicised trials in the 1920s, and the CPI had been banned from the mid-1930s. But for anyone attracted by communism in the Punjab and the NWFP, Kirti was a natural home. Kirti had always had close relations with Naujawan Bharat Sabha and, given Silver's association with the Sabha since his school days, he was familiar with many of its members. Perhaps the crucial factor in his joining was that one of Kirti's most prominent leaders was Silver's mentor, Ram Kishan. And Ram Kishan had an urgent task for his disciple. This was to help party workers coming back to India from America and other parts of the world, often using forged passports. His assistance was also needed by those who wanted to leave the country via the tribal areas for Afghanistan, Soviet Union and other countries. Having no first-hand knowledge of the area in August 1939 Silver decided to explore the region and headed for Chitral.

The choice showed his sense of adventure. Silver had never been out of India, indeed never further than Lahore in neighbouring Punjab, while Chitral was more than 200 miles away from Peshawar. But for Silver Chitral was ideal. Curzon had described it as 'this small chink in the mountain palisade', the northernmost town of any size where Britain's Indian frontier practically touched the Russian border. Russia was said to covet it and the British were determined to hold on to it. It was the attack on Chitral by rebellious tribes in 1895 that was the background to the war that had brought Churchill to the region in 1897. A princely state that had a treaty arrangement with the British, Chitral was ruled by the Mehtar, who received a subsidy with the British maintaining a fort in the area. As in all such princely states, the British allowed the rulers to do much as they wanted as long as they never upset the overall British control of the subcontinent. Chitral, whose inhabitants were predominantly Sunni Muslims, allowed its small minority of Hindus and Sikhs to trade but not to openly practise their religion or have places of worship. Other Muslim sects, such as the followers of the Aga Khan, also faced similar discrimination and many of them had fled. But religion had never mattered much to Silver: what was of greater interest for him was that Chitral, as a princely state, did not have the communications that a British-controlled province would have. The car and the telegraph line had only reached Chitral a decade earlier, and he felt this gave him scope for developing his contacts without much scrutiny.

His decision to go to Chitral was also influenced by the fact that, after a decade of hostility, it had once again become friends with Afghanistan. Silver was keen to explore the river trade route between the two countries, and he was in the middle of doing just that when he heard that the Second World War had broken out.

He hurried back to India to find the Indian political scene in turmoil. Within hours of Neville Chamberlain's broadcast that Britain was at war with Germany, Lord Linlithgow had, without consulting a single Indian, plunged 400 million people into a European war of which they knew little and understood even less. The question for the Indians was, if Britain was prepared to go to war to safeguard the freedom of Poland, should it not free India or at least say when it would give India freedom? In Nehru's vivid phrase, how could Indians fight for freedom when they themselves were not free? With Britain in peril Linlithgow felt such questions were irrelevant. The Congress responded by deciding it could not support the war effort and launched yet another campaign to free India. There was a split in Congress ranks about the war with Gandhi, after the fall of France, giving Linlithgow the extraordinary advice that the British should allow Hitler to 'take possession of your beautiful Island', even allow the German dictator to slaughter them. However, Nehru was a dedicated anti-fascist and would have joined the war effort had Linlithgow showed any inclination that the British planned to free India after the war. For Silver and his communist comrades what mattered was not what the British did in India but what the Soviet Union decided.

With Stalin having signed his infamous pact with Hitler weeks before the Nazi planes unloaded their bombs on Warsaw, the diktat from Moscow was that this was an imperialist war, one which they should not support. The Kirti leaders, like communists all over the world, slavishly accepted Moscow's advice although it brought a swift retaliation from the British. It meant the party could no longer operate openly and the party's two magazines, *Chingari* and *Kirti*, which the British felt had developed an 'increasingly vehement and unlawful tone', ceased publication. The result was, as one secret British memo put it, 'all revolutionary plotting and planning was forced to go underground'.

The impact of this on Silver's life was dramatic, as he realised when he met his guru Ram Kishan. Clearly impressed by the way the young man had gone to Chitral, Kishan had decided he would be his frontier 'contact'. His orders were succinct and clear: Silver should abandon political work, should no longer be in the public eye organising meetings and protests, and should go 'underground'. Ram Kishan was asking the 31-year-old to make a huge change in his life. Having been a man very much in the public eye who revelled in organising publicity and propaganda and boasted about being jailed by the British, he was now required to go underground and at all costs avoid being arrested. It took many hours of meetings spread over several days in various towns of the North West Frontier, Mardan, Peshawar and Nowshera, before Silver accepted his guru's orders.

Ram Kishan was well aware his disciple would need some tutoring for this new life and in the space of little over six months introduced him to three men who knew much about this secret world. Two of these were on the run from the police and the third had supplied guns to Punjabi terrorists. All three would be jailed before the end of the war. For Silver, working with these three was a crash course on how to be secretive, keep out of the clutches of the police, and secure safe hiding places, both for sanctuary and the storage of valuables.

Harminder Singh Sodhi[1] was the first to enter Silver's life when in February 1940 Ram Kishan summoned him to a meeting in Mardan. Silver had never met someone with such experience of the world of international revolutionary activity, and he listened with wide-eyed wonder as Sodhi told him the story of his life. A clean-shaven Sikh and treasurer of the Kirti party, he claimed to be a man of the world, having worked in the United States, as a paid apprentice at the Ford factory in Detroit. There he had been recruited by the Ghadar party and sent to the Soviet Union for training as a communist. In 1937 Sodhi, as a British secret intelligence note put it, 'surreptitiously arrived in India from Moscow' and had initially run an eponymously-named party publication. Then as the war began Sodhi decided to preach sedition to Indian troops who had pledged themselves to fight for Britain.

Silver listened with rapt attention as Sodhi described how he had worked to suborn the Sikh soldiers of the Central India Horse, a cavalry regiment stationed in Meerut in the United Provinces. Sodhi so successfully indoctrinated their leader Bishan Singh that he had told his men:

> British rule in India would collapse ... The right place for Sikh soldiers, therefore is at home in the Punjab, guarding their wives and families, not fighting Britain's inevitably losing battle against more powerful European enemies in Egypt.[2]

In 1940, as the regiment was ordered to the Middle East, two thirds of the Sikh squadron refused to go. The regiment sailed without the Sikhs and, after a court-martial, the leaders were transported to the Andamans where they fell into the hands of the Japanese after Japan's conquest of the island. By this time Sodhi had left Meerut and headed back to the Punjab, proposing to carry on with his anti-war activities. He had come to the NWFP in the hope of persuading Ram Kishan and Silver to help organise a local branch in the province and also distribute copies of his new publication, *Lal Jhanda* [Red Flag]. Silver readily agreed.

Sodhi hoped to use his propaganda sheet to persuade more Indian troops to mutiny, and for this the Punjab and the NWPF were hugely significant. This was because the British recruited Indians on the basis of a racial policy called the 'martial race' theory, which laid down that only certain Indians were racially capable of being soldiers. So not every Indian, even if he wanted to fight for the British, was allowed to join the Indian Army. The Punjab was considered to be full of racially suitable men and provided the majority of troops, while other provinces much bigger than the Punjab did not have a single soldier in the Army. Just before the war began the Punjab provided 43.72 per cent of the Army, and the NWFP 4.67 per cent, when the two provinces together made up just about 7 per cent of India's total population. In contrast the British believed the 'effeminate' Bengalis of the east were more capable of being clerks—in Macaulay's words: 'During many ages he has been trampled upon by men of bolder and more hardy breeds. Courage, independence, veracity are qualities to which his constitution and his situation are equally unfavourable.' So, despite the fact that Bengal had 14.6 per cent of the country's people, there were no Bengali soldiers in Britain's Indian Army.

But while Sodhi was confident of suborning troops in the Punjab and NWFP what was to be done with the soldiers who mutinied? 'It was proposed,' says Silver, 'to explore the possibility of shifting them to tribal areas for training in anti-British sabotage'.[3] Soon after this meeting Silver was despatched to the areas, meeting several tribal leaders, and discussing whether land could be purchased to set up a colony where these soldiers could be housed and trained in anti-sabotage work. But while the tribal leaders were never shy of fighting the British they were not keen to train soldiers to fight the British in India. They were also not keen to have immigrants from India in their midst. One of them told Silver that with the British having their agents among the tribes, these soldiers would be easily detected, and it was best to wait until there was a war between the tribes and the British, as there often was. Silver returned to tell Ram Kishan the plan would not work, and 'as an alternative these men [should be] distributed in small groups and deployed in different parts of the country to do the underground work of our party'. This anti-British activity may have come to nothing, but Ram Kishan was impressed with the speed with which he had established relationships with the tribal leaders and learnt secret routes back and forth to the tribal areas. He decided Silver would be ideally suited to help the Kirti party deal with a crisis so serious that it threatened the very existence of the party. Very simply, Kirti had run out of money.

For the first decade of its existence Kirti had been able to flourish as a regional party independent of the CPI because of generous funds provided by the Sikhs in North America. So the expat Sikhs had provided Rs 10,000 to fund the publications that Sodhi produced. The wartime restrictions imposed on the transfer of money from abroad meant the Sikhs in America could no longer send funds. The only alternative was merger with the CPI. In April 1940 Ram Kishan had had merger talks with the CPI, but negotiations broke down when the larger party proposed that the Kirti dissolve itself and merge with the insignificant Punjab branch of the CPI, a proposal Ram Kishan contemptuously rejected. There was, he decided, only one alternative: go to Moscow to convince the Soviets that it was the Kirti that should be recognised as the true communist party in India. He also felt that the trip would be useful to seek Moscow's guidance as to the war policy the communists should follow. However, making a trip to the Soviet Union via Afghanistan required a great deal of planning, and this is where Silver came in. Ram Kishan had seen enough of his work to be convinced that he would be the ideal person to act as a contact and guide for him and other Kirti party workers who wanted to use this route to reach their communist paradise. In late May 1940 Ram Kishan arrived in Ghalla Dher to discuss the new role he had for Silver.

Now, in theory, Ram Kishan could not have arrived at a worse moment. Two weeks earlier Silver had got married. It is, however, a real insight into Silver's character that, far from showing Ram Kishan the door, he could not wait to hear what this new job was and how soon he would start. And here the biographer of Silver is faced with a very difficult task. In his 267-page biography Silver devoted just four lines to his marriage. He does not even mention his wife's name. We only learn of it from the caption in a photograph showing Silver posing with a woman. The caption reads: 'The author, Bhagat Ram Talwar [Silver], with his wife, Shrimati (Mrs) Ram Kaur'. The picture shows the couple in middle age when his life as a spy was history.

It was clearly an arranged marriage, as Silver makes no secret in his memoir that he did not want to get married: 'The nature of my political work that lay ahead was not quite suitable for such a step'. But he gave in to family pressure: 'However because of social customs prevailing in the family and among my relations I had to agree to this marriage'.[4] As far as his family was concerned a 32-year-old man could not be single. Nothing illustrates better the hugely contradictory world Silver inhabited.

Politically he could not be a more dedicated communist, a man keen to drastically reorder the old feudal world, yet in his private life he had to accept the age-old ways of Indian society. It must be said that Silver was not unique in this. In 1968 his political hero Ghaffar Khan, when asked by an Indian scholar about the names of his sisters, rebuked his questioner: 'Why speak their names?' And Rajagopalachari, one of India's foremost politicians and the first Indian to be Governor-General of India, while keeping a prison diary to record his experiences in a British jail, did not mention his wife's name. Echoing Khan, he wrote: 'Why speak their names now?' As far as Silver was concerned marriage was something men went through, and the wife could be left at home if a more thrilling adventure beckoned. Nothing Ram Kaur and family life offered could match the excitement of this new assignment.

Ram Kishan had arrived in Ghalla Dher accompanied by a man posing as a student. Silver soon discovered the stranger was no student but a high ranking Kirti comrade called Achhar Singh Cheena who knew Sodhi well. A Sikh, and the son of a rich Amritsar landowner, he had, against his father's wishes, abandoned his engineering studies at Berkeley University in California, to work at the Ford factory in Detroit. That is where he had met Sodhi, and like him he had joined the Ghadar party and gone to Moscow for training. Then, after a time back in America, he had returned to India at the end of 1935 using a false passport and with money from Sikhs in North America, to organise Kirti along mass revolutionary lines. Like Ram Kishan he had also tried to organise a merger between the Kirti and the CPI. But despite offering what was a substantial sum for those days, Rs 1,200 as 'a token of Kirti goodwill and earnestness to form a united front', the talks failed. By the time Cheena met Silver he had been on the run from the police for nearly two and a half years, having run into trouble in March 1938 when he had presided over a political conference near Amritsar which resulted in a fight between two rival groups and the death of two men. The police had charge-sheeted him and, as the intelligence note put it, 'He absconded before he could be arrested'.[5] In order to avoid detection he had shaved off the beard most Sikhs have and made sure that, as he criss-crossed India, his clothes blended in with those of the locals so that he did not stand out. If meeting Sodhi had made Silver realise the sort of anti-British activity the Kirti party was keen on, Cheena proposed something that was quite remarkable and totally unexpected. He told Silver that the party wanted him to escort 'a very important person of international eminence to the Soviet Union',[6] taking him over the land route via Afghanistan. Cheena did not reveal who this important person was and Silver, having quickly picked up the secret ways of the shadowy world, did not ask. It was many months later that Silver realised who this 'very important person' was.

The person Cheena was referring to was Subhas Bose, whom Cheena had met a few weeks previously while in Calcutta. At that meeting Bose had asked for the Kirti party's help to get him across the tribal areas into Afghanistan and then over the Oxus river into Russia. He wanted to go to the Soviet capital to get Stalin and the Red Army's help to invade India and drive out the British. That Bose had approached a party struggling to survive showed how desperate he had become. He had lost control of the Bengal Congress, his political power base, been expelled from the national party and after nearly twenty years of trying to free India from British rule had nothing to show for his efforts. What he was proposing was curious, since the Soviet Union had in the past rebuffed his efforts to visit the country. And it was undoubtedly opportunistic, based on the principle of 'my enemy's enemy is my friend', irrespective of the nature of the enemy whose help he was seeking. Bose had initially approached the CPI leadership, who had turned him down as they suspected that he was, at heart, a fascist and could not be trusted. So it was as a last resort that he had turned to this fringe communist party.

Cheena was initially staggered by Bose's request. Major politicians, who had based their entire political life on public agitation, did not suddenly plan to escape from India as a fugitive, certainly not politicians of the stature of Bose. But Cheena quickly saw much merit in the idea, and it was ideally suited to the plans he was himself formulating. If the Kirti helped Bose get to Moscow they could show the Comintern, the Soviet organisation that guided overseas communist parties, that they were not a puny party but one trusted by a major political figure, something that at that moment the CPI could not claim. And by this time Cheena had become very tired of always looking over his shoulder; even during his brief stay in Calcutta he had to change his hide-out twice to evade the police. Even before he had met Bose Cheena had decided that to avoid arrest he must return to the Soviet Union and that he would take Ram Kishan with him. He now told Bose of these plans, who immediately gave Cheena Rs 200 to cover his expenses. The two men parted on the understanding that Cheena would return to the NWPF, make plans to spirit Bose out of India and then return to Calcutta to fetch Bose. And having heard much praise of Silver from Ram Kishan, Cheena had hurried to Ghalla Dher to recruit him.

Silver could barely contain his excitement, and the very next day he bade goodbye to his bride of two weeks and accompanied Ram Kishan and Cheena to Peshawar, where he stayed in a safe house that Ram Kishan had arranged for them. Cheena, still keeping Bose's name a secret, told Silver that he was off to fetch the 'very important person' and Silver should help Ram Kishan prepare for the journey. There was much to do.

The house they were in was not considered suitable for the very important person so another one had to be found for him to stay in when he arrived in Peshawar. Also they had to get a Pathan guide for the journey through the tribal areas. Silver's role was to help Ram Kishan in this, and he was impressed by how his guru went about finding the house and hiring a guide called Mir Zada. Ram Kishan also devised cover names for himself and Cheena. Ram Kishan was to be called Zaman Khan, and Cheena Nawaz Khan. These were, of course, Muslim names, as Hindu names were deemed suspect for the journey through tribal territories. Ram Kishan told Silver that they must always take care to use these Muslim names when speaking in front of Mir Zada. At this stage Silver was not given a Muslim cover name because he was not expected to have a role beyond the Indian border. He was seen as a helper, not a central figure in this adventure. A few days later Cheena returned and Silver was devastated to hear that the very important person was not coming and had changed his mind. Even at this stage details of what took place between Cheena and the important person were not disclosed to Silver, and it was many months later before he learnt the whole truth.

What had happened was that on his return to Calcutta Cheena was told by Bose that, worried his plans had leaked, he had decided not to escape but instead launch an agitation against the British. Cheena's Calcutta contact told him that Bose would almost certainly be arrested and there was no way he could now think of undertaking such a journey. Bose was also not impressed when Cheena informed him that he had himself never been to Kabul, and while Ram Kishan knew Kabul well he had never been to the Soviet Union and would not know how to get to Moscow. Bose was left with the thought that while Cheena and his friends might get him to Kabul, he could very well find himself stranded in the Afghan capital.

Depressing as this news was, Ram Kishan told Silver that he would not change his plans to go to Kabul and on to the Soviet Union. Indeed he was going to leave the very next day for the Afghan capital. And now he gave precise instructions to Silver as to what he wanted him to do. He was to go back to his village and wait for a message from Ram Kishan. This would come in the form of a letter, telling him how Ram Kishan had got on with the Soviet Embassy in Kabul. The letter would be signed Zaman, and Cheena would be addressed as Nawaz Khan. A special messenger would bring the letter. Ram Kishan did not say who the messenger was, but emphasised to Silver that after receiving the letter he must do nothing but wait for Cheena to contact him and then disclose the contents of the letter and the steps to be taken. Silver, still learning about the world of subterfuge and code names, listened carefully and by the time Ram Kishan left he was confident he could do as required. Then, after bidding his guru a very affectionate farewell which involved touching Ram Kishan's feet in the mark of respect younger men show their elders in India, Silver returned to Ghalla Dher. A month later, just as he was getting to know his wife for the first time, a messenger arrived with the letter from Ram Kishan. Silver had to strain to listen to the messenger, a stout, well-built man with a hoarse voice as well as a stammer. The letter he carried was to have important consequences for Silver, and the messenger would prove to be the third man, after Sodhi and Cheena, who would play a vital role in helping convert Silver from a mere courier into a spy.

The messenger was Abad Khan. In contrast to Sodhi and Cheena he was a Muslim but an old friend of Ram Kishan who lived a very intricate double life. Most people knew him as a transport contractor who hired out lorries for use on the Peshawar-Kabul route. But that description did little justice to a man whose political views were very much to the left, who was a gun-runner for various Indian revolutionaries and had provided information to the Russians in Kabul. He was also employed as an agent by the British intelligence operation in the region and had brothers who served in the Indian Army. From an early age, Abad had been influenced by a headmaster who 'held strong political views and impressed on me that the English were plundering India by taking away the products of our country, and ever since my sentiments have been anti-British'.[7] Despite this, in the last year of the First World War Khan, then a 21-year-old, joined the Military Transport Department as a driver, and with the British using Indian troops to secure Iraq, was drafted to Basra. He served with the Indian Army in various parts of the Middle East, including Baghdad, Khanke and Kermanshah.

In the years leading up to the Second World War Khan had done various jobs, including working as a driver for several military contractors. This had given him enough money to ply his own lorries between Peshawar and Kabul and make it such a successful business that he owned a very comfortable home in Peshawar. He had often been to Kabul, becoming very friendly with an Indian café owner, Ghulam Mohd, who was an agent for the Russians. Abad, who would later confess to the British police, 'I had incurred a hatred for the British Government and cherished a desire to participate in any movement directed against them',[8] readily worked for the Russians. This included providing reports on the various political movements in the Punjab, military information and maps. With funds supplied by Modh, Abad Khan also purchased arms for Indian revolutionaries, took part in the Frontier Gandhi movements and was even arrested. But, reflecting the often contradictory world of Indians and their relationship with the British, he also acted as an agent for Mian Abdul Hanan, who worked in the Quetta intelligence, part of the elaborate and extensive British spy network in the region. They had developed such a good relationship that he counted Abad Khan as one of his friends. To complete the complexity, two of Khan's brothers served as fitters in the Indian Army and, even as Silver met Abad Khan, one was fighting the Italians in Libya, while the other was based in Singapore.

Abad, who knew Ram Kishan well, had arranged for his journey from Peshawar to Kabul and agreed that he would personally act as his messenger and take the letter he sent from Kabul to Silver. Delighted as Silver was to meet Abad, the contents of the letter dismayed him. When Ram Kishan had left Peshawar for Kabul his great worry was that as an Indian with no papers it would be very risky to carry any money or clothes with him while travelling through the tribal areas. However, Mir Zada had an Afghan travel permit and could take the regular lorry service from Peshawar to Kabul, and he asked him to carry the money and clothes. It was agreed the two would meet at an Afghan village Ram Kishan knew well situated just over the border with India. But when he got there he found neither money nor clothes. Mir Zada had just disappeared. And to make his life in Kabul almost impossible he could not get anywhere with the Russians. The Embassy officials did not trust him, refused to believe he was a communist in need of help and would not even talk to him. So desperate was Ram Kishan's plight that his instructions to Silver had changed. He could not wait for Cheena to contact him, he must find him and ask him to come to Kabul immediately.

For days Silver agonised about how he could help his political mentor. With Cheena always on the move to avoid the police, Silver just did not know where to contact him. Fortunately Cheena, getting restless, came back to Peshawar, contacted Abad and, hearing the grim news, immediately rushed to see Silver in Ghalla Dher. He only had to read Ram Kishan's pitiful letter to realise that that as far as Kirti was concerned, Bose was now an irrelevance. For the survival of the party Cheena had to go to Kabul and establish contact with the Russians. Cheena headed back to Peshawar, accompanied by Silver, and immediately met Abad and asked him to help organise his trip to Kabul.

Abad was ready to do so but the only problem was money. There was the cost of an Afridi guide and also clothing that would make sure Cheena looked like a Pathan as he went through the tribal areas.

Now Sodhi, who had by this time also joined the group, proved the saviour. Living up to his reputation as a resourceful treasurer, he produced the necessary money, Rs 200. But lest Abad get the wrong impression, he emphasised that with the war going on and no remittances from America the party was broke. Silver carefully went through the route Cheena was taking, and it was agreed that this should be established as the preferred route for other Kirti workers who wanted to go to Kabul. But even as Silver helped out he could not conceal his worry about what was happening to his political mentor in Kabul. Cheena reassured him that the first thing he would do on his arrival in Kabul would be to take Ram Kishan to the Soviet Legation and ask for help in getting to Moscow. Once there they would obtain the Comintern verdict on what Kirti should do during the war and how it should finance itself. The pair would then immediately return to India and report to the party leadership. Silver bade goodbye to Cheena with great affection, urging him to convey his best wishes to Ram Kishan and how eagerly he was looking forward to his return. Little did he know that he would never see Ram Kishan again and, when he finally caught up with Cheena, long after Indian independence, he would hear a totally fabricated story about how Ram Kishan had met his end. In this case it was Silver, the master spinner of lies, who was deceived by Cheena.

After Cheena's departure, Silver returned to Ghalla Dher to resume his already much interrupted married life with Ram Kaur. Still unhappy with it when, in September 1940, he heard that Sodhi was back in the NWFP and staying in Mardan, he rushed to see him. Sodhi had been put up by a relative who was a Tehsildar, revenue officer, in the area. The fact that Sodhi, wanted by the British for organising a mutiny, could stay with someone who was an essential part of British colonial rule showed how rebels and collaborators co-existed in the Raj. Sodhi brought news that plans were being made to hire a safe house for the party in Nawakot, a suburb close to Lahore City. This, Sodhi explained, would serve as the rendezvous point for Kirti workers in Lahore.

In the 15 months since the start of the war there had been major changes in Silver's life. From being a skilful propagandist for the party, he was now an intimate associate of men who led double lives and operated in the shadows. But Silver still had a walk-on part and hardly any lines. He craved the big stage. As he would later tell the British:

> ... the spirt of adventure appealed to me compared with the narrow rut of subversive politics in Peshawar and Mardan. Having quarrelled with the Red Shirts the latter prospect offered little scope in any case.[9]

Now a series of events would provide Silver with the adventure he sought. It was triggered by another visitor who called on Silver in Ghalla Dher, a very different man to the many who had come calling in recent months. He was not living in the shadows, always looking fearfully over his shoulder, but a major political leader of the region and, what is more, not from Kirti but from Silver's old party, the Forward Bloc. The task he set Silver ensured the stagehand would indeed take centre stage in the drama that unfolded and end up completely overshadowing Cheena, Sodhi, Abad Khan and his own hero, Ram Kishan. It is a testimony to Silver that, far from fluffing his lines, he seized this totally unexpected opportunity as if he had always been destined to play the starring role.

Searching the Road to Kabul

The visitor who arrived in Ghalla Dher in the third week of December 1940 was a Nowshera lawyer called Mian Akbar Shah. He was probably the most colourful politician ever to come there. In his youth he had joined the Hirjat movement of the Frontier Gandhi and gone to Afghanistan. There, however, he had been attracted by communism and decided to go to the Soviet Union, where he studied in Moscow at the 'University of the Toilers of the East'. On his return to India he had been charged in the Peshawar conspiracy case, one of several brought by the British against communists who had slipped back to India from the Soviet Union, and after three years in prison he had decided to shed his communist associations. By the time he travelled to Ghalla Dher his professional time was spent getting communists released from Peshawar jail, while politically he was an important leader of Bose's Forward Bloc on the North West Frontier.

Shah had just come back from Calcutta where he had met Bose, who had recently been released from jail after going on hunger strike and threatening to fast unto death. One cynical government view was that the hunger strike would do Bose good: 'as he has been suffering for some time from over-eating and insufficient exercise, it seems likely that a little starvation will improve his health'. However, the British did not want his death on their hands, and had decided on a cat-and-mouse policy: the moment he recovered, he would again be jailed. Unconditionally released, Bose was now free to go where he wanted, though the Calcutta CID kept a round-the-clock watch on him and also had a spy, a distant cousin, inside his home. Bose was due back in court on 27 January 1941 and both the British and Bose knew what would happen. Bose would be asked to keep the peace, he would refuse, and this would mean yet another spell in jail. Mortified by the idea that he would spend the war, which could decide India's destiny, in a British jail, Bose decided to revive the idea he had first discussed with Cheena. He would disguise himself as a Muslim, surreptitiously leave Calcutta in the dead of the night and make sure he got to Kabul before his scheduled court appearance. But with Cheena no longer an option Bose had turned to Shah. Although Shah had no clue of how he could get Bose to Kabul he had got to know Silver, particularly during the pre-war Ghalla Dher agitation, been impressed with him and decided he was the man to turn to. He was all the more convinced he had made the right choice when during their meeting in Ghalla Dher Silver, far from showing any surprise at Shah's approach, told him that detailed plans for the escape were already in place. It was during this meeting that Silver finally learnt that the very important person to be transported was Bose. The next day the two travelled to Peshawar and that evening went to Abad Khan's home confident the arrangements would not be a problem. But that was not to prove the case.

For a start there was Abad's attitude. Gone was the affable, friendly, willing man Silver remembered from his previous trip. Now he appeared very reluctant to be involved in this adventure. It didn't help that during the conversation Mian Akbar Shah revealed that the 'important person' for whom Khan was to organise a reliable, safe journey to Kabul was Subhas Bose. And with the court date looming it had to be done quickly. For Khan the casual way Shah had revealed Bose's name suggested he was dealing with amateurs who did not know how to keep secrets. He flatly refused to help. Silver had to work hard to convince him, and eventually persuaded him to 'find a reliable man' to escort Bose to Kabul.

But then there was the problem of finding a good guide, essential with the British enforcing a strict check at Jamrud, the town that was the doorway to the Khyber Pass. Abad had had in mind, Ghairat, who worked as a cleaner, but he was nowhere to be found. 'Again and again', Khan later confessed to the police, 'they pressed me to make this quick arrangement, but I could not find a reliable man'. The clock was ticking for Bose's appointment with a Calcutta court, and 'At last, without having made any arrangements, I told them to send for Bose'.[1]

During this period of waiting there was one question on which everyone was agreed. Bose could not be allowed to make his own way to Kabul: he would simply not be able to cope. With Abad Khan refusing to accompany him and other candidates rejected, that left Silver as the only option. Though growing in confidence that he could get Bose to Kabul, he was soon confronted with problems he had not anticipated. The first was Sodhi's sudden arrival from Lahore. He had learnt that the police had worked out who was behind the mutiny of the Sikh soldiers of the Central India Horse, and had charged him with abatement of mutiny, a capital offence. Eager to escape the hangman, Sodhi had decided to follow Cheena to Moscow, and it was agreed that he would accompany Silver and Bose to Kabul.

A few days later Silver was told Bose would arrive in Peshawar by the Frontier Mail on 19 January. That evening Bose checked into room six of the

Taj Mahal hotel and was moved the next day to a house rented by Abad Khan where, on the evening of 21 January 1941, Silver met him for the first time. For both men it was to prove a rather disappointing meeting.

Bose had been told he would be in the hands of a revolutionary Pathan, so assumed that Silver would be stereotypically tall, big and imposing. But the great revolutionary guide who stood in front of him, Bose would later confess to Silver, was disappointingly small and thin and looked incapable of fighting anyone.

By contrast Bose did not appear remotely like the man whose visit to Peshawar Silver had helped to publicise. In place of the traditional dhoti and Bengali *chaddui* (garments covering the lower and upper parts of the body) he had worn then, he was wearing broad pyjamas, a long coat and a black fez, clothes worn by Muslims on the north-west frontier, and posing as one. He was carrying a business card which read: Mohd. Ziauddin, B.A., LL.B., Travelling Inspector, The Empire of India Life Assurance Co. Ltd., Permanent Address: Civil Lines, Jubbalpore.

Silver could not help noticing how jumpy Bose and even Abad Khan were: Bose wanted to get out of Peshawar as quickly as possible, fearing that the moment news of his escape leaked out the place would be swarming with CID officers. It was also understandable that Bose, a 43-year-old politician who had been in the limelight all his life, was not finding it easy to adopt to life as a fugitive. It was barely a week since he had been spirited away in the dead of night from his Calcutta residence by his nephew, boarded a train for Delhi at a wayside station and, on the final lap of his journey to Peshawar, had to restrain himself from disclosing his real identity to a fellow passenger who was regaling the compartment with stories about the finances of the Indian princes.

Abad, increasingly worried curious neighbours may discover Bose's presence, decided to shift him to a more secluded, if more costly, house. Such was his paranoia that he moved Bose only after darkness had fallen. There Bose was kept under virtual house arrest. Abad came every morning with vegetables, meat, tea, etc., to see that he had enough to cook for himself. He would then lock Bose up and go to work. Bose, suspecting him to be a fraud, offered Abad a bribe of his gold watch which Abad refused, reassuring him that, 'None except God could arrest [him].' For the first few days Abad did not even tell Silver where Bose was. When Silver did visit Bose he decided it was best if he came only in the evenings, spending the day wandering round Peshawar buying clothes for Bose to make him look like an authentic Pathan: a Malaysia cloth *salwar, kamiz*, Pathan leather jacket, a Postin waistcoat, khaki *kulla* and *lungi* as headgear and Peshwari *chappals* as footwear. He also decided Bose should carry a Kabuli blanket. Bose, by now, had a beard about an inch long and Silver, keen to cheer him up, reassured him that this, combined with his build, sharp features and fair complexion, would certainly make him pass as a Pathan. He also organised Afghan currency and medicines, the last of which was obtained from Dr Charu Chandra Ghose, the President of the NWPF Congress Committee, though he never dreamt of telling him—a Bengali to boot—that Bose was in Peshawar.

Sodhi was also a visitor and Silver listened keenly to their conversations. Bose, seeing the Soviet Union as virtually in an alliance with Germany against the British Empire, suggested to Sodhi that, surely, Stalin would not hesitate to invade India and help eject the British. Sodhi countered that if India rebelled, the Soviet Union would support the revolt, certainly help with revolutionary propaganda and perhaps provide money. But he did not think Stalin would send the Red Army to invade India, thus entering the war on the Axis side, unless conditions became much more favourable and India appealed for help. Sodhi was also not convinced that Bose was not a fascist sympathiser, at which Bose protested vigorously that he had written many articles against fascism and even supported the Russian invasion of Finland. But, despite their evident political differences, Sodhi and Bose had one thing in common, both were very worried about being arrested and Sodhi made it clear he must accompany Bose and Silver to Kabul. However in the end it was agreed that as neither he nor Bose spoke Pushtu, the Afghan language, it was too risky for Silver to take both of them. Sodhi would wait for Silver's return from Kabul and then go later.

By now Silver had decided on how Bose should behave during the journey. Bose was to pretend to be a deaf and dumb Muslim gentleman going to Adda Sharif on a pilgrimage. He would continue to be called Ziauddin but, Silver warned him, on no account was he to open his mouth in public as he did not know Pushtu. Silver was also aware that he had to acquire a Muslim name to pass off as a Pathan in the tribal areas and in Afghanistan and choose the name Rahmat Khan, the one he, as we have seen, later gave to Quaroni when they met. Silver was also conscious that both he and Bose would have to be careful when they prayed so as not to give any hint they were not Muslims. He feared that if the tribals suspected they were not Muslims they would be stripped, revealing that they were not circumcised and could not, possibly, be Muslims.

Then Silver hit an unexpected problem. He had decided that his route would be the one Ram Kishan had taken: Peshawar to Shab Kadar, Gandab Valley, then Lalpura, Jalalabad, a detour to Adda Sharif to make sure the story of Bose the pilgrim was convincing, and then a quick backtrack to Jalalabad and the final stretch to Kabul. But then he heard that the British police had arrested a stranger, said to be an enemy spy, on the Indian side of the border, and this convinced him that the route was being watched by British CID agents and must be abandoned. With Abad Khan he devised an alternative route: from Peshawar to Jamrud, then on to the Khajuri Maidan British military camp, leading on to the Afridi and Shinwari tribal areas, where they would cross into Afghan territory at Garhadi on the Kabul–Peshawar road. From there via Bhati Kot to Jalalabad, the obligatory detour to Adda Sharif, back to Jalalabad and then to Kabul. This new route, 13 miles south of the Khyber Pass, had its problems: it was shorter but steeper, but what clinched it for Silver was that as none of his colleagues had ever used it, no-one knew about it, so even if there was a spy in their camp, something Silver was always concerned about, he could not disclose any details of the route to the British.

Silver also asked for a guide to take them through the tribal areas, and the evening before their planned departure Abad introduced him to a 40-year-old Afridi. Silver, aware of how Mir Zada had cheated Ram Kishan, went to meet the guide in some trepidation but instantly liked the look of him: medium build and height with a small pock-marked face and beard, a wheatish complexion and blue eyes. However, Abad Khan could not completely trust the Afridi and it was agreed that he would spent the night with Silver and only meet Bose the next morning.

At 6.30 the next morning, as Silver was waiting with the guide on the bank of the canal opposite Peshawar's Sessions Courts, stocked up with *parathas,* fried eggs and blankets, Abad drove up in a Chevrolet he had hired that morning on the pretext of taking some guests to the Khajuri plain with Bose in the back seat. The route Abad Khan's driver had taken suggested this was just an everyday car journey, and not the first leg of helping a rebel find foreign support to eject the British from India. At one stage the car had gone past the local police station where there was a three-minute wait in a traffic jam. As if this was not sufficient defiance of British might, after collecting Silver and his party the car drove through the Cantonment, where the British military was based, towards Bara Fort. There could have been a potential problem at the levy post when the Khassadar, one of the tribals the British paid to be loyal to them, presented the register, but Abad Khan made a false entry and signed it, and they drove on towards Fort Salop. To the right of the fort a hilly track led towards Afridi tribal territory, and here Bose, Silver and the guide got out.

As they were preparing to bid goodbye Bose took out his wad of notes, Rs 450, peeled off Rs 100 and gave it to Abad Khan for his expenses. Aware of how Ram Kishan had been robbed by his Afridi guide, Abad sternly warned Bose and Silver not to show their money to the guide or anyone else in the tribal territory. And then, to make sure the guide believed that neither Bose nor Silver had any money, Abad Khan made a great show of giving Silver 100 Afghani rupees for the journey. Abad told the guide that if anyone questioned him about Bose and Silver he was to say they were guests of Latif Malik of Tirah; he was to take them to Adda village, and on his return would receive a reward of Rs 30. Then just before he took his leave of Silver and Bose, Abad suddenly turned to Bose and said that he should take off his glasses: they were far too conspicuous for the tribal areas.

The British explorer Robert Byron, coming the other way from Kabul to Peshawar a few years earlier, recorded how the British had brought modernity to the area, supplementing the historic road now used by camels with two roads, one of 'asphalt as smooth as Piccadilly and glanced by low battlements' and:

> Intertwined with these comes a third and larger thoroughfare, a railway, leading to the head of the pass and soon to extend beyond it, glinting from tunnel to tunnel whose black mouths, framed in pylons of red masonry, recede into the savage grey distance. Roads and railway are embanked on shelves of hewn stone linking mountain to mountain; iron viaducts carry them across the valleys and each other. Sheaves of telephone wires fastened to metal posts by gleaming white insulators, red and green signals jewelled in the torrid haze, drinking-troughs fashioned like antique sarcophaguses, and milestones proclaiming, at intervals of thirty yards, that the distance to L, J, and P—Landi Kotal, Jamrud, and Peshawar—has decreased, all complete the evidence of the neat grey block-houses perched on every ledge and peak: that if the English must be bothered to defend India, it shall be with a minimum of personal inconvenience.[2]

Bose and Silver, seeking to bring down the English, could not minimise their personal inconvenience by using such British inventions. Their first concern was that the hilly track they now slowly negotiated was only a furlong from the British military camp but with the three posing as devotees going to a Muslim shrine nearby nobody paid them attention. It was when they had come little more than a mile from the shrine that Silver realised that the problem of getting to Kabul was not going to be just avoiding British and Afghan checkpoints, but Bose himself. A politician used to a sedentary life, Bose had never done anything like this before. Travelling in this region was demanding: the route traversed a fiercely hot, stony desert with no trees, no grass, occasionally a few thorny bushes. Now and then there would be a couple of mud houses, but it was mostly just an arid, empty landscape. Even though it was winter, the dry, intense heat of the day was unlike anything Bose had experienced in the Indo-Gangetic plains. They seemed to be forever climbing and descending hills: a climb of about 130 metres, followed by a descent of some 200 metres, then a climb again. Though not much older than the Afridi, and despite what the British had thought about a hunger strike being good for his weight, Bose was still a fairly heavy man. As a result, even though the journey had barely begun, he suddenly sat down, clearly exhausted.

Silver knew he could not order Bose to continue. For all his revolutionary views, when it came to social matters he was a conformist, religiously observing the Indian custom of respecting older men. Even as a grown man he had touched the feet of his parents and other elders, and he always addressed Bose with the correct Indian form of the personal pronoun: not *tu*—for very close friends—or *tum*, for acquaintances of a similar age, but *aap*, for older people and those of distinction. What is more, he would never refer to him as Subhas, but rather Subhas Babu, a term of respect often used to address political leaders. So with Subhas Babu unable to move Silver decided this would be a good place to have lunch, collected some dry wood and got a fire going to heat the *parathas* to have with the eggs. And to cheer Bose up, he told him he was now in tribal lands, 'independent territory not under the domination of a foreign power'.

Bose was instantly revitalised. All the frustration, uncertainty and fear he had felt since leaving Calcutta a week earlier evaporated. He jumped up, stamped his feet and shouted, 'Here I kick George VI!'[3] Back in October 1939 Bose had met Linlithgow in Delhi's Viceregal Palace, the only time he had had such a meeting. Linlithgow did not believe Indians could rule themselves; Bose wanted the British to leave immediately—but, as Linlithgow's secretary recorded, 'the Viceroy liked him personally and the talk was quite friendly'. Now Bose laughed, and spat out a globule of spit. 'Here I spit on the face of the Viceroy,' he shouted.

From that moment Bose did not find the journey quite so trying, and by midnight they had reached the village of Pishkan Maina. The Afridi guide knew the local custom was for strangers to be accommodated in the mosque or a place called *Hujra*, a common sitting-room. It was like no hall either Silver or Bose had ever seen: no windows or ventilation, no furniture, let alone beds, and 25 men sleeping, talking or lying on a floor cushioned with a thick layer of dry grass. Silver knew they only had to say they were hungry for food to be provided and, what is more, Pathan custom dictated there would no charge—indeed, an offer of payment would be deemed an insult. The food was simple: pots containing sugary, milky tea and cakes made of salted maize bread.

However, Bose found the stuffy, smoke-filled room very uncomfortable and woke Silver up with a jolt saying he needed to go outside for air, where Silver had be a nurse to him, giving him water and putting drops in his nose and throat. The men in the hall had been very incurious as to who they were and had left them alone, but with Bose going outside for air frequently Silver got worried that the tribals might become suspicious—they might think the strangers in their midst were spies trying to make contact with their agents. He was very relieved when the night was over.

Silver knew the next morning the villagers of Pishkan Maina would be curious about the strangers and told Bose they would pretend to be masons from Peshawar going to the next village to construct the house of Malik

Latif Khan. But while the villagers were easily convinced, they had barely left the village when Bose declared he could not cope with all the walking: could he have a mule? Having just said they were going to the next village only three miles away, Silver explained, a request for a mule would look odd. They would have to wait till they got to the next village. Bose, reluctantly, accepted although this meant a very slow walk with the journey taking three long hours. Fortunately the village turned out to be bigger than the one they had left, and Silver quickly found an Afridi shopkeeper who was also a Sikh. He had mules, agreed to hire them one to take them to a village just over the Afghan border for only Rs 8 including cushions.

Just before they left, Silver reminded Bose that he was not to talk if anyone else was around, as he did not speak the local tongue. It helped that they were going through an area where many of the inhabitants lived by smuggling goods between Afghanistan and the tribal areas: they didn't want strangers to be curious about their business either, and the less everyone talked the better.

With the route taking them across the mountain range that formed the border between the tribal area and Afghanistan, Silver was now wholly dependent on the guide and the mule man. Towing Bose as he sat on the mule also made progress slow. To add to the complications, the mountain pass was at a considerable altitude, and it was nine in the evening before Silver and his party reached it. The journey up to it, on the sunny eastern side of the mountain, had been comfortably negotiated, but as they began to descend on the western side what light there was totally disappeared as they entered dense forest and encountered snow for the first time. This so disorientated Bose that he slipped from his mule. Fortunately he was rescued by the mule man and the guide and a quick examination showed he had a few bruises but no serious injury. But it was clear he could no longer ride the mule while descending the mountain and must dismount and walk, which made the journey even slower, and it was one in the morning before they reached the first Afghan village on the foothills of the mountain, a small settlement inhabited by the Shinwari tribe. The guide and mule-man assured Silver that it would be easy to find shelter as they knew one of the villagers. Silver, inventive as ever, quickly came up with the story to tell the villager: that he and Bose were strangers who happened to be travelling together as they were both heading for the village of Garhdi. All they wanted to do was spend the night in the village.

Silver's group could not have arrived at a more awkward time. That very day the villager the guide knew had got married, and was just settling in with his bride to celebrate their wedding night. Moreover, the couple lived in a single-room house. Nevertheless, Silver and his group were welcomed in and, with almost a spring in his step, the villager flung open the door to the room and lit a kerosene lamp to provide some light.

The scene that presented itself was probably one of the most unusual Silver, and even more so Bose, accustomed to an affluent life in India, would ever have encountered. In one corner were several goats, and in the middle two beds, on one of which the bride, still in her wedding dress and wearing the jewellery she had been given for her wedding, was asleep. The man motioned Silver, Bose and the others to settle on the vacant bed while he woke up his wife and, writes Silver:

> ... she seemed pleasantly surprised to see us and offered to cook for us. We were hungry and therefore we readily agreed. We certainly did need something to eat.... We were amazed at the promptness with which the newly-wed bride cooked and served us food. She gave us scrambled eggs and parathas.... Though she was modest, she never displayed any undue shyness and behaved as if we were her own kith and kin.[1]

Indeed, the newly-wed took such a liking to Silver that later that night she helped him further. Throughout the trip Silver's one great dread had been that the Afridi guide would rob them: now he wanted to scribble a message of thanks to Abad Khan complimenting him on his choice of the guide—but he neither had pen nor paper.

> When this bride guessed my problems she took out a ball of thread, removed its wrappings and handed it over to me for writing my message. She poured a few drops of water in her palm and added some indigo to serve as ink and gave me a small stick to be used as a pen. I scribbled the message on the piece of paper and handed it over to the guide who left along with the mule-man.[5]

After the excellent meal Silver wanted a night's rest, and clearly Bose too, but the villager insisted they leave while it was still dark. Clearly he did not believe that Bose and Silver were on their way to the Adda Sharif shrine—Silver got the impression he thought 'that like many other people in the border area we were also in some sort of a business of dubious nature'[6]—and possibly he didn't want them still in his house at daybreak to arouse suspicion in the village. So at five in the morning, barely four hours after they had arrived and with the village shrouded in darkness, Silver was back on the road. At this stage, having bid goodbye to the Afridi guide the rest of the journey to Kabul should only have been the two of them, but with Bose still requiring a mule and the villager also having some it was decided to hire one from him even if his price of Rs 13 was on the high side. It also meant the villager and one of his men came along with them but to Silver's relief, the track ran on level ground and this time Bose had no problems on the mule.

As they neared Garhdi the villager, as though testing their claim to be Muslim pilgrims, told them there was a sacred shrine called Garhdi Baba, also known as

Gardhi Gaus, which they should make for. There, while the villager looked on, Silver and Bose went through the motions to suggest they were indeed devout Muslims. Apparently reassured, the villager told Silver that should he need help on the return journey he could ask for it. However, before they parted he did warn Silver that if anything happened to the pair they must not disclose they had spent the night with him. This was a jarring note on which to part but what reassured Silver was that despite pretending to be a Muslim accompanying an Indian political leader, who for the last week was being furiously sought by the British police, he was now thirteen miles inside Afghanistan and had not been apprehended. He felt he had every reason to congratulate himself on what was a major coup.

The easy way to reach Kabul now would have been to take one of the many buses plying between Garhdi and Jalalabad, but Silver decided that would be too risky. There might be CID officers on board, or he might meet men he knew in Peshawar, and sitting by the roadside waiting for the bus might also encourage passers-by to start asking them questions. He decided the only way to get to Jalalabad was to hitch-hike on a passing truck. Bose was not used to hitch-hiking, but apparently lifted by being in Afghanistan, a country that had always resisted the British, he felt so elated that he now almost danced and skipped as he and Silver sauntered down the road happily discussing politics. Their joy lasted a mere two miles when Silver was suddenly faced with the grim possibility that he would be caught out and his lies exposed.

They had just sat down for a rest by the roadside when around the bend from where they were sitting emerged almost a comic-book Pathan—huge, with a handle-bar moustache. Clearly surprised to see them he started asking questions forcing Silver to spin more lies.

In response to the Pathan's first question as to where they were from Silver had jauntily answered they were Lalpura, a small village just across the river from Kabul about six miles away. Although Silver had never been there he had heard many stories about the village from fellow inmates in Peshawar jail and was convinced he had invented a reliable tale. The Pathan's response was thunderous: they could not possibly come from there, he was from Lalpura himself and had never seen them there. Silver realised he had to admit to the lie, but came up with another—that the pair were actually from across the border and in Afghanistan because Bose, his uncle, was deaf and dumb and they hoped he could be cured by making a pilgrimage to Adda Sharif.

This pacified the Pathan somewhat, but there was another problem. The Pathan claimed some medical knowledge and demanded to see Bose's tongue. Until now Bose had played the deaf and dumb very well; now Silver had to persuade him to show his tongue to the Pathan. Not knowing any sign language, Silver gestured with his own tongue to make Bose realise he had to stick his tongue out. The Pathan wiped his hand on his long *kurta* shirt and felt Bose's tongue.

Silver waited apprehensively for the Pathan to declare that there was nothing wrong and the two were clearly involved in some scam. But to his relief the Pathan declared that Bose's tongue was really stiff and that, while a visit to the Adda Sharif shrine was a good idea, Bose should also try some treatment—alum in hot water which should be held in his mouth for some time three or four times a day.

The Pathan did not seem to want to let them go, and as they got up to resume their journey so did he, telling them they should come to Lalpura and he would help them in any way he could. Silver, keen to get away, underlined the urgency, for devout Muslims such as themselves, of reaching the shrine, but promised to do so on his return. This seemed to satisfy the Pathan who, to Silver's immense relief, finally departed.

For a time it seemed they would have to walk all the way to Jalalabad, but fortunately they were able to thumb a lift with a truck carrying boxes of tea, albeit perched precariously on top of them. There was a further scare when the truck was stopped by two policemen looking very stern, who told the driver he had to wait until a district official arrived. For two hours Silver and Bose sat on the tea boxes not knowing what the official might do. But when the man arrived it seemed all he wanted was a lift to Jalalabad and since being an official he could not perch on the boxes the driver found him a seat in front.

In the history of Britain's involvement with Afghanistan, Jalalabad stands for the worst defeat suffered by them in the nineteenth century, during the first Afghan War. It ended with a lone Scotsman, Dr William Bryden, arriving at the walls of Jalalabad on a bedraggled and exhausted pony, saying he was the only survivor of an Indus Army of 20,000 and twice that number of camp followers who had been sent to conquer the Afghans. By the time Silver and Bose arrived it was one of the largest cities in the country, with broad roads and alleys, and capital of the eastern province, with the British having a consular office right on the bank of the River Kabul. Silver, taking care to avoid it, headed for the crowded bazaar to find a hotel.

He soon discovered that Afghan hotels were not like hotels in India or many other parts of the world. Clearly Afghans did not believe that guests required their own rooms or even beds: everyone was accommodated in a large hall, sleeping on thick, beautifully designed rugs, made quite cosy by a system of heating Silver had never encountered before. The *bukhari* system used wood burned in a drum-shaped steel hearth to heat a water drum above it, an exhaust pipe connected to the water drum taking the smoke away. The hotel did have the odd private room and Silver had to work hard to convince the hotel owner that his uncle was so unwell that they needed one.

Next morning they were off to Adda Sharif, a little over four miles from Jalalabad, ostensibly to offer prayers but in reality to go and see Haji Mohd Amin who lived in a village called Lalman, a mile and a half outside the Adda

Sharif. Silver had met him in jail in Peshawar in 1930 eleven years earlier, and Amin was a useful contact who combined his belief in Islam with a fervent hatred for the British.

Amin was delighted to see the pair and embraced them both. Silver, very aware proper decorum must be maintained, addressed him respectfully as Haji Sahib and spoke in Urdu so that Bose could follow the conversation. With Amin Silver felt he could drop the pretence that Bose was his deaf and dumb uncle and let him on their mission—but even then only partially. So he did not reveal Bose's identity, introducing him as a very important figure in Indian political life who was heading for the Soviet Union. Amin, in turn, warmed Silver's heart by saying that he knew all about the great sacrifices Silver's family had made, a reference to Hari Kishan's execution by the British, that 'he always considered the British the enemy of his people' and 'would consider my [Silver's] word as a command for him in the struggle against the British'.[7] His advice on the best route to Kabul was to retrace their steps to Jalalabad and hire either a truck or a tonga. He warned, however, that with Jalalabad having 'all sorts of people' they shouldn't stay too long. If they ran into problems they should say they were men of Naqweb Sahib, a religious leader in the Afghan administration widely regarded as pro-British.

Back in Jalalabad Silver decided a tonga was best. But they could not just hire one to head straight for Kabul: they had to pretend to be locals just travelling from one village to another. So when they reached the next village, Sultanpur, nine miles away, they got out as if this was their destination, and when Silver saw the tonga start on its return journey to Jalalabad he hired another one to go the other way to Kabul. Every step on the journey had to be measured: who was watching—was he an Afghan spy or a British spy? After a delicious lunch at Fatehabad of *pulao*, chicken and *naan-i-khushik* which Bose, who liked his food, much enjoyed, the pair took to the road again and reached Mimla, a local beauty spot famous for its orchards and running water. The Mimla Hotel was by far the best hotel they had seen since leaving Peshawar, and Silver was very 'tempted' to enjoy its comforts. But he felt 'it looked like a rather posh government hotel for tourists, officials, foreigners and state guests', and two strangers with enough money to stay there would arouse immediate suspicion. In any case, a truck was approaching, and Silver quickly signalled for it to stop.

Once again they had to perch themselves on top of boxes of tea, and this time they weren't the only passengers. Night descended on the mountain road to Budhkak, the main town before Kabul, and travelling in the open sitting on a tea box was no longer the rather breezy drive it had been: the road led through the Lataband Pass, where there was snow on either side, and it grew almost unbearably cold. Bose had never experienced such weather before, and even for Silver, who had grown up on the north-west frontier and was used to cold winters, this leg of the journey was 'very difficult and strenuous'. The five-hour drive to Budkhak seemed never-ending, and it was four in the morning before they arrived in what the Afghans proudly called their country's fruit capital.

This was the only place in the world where good-quality Sarda, the country's favourite fruit, is grown. But for Silver the immediate concern was that Budkhak was also where the government's customs and excise officials checked both foreigners and locals. Foreigners had to show their passports, others had to have their names and addresses recorded. Truck drivers, though, were allowed to pass through without giving their names, so Silver told Bose to follow them and pretend he was one of them. He himself went to the booth prepared to give a fictitious name and address, but found the official fast asleep. A few minutes later as Silver joined Bose in their hotel the two men could not stop laughing as to how easy it had been and with Bose convinced he had negotiated the final checkpoint before Kabul.

Budkhak is only thirteen miles from Kabul and at 8 a.m. the next morning their truck driver announced he was ready to leave. But the truck had to pass through a customs barrier, and passengers on trucks were often assumed to have come from Peshawar so Silver decided it was much safer to take the tonga to Kabul. It was not hard to find one and they arrived at its Lahori Gate at about 11 a.m. on 27 January 1941.

Bose, who had always taken a keen interest in history, knew all about how much Barbar, the first Mughal Emperor of India, had loved Kabul. Babur may have conquered Delhi, and established the Mughal dynasty in India, but he had insisted that he should be buried in Kabul. The city that lay before them had come a long way since the sixteenth century. While it still had an easy, unpretentious character it looked more like a Balkan town. Silver and Bose could see how it clustered round a few bare rocky hills which rose abruptly from the verdant plain and acted as defences for Kabul. In the distance they could see the mountains covered with snow.

Silver was immediately taken by the fact that the location of the city, 'in a valley surrounded by hills', made it easy to defend:

> The city at the foothill is protected from enemy attack from outside by a huge wall constructed many years ago. It is an old wall constructed on top of the hill on three sides of the city. The wall is used as protection for the army defending the city from invaders. There are a number of gates in the wall around the city, but no such gates have been provided in the wall along and on top of the hill.[8]

This defensive strength was enhanced by the natural beauty of the river Kabul cutting through the city with bazaars along the banks. However, the setting could not compensate for the fact that that Kabul, which at a height of 6,000 feet was always going to be cold, was in the middle of a severe winter. It had snowed heavily in the week preceding the pair's arrival and snow lay thick on the ground. And Silver knew in bringing Bose to Kabul he had done only part of his job. Now he had to find a place to stay, and then knock on the doors of the Soviet Embassy.

This became all the more urgent when, a few hours after their arrival, as Silver and Bose wandered the streets of the city, they heard a radio broadcast saying Bose had disappeared from his Calcutta residence, with conflicting reports of where he had gone, some saying he had, like the classical Hindu sages, renounced life to go and live in an Ashram. Silver had no clue where the Soviet Embassy was or how he could get Bose inside it. The journey to Kabul had been an adventure. But this was a prelude to an even greater one: something beyond his dreams.

Seeking Stalin finding Hitler

In many ways Kabul in 1941 was little more than a glorified village.[1] There were only about 15 modern brick and cement buildings: the King's palace, a few apartment buildings, the embassies and consulates. The majority of its population lived in mud houses, and while there were some decent hotels Silver felt that in such a hotel their cover story of being visitors from a village would not wash and that the only safe option was the *serai*: a sort of café where most people ate on the pavements and slept on charpoys or beds in a large communal hall, though serais also had a few private rooms. It was at such a *serai*, near Lahori Gate, that Silver secured a room. It provided some privacy and a couple of beds but nothing else. They had to acquire bedding, fuel, candles as there was no electric light, and some cheap second-hand woollen garments for Bose.

The Indian food they both liked was very different to what most Afghans ate, so, the better to blend into the local landscape, rather than eat in restaurants Silver and Bose bought food and ate it in their room. However, as Silver soon discovered, lack of knowledge of the local customs caused problems. Passing a roadside café they saw some very tempting hot *halwa*, a popular sweet, and katalmas, huge round white parathas lavishly fried in *ghee*. Silver ordered half a *pao* [a pao in India is about 200 grams] of each for both himself and Bose, thinking it would just about fill a plate each. But an Afghan *pao* was 450 grams, a pound. The shopkeeper seemed surprised the two men should want so much food and, sensing he might think they were strangers, Silver quickly told him to pack up the food after he had filled their two plates.

As long as they kept their distance from the locals Silver and Bose could wander round Kabul in peace and soon they were visiting the city's many bazaars, the great beauty spot, the garden on the Shah-i-Kabul hill overlooking a stream and a vast meadow where Babur was buried in an open grave looking up at the snows of Paghman mountain, a place Silver would get to know well in the next few months.

However, even as they wandered round Silver always had to be on his guard. When Bose noticed a photographer and suggested they take a picture Silver told him they should do no such thing—by now his photograph must have been published in thousands of newspapers, even the Afghan press. The photographer in developing the photograph would look at the film minutely, retain the negative and should he then glance at a paper he would immediately identify Bose. And for all he knew, said Silver, the photographer may be an Afghan or even a British agent. Bose, never having thought of such complications, sheepishly confessed 'he had very little experience of underground life and was not aware of its technical aspects', and expressed his happiness that he had a man like Silver 'so well experienced in the work of such a nature'.[2] Silver did not admit that this was his first spying venture and the incident shows what a quick learner he was. In contrast Bose, for all the talk of being a revolutionary and, in the British portrayal of him, a man who worked with the underground movement, was in reality a politician at his best when arousing the masses at public meetings.

But while teaching Bose how to behave like an undercover operative was not impossible, contacting the Russians in Kabul seemed an insurmountable problem. It was more than six months since Ram Kishan and Cheena had left for Kabul and Silver did not know if they had succeeded in getting in touch with the Russians or whether they were even still alive: 'During this period we had no contacts with that country through their embassy in Kabul or through any other source'.

The two men debated at length about how to get into the Soviet Embassy. Should they just go to the front gate and demand to be let in? They decided this was far too risky: not only would the embassy have Russian guards, but there were also Afghan policemen outside, and Silver and Bose did not look important enough to suddenly arrive unannounced at the embassy gates. Silver also quickly concluded that the various individuals he'd noticed on the approach to the embassy were spies working for other embassies in Kabul, in particular the British Embassy, whose task would be to report back the coming and goings on at the Soviet Embassy. Bose was also particularly worried that, with the Afghan government very pro-British, if he was apprehended he would immediately be handed over to the British. Silver was confident Bose would be allowed to travel to any country he wished to, but with Bose claiming to know how international politics worked, Silver had to defer to him.

The plan Silver devised to contact the Russians may not be recommended in many training manuals for spies, but was quite ingenious. The pair would monitor the comings and goings at the embassy, and every time a white man or woman appeared they would know these must be Russians. The pair would then follow these officials around Kabul, and Silver would approach them with Bose's letter to the Soviet Ambassador saying who he was and that he wanted to go to the Soviet Union. There was no guarantee, of course, that the Russians could speak English, but Silver decided that Soviet staff in this part of the world must speak Persian, one of Afghanistan's main languages. The Afghans use a form of Persian called Dari, very similar except it uses more Arabic words and some Persian words no longer used in Iran. Silver, having studied Persian at school, could make himself easily understood in Dari. So, from the morning of 28 January 1941, Silver's 'catch a Russian' operation began.

The two-storeyed Soviet Embassy on the right bank of the River Kabul was surrounded by high walls. However, the gate was clearly visible from the bank opposite. Silver selected a good vantage point which had another very attractive feature. During the day the sun shone brightly and many Afghans came here to take the sun. Silver and Bose could easily pass for locals and not arouse suspicion.

The pair had to wait a day before a Russian emerged. Silver and Bose watched where he was headed, and as he was walking down a street that led to Bazar Labe Darya, Silver made his move. He sidled up to him and, in Persian, told him he had a letter for the ambassador. Treating Silver as yet another Afghan trying to sell him something, the official murmured something in Russian and quickly walked away.

The next day two Russian women emerged, distinctive not only for their skin colour but also, in a city where women were always veiled, for their frocks. They too were heading for Bazar Labe Darya. But the women just shook their heads, said nothing and quickly moved on, convincing Silver that the embassy staff were under strict instructions not to have any dealings with the locals.

He soon came up with an alternative plan. Before leaving India he had discovered that the Soviets had a trade agency about half a mile from their embassy. On 31 January, having spent three fruitless days seeking a friendly Russian, Silver headed for the trade agency and found it conveniently located near a fruit shop. Silver engaged the proprietor in conversation and asked how he could see the Soviet trade agent. As they were speaking an official came out: this, the shopkeeper told Silver, was the trade agent. However when Silver approached the official he was brusquely told that if he wanted to send a message to the Ambassador he should go directly to the embassy.

The situation had an element of comedy about it: two Indians, one a major political figure, pretending to be Afghans staying in a dosshouse, unable to contact the Russians. But for Bose it was also very frustrating and, after two days of head-scratching, he decided he would approach the Germans. They were after all at war with the British. In the thirties when the British had exiled him from India, and stopped him from coming to Britain, he had lived in Vienna, been to Germany often, met high-ranking German officials, and could even speak the language. He had also secretly married an Austrian woman four years earlier. In contrast the Russians had never shown any interest in him.[3]

The plan the pair worked out was that Silver would accompany Bose to the German Embassy. But only Bose was to try and enter, and if Silver did not hear from him during the day he was to assume the Germans had taken Bose under their protection and would arrange for him to travel on to Germany. Just to make sure, though, Silver was to wait at the bridge on the River Kabul near the customs office at 4.45 p.m. for a message from Bose to confirm everything had gone all right. Bose wrote a letter in Bengali for his older brother Sarat, and an article in English on the Forward Bloc, and explained to Silver how to contact his family in Calcutta.

The walk to the embassy on 2 February provided another twist. They had just gone past the Japanese Embassy when they noticed a car flying a flag approaching them. Silver quickly realised it was the Soviet flag and assumed the person sitting in the back was the Soviet ambassador. Silver was right. He was Moscow's envoy in the Afghan capital, Konstantin Aleksandrovich Mikhailov. As luck would have it, around the bend they found the car temporarily immobilised in the Kabul snow. It seemed a godsend. Silver knocked on the window and in Persian, a language the ambassador was likely to know, said, 'I have Subhas Bose with me and he is seeking asylum in the Soviet Union.'

Not surprisingly Mikhailov asked, 'How do I know you have Subhas Bose with you?'

'Well,' responded Silver, 'take a good look at him. He is standing next to me dressed as an Afghan. In any case, it can be checked with photographs that have been published.'

Mikhailov looked at Bose for a long time. Was this a British plot? He had grave suspicions that the British had allowed Bose to escape in order to create trouble between Russia and Afghanistan. In any case, he could not act without instructions from Moscow. As Silver watched in dismay, the ambassador looked away, and eventually the car drove off. The Russian connection had failed. Evidence that has since emerged shows that Mikhailov not only knew Bose was in Kabul but had also been told by Moscow that he would probably go over to the Axis and it would be best to have nothing to do with him.

By now Cheena and Ram Kishan were in Moscow, although it had not been easy to get there. After Cheena's arrival in Kabul he and Ram Kishan had managed to contact the Soviet Embassy, but it had refused to help and told the pair to make their own way to the Soviet border by crossing the Oxus River and try their luck with the first Soviet outpost. Faced with the appalling prospect of being stranded in Kabul the pair decided they had no other option but to make their own way to the border. After a journey that involved a horse ride of three days they crossed over safely, only to find that when they got to the Soviet side they were taken to be criminals and locked up. Cheena needed all his powers of persuasion, including reminding the Russians of his Comintern pseudonym, Larkin, before they managed to get through to Kozloff, considered the Comintern's expert on India. To Cheena's great relief he recognised the Indian.

Kozloff apologised for locking them up and tried to make amends by putting them up in a hotel, giving them warm clothes and taking them to Moscow. When Cheena told Kozloff how Bose had given him money and asked for help to arrange his trip to see Stalin, but had had to be left behind, Kozloff's response was it was just as well they had not brought Bose 'as this might have led to international complications which the Russian Government did not want'. Kozloff seemed very well-informed on India and Bose, and had asked Cheena why Bose was planning to visit Russia when one of his lieutenants, a man called Shankar Lal, 'was flirting with the Japanese Government'. This was highly secret information which only the British knew, and it is likely the British had tipped off the Russians. At this stage of the war the British were courting the Russians and feeding them information, including warnings of Nazi attacks—within weeks Churchill was to send a message to Stalin that Hitler had moved large forces to the east—and there could well have been titbits about Bose amongst all this. On hearing news of Bose's escape Kozloff had told Cheena that he thought Bose would join the Axis, and all this must have been passed on to Mikhailov, increasing his suspicions about a man the Russians had always thought was a fascist at heart.

The German Embassy was no different to the Russian one, at least outwardly: high perimeter walls and gates manned by Afghan police. As Silver and Bose approached the embassy they agreed that in the event of the guards asking questions Silver would explain that Bose was ill and deaf, had a nephew who worked for the German legation in Tehran, and had come to request the legation make some enquiries from Tehran about him. But the guard made no enquiries and Bose was allowed in.

However an Afghan had been watching and, as Silver turned to head back to the *serai*, he was followed. Silver's response has more than a touch of Rudyard Kipling's hero Kim, learning on his feet and adapting brilliantly to any new situation.

I suspected him to be a British spy watching the German legation. He continued to dog my steps but as soon as I took a turn towards the bazaar from the Japanese embassy from where he could not see me, I took long and quick strides to enter the bazaar and mingle with the crowd. Meanwhile I managed to wear my coat inside-out (as the colour inside was different). I then walked some distance through different roads and came back to the bazaar. I did not find the man chasing me anymore.[4]

A relieved Silver decided to celebrate by going to a good restaurant and eating to his 'heart's content' quite the best meal since leaving Peshawar. But he returned to the *serai* to find Bose sitting outside looking very upset, convinced that either Afghan government spies or agents of other embassies had seen him and that he might be apprehended any moment.

This was despite his having just met Hans Pilger, the long-serving German ambassador, who not only knew about him but had met him on one of Bose's visits to the German Foreign Office. Pleased as he was to see him, the ambassador was horrified that Bose had just walked into the embassy— given that Kabul was crawling with agents of both the Afghan and British governments this, he told the Indian leader, had been very rash. When Bose replied that this was why he should be sheltered at the embassy until he could be given a safe escort out, Pilger grew very nervous and spoke of the many Afghans working at the embassy, and how there was no knowing which of them were spies. He promised to immediately contact Berlin and, while hopeful of a favourable reply, warned that Bose must not come to the embassy again, but keep in touch with a Herr Thomas of Siemens.

Pilger knew arrangements to get Bose out of Kabul would take time. The Afghan government conducted very thorough border checks, and there was very little traffic across the border. Soon after Bose left, Pilger contacted the Italian and Russian ambassadors, and telegraphed Berlin. Pilger was well aware that Bose could only get to Berlin with Russian help and with the Nazi-Soviet honeymoon still continuing had no problems having a chat with Mikhailov about Bose. The Russian warned his German counterpart that he suspected that Bose turning up in Kabul in this manner was a British plot designed 'to bring about a conflict between Afghanistan and Russia, because Bose could be taken only very secretively across the border in view of the local situation, hardly any communication, strictest passport and border checks'. However he could not disregard Pilger's request and soon after receiving it telegraphed Moscow and asked for instructions. Pilger's parting words to Bose had been 'to keep himself hidden among Indian friends in the Bazaar'. And it was this that had depressed Bose for it meant condemning Silver and him to a precarious existence in the *serai*.

They had already spent six days there—far too many for travellers stopping at a place meant for itinerant drivers of mules and horses. They made a curious pair: one older, heavier in build and pretending to be deaf and dumb; the other younger and fitter—both wandering about Kabul all day and returning to the *serai* in the evening. They looked suspiciously like agents waiting for a contact, and could even pass as smugglers.

One Afghan government spy had, in fact, been watching them very closely. The evening before they were to meet Herr Thomas he struck. He wanted answers to a whole series of questions. Who were they? What were they doing here? How long were they going to stay? Silver tried to bluff, telling the Afghan policeman they came from Lalpura and, through a judicious mixture of piteous explanation (his uncle was deaf and dumb, had come for treatment in Kabul and was waiting to get into hospital) and an appropriate bribe, saw him off: 'We did not like the officious tone of the talk of this new visitor and, in fact, it gave us the creeps'.[5]

The next morning Silver and Bose set off to see Herr Thomas. Initially it seemed that Silver would be of little use. The man who met them at Siemens, a young German who Silver later learned was a radio engineer, did not speak Persian, and in answer to Silver's inquiry said something in German. Bose who knew the language had to take over. He also did all of the talking when they met Herr Thomas. Although Berlin was very happy about getting Bose out of Afghanistan, Thomas refused to give him sanctuary in the German Embassy and told him to come back in three days. Bose said he might not, but his secretary—referring to Silver by his Muslim name Rahmat Khan—would.

This was the first time Bose had referred to Silver as his secretary. It was also the first time in his life that Silver had been part of a conversation with a white man. He had seen many of them in India, but at a distance, and, as we have seen in Kabul, tried to contact them on behalf of Bose. But none were sit-down meetings where he was treated as a fellow human being. From now on the Germans would always address him as Rahmat Khan and refer to him as Bose's secretary, and since they saw Bose as, potentially, a great catch, they began to feel Rahmat Khan was also an important man.

Silver was not to become aware of that for some months, and his immediate problem was that the very next day the Afghan spy reappeared in the *serai*. He could not understand why it should be so difficult to get seen at the hospital, was convinced they were smugglers, and insisted they come to the police station at once. When Silver increased the bribe the man left, but Silver knew this was only a temporary reprieve and he had to do something. Clearly he had to find a safer place in Kabul, but he did not know anyone. Suddenly it came to him that he did know of a man called Uttam Chand Malhotra, with whom he had been in jail in Peshawar in 1930, who was related to a Hindu family from his village and after his release had moved to Kabul and opened a shop. On one of his visits to the bazaar Labe Darya, where he had tried to speak to the Russians, Silver had noticed a sign on a shop which read M. C. Uttam Chand, but he could not be sure if it was the same man.

By now Silver had a keen sense of what people in Kabul looked like, and was aware that Bose's clothes were not quite what the ordinary Afghans wore. He decided to buy Bose an overcoat that would cover his clothes—in any case, Kabul was by now very cold with regular snowfalls and they needed more woollen garments. From a Hindu Afghan garment dealer he bought a second-hand overcoat for Bose and socks, pyjamas and used galoshes for both of them. Having established a rapport with him, he casually asked the shop keeper if he knew Uttam Chand Malhotra. To Silver's great delight he responded that there was an Uttam Chand Malhotra who had a crockery and radio shop with a sign reading M. C. Uttam Chand.

He was barely back in his room an hour when the spy reappeared. Silver pleaded that he was unable to get a hospital bed for his uncle but the man was not convinced, and told Silver he had informed the police about their presence. This time Silver gave him four times the money he had previously, eight Afghanis. The man warned that if they did not succeed in getting a hospital bed someone else might come after them: 'From his talk we gathered that he genuinely suspected us of being some kind of smugglers or fishy people indulging in some illicit trade'.[6]

The visit of the spy caused such panic that Silver and Bose thought of leaving Kabul for a village near the city, or finding another *serai*. Silver even rented a room in another *serai* and while he did so kept Bose locked up his room as he did not want to lug him around and feared if an Afghan wandered into the room the game would be up. Then another visit by the spy made them realise the only realistic alternative was Uttam Chand.

On the spy's previous visits Silver had been very supplicant. But now he decided he would no longer be meek and submissive. Instead, in response to the Afghan spy demands that the pair come with him, a furious Silver shouted declaring that they would not go to any police station. Suddenly the spy became very polite and told Silver he should not be angry with him as they were fellow Pathans: they should be friends—and he launched into a long sermon on the brotherhood of Pathans. What he was looking for, he told Silver, was a token of friendship—something of a lasting nature that would always remind him of the special bond between two fellow Pathans.

Silver noticed him looking at the wristwatch he was wearing: an old watch with thick glass and the number 12 picked out in red. It had actually been Bose's watch, a gift from his father to which he was sentimentally very attached, which he had given to Silver as they were going through the tribal area as his own gesture of friendship. Silver knew it would break Bose's heart if he gave it away. Bose gestured to Silver to hand it over. Suddenly the spy was all smiles, and departed saying that Silver could always turn to him in time of need.

It was evident they could not stay in the *serai* any longer, and now Silver told Bose about Uttam Chand. He was not sure what had happened to his old jail mate during the last eleven years: he might no longer want India to be free—indeed, might have decided it was best to collaborate with the British and could even be working for them. But Silver decided to take a chance, and they agreed that if the next day Herr Thomas could not provide any definite news about Bose's move out of Afghanistan then Silver would contact Uttam Chand.

The next day as soon as Herr Thomas confirmed there was no news from Berlin Silver headed for Uttam Chand's shop and found him reading a newspaper. Despite the years that had passed he recognised him immediately, but seeing that there was a young assistant in the shop Silver decided it would be unwise to speak in either Punjabi or Hindi, the two languages of India, and instead asked him in Pushtu whether he was from Peshawar. Uttam Chand replied yes and asked Silver sharply what he wanted. Silver glanced at the boy and Uttam Chand took the hint and sent the boy out to get some tea. Now Silver revealed his identity, and reminded Uttam Chand that they had been in the same cell in Peshawar jail. Uttam Chand broke into a smile, shook his hand vigorously and embraced him. Silver told him how he had brought Bose to Kabul and now needed a safe place to stay. Initially Uttam Chand offered to put them in touch with some old revolutionaries in Kabul, but Silver explained that they didn't have much time. Then he offered to put them up in his own home, reassuring Silver that it was in a very safe area and nobody there knew anything about his political views. It was agreed that Silver would come with Bose the next day to the shop at precisely 4.45 in the afternoon.

Uttam Chand lived on the first floor of a two-storey building whose very name, Mohalla Hindu Guzar, indicated that this was where the Hindus of Kabul had their homes, a sort of Hindu ghetto. On the ground floor lived another Hindu, Roshan Lal, who was also from Peshawar. Everything seemed to go well: Silver and Bose had their own rooms, furnished in the style common to central Asia: a floor covered with durries and carpets with a *sandli*, a wooden stand, under which there was an oven to keep the quilts in the room warm. There were thick low mattresses with cushions which could be used to sit on during the day or made into beds at night.

Much to Bose's delight there was Bengali music on the radio, and Uttam Chand could provide food Bose was used to rather than the heavy Afghan food that gave him a stomach ache. Soon Roshan Lal came to pay a visit. However, the next day Silver noticed that Roshan Lal and his family had suddenly vacated their flat. Had he perhaps recognised Bose—and gone to the police? This so worried Uttam Chand that he turned to a close friend of his, Haji Abdul Subhan, who had a reputation for being an experienced revolutionary. (He was in fact a German spy, although Uttam Chand did not know that.)

His story was broadly similar to that of Cheena and Sodhi. An Indian from Mardan, Subhan had gone to America to study and become friendly with the leader of the Ghadar party. The outbreak of the First World War saw Subhan return to Afghanistan to try and foment rebellion against the British, and after the war he travelled to Manchuria and then Germany, where he had married a German lady. By then he had also developed close contacts with the Afghan royal family and decided to settle in Afghanistan starting a factory producing woollen hosiery.

The four met for lunch at Uttam Chand's home, and while Subhan not surprisingly praised Bose's decision to seek foreign help, he confirmed Uttam Chand's fears that there was something deeply suspicious of Roshan Lal's sudden departure. Silver was the only one sure that Lal's departure did not mean he was about to betray Bose to the Afghan police and sought to reassure Bose that there was nothing to fear. But, he told his old jail mate, 'we do not want to be selfish, and if you are still apprehensive of any danger to us at all we will be prepared to shift immediately to some other place'. Silver would later learn that his view of Roshan Lal was spot on: Lal told a friend he had left the house as he felt it was under some kind of spell, possibly under the influence of evil spirits. But Uttam Chand and Subhan remained apprehensive, and the next day Silver found a *serai* used by truck drivers and their passengers, for him and Bose to move to.

Despite this Uttam Chand had now become part of the group and with Bose falling ill, he had stomach problems, it was decided he would take over liaison with Herr Thomas. Soon Bose had a new task for him. With Thomas having no information from Berlin an increasingly anxious Bose suggested that Uttam Chand and Subhan explore their contacts to see if he could make the journey to the Soviet border on his own. Uttam Chand readily agreed to help as he knew a man called Yakub, originally from Peshawar, who had married into a family in a village in the district of Khanabad, an industrial city on the border of the Soviet Union, and whose brother-in-law lived near the border, doubling up as a bandit and a smuggler. Uttam Chand was confident that it would be possible with Yakub's help to cross the border at the Oxus river and take Bose far enough into the Soviet Union. Silver agreed Uttam Chand should talk to Yakub, but not mention that the person seeking to cross into the Soviet Union was Bose. Yakub was very keen and sure his brother-in-law, who was going back and forth across the border all the time as part of his 'trade' of smuggling, could handle this easily.

However, neither Silver nor Bose had lost hopes that the Germans might come up with something and Thomas reassured Silver that all three Axis powers, Germany, Italy and Japan, had made a joint request to the Soviet Union to grant a transit visa to Bose. By this time Silver's role as secretary had expanded as Bose, still plagued by stomach problems, developed serious dysentery. He obviously couldn't go to a doctor, so Silver described his symptoms to Uttam Chand, who relayed them to a physician and got him some medicine. Bose was also missing the Bengali food he was accustomed to and Uttam Chand got his wife to cook Khichiri, a mixture of rice, dahl, eggs [which the British in India had transformed into kedgeree] and curds. Silver now acting as a bearer brought this food to Bose every day from Uttam Chand's shop.

Unaware that Subhan was a German spy, Silver tried to use him to contact the Russians. Russian embassy personnel came to his factory to purchase garments, and he agreed to give them a letter from Bose to the ambassador. A few days later two Russian ladies, possibly the same ones Silver had tried to talk to, came to the factory, and Subhan gave them the letter. When there was no response Subhan's explanation was that the ladies had never come back. There was now nothing for Silver and Bose to do but wait for word from Berlin. However Subhan's influence with Uttam Chand did come in useful when he persuaded the shopkeeper that Roshan Lal had clearly not shopped Bose to the police enabling Bose to move back to his house. Silver organised the move in a deliberately circuitous series of tonga rides.

Bose, increasingly, fretful, pressed Silver to pursue the Yakub option and on 16 February 1941 Uttam Chand arranged a meeting between Silver and Yakub, introducing Silver as a good and long-standing friend whom Yakub should help as much as he could. Yakub was more than willing, and confident his brother-in-law could help Bose cross the river. Silver, now a practised liar, told Yakub that his friend was still in India, but once Yakub had made all the arrangements he would come to Kabul for his onward journey to the Soviet Union. Silver gave Yakub 300 Afghanis for the trip and some more money to buy a present for his brother-in-law. He also went round to the Siemen office and gave Thomas a letter addressed by Bose to Pilger saying that, as Bose had heard nothing from the Germans, he was now making his own plans to cross the border.

It was more than a month since Bose had made the midnight escape from his home in Calcutta, and by now he was running into money problems. He had not anticipated staying so long in Kabul and spending quite as much as he had, and asked Silver to try and obtain some funds from Thomas. The reply was the usual one: come back in three days. It was agreed, therefore, that Silver and Bose would leave by bus on the morning of 23 February 1941, and three tickets were purchased for Khanabad: two for Bose and Silver and one for Yakub. The day before their scheduled departure, Silver met Yakub again and gave him more money to buy food and other provisions for his family for the month that he would be away, and also a *lungi* and other presents for Yakub's brother-in-law. Silver also studied the terrain they would travel having left Peshawar with a road map covering Afghanistan right up to the Soviet border. Uttam Chand provided further help giving him a guide book for Afghanistan which also had a useful map.

Before they left, however, Bose wanted a reply to his letter to Pilger and Silver went back to see Thomas. It would prove to be Silver's last encounter with the German and a significant one. Instead of the usual reply of 'come back in three days', Thomas told him to go and see Signor Quaroni, the Italian minister. Silver's immediate reaction was this was yet another attempt by the Germans to fob him off. He didn't know the Italian minister, but Thomas assured him that he would see him, and with some reluctance Silver agreed to go to the Italian Embassy. It could, he felt, be a futile mission, but there was nothing to lose.

Silver did not know where the Italian Embassy was, but as he left Thomas he recalled that in his wandering round Kabul he had once strayed into a blind alley in new Kabul and seen a small sign for the Italian legation. Silver headed for the alley, discovered it was the back door of the legation, and a number of its Afghan employees were sitting around having a smoke. As we have seen, Silver quickly invented the story that he was a cook sent by Herr Thomas, and was ushered into Quaroni's office.

Silver's life would never be quite the same again.

The Italian Job

Quaroni's meeting with Silver revealed how far the Indian had come in the three weeks he had been in Kabul. He now had the confidence to deal with a foreign ambassador and his instincts as a spy were sharply honed. So, Silver started the conversation with Quaroni by putting the Axis, and in particular the Germans, on the back foot, talking of the many meetings with the Germans which had got nowhere and how increasingly worried Bose and he were about such a long stay in Kabul. Indeed, he said, it was potentially so dangerous they had decided to make their own arrangements to travel to the Soviet Union.

Silver was not to know that he was talking to a man who had little time for the Germans in Kabul, and listening to the Indian confirmed Quaroni's view that you could always trust the Germans to mess things up. Hans Pilger, his German opposite number, had never much impressed people. When in 1937 he had been appointed as Minister to Kabul the British ambassador in Berlin had described him as having a 'somewhat scrubby and unprepossessing appearance' who, said the ambassador, viewed his 'promotion ... without enthusiasm'.[1] Quaroni, having observed him for nearly four years, was even more dismissive and would later tell Connor-Green, the Special Operations Executive's (SOE's) man in Kabul, that he was 'completely bone-headed':

> I tell you frankly that I have been astonished that I should have to deal with such a set of fools. Their organisation of intelligence—the word indeed can only be used on the principle of lucus a non lucendo [absurd derivation]—is childish—in fact it hardly exists either in this country or in India.[2]

What really upset the Italian was that the Germans were very indiscreet, and their planning was bad in both conception and execution. It did not please him that they often tried to keep him in the dark, but being half German himself he was sure he got everything out of them without their realising it:

'They are not even intelligent enough to read between the lines of their own propaganda, much less do they listen to news from other sources'.[3]

Quaroni accepted that the Germans were able to gather accurate information about military matters as far as the line of the Indus, although not beyond. This was largely from deserters who proved most useful. But the problem was information about the general situation in India. He was convinced the German information was meagre and the sources of very poor quality, in contrast to his own information, which he was sure was well informed. Interestingly, the reason for this was, as he would later tell the British:

> we got 89 per cent of our information from a study of the newspapers, including the advertisements and specially of small provincial newspapers which you people in your legation have probably never even heard of.

Connor-Green would underline the word 'advertisement' and comment that, 'What he says corresponds with the universal experience of intelligence services'.[4] Quaroni's favourite read was the British-owned Calcutta newspaper, *The Statesman*, which he bought in Kabul every day for five Afghanis, never missing an issue.

Listening to Silver Quaroni was convinced that he must step in to, in effect, take over from the incompetent Germans, and he immediately set about trying to convince Silver how dangerous it would be to go with Yakub's brother-in-law. Did he know, the Italian told Silver, he would have to negotiate with a number of Afghan customs posts and other barriers before they got to the border, and even if they managed to cross into the Soviet Union there was no guarantee as to how the Soviet border guards might react? They might take them to be outlaws, robbers or smugglers and shoot them on sight. Then, concealing his dislike for the Germans, he said that the delay was not because the Axis did not want to help Bose. Indeed, all three Axis powers had made a joint request to the Soviets and, given the Nazi–Soviet pact and the excellent relations the Germans and the Italians had with the Soviets, he was very confident there would be a favourable reply. When Silver dismissed this as much the same talk he had heard from the Germans, Quaroni emphasised that they were expecting Italian diplomatic couriers to arrive shortly in Kabul. If that failed they could take Bose through Iran and Syria to Rome or Berlin, and the Italian and German diplomatic missions in the two countries had already been contacted to pursue this option.

Silver refused to be convinced, saying that the Germans had taken so much time it had made their stay in Kabul almost impossible. They could be arrested any day and felt they were only just keeping ahead of the Kabul police. They had to go with Yakub, but the Italians could help by giving some money for the journey as they were now very short of funds.

Silver's obduracy may or may not have been genuine, but it certainly had an effect on Quaroni and he requested a meeting with Bose. Given how hard Silver and Bose had tried to meet the Russian ambassador it might be expected that Silver would jump at the idea but, playing hard to get, he told Quaroni that as Bose was unaware he had come to see him, he could not be sure he could persuade him to come. They had already purchased tickets for the bus journey and they were ready to leave for the border the next morning.

It is astonishing to consider how confident Silver was in this very first meeting with Quaroni. Before his arrival in Kabul he had always been forced to see all Europeans as masters, had never sat down and chatted with a European on equal terms, let alone met an ambassador of a major European power. Yet here he was behaving as if he was a diplomat representing a sovereign nation. And this from a man who was essentially a bag carrier for a politician fleeing in great secrecy from what was then the greatest empire in the world. That Silver could now cope with this situation showed that his boast that he was indeed a true Pathan who was overawed by nobody was not without validity.

Quaroni, keen to meet Bose, would not give up, and introduced Silver to Enrico Anzilotti, the Secretary of the Italian Legation. He also dangled the bait that when Silver came back with Bose he would not have to take the back alley entrance but Anzilotti would be waiting for him at the front door. All Silver would have to do would be to knock and Anzilotti would open the door himself. There would be no question of Afghan gatemen asking them questions. Silver nodded, but warned Quaroni he could not promise. If he did bring Bose back with him, he said, it would be between seven and eight that evening.

Silver was right to be cautious, for the Indian leader was so disenchanted he had given up on the Axis powers. Bose was sure Yakub's brother-in-law was a better bet and was not best pleased that Silver had been to see the Italians. Silver not only justified what he had done but managed to convince Bose to accompany him to the Italian legation. Bose, realising his appearance was rather slovenly, spruced himself up, clipping his beard and moustache, discarded his Afghan clothes for one of Uttam Chand's European suits and, then borrowing a triangular, peaked, karakul cap made of karakul sheep skins, set off to see Quaroni.

For the first time since the pair had arrived in Kabul they were met with the sort of respect that Bose, who had met Mussolini and Ciano (Mussolini's son-in-law who was also the Italian foreign minister), felt he deserved. The moment Silver knocked on the front door Anzilotti appeared and escorted them to Quaroni's room. At this point Silver, having acted as courier, should have taken a back seat, but he did not. As Quaroni, after congratulating Bose on his successful escape from India, started a discussion on the political situation in

India, the effect of the war and how a strong anti-British resistance movement in India and the tribal areas could be built up, Silver interjected. Convinced that the two 'were getting lost in political discussions [and] forgetting the immediate practical issues at hand', he reminded them that there was still the question of Bose's safe passage out of Kabul. He also told Quaroni that they:

> ... had to take a decision immediately as to whether we were going back or staying the night at the legation because it was dangerous to move about in Kabul late at night.[5]

The sheer chutzpah of Silver is quite breath-taking. He was sitting in the office of the Italian ambassador, whose diplomatic career had begun back in December 1918 as 'Italian Officer attached to the person of General Pershing,'[6] Commander of the American Forces in Europe. In the two and half decades since, Quaroni had met Stalin, Trotsky, Chaim Weizmann, then leading the campaign to have a Jewish state (and later the first President of Israel), King Zog of Albania, foreign ministers of various countries and been an interpreter at a meeting between Hitler and Mussolini. And, as we have seen, Bose was one of the leading politicians of India. But despite the fact that Silver's English was halting he now had such confidence that if he felt something needed to be said he would not shy away. It helped, of course, that the 33 year-old Silver, as we have seen, was an experienced political operator who had dealt with vicious jail warders and obdurate politicians some of them at the highest level in the Indian freedom movement. Now that experience stood him in good stead.

Quaroni, who was keen to have a long discussion with Bose on how he saw things in India and the world in general, wanted both Silver and Bose to stay the night at the embassy. But Silver immediately vetoed the plan. Jiwan Lal, a friend of Uttam Chand, was supposed to come and see Bose that night, and the absence of both of them could lead to Jiwan Lal drawing 'undesirable and harmful conclusions'.[7] Silver made it clear Bose could stay but he would have to return to Uttam Chand's house.

Quaroni, keen to be helpful, turned to Anzilotti and asked him to take Silver wherever he wanted to go. Silver's response showed how sharply his spying instincts had developed during his stay in Kabul. He immediately rejected the offer, saying that if spies from the Afghan government, or other embassies, were watching the Italian legation they would wonder why two Afghan-looking men had entered the Italian Embassy at seven in the evening and only one had come out two hours later. It would be better if both Bose and he leave together. They would travel some distance on foot and then Anzilotti should pick Bose up from a spot they could agree on and bring him back. Silver also suggested that they should fix a place and time for the next afternoon where he would come to pick up Bose.

Silver returned to Uttam Chand cursing his host for inviting Jiwan Lal. That, he felt, showed that the shopkeeper did not understand the nature of undercover work. But he dealt with Jiwan Lal, making sure he left without harbouring any suspicions as to why Bose was not there. By the next afternoon he had also resolved the potentially trickier situation with Yakub. Silver realised Yakub would be happy if he was offered some money for doing nothing and told him that, while the trip had to be cancelled, he could keep the refund he would get from the tickets. He was now ready to collect Bose, and this meant a journey, in effect, to a new city.

The Italians had told him to come not to the Legation but to Amanullah's abandoned capital. The deposed King had built this new Kabul six miles from the old in the hope that it would match the British-built New Delhi. Silver had never seen anything like this and quite marvelled at it.

It was joined to the old city with four miles of long, wonderfully beautiful, dead straight avenues, lined with tall white-stemmed poplars, in front of which ran streams confined by grass margins. Behind them were shady sidewalks and a tangle of yellow and white roses.[8] There was also a narrow-gauge railway connecting it to the centre of Kabul.

After Amanullah was forced to flee his successor moved the capital back to the old city, renaming the deposed king's capital as Darulfunun or the Abode of the Arts. However, there were still villas for high government officials and diplomats, and Silver was told to come to the Italian villa. Silver arrived, full of wonder of what the man he had read so much about in the Har Bhagawan school library had built, and was met by Crishnini, second secretary of the Legation. He had been close to Mussolini, and this meant Silver, the anti-fascist, had to listen to tales of how the Italian fascists had seized power in the 1920s. A keen photographer, he also took pictures of Bose, who was still wearing the suit he had borrowed from Uttam Chand.

Silver could see that, in contrast to the Russians who would not see them and the Germans who could not make up their minds, the Italians were eager to help. This was because Bose was a godsend for Quaroni. For a start, his arrival provided relief and excitement in a place he saw as a wilderness. He was to consider his time in Kabul so dreadful that when he came to write his memoirs after the war he did not even mention his eight years as Italian ambassador in Afghanistan. Quaroni had been sent to Kabul because Mussolini had not forgiven him for what he had done back in September 1935, when he had expressed disapproval of Mussolini's policy about Italy's withdrawal from the League of Nations in the weekly publication, *Affari Esteri*. He had first been posted to Thessaloniki as General Consul and then, in December 1936, made Italian minister plenipotentiary in Kabul. Bose was by far the most significant person to walk through the doors of the Italian Embassy in Kabul while Quaroni was there.

There was another reason why Quaroni was excited by Bose's arrival. He saw him as an ideal weapon to use against the British in India. By this time Quaroni was very confident he understood how the British operated in the country they considered their crown jewel. In 1938, two years after he had taken up his hardship posting in Kabul, he had persuaded the British to let him visit India. However:

> ... the English were not particularly keen at this time for foreigners to wander about India ... you were always aware of someone at your elbow, of an atmosphere of discreet supervision.[9]

Interestingly, he devoted a whole chapter in his memoir to the visit, calling it 'The Indian Viceroy', while omitting to mention he had gone there while ambassador in Kabul. The Viceroy was Linlithgow, who entertained him to lunch in the Viceregal Palace and told the Italian that 'these people [Indians] are not at all difficult to govern ... they'll obey if they know whom to obey'. The problem was, 'It's in London that they forget how to rule', with the result that if he forbade 'someone here to do something, the fellow then uses his influence in London'.[10]

Quaroni had returned to Kabul with the shrewd impression that England had two faces: a metropolitan face of the Magna Carta, the habeas corpus, the Mother of Parliaments, which only Westerners saw. Then there was the face the Orientals saw: the imperial face presented in the British colonies 'of how to rule and how to ensure obedience. With this second England it is unwise to take liberties'.[11] Now, having met Bose, Quaroni began to ponder that, while not taking liberties, he could at least do enough to shake up the confidence of this imperial face of England. As he put it to Rome:

> Bose is a type that we all know from his works and his actions. Intelligent, able, full of passion and without doubt the most realistic, maybe the only realist among the Indian nationalist leaders ... what he says about the Indian situation tallies with what...can be made out of the very censored Indian Press; which is a sign that his statements do not sin of optimism and this is a thing in his favour.[12]

During their discussions, starting that first night they met, Bose had sketched out his plans. A government of Free India should be set up in Europe and, once it had obtained a guarantee of the freedom, integrity and independence of India from the Axis powers, it would immediately begin a special radio campaign beamed exclusively to India and try to foment revolution there. The help given would, of course, be in the form of a repayable loan, and Bose for his part would start broadcasting only once he was convinced of the Axis' good faith. Bose, who had always been a good propagandist, now sold himself to Quaroni as a unique Indian: 'In Indian political left [wing circles] today he is the person whose words carry most weight in foreign politics'. He told Quaroni how at the Tripuri Congress in 1939:

> ... I prophesied that the European war would start within six months ... war did actually break out exactly within the six months, thereby I have risen to fame of being a person who can see more clearly than anybody else the international events: that is why ... the day I can say over the wireless, 'Friends of India, I have come to Europe, I have studied the situation and I am convinced that the Axis Powers will win,' there will be more belief in my words than of anybody else.

Quaroni went on to tell the Italian Foreign Office:

> According to Bose India is morally ripe for the revolution, what is lacking is the courage to take the first step: the great obstacles to action are on one side the lack of faith in their own capabilities and on the other the blind persuasion of British excessive power. He says that if 50,000 men, Italian, German, or Japanese could reach the frontiers of India, the Indian army would desert, the masses would uprise and the end of English domination could be achieved in a very short time ... Bose is of the opinion that the main obstacle to the possibilities of a revolution in India is the great fear of England ... If in June 1940, that is at the time when the defeat of England seemed certain, we had a ready organisation like the one Bose proposes now, it could have been attempted to liberate India, and it might have been possible. Politically and militarily India is a cornerstone of the British Empire. Last year's chance is gone but a similar one could come this year also: one should be ready to take full advantage of it. To put up this organisation money will be required, probably not little of it. In the past, we have spent big sums of money, for instance on Press propaganda in the two Americas, with the results we can see today: here one can work on a much more solid terrain. If what is being attempted should work out even in part, probably several months of war, human lives, millions worth of materials will be saved. Our enemies, in all their wars, the present one included, have always largely used the 'revolution' weapon with success; why should we not learn from our enemies?

Bose wanted to 'intensify internal propaganda for the desertion from the army', not the odd soldier Sodhi had managed, 'but mass desertion of entire divisions'. Quaroni concluded his report:

> Two things are necessary to make revolutions: men and money. We do not have the men to start a revolution in India, but luck has put them in our

hands; no matter how difficult Germany's and our monetary situation is, the money that this movement requires is certainly not lacking. It is only a question of valuing the pros and cons and to decide on the risk.

Quaroni's enthusiasm for Bose meant that after weeks of inaction events now began to move unexpectedly quickly. Silver had little time to reflect that, a mere 24 hours after he was pretending to be a cook gaining entrance into the Italian Embassy through the back door in a little alleyway, he could now march up to the front door any time he wanted and, as often as not, Anzilotti was there to greet him. And the Italians now came to Uttam Chand's shop posing as customers. If a message had to be conveyed, Silver would go to Crishini's residence in new Kabul and the Italians, in turn, sent Quaroni's Russian-born wife to Uttam Chand's shop. Released from the dreadful burden of living incognito, for the first time Silver and Bose began to act as tourists, wandering round Kabul.

But Silver always had to be on his guard that Bose might do something that would blow their cover, and this nearly happened when Bose went shopping. While Uttam Chand's suit just about fitted Bose, his shoes did not, and he decided to get a new pair. Until now the iron rule of any contact in a public place was that Bose would pretend to be dumb and Silver would speak. But, boosted by his meetings with the Italians, Bose forgot the role assigned to him and asked the shopkeeper to show him some shoes. The shopkeeper, who was Indian, quickly guessed from Bose's accent that he was also from India, and began to ask him fairly pointed questions as to where in India he was from. Bose, trying to make up lies but not being as accomplished as Silver, slipped up badly, saying that he was from the eastern part of the United Provinces and had just taken up a job in Habibya College at Kabul. The shopkeeper, who knew all the Indian professors at the college, wondered why he had never seen Bose there. Bose replied that because of language problems he did not move about much and, also, he had only recently arrived in Kabul. The shopkeeper, clearly very intrigued and keen to know more, invited Bose and Silver to have tea. Silver intervened, to say that while they would love to do so they were in a hurry and had to go but would come back later. He quickly paid for the shoes and both Bose and he left immediately. Fortunately for Bose, efforts to get him out of Kabul were finally moving in the right direction.

On 3 March the Commissariat for External Affairs informed the German ambassador in Moscow that the Soviets were prepared to give Subhas Bose 'the visa for journey from Afghanistan to Germany through Russia. The Commissariat has been requested to instruct the Soviet Embassy in Kabul accordingly'.[13]

But the Germans, as Quaroni cabled Rome, had only done half the job:

German Ambassador had asked transit visa but he had forgotten to make arrangements with the Soviet government about how to get him [Bose] out from Afghanistan as he had earlier illegally entered Afghanistan and was therefore without documents.[14]

For Quaroni this was yet another German mess and, as he put it to Rome:

Not to prolong this situation which [has] become extremely sensitive, I gave to Bose the Italian passport in the name of Orlando Mazzotta, radio operator of this Legation, where I changed the photo after obtaining an exit visa from Afghanistan. Please excuse me for having done so without permission but the Soviet Ambassador [in Kabul] was only willing to put a visa on a document provided by us and the one from Germany would not act [work] without precise instructions from his government. On the other hand [given the] dates and circumstances the risk [of not doing] was greater than it seems. Please collect if necessary the passport in Berlin, informing me.

Quaroni would later tell the British that the Russian ambassador in Kabul was fully aware of Bose's identity when he gave him the transit visa on a false passport in the name of Mazotta.[15]

It is puzzling why Quaroni did not make it clear to Bose and Silver that Bose would travel on the passport of the Legation's radio operator. Instead the Italians spun a story to them that two Italian diplomatic couriers were expected to arrive in Kabul almost any day now. The plan, said the Italians, was that one of them would stay back and his diplomatic passport with a visa would be used by Bose to leave Afghanistan and cross the border into the Soviet Union. Within a week Mrs Quaroni came to Uttam Chand's shop to tell him these Italian couriers had arrived in Kabul and that arrangements had to be made for taking a photograph of Bose to be used in the passport of one of the Italians, and that Bose should also get a bag of clothes to take with him during the journey. Crishini was again the photographer, with the clothes provided by Subhan, who also arranged for a tailor to measure Bose for suits and shirts. The only thing the tailor could not get ready was a vest for Bose but this was later on sent to him by Subhan's German wife through her sister in Berlin. Silver procured towels, pyjamas, toilet and shaving articles and a suitcase was made ready.

On the afternoon of 15 March Bose and Silver were having tea with Subhan and his wife when suddenly Uttam Chand arrived. He had a message from the Italians. They wanted Bose's luggage to be at his shop the next afternoon and Bose to be at Crishnini's residence on the evening of 17th, with his departure fixed for the morning of 18 March. But the Germans again proved inefficient, and Quaroni had to make arrangements without getting prior authorisation from Rome. This meant a telegram asking for retrospective approval:

Since Bose started as an employee of this Legation, I paid for him to drive to the border and equipped with the bare minimum for the trip: Please telegraph how I have to record this amount of 1,500 Afghanis. I advised Bose to go immediately to the embassies of Italy and Germany in Moscow and wait for instructions that will be given on how to continue the journey and how to get out from Russia as soon as possible. He thanks you for your help and your message.[16]

The night before he left, Bose sat down with Silver in Crishnini's guest room. Silver went in expecting this would be goodbye, but Bose had no plans to let go of him. He had been given an idea by Quaroni and was keen to develop it further. This had arisen from Quaroni's questioning of Bose about terrorism in India. Bose had replied that while there were terrorist organisations, terrorism was useless. But have you thought, asked Quaroni, of changing these organisations from individual terrorism to 'organised sabotage'? Bose hadn't but, as Quaroni informed Rome:

> ... he liked the idea very much and through his secretary has sent instructions to the chief of the organisation in Bengal to work on this new way, who according to what he says is in close touch with him. I have told him in Berlin and Rome he could get all the practical advice on the mode of action and also the technical means for action. It is clear that if large scale sabotage could be organised at a moment when India plays such an important part in the war supplies of the British army in the Middle East, it could be a thing of no mean importance.

Bose now told Silver that he should see the escorting of Bose to Kabul as the start of a great mission. He wanted Silver to be his link between India and Kabul. He added that he had already spoken to the Italians, and they had agreed that they would provide him the means of communicating with Bose. Kabul would be the centre of this operation, with the Italians giving Uttam Chand news of what Bose was up to in Europe. Silver was to come back to Kabul after his visit to India. Bose gave him Rs 600 and also told him that Sarat would give him more money.

Bose, of course, had grossly exaggerated to Quaroni the extent of his movement, and the idea that all it required was Axis money to convert it almost overnight into an organisation capable of carrying out sabotage in India was a fantasy. For a start, to describe Silver as his secretary was stretching the definition of secretaries. While Silver had worked for the Forward Bloc in the NWFP, he was no longer a member, having joined the Kirti party, and he had no overall knowledge of Bose's organisation. As we have seen, Bose had only met him for the first time less than two months previously. Bose had told him something of his movement during their time in Kabul, but Silver had never been to Calcutta, the headquarters of Bose's party. Nobody in Calcutta even knew who Silver was, and before he left Kabul Bose had felt it necessary to give Silver a letter in Bengali to his brother Sarat to introduce Silver and request that he be put in touch with Satya Ranjan Bakshi. He worked as a clerk in Sarat's chambers and was also Subhas Bose's contact with the underground revolutionary movement in Bengal.

That night's conversation with Bose marked the moment when Silver became a spy. Bose, seeking to foment revolution and influenced by an Italian diplomat, now provided a courier with the opportunity to become a great deceiver. What is more, the circumstances were such that it made it impossible for anyone to suspect Silver was a spy. As the British would record when they finally caught up with Silver:

> He admits that his own contacts with the Axis in Kabul developed purely fortuitously as a result of Bose's journey, and Bose having subsequently nominated him as his link with India. He is absolutely confident the Axis in Kabul has no other Indian agent working for them in India, and no independent means from Kabul of checking up on his completely non-existent contacts with Bose's organisation in India.[17]

Quaroni, who was hugely impressed by Bose, saw what he wanted to see and clearly felt Silver was just the sort of Indian agent the Axis had long been looking for. The Italians gave him money for travel and told him that they wanted him to bring back some Survey of India maps. For a restless man like Silver, who had by this time got bored with the politics of the NWFP and was always looking for new adventure, nothing could have sounded sweeter.

The next morning while it was still dark a big four-door car arrived at Crishini's house. In it was Dr Herren Wenger of the Todt Organisation. This was a large semi-military Nazi organisation which had won the contract for supervising road construction all over Afghanistan, and part of the wider German plan to establish itself in Afghanistan to rival the British and the Russians. Wenger knew the road to the Russian border intimately. In the car there was also another member of the German legation, and it was being driven by a European. The choice of a European driver was very significant, as the Germans and Italians wanted no Afghan involvement in a journey which was effectively deceiving the Afghan government.

A very emotional Bose embraced Silver, affectionately joking, 'You have to put [find] some other comrade to establish contact with the Soviet embassy'.[18] He grew so sentimental that he could hardly speak. Silver could not take his eyes off him, and began to think that the man he had always thought of as the classical Bengali did have some Sicilian looks and could pass off as Orlando

Mazotta. What neither Silver nor Bose ever knew was that it had been a close shave getting Bose out of Kabul. The British were well aware that he was there and had discussed several measures to deal with their 'implacable foe'.

The British had always had a huge intelligence operation in Afghanistan, in the shape of locals in various branches of Afghan society providing both hard intelligence and bazaar rumour. In addition, through judicious use of bribes, they had established excellent contact with key officials. Before the war the War Office had thought of establishing a link with the Afghan security system and taking over Afghan Police Intelligence, but MI5 advised that this was unwise. In any case, as far as Kabul was concerned this was not particularly important, as by 1941 the British had decoded both Italian and Japanese diplomatic messages from Kabul which were communicated entirely through cable. The Germans, though, had their own transmitters, and the British only succeeded in penetrating the German code in 1943 through Operation Pandora.

Whether through reading the Italian cables, or from one of their spies, the British legation in Kabul knew that Bose was in town. Sir Kerr Fraser-Tytler, British Minister in Kabul, asked Delhi whether he should do something about Bose. London was consulted, and Peel at the India Office wrote to Sir Olaf Caroe, Foreign Secretary to the Government of India, that no action should be taken 'for fear of compromising a source'.[19] We do not know what this source was. It must certainly have been at a very high level for the British to decide not to ask the Afghan government to arrest him. However, the British information on Bose was not always up to date, as evidenced by the government of India's conviction that he was still in Kabul as late as May 1941, two months after he had left.

But if the British in India did not want to do anything about Bose for fear of upsetting the Afghans, another branch of British intelligence was busy making plans to eliminate him. As we have seen, the cables Quaroni had sent to Rome soon after meeting Bose had discussed how the routes Bose might take to get to Germany could involve travel via Iran, Iraq, and then Turkey. This led the SOE to ask its agents in Istanbul and Cairo, 'what arrangements you could make for his assassination'. But by the time SOE sent this message it was 7 March 1941 and, as we have seen, the Germans and the Italians had found a way of getting Bose to Europe without having to go through any of these countries. So while murder was discussed there was no chance of its implementation.

Silver remained oblivious of all this, and in his memoirs he bragged that he had been in Kabul for 52 days:

> ... a small city with scope for very limited movement. It would not have been difficult for the British police to locate and put us into trouble in that

city if they had wind of our movement up the north-west of India. Our arrangements of escorting Netaji [the name Bose would be given by admirers during the war] to Kabul were so reliable that no word leaked out and even the strong force of British CID could not get a smell of our movements and activities ... About me the police never suspected even up to the time of my return to India that I had escorted Netaji to Kabul.[20]

He was right that the British did not know he had escorted Bose and, as we shall see, would not learn of this for another two years, and then from a totally unexpected source. Basking in what he had achieved, and having seen off Bose, he returned to Uttam Chand's house, and had his first proper bath since leaving India. He felt so relaxed that he was even ready to forgive Uttam Chand for not realising the need to be discreet in undercover work.

Wars create huge changes that can never be predicted, but that this deception of the Nazis and Italians was engineered in this fashion is truly extraordinary. It is as if the Axis powers were almost wanting to be deceived. It has generally been conceded by historians that the Italians had the ablest Axis intelligence service, with one historian calling the Japanese buffoons in comparison. Quaroni, who felt very frustrated in Kabul, wanted to prove that he was superior to the other Axis diplomats, and to him Silver was just the man he had been looking for. The Japanese, who will only emerge later in our story, did not on the whole rate intelligence, although there were exceptions which impacted the Indian Army in Singapore and Malaya. The surprising part in this Axis package were the Germans. They cared about intelligence and had in the Abwehr supposedly a very superior intelligence agency. The Silver story, however, proved them to be not far behind the Japanese in intelligence incompetence. But to understand why Silver's relationship with the Axis developed in Kabul we need to focus on the Axis strategy in that part of the world, how Hitler saw the British and their empire and, in particular, the extraordinary relationship Hitler's men developed with a Faqir. Today this Muslim holy man would easily be portrayed as a dreadful Jihadist, but that would be to do him a great disservice. He was in reality a classic rebel, and one who, even before the war, had proved a dreadful thorn in the side of the British.

Hitler, the Faqir and the Nazi intrigues

On 17 February 1941 Hitler gave an order to the Operations Staff of the German High Command to prepare a study for an invasion of India via Afghanistan.[1] Historians now agree that if Hitler had concentrated on the Mediterranean and Middle East in the spring of 1941, instead of invading Russia, the British could have been dislodged from there and, as Churchill admitted in his war memoirs, the Germans could have threatened Syria, Iraq and Iran, and 'Hitler's hand might have reached out very far towards India and beckoned to Japan'.[2]

The German targeting of India was not a new idea. In May 1939 Franz von Papen, German ambassador to Turkey, who had helped Hitler come to power, had written that, in order to defeat Britain, Germany 'must hit her in her most vital point: in India'. In 1940 Herbert Tichy, an Austrian who a few years previously had travelled widely through Afghanistan, India and Tibet, had in his book *Afghanistan—The Gateway to India*, described it as 'the navel of the world', a country on the land route from Europe to India. He went on to say that for world domination India was crucial, 'for who rules India, rules the international trade and through it the whole world ...'[3] In 1941 the Abwehr had considered Tichy for intelligence work, but the publicity his book received made them abandon the idea.

The 1939–1941 honeymoon between the Germans and Russians had seen Joachim von Ribbentrop, Hitler's oily Foreign Minister, try hard to get the Soviets interested in carving up the world, with various roles assigned to India. On 6 January 1940 General Alfred Jodl, chief of the Oberkommando Des Heeres (OKH) operations staff, argued for joint German–Soviet action in Afghanistan and India. Later these plans developed further, and by 30 June 1940 Jodl had provided for direct action against India and Afghanistan.

But Hitler's plan for an invasion of India was an entirely different matter. This was not Hitler working with Russia but planning for post-*Barbarossa*, and was part of his scheme to become the master of the universe. However, having failed to meet his target to annihilate the Russians by the autumn of 1941 the German forces got nowhere near India, and nothing more was heard of Hitler's Indian invasion idea. Whatever prompted Hitler to issue the order, it remains one of the great paradoxes of the war, for the German Führer was a great admirer of the British and their Empire. He repudiated the theory that the British had acquired their empire by fraud, a view that Bose and many other Indian revolutionaries took, and saw in their subjugation of India the model for the German empire he wanted in Eastern Europe. Indeed, just before he unleashed his forces against the Soviet Union he told them to copy the British in India, where a small number of white people ruled vast swathes of brown people. For Hitler the fact that the British with 250,000 white men, and 50,000 white soldiers, controlled 400 million Indians was very impressive, and as his forces swept into Russia he told them: 'Our role in Russia will be analogous to that of England in India ... The Russian space is our India. Like the English, we shall rule this empire with a handful of men'.[4]

For good measure, in his meeting with Halifax he had advised the British Foreign Secretary that the way to deal with Gandhi's non-violent campaign was, 'Shoot Gandhi, and if this doesn't suffice to reduce them to submission, shoot a dozen leading members of Congress.'[5] Halifax, who as Viceroy had negotiated with Gandhi, prompting Churchill's infamous jibe of Gandhi posing as 'a half-naked fakir', could not have been more astounded. In *Mein Kampf* Hitler had dismissed the Indian freedom fighters as 'Asiatic jugglers' and predicted that:

> England will never lose India unless she admits racial disruption in the machinery of her administration (which at present is entirely out of the question in India), or unless she is overcome by the sword of some powerful enemy. But Indian risings will never bring this about. We Germans have had sufficient evidence to know how hard it is to coerce England. And, apart from all this, I as a German would far rather see India under British domination than under that of any other nation.

When in May 1942 Bose during his meeting with Hitler challenged him on these racial slurs Hitler, for the only time during this dismal meeting, lost some of his fluency, and justified his utterances by saying that weak subject nations could not 'build up a united front against the oppressors', and that he had wanted to discourage passive resistance in Germany along the Indian pattern, 'which in any case was a completely wrong doctrine'.[6]

In May 1930, three years before he was elected Chancellor, Hitler had told Otto Strasser a party member, that:

> You have spoken in favour of the so-called Indian 'Freedom Movement' but it is clear this is a rebellion of the lower Indian race against the superior

[*hochwertige*] English–Nordic race. The Nordic race has the right to rule the world and we must take this racial right as the guiding star of our foreign policy. It is for this reason that for us any co-operation with Russia is out of the question for there on a Slav–Tartar body is set a Jewish head ... The interest of Germany demands co-operation with England since it is a question of establishing a Nordic–Germanic America, over the world.[7]

Before the war Hitler had often offered to guarantee the British Empire, and during it he renewed this proposal several times. In one of his wartime table talks he said that the 'loss of India by the British Empire would be a misfortune for the rest of the world including Germany itself'. And despite the fact that Japan was an ally, as they advanced to India's border Hitler felt unhappy about the decline of the white man, and spoke of giving the British 20 divisions to 'help throw back the yellow men'. He would go on to describe, in his table talk of 16 December 1941:

A very strange thing that with Japan's help we are destroying the position of the white race in East Asia.

He also forecast that:

If the English give India back her liberty, within twenty years India will have lost her liberty again.[8]

This love for the British Empire was the one thing Hitler shared with his fellow dictator Stalin. During the Teheran Conference in 1943 Roosevelt, trying to get Stalin on his side to pressurise Churchill, suggested that the British could be removed from India through a process of 'reform from the bottom, somewhat on the Soviet line'. But Stalin, who was getting on famously with Churchill, rejected this and instead proposed expansion of the British Empire by giving the British trusteeship over certain bases and strong-points throughout the world.[9]

Despite this, there were various German officials who did think of encouraging revolt amongst the subject peoples of the world, in particular the Indians. Contrary to the widely accepted view, Hitler's Germany was not a monolith, in fact was less of one than Stalin's Russia, as Bose found when he arrived in Germany. In Berlin the German Foreign Office department which liaised with Bose was the *Arbeitskries Indien*, India Working Group, later becoming the Special India Department of the Wilhelmstrasse, all of whose officials hated the Nazis. While the department's nominal head was an old Nazi party hack and Hitler's financial adviser, the three men who really ran it could not have been more dedicated anti-Nazis. They were Adam von Trott zu Solz, Dr Alexander Werth and Franz Josef Furtwängler.[10] Werth, having survived Colombiahaus, one of the Nazi SA's torture chambers in Berlin–Tempelhof, went to England with his Jewish stepfather, where he qualified and practised as a lawyer before returning to Germany just before the war. Furtwängler was a trade unionist and a Social Democrat, but the leader of this group, Trott, was the most remarkable German of his generation. His life summed up how it was possible to live under the gaze of the Nazis, even work for them, yet seek to undermine them. Giles MacDonogh entitled his biography of Trott *A Good German,* and Trott's friend Isaiah Berlin would sum him up as:

> ... a brave and honourable man, a passionate patriot, incapable of anything ignoble or unworthy, and he served what he regarded as being the deepest interests of his own countrymen and of decent people everywhere.[11]

A Rhodes Scholar at Balliol in the 1930s, he had many British friends, some of whom would become prominent in the Labour Party, and was close to Stafford Cripps. During the war Cripps defended him against charges of dishonesty by his Cabinet colleague Anthony Eden. When Gandhi visited Balliol, Trott met him, was photographed with him, sat in the first row as Gandhi gave his lecture and treasured his memory of that occasion. He had no fondness for the British Empire, and would often upset his English friends by telling them that the pink blobs on the map would have to go.

It is one of the great ironies of the Silver story that Peter Fleming, who was helping him deceive Germans, had been a friend of Trott before the war and even endorsed some of his ideas. During his travels to China in 1938 Trott had sought out Fleming's friendship. Fleming, then working at *The Times*, took back a paper Trott wrote arguing for Anglo-German political co-operation to stop Japan, then engaged in a brutal conquest of China. The paper, widely circulated in the higher reaches of the British Government, made a favourable impression. The Fleming archives list a letter Trott wrote to him on 4 November 1938 from Singapore when his ship, the SS *Ranchi*, bringing him home, stopped there. It was on the situation in China and Inner Mongolia, and described the atmosphere in the Treaty Ports controlled by the European powers. The letter does not survive, and it is interesting to speculate, had Trott survived the war, how the German and the Englishman would have compared their contrasting war-time experiences. There was Trott in Berlin, working alongside Bose, receiving messages from Silver, without realising this was fiction dreamt up by Fleming's deception unit in Delhi. And Fleming had no idea Trott was working with Bose.

Bose's arrival meant Trott's department received lavish money from the German Foreign Office, giving him a free hand to work against the Nazis while being financed by them. He could hire friends of his who were sympathetic to resisting Hitler. He could also use the Free India mission to travel in Germany and around Europe, visiting neutral countries where he could contact British and other Western powers to convince them that there was German resistance to Hitler. Indeed, just weeks before the July 1944 Count Stauffenberg bomb plot against Hitler, he used the excuse of conducting Free India business to go to Holland and contact the Dutch resistance in an effort to make the Allies believe that they could do business with the plotters. The failure of the plot saw Trott brutally murdered by the Nazis, slowly asphyxiated with a thin cord.

But, for all the effort by Trott and others to organise German help for Indians seeking freedom, Hitler's racial ideas meant no coherent policy could develop, and Afghanistan was a classic example of this. By the time the war came Germany had a substantial presence in Afghanistan, becoming, as Hauner puts it, the third power in the country after the British and the Russians, with the British initially welcoming the German presence as a lesser evil than the Russians. There were several German engineers and teachers, often prepared to work in conditions the British and the French found beneath their dignity. By 1938 the German Colony was the largest European one in Afghanistan, and by January 1941 there were 122 Germans in the country, excluding the wives, children and members of the German legation, compared to eleven Italians and just four British. The German school in Kabul was the largest foreign school in the city and the largest of its kind outside Germany; members of the Todt organisation supervised road construction all over the country; Lufthansa had a weekly flight to Kabul from Berlin and Germany gave trade credit to Afghanistan. In 1938–39 Germany's share of import of machinery by the Afghan government was 69 per cent, compared to the British share of 4 per cent.

The Germans set up a meteorological station in the Hindu Kush. A wireless telegraphy station was established at Kabul's Sherpur airport, operated by three German engineers, and a petrol and storage tank and pump were also installed at the airport. Many Afghan cities were visited to inspect possible landing grounds. By 1936 Afghans had ordered 500 radio sets from Germany and in 1939 imported 97 of them from Germany compared to only 10 from the UK. 1939 also saw Siemens erect in Kabul a civil broadcasting station of 20 KW which could be heard in Northern India.

The German contingent included several key people.[12] There was Major Schenk, instructor at the Kabul Military Academy, Professor Fischer, a specialist in tropical diseases and the Legation's doctor, and, most important, Kurt Brinckmann, a member of the SS Sicherheitsdienst [SD]. This group, again demonstrating the intelligence confusion the Germans suffered from, overlapped with the Abwehr in some areas. Brinckmann arrived at the end of 1940 and opened a dental surgery in Kabul. Rated by Quaroni as the only intelligent German in Kabul, he was an ambitious SD agent, very clued up about what the Nazi party thinking was, and made much of a remark by Hitler: *Wir schlagen England wo wir es treffen* [We beat England where we meet]. As a committed Nazi who accepted the party's racist ideology he identified who among the Germans in Afghanistan was a Nazi party member, and Schenk was always suspect as he was half Jewish. Brinckmann, not given to modesty, felt he was in a unique position to lecture everyone because from 1 April 1941 he had become the dentist of the Afghan Prime Minister, treating his troublesome teeth every other day. Clearly Hashim Khan, while sitting in the dentist's chair, spoke volubly, for Brinckmann was convinced that it was 'absolutely out of the question' that the Prime Minister was pro-British. How reliable this was can be judged from the fact that Quaroni would later tell the British that 'the Prime Minister has been consistently pro-British ... except for 15 days after the collapse of France, the Prime Minister has never wavered in his conviction that the British will win the war'.[13]

Brinckmann also suggested to Berlin that Germany should give a guarantee to Hashim Khan that should Amanullah return as king he would still remain Prime Minister. He took careful note of the comings and goings at the British Embassy and quickly identified Major Fletcher, the man the Special Operations Executive had sent to Kabul, as 'their local SS man'. In February 1941 Berlin also sent a trained secret service agent, Herr Weiland, whose cover was that he was a businessman but his mission was to organise military espionage in India.

Astonishingly, despite Nazi racial policies, and unlike the British who shunned inter-racial marriage, many Afghans had married German women. As many as ten highly placed Afghans had German wives, including the President of the National Bank and Minister of Commerce, Abdul Majid Khan. He felt so much at home in Germany that, having arrived in Berlin in February 1941 for an abdominal operation and to conduct trade negotiations, he stayed for six months and then spent the rest of the war in Switzerland. As the war loomed the German presence in Afghanistan worried the British sufficiently for Lord Zetland, Secretary of State for India, to say he thought the Germans were trying to build up their influence in Afghanistan, which would be used when there was conflict with the British.

Zetland was not far wrong. In the early days of the war Ribbentrop met SS-Sturmbannführer Dr Ernst Schafer, who saw himself as a sort of German Lawrence of Arabia, and who had organised a number of German expeditions to Tibet. He offered to lead 'his mountain tribes for a parallel action against India'. But as this would take two years Ribbentrop, keener on something more immediate, suggested guerrilla-type incursions into British India from Afghanistan, on the proviso that the Soviets would support such a move.[14]

Then quite by chance the Germans found there was a guerrilla leader they could back to create problems for the British. That man was the Faqir of Ipi, easily the most extraordinary guerrilla leader of the Second World War. The Faqir of Ipi, says Hauner, 'was unique. He was the most determined, implacable single adversary the British Raj in India had to face amongst its own subjects.'[15]

The Times obituary on his death in 1960 described him as:

> ... a doughty and honourable opponent ... a man of principle and saintliness ... a redoubtable organizer of tribal warfare ... many retired Army officers and political agents ... will hear the news with the tribute of wistful regret.

Operating from inaccessible hideouts in Waziristan he was:

> ... uncompromising, unyielding, obstinate and unscrupulous in the choice of combat methods against his opponents. These included traditional methods of tribal warfare such as ambush, kidnapping and mutilation.[16]

His unrelenting hostility meant the British had to maintain a large Army on the North West Frontier all through the war. At one stage some 40,000 British and Indian troops were engaged in trying to capture him. This was a fair proportion of the 187,000 men—140,000 Indians—who formed the Indian Army at the outbreak of the Second World War. And it should be emphasised that this Indian army constituted the largest segment of British imperial troops. But like the Scarlet Pimpernel he proved elusive. Indeed, a couplet called the 'The Scarlet Pimpernel of Waziristan' was written: 'They sought him here, they sought him there, those columns sought him everywhere'.[17]

In the classic mould of guerrilla warfare against an organised army, the Faqir of Ipi never had more than a thousand tribesmen, whose armaments hardly compared to those at the command of the British Army. The British had tanks, airplanes and artillery. Ipi's main weapons were pre-First World War rifles, a few machine guns and one or two pieces of old cannon. He was often short of ammunition, and he gathered intelligence not through the radio, or any other twentieth-century invention, but the old tried and tested method of humans transmitting information across often very difficult terrain. Remarkably, he never acquired a radio set.

And as the Second World War devastated Europe in a fight described as one between civilisation and barbarity, out in the mountains between Afghanistan and India the Faqir of Ipi was the twentieth-century version of the warriors Churchill had encountered in 1897. In the great man's words these were people fighting 'in the unpenetrated gloom of barbarism' and striking 'a blow at civilisation'.[18] The Faqir did not care or know about fascism or communism and neither did his fellow tribesmen. But, while they may have represented barbarism, their fight with the British was also a fight for freedom. They wanted to preserve their historic freedom.

> Classic anarchists who accepted no overlord, they had successfully resisted all British efforts to conquer them and looked with disdain if not outright hostility at British attempts to civilise them by building roads and railways.

The Faqir for them was, as Hauner writes, a Muslim holy man, 'their supreme religious authority as one endowed with divine rights'.[19]

The British had cultivated links with tribal maliks (chiefs) and mullahs (priests) by paying cash allowances to the tribal maliks. In 1940 this amounted to nearly one million Rupees for the whole Tribal Territory. In theory this was payment for road and camp protection, but in effect bribes to khassadars (untrained men), either young boys or old men selected by their local maliks. But those who followed the Faqir were not tempted by such bribes, reasoning that the shortest cut to lucrative allowances was not through loyal service, but attacks on British-built fortified posts before taking to the hills. The Wazirs, inhabiting the barren and inaccessible country across the Durand Line, played this game brilliantly.

The British estimated that as of 1 April 1940 the tribal areas had 414,000 fighting men armed with 233,562 breech-loading rifles or carbines, which meant the tribes had more fighting men than in the entire Indian Army. The British response to tribal warfare was just as brutal as in the days when Churchill had fought them. Then villages were burnt, now they were bombed, on the principle that if the warring tribes sheltered in a particular village, the entire village population must be held responsible. And just as Churchill had justified village burning, so the British government brushed aside objections from men like C. F. Andrews, the Quaker friend of Gandhi.

The Faqir of Ipi was born Mirza Ali Khan about ten years before Silver, anywhere between 1892 and 1897, into the Bangal Khel clan of the Madda Khel section of the Tori Khel Wazirs, part of the greater Utmanzai branch concentrated in Northern Waziristan. His education was classically tribal, starting at Islamic religious schools on the British side of the border, then moving across the border into Afghanistan and becoming a pupil of the Naqib of Chaharbagh, at the time the most famous and influential religious leader in Afghanistan. Then, after performing Haj in Mecca, he made the village of Ipi his base, near the British-built military road connecting Bannu and Razmak. He acquired a saintly reputation among the local Daur tribe but gave no political trouble to the British for many years. He graduated from being the saint of Ipi to guerrilla leader in March 1936 after what the British called the Islam Bibi case, an alleged abduction and forcible conversion to Islam of a minor Hindu girl. Islam Bibi was the adoptive name of a young Hindu girl who had married a Pashtun student. Her Hindu relatives claimed that she had been abducted. The British Political Officer in Waziristan responded with a show of force and removed Bibi and her relatives to the Punjab. Her husband was found guilty of abduction and sentenced to two years' imprisonment. This provoked local protests. The Faqir of Ipi launched a violent anti-British agitation. When the local Daurs disappointed him by dispersing in the face of another British show of force, he fled and established a house and a mosque in an area inhabited by the warlike Mahsuds and raised a force of five hundred, most of whom were Afghans. The British sent two columns of troops, imposed fines and destroyed houses, but he organized a successful ambush which caused heavy British casualties and then escaped. In what the locals saw as a miracle, the normally warring tribes, the Tori Khel Wazirs, the Mahsuds and the Bhittannis, united to oppose the British, and the Faqir was transformed from holy man to warrior. But while religion played a huge part in this conflict he cannot be compared to the Islamic fundamentalists of our time. This is well summed up in his letter to Nehru in September 1937, where he addressed the Indian leader as 'the leader of the liberty-loving people and the distinguished Head of the Indian Nation':

> Islam does not countenance strife and war in the world. Still it is against the spirit of Islam not to resist tyranny or to submit like a coward to a tyrant. Islam has threatened cowards with worst punishment. You, Sir, should clearly understand that the war between us and the tyrannical [British] Government is entirely due to their unwarranted attack on our liberties and not because of our proselytising mania. God has plainly instructed us in the matter of religion and taught us in the Holy Book that 'there is no compulsion in religion'. This means that every person is free in the choice of religion. He can choose to be what he likes—Muslim, Hindu or Christian. Hence it follows from the Koran that religion is a matter of temperament, instinct and spiritual outlook. This is why a day of reckoning is fixed after death when God, not man will award punishments and rewards for acts in this life. You should take it from us, Revered Sir, that the present situation in Waziristan is a result of [British] excesses and the policy of aggressive conquest adopted by the Government of India and is due to nothing else. Hence as long as there is the breath of life in us it is impossible for us to submit to slavery. With God's help may India emancipate herself from their [British] hands and we free our land at the point of our sword. So be it! Amen! [20]

A few months after Faqir had written to Nehru, in December 1937, British forces withdrew to their cantonments. However, in the years leading up to the war the British would return to conduct other operations, and the Faqir's ability to lead the British a merry dance meant that by June 1939 the British had spent an estimated £10 million but failed to capture him. A number of Waziri mullahs demanded complete British withdrawal from Waziristan, and common people readily believed the Faqir had miraculous powers. Among their beliefs were the ideas that if they cut branches from trees the Faqir could convert sticks into rifles, and like Jesus he only needed a few loaves of bread in a basket to feed his people. Should the British use gas, this could be dealt with by divine breezes, and bombs dropped by the British would be made into paper. The Faqir could claim he had demonstrated his miraculous powers given that, as we have seen, the British planes dropped warning leaflets before the bombs came. The faith in the Faqir's powers was not confined to his tribal followers but was so extensive that stories of what he was doing to the British were even heard in the bazaars of India many hundreds of miles to the south.

Destructive as British bombing was, often killing many innocent people, no bomb ever touched the Faqir. When British bombers flattened the Mahsud village of Arsal Kot the Faqir escaped by taking shelter in a nearby cave. His followers, not being on the British khassadari bribe system, continued to flock. Although he failed to unite the warring tribes his lashkars [soldiers] achieved quite a few stunning successes by blocking British lines of communication. The British tried bribing him, offering land outside Waziristan, even tried to get Afghan government help, but all their efforts failed. It is remarkable that, for all the bombing and other military measures against tribes that sheltered the Faqir, they continued to hide him. He sheltered finally with the Madda Khel Wazirs in inaccessible caves in the mountain cliff at Gorwekht, a little over a mile from the Afghan border. This meant that when British efforts to destroy his shelter proved too uncomfortable he could slip easily into Afghan territory.

The Faqir's actions may have prompted the British to promote a rival Muslim leader, the mysterious Shami Pir, another holy man but from Syria. Born Muhammad Saadi al Keilani, a family that claimed direct descent from the Prophet, he was the spiritual leader of one of the most important Islamic fraternities: the Quadiria. Unlike the Faqir of Ipi the Germans could claim to have shaped this Pir. He had studied in Germany and married a daughter of a senior police officer from Potsdam. Observe how, in contrast to the British, and despite German racial attitudes, such an inter-racial marriage was not taboo in Germany. He was also very well connected, being the first cousin of Amanullah's wife Souriya. The British believed he had kept in touch with Amanullah during his exile in Rome. In January 1938 Keilani arrived in the North West Frontier Province. The reason given was that he was collecting shukrana, donations from his followers customary among religious leaders. Having travelled to Southern Waziristan he initially preached, tried to settle tribal disputes and unite the Wazirs and Mahsuds. This is when he was given the name of the Shami Pir. Then without warning in June 1938 he denounced the ruling Afghan King Zahir Shah as a usurper, claimed Amanullah as the rightful ruler and, having gathered an army of Mahsud tribesmen, set out on a march to Kabul. In the complex way Afghan society worked, the same Mahsuds had nearly ten years earlier brought down Amanullah. It seemed Zahir might fall, but the British, not keen to see Amanullah back, worked hard to stop the Shami Pir and persuaded him to go back to Syria. Caroe would describe it as 'the most determined use of force combined with cajolery'.[21] This involved RAF bombing of the Pir's lashkars and the use of Indian soldiers, with the 'cajolery' being a bribe of between £25,000 and £50,000. In his diary entry for 29 June 1938 Sir George Cunningham, Governor of NWFP, revealed that he himself had to draw a cheque for the Shami Pir from his own bank.[22]

The Faqir of Ipi did not ally himself to Pir, and it has never been worked out whose agent Shami Pir was. Could he have been a British one used to destabilise the Afghan government as part of a wider strategy against the Soviets? At that stage, a year before the war, the British still regarded the Soviets as the greater threat in Afghanistan. If he was German then it is hard to explain why Pilger was baffled by the whole affair. But with much rivalry in the various branches of the German government the hapless Pilger may not have been told. During the war there was known German Foreign Office and Abwehr contact with the Shami Pir. Their agents visited him often, but the Pir rebuffed all Axis requests to be part of a plot to restore Amanullah. Caroe, in charge of India's external relations during the war, was certain he was part of a wider Axis intrigue in the whole of the Middle East whose leader was the Grand Mufti of Jerusalem, a man Hitler met, and Caroe blamed Indian intelligence for not discovering the secret. Hauner believes that the Shami Pir's movement must have had 'some British connivance' and has no doubts:

> there is precious little evidence to show that he had been recruited by the Germans at any stage prior to or during the war to work for them for the restoration of Amanullah to power in a pro-Axis Afghanistan.[23]

Until Silver arrived in Kabul and was christened the Axis spy, the Faqir of Ipi was the only game in town for the Axis, and in a remarkable development it was the Italians, not the Germans, who took the lead in trying to persuade the Faqir to work for the Axis, with Quaroni playing a crucial role. The Italian had barely reached Kabul when the British media began to highlight that the Italians were up to mischief. On 16 April 1937, at the height of the war with the Faqir, a front page *Daily Herald* story claimed that 'Mussolini was behind the revolt on the NWFP'. *The Sunday Chronicle* of 26 February 1939 implied that a radio link between the Faqir of Ipi and the Italians had been established, and added, for good measure: 'Meanwhile Hitler is active in Kabul ... where more and more German airmen are being sent as instructors'. In fact these were media stories without foundation, based on the fanciful tales told by many British agents in Kabul, and were certainly not believed by Fraser-Tytler. What was nearer the mark, as Fraser-Tytler reported to London, was that Quaroni was using unscrupulous methods to spread extremely bellicose anti-British propaganda among Indian visitors. And he was looking into what the Axis could do to exploit British problems on the North West Frontier.

In essence Quaroni was revisiting the plan the Germans had tried during the First World War, promoting strife amongst the frontier tribes which would force the British to maintain strong forces to protect the back door to India. This was the substance of his chat with Dr Georg Ripken when, in the summer of 1939, he came to Kabul as leader of a German trade delegation. But Quaroni's suggestion that the Germans and Italians should co-ordinate their operations in the country, given how important Afghanistan would be should there be conflict with Britain, did not meet with Ripken's favour. Quaroni persisted. In June 1939 he was reported to have declared in front of two Indian visitors that the Frontier tribes should be worked up and, in the case of war, led against the British. 'We could not defeat Great Britain in a war in those areas,' he said, 'but seriously injure them, and we possess adequate instruments for the purpose.'[24] A month later, Quaroni told the Germans in Kabul that the Axis powers should co-ordinate their political activities in Afghanistan with a view to using Amanullah, as well as promoting unrest among the tribes on the Frontier in the event of war with Britain. As we have seen, this was about the time the Faqir of Ipi was having his first major clash with the British. However, with both Rome and Berlin procrastinating over Quaroni's plans, the Axis played no part in this fight the Faqir of Ipi had with the British. It was not until March 1941, just as Quaroni was meeting Silver, that his proposal to send the first payment to the Faqir was finally accepted.

The Italian soon discovered that for, all his holiness, the Faqir knew how much he was worth. Through his intermediaries, the Axis legation in Kabul received the following price list: £25,000 to be paid every other month to keep the pot boiling; This sum would double if tribal unrest should be extended to other areas; in the event of a general uprising on the Frontier the price would have to be tripled. The money was in addition to supplies of weapons and ammunition which the Faqir also required urgently. Pilger admitted that to keep the tribes in the field against the British was just a question of spending money. But even if the Faqir's annual requirements amounted to around half a million Reichsmark it would still have been quite a cheap price considering what the government of India had to spend on each punitive expedition into the Tribal Territory. The Axis had money, and no problem forwarding foreign banknotes to Kabul from Rome or Berlin. And, with Germany still allied to the Soviet Union, Russian territory could be easily used for this purpose. The problem was converting pounds and US dollars into a convenient currency, like Afghanis or Indian Rupees. The Afghan government put restrictions on this, and without rupees the money was useless to the Faqir and his men.

Quaroni would later admit to his British interrogators that even though the Axis talked money to the Faqir in the summer of 1941 any plan to use the Faqir of Ipi would have been a sheer waste of time and money. The most propitious time, he maintained, to start action against the British on the Frontier would have been in the autumn of 1940. For this he blamed the Germans in Kabul, who he saw as generally incompetent, taking too long to collect information, often working at cross purposes, and more interested in telling Berlin how useless their fellow Germans in Kabul were rather than working against the British.

This is where Silver and what he offered was so enticing. Silver could provide intelligence on what was happening in India and was ready to subvert the British Raj. The Faqir of Ipi could certainly tie down British troops, but he could do nothing in India. The Axis had never had an agent like Silver at the heart of Britain's most prized colonial possession, and it is understandable why Quaroni was so excited by the prospect of working with him. The fact that he knew nothing about Silver, and had no means of checking who he was and whether his claims amounted to anything, did not seem to worry the Italian, and nor did it worry the Germans when they took over from Quaroni.

As for the Faqir, he long outlived the Axis powers. In February 1944, a year after Quaroni had left Kabul, with Italy now on the side of the Allies and no expectation of support from the Germans, the British still had to threaten tribes harbouring him with massive reprisals. The North West Frontier weekly intelligence summary reported in a telegram to the Foreign Office on 2 February that the:

> Ipi was moving in the Shaktu Valley and the political agent in South Waziristan has been asked to tell the Shabi Khel, Kikari and Marsangsai tribes, that unless they expel the Ipi within 48 hours, 'We will bomb any village in Shaktu or Buazha Basins which has helped Ipi (Faqir).'[25]

The Fakir proved an unfinished part of the British legacy to Pakistan after its creation following the British withdrawal from the subcontinent in 1947. He joined Silver's mentor, Abdul Ghaffar Khan, in campaigning for an independent Pashtun state. The latter's political efforts were defeated, but the Fakir continued his guerrilla struggle, with verbal backing from the Afghans and the Soviet Union, until his death in 1960—the same year as ex-King Amanullah, by then a forgotten exile in Zurich. That is when *The Times*, as we have seen, wrote with typical British romanticism about a former foe.

Unlike the Grand Mufti of Jerusalem the Führer never got to meet the Faqir. But he was at the centre of some of the most bizarre intrigues dreamt up the Abwehr in Kabul. And Silver, as their main agent, was, inevitably, drawn into these schemes.

The Phantom Italian Spy

Silver headed out of Kabul on the morning of 19 March 1941 in a carefree, relaxed mood. Not having to worry about looking after a portly political leader who could not speak the local language, he could more easily be a natural Afghan Pathan blending in with his surroundings and talking freely to his contacts about Subhas Bose. So, as on the outward trip, he made a detour to Lalman to see Haji Mohammad Amin again, walking all the way. Once there he told him that the man who had previously accompanied him was neither deaf nor dumb, or his uncle, but Subhas Chandra Bose. Ah, said the Haji with a laugh, 'You are a mischievous person.' But while this was followed by some serious talk about 'a final assault on the British for the independence of our country', and organising anti-British movements among the Shinwari and Mohmand tribes, Silver's real reason for seeing Amin was that he needed help to get to India.

The simplest, direct way was to take the bus back to Peshawar, but this could be dangerous. Many people he knew from the Peshawar area often took the bus, he was convinced the police were looking for him, and along the way there were also checks for passports—which he did not possess. The route he had selected, therefore, would take him from the village of Arkhi through the tribal territories of Kudakhel, the Gandab valley, Shabkadar and on to Peshawar. Haji Amin secured him an Afghan guide who helped him cross the River Kabul and reach the road to Shabkadar on the Indian side of the border. He could not afford to wait for the bus in Shabkadar as many of those with whom he had been in jail lived here, and decided instead to take a tonga, which meant he did not reach the outskirts of Peshawar until three in the afternoon. Keen to find shelter until it was dark, he quietly slipped into the tailor's shop of his relative Arjan Das, crept into a corner and went to sleep. Silver had often done this before so Das was not surprised to come upon him, but what he told Silver when he woke up was worrying. While he had been asleep a Peshawar CID sub-inspector, Kucha, whose speciality was tracking down political workers, had come to the shop asking for Silver—and this was not the first time he had come, as he knew they were related. Silver decided his best response would be to sound as casual as possible. Whenever the police did not see him for a few days, he assured Das, they became uneasy for no reason and started asking all his friends and relations about him.

But it confirmed to Silver that he had to stop playing the Afghan and begin to look like an Indian again. He had begun to clip his beard on his way back to Peshawar; now he had a clean shave. He also needed to discard his Afghan clothes, which meant turning to Abad Khan. That evening, after Arjan Das had gone to sleep, Silver slipped away just as quietly as he had come and headed for Khan's shop.

Silver knew that Abad Khan would be keen to hear what had happened to him, but even though he had barely begun his spying career he decided not to tell the whole truth. Some of his lies seem curious—Abad was told that Silver had pretended Bose was his deaf and dumb brother, not his uncle. Some were more calculated. While he mentioned meeting Quaroni and dealing with the Italians, and Uttam Chand's help, he omitted anything about his association with the Germans, perhaps because he knew in Abad's eyes it was the Germans, not so much the Italians—of whom little was known in India—who were seen as real fascists. He also lied about how he got to see Quaroni. In this version he had not pretended to be a cook sent by the German Thomas, but rather a servant bearing a message from the Persian minister in Kabul.

By now the transport contractor was quite suspicious of Silver. He had already warned his brother that 'Silver was a dangerous man' and advised him not to mix with him. What is more, he also 'knew the CID had connected Silver's disappearance with Bose' and decided he would now distance himself from both of them. This meant breaking his promise to Bose that, should Silver return with a letter for Sarat, he would take it to Calcutta himself. However, he did advise Silver not to give himself up to the police: 'I told him to continue his underground activities and remain in the Punjab and down country'.[1]

He was, however, prepared to help Silver get new clothes, and took him to Kripa Ram Bros, a well-known firm of Indian tailors, to buy a warm suit and a felt hat, in an instant transforming Silver from a tribal Pathan into the kind of Indian readily seen by the British as loyal to the Raj. That this shop was in the cantonment where the British Indian Army was based did not worry them—an indication of how the British caste system, which kept the civilians away from the army, meant they had no fear of meeting CID officers or police informers in that part of Peshawar. Abad also had no problem going with Silver in one of his taxi lorries, a sort of Indian minibus, to meet Akbar Shah in Nowshera.

This meeting underlined the compartmentalised life Silver had begun to lead as a spy. Normally in the traditional Indian style of hospitality all three would have got together and chatted over tea and sweets. Now Abad waited outside, while Silver and Akbar Shah withdrew to a side room. There Silver, aware Shah was part of Bose's political party, was more forthcoming. He agreed with Shah that Bose had tricked them by heading to Berlin rather than Moscow, although in Bose's defence he did point out that the Russians had refused to see him.

For Silver the most important thing before he signed up officially to be an Italian spy was to get the approval of Kirti party leaders. With the Hitler–Stalin pact still in existence the communists' view that the war was an imperialist one had not changed. But, wondered Silver, would they approve of actual collaboration with the main fascist ally of the Nazis? This meant a trip to Lahore. He could not just jump on the train at Nowshera, so he took a tonga to a wayside station which was on the bus route from Peshawar to Rawalpindi. The bus ride filled him with dread as the police and many people in the area knew him, but he was not spotted, and in Rawalpindi he easily managed to catch the night train to Lahore.

So much had changed in Silver's life in the previous two months that he now found himself in a very curious position. He could claim to know the back streets of Kabul, but he had never been to the capital of the Punjab. The money Bose and the Italians had given him meant he could book into a decent hotel; the bigger problem was that most of the Kirti leaders were by now in jail. One of the few leading communists who was not was Gurcharan Singh Sainsra, whom Silver was keen to see, having met him some months earlier at Abad Khan's place when they were planning to organise the Kabul trip for Cheena. Like Silver, he was using a Muslim pseudonym, in his case Hidayat Khan. Back in August 1940 when Cheena, Sodhi and other Kirti leaders had held a series of meetings to tell Kirti workers they should concentrate on winning over Sikh soldiers who were on leave, Sainsra had taken an active part and been placed in charge of a special subsection of the Kirti party for military work. He was also a writer for the *Milap* magazine that specialised in Punjabi literary fiction, Punjabi being his mother tongue. Silver had a contact in the magazine, Pandit Balbhadar but with the communists trying to keep out of the clutches of the police Balbhadar did not know where Sainsra was.

After several days, Silver was directed to be at a small park in the city. He approached the park with care. Sainsra, a 40-year old Punjabi, would have been easy to miss. He could easily blend into his surroundings: medium build, medium height, clean shaven, his wheatish complexion common to this part of the world, and wearing, like most Punjabi men, *kurta* and pyjama. But even from a distance his spectacles that concealed small eyes, and his Karakuli Afghan hat convinced Silver that this was the man he had met at Abad's place. To Silver's great relief Sainsra told him the party had set up a secret underground headquarters in a large house in the suburb of Nawakot owned by a doctor who was a Communist Party sympathiser. Silver arrived to find quite a few of the party leaders there and also Sodhi, who had been summoned from his own hiding place in Lyallpur. As party treasurer it was important for him to hear what Silver had to say.

As with Abad, Silver was selective in what he told his party comrades, and the way he told the story showed how he had learnt that the odd, often meaningless, bit of colour could beguile the listener into believing he was getting the full truth. So he gave some details of the journey, including the mule ride with Bose, but did not disclose his route to Kabul. As for the Italians, Silver 'did not give full details of their various discussions' but dropped the tantalising titbit that none of the discussions took place in the Italian Legation, but rather the summer residence of the Italians at Paghman.[2]

Instead, Silver stressed how the Soviets had refused to help, and that the Italians had paid all his expenses and given Silver money to return to India. For Sodhi, Sainsra and the other Kirti leaders this was the crucial news. Silver would later tell the British that opinion was divided over whether this Axis money should be accepted and if Silver should obey Quaroni's orders to return to Kabul, but Sodhi makes no reference to this. And there was never any doubt about the outcome of the debate: with American funds having dried up, and the party on its uppers, as Sodhi the treasurer knew only too well, a completely unexpected source of cash had miraculously opened up and Kirti, for all its belief in communism, was not about to turn the money down even if it was from the hated fascists.

This meeting, and its decision, marked an important moment in Silver's spying career. Sainsra would be invaluable in concocting fictitious stories, and the house in Nawakot became a home away from home as he and Sainsra worked on documents designed to fool the Italians and later the Germans. It was in this house that the British would finally catch up with Silver—but that was another twenty months away.

The meeting also had to decide what to do with the letters Bose had given Silver. Should they be delivered, or destroyed, and Silver return to Kabul and pretend he had done so? In the end it was decided that Silver should fulfil this part of his role as Bose's secretary. The delivery of one letter was not a problem, just a trip to another part of Lahore where Sardul Singh Caveeshar, the leader of Bose's party in the Punjab, lived. Sainsra accompanied Silver, but Caveeshar, aware that following Bose's escape his house was being watched by the CID, reacted with fright to Silver's visit, claimed the letters were not in Bose's handwriting and sent them both packing.

The more interesting journey was to Calcutta to deliver Subhas' letter to Sarat. This involved Sodhi, and resulted in another elaborate deception by Silver and the Kirti party. Bose and the Italians had told him to return to Kabul with two reliable men—one of them from among Bose's revolutionary supporters in Bengal—who could be trained in sabotage techniques and wireless work. Silver would obviously have to go to Calcutta to get the Bengali revolutionary, but who should be the second one? According to Silver's memoir he asked Sainsra to find him one, and the latter came up with Sodhi, leaving the reader with the impression that this is how Sodhi came into Silver's life. Indeed, the first mention of Sodhi's name in Silver's memoir comes when Silver describes their journey together to Calcutta and how Sodhi was later selected as the revolutionary comrade from Punjab. When Silver made this disclosure in the mid-1970s he could not have anticipated how the subsequent opening of British archives, containing Sodhi's confession, would expose his lie.[3] Sodhi had no desire to be the second revolutionary in Bose's plans and come back and organise anti-British sabotage. All he wanted to do was escape from the police in India, aware that he faced the noose should he get caught. As Silver was very much the junior person in the party, he had to accept Sodhi's decision whether he liked it or not.

However, aware that the British were hunting Sodhi, Silver realised his name had to be tweaked, so decided to introduce him to Bose's associates as Sodhi Mohinder Singh, converting his surname into his first name. Bizarrely, Silver used this name for Sodhi as late as 1973 when he presented a paper at an international seminar on Bose in Calcutta, where he publicly described for the first time how he had helped Bose.

Travelling with Sodhi to Calcutta did make the journey more difficult. Both the main stations at Lahore and Calcutta would have had police informers carefully watching long-distance trains, so when the pair headed out to Calcutta on the evening of 28 March they took the train not from Lahore but from a small station a few miles away. And, instead of going on to Howrah the great central station in Calcutta the British had built for a city which only a decade earlier had been the capital of India, they got off at another wayside station and took a local train in.[4]

Sarat's house was situated in Woodburn Park, a part of the city previously known as 'white town' when only the British were allowed to live there. Now there were some well-off Indians there as well and the house reflected Sarat's status as one of the city's most successful barristers. Like his brother, Sarat wanted the British out of India, but like many Indians of his generation he also admired the British and lived in the style they did in India. The large three-storied dwelling was fronted by a spacious lawn with flowering shrubs on the far side, and flower beds of English annuals. One of the photographs on the staircase was of Sarat in impeccably tailored morning dress complete with top hat, which had much amused Gandhi, who had discarded such British clothes for his loincloth.

This was Calcutta's *Downton Abbey*: Silver had never encountered such a house, but, characteristically, having got past the guards at the Italian

Embassy he was no longer daunted. With Quaroni he had had to pretend he was a cook; now he could be himself. So when the servant, discovering he did not have a visiting card, as most visitors who called on Sarat did, gave him a slip of paper on which to write his name, he wrote with a flourish, 'Bhagat Ram, I come from the frontier'.[5]

Silver was met by Sarat's son, Sisir, the nephew who had helped spirit Subhas Bose out of that house back in January. Silver duly gave him the letter Subhas had written to his father and the two articles he wanted published. Later Sarat appeared and Silver had a chat with him. But with the house being watched by the police, Sarat warned Silver not to come again to his place but meet him the next morning while Sarat was having his morning stroll, in the garden of Victoria Memorial, the great monument to Queen Victoria built by Lord Curzon as a symbol of British rule and situated directly opposite the Calcutta racecourse, another British import into India.

It was in this very British setting that Silver told Sarat about his younger brother's journey from Peshawar to Kabul and beyond. Sarat was keen to know every detail, and that meeting illustrated the two faces of Sarat. Much more than his brother he was the great constitutionalist. He was a member of the Bengal Legislative Assembly the British had set up, loved the cut and thrust of debating there and was, at that very moment, planning to become a minister in the local Indian-run Bengal government. Yet after years of failing to persuade the British to negotiate withdrawal from India he also supported his brother's move to secure foreign help, seeing the war as the great and last chance for India. Calcutta also meant money and Sarat gave Silver 200 rupees.

Silver also met Satya Ranjan Bakshi, Subhas Bose's close confidant, at Princep's Ghat by the Hooghly river, and it was agreed that Bakshi would send a Bengali 'comrade' to Lahore to accompany Silver on his return trip to Kabul. Silver was now so relaxed that he even did a couple of days sightseeing before returning north. By mid-April 1941 everything was ready for his return to Kabul. Silver, Sodhi and the revolutionary sent from Bengal gathered in Peshawar where Abad Khan had arranged a house for the trio. The newcomer from Calcutta was 'a tall, thin Bengali youth' called Santimoy Ganguli, whose organisation, the Bengal Volunteers, fervently believed that only violence could free India. Silver told Sodhi and Ganguli that for the trip they would have to assume Muslim names. He would revert to Rahmat Khan, Sodhi would be Mohammed Khan and Ganguli Sher Zaman.

On the morning of 20 April 1941, Silver jauntily set off on his second trip to Kabul. He was now so confident that the only help he needed from Abad was a taxi to drop him and his two companions near Jalala, a busy bazaar on the road to the Swat Valley. There Silver had arranged five Pathan guides to meet them. This time the route was longer via Lalajan Koruna, Barang and across Mohmand tribal territory, but Silver justified it to his companions on the grounds that it would take in more tribes, extend the influence of the anti-British movement and lay the foundation for a widespread struggle in the future. In reality, having decided that as a spy he would often have to go back and forth from Peshawar to Kabul on foot, he also wanted to explore new routes. In Kudakhel they met Mirin Jan, a resourceful, educated tribal chief who lavishly entertained Silver's party. But while he was ready to die fighting the *feranghis*, the subcontinental term for white foreigners, Jan told Silver and his colleagues that he was a realist: the tribes could be easily persuaded to take up arms, but he would not indulge in rash action against the British, only in operations with some chance of success. He was also keen to know how a free India would treat the tribal people—if it behaved like the British, then replacing the British with Indians did not make much sense.

Though Silver was no longer escorting a prominent leader with no experience of the terrain who could not be easily ordered about, Sodhi and Ganguli tested Silver's patience to the limit. Neither understood let alone spoke the languages of the tribal areas and Afghanistan, Pashto (the language of the largest Afghan ethnic group, also called Pakhto, Pashtu or Pushtu), and Persian, or knew the local customs. There was a problem with the way Ganguli ate his rice. Like most people in India all three ate with their fingers, but Ganguli, brought up in Bengal, made balls of rice and threw them into his mouth. Silver advised him to watch how the Afghans were eating and copy them. Ganguli, the junior of the party, at least was biddable. Sodhi, the man of the world, was not.

Afghans like green tea without milk, with a bit of sugar in the first cup—but if they have refills, they do not add any more sugar. Sodhi kept asking for more sugar, and when Silver advised him not to they had a huge row. Sodhi had lived in America, been to the Soviet Union and was in no mood to listen to someone he considered a very minor party worker. He remonstrated that Silver was preventing him from eating and drinking and the pair often had rows. Also, in public Silver could not allow either Sodhi or Ganguli to open their mouths:

> And that meant that this time I had two deaf mute persons with me. I succeeded with that story in this mission also though technically it was very wrong. But I had no choice in the matter.

When he met Uttam Chand in Kabul the shopkeeper asked, 'Are they deaf and dumb as well?'[6]

The terrain had been enough of a problem to Bose: with Ganguli it was nearly disastrous. When he decided to take a plunge in the Dir river to relieve the uncomfortable heat, not realising that the water was ice-cold, he nearly froze to death. At one stage, with Ganguli struggling to walk, it was decided to hire a donkey:

... but we had gone only a few hours along a good path along the foot of the hills when Santi Babu's donkey saw some other donkeys at a camp pitched by a caravan, and all of a sudden took off at a tremendous speed with Santi Babu on its back. We really got worried and all of us ran after the donkey to save Santi Babu. When at last we caught up with it we found Santi Babu with his arms round the donkey's neck and very much alarmed. Actually I was rather more terrified than him because the track was such that on one side was the river Kabul and on the other side a wall of mountain range and the track also was rough and rocky. So anything could have happened to Santi Babu. We dispensed with the donkey.[7]

In Kabul Silver settled his companions in the same *serai* he had stayed at with Bose, and visited Crishnini to tell him about Sodhi and Ganguli. The next morning Madam Quaroni left a message with Uttam Chand that Quaroni wanted to see him in the Italian Embassy summer residence at Paghman and Silver was quickly on his way. Amanullah had seen Paghman as his Simla and Byron had described it as 'spread over a wooded slope two or three thousand feet above the plain where grassy glades interrupt the poplars and walnuts, an orchestra plays of mountain streams, and the snows appear through the streets unexpectedly close'. However the Englishman had found the houses themselves 'appalling', like 'back parts of Pimlico ... shoddy and obscene they defile the woods and streams and the view of the plain beneath.'[8] But Silver loved it. And Quaroni, having waited anxiously for him to return—in the preceding weeks sending his wife to see Uttam Chand for any news—laid on quite a party.

There it was confirmed that Bose was in Berlin working with the Axis on setting India free. The news was not pleasing but, as the Kirti leaders had decided at their meeting in Nawakot, the party needed money, and nothing should be done to show any displeasure with such Nazi association. Once contact was established with the Russians Kirti could explain why they had appeared to help the fascists. So, laying it on with a trowel, Silver told the Italians to tell Bose that his 'followers in India were enthusiastically continuing their work [disrupting the British war effort], and that they were glad to know Bose was negotiating with Axis leaders'.

For Quaroni Silver's return was encouraging. Rome had always talked of stirring trouble in the tribal areas, but Quaroni had stressed to his masters the special qualities required of anyone sent into the field on such a mission:

... it is necessary to choose people who are above all genuinely able to pass themselves off as natives ... We must therefore choose people who are truly capable of doing anything and to be prepared to send them out when it is really useful and necessary to do so. We are dealing with a problem that is much more difficult and delicate than it might seem and the smallest imprudent act runs the risk of compromising everything.[9]

And Silver for Quaroni was not only that ideal person, who could truly pass himself off as native, but seemed also to combine shrewd political judgement with encouraging news of what was happening in India. When Rome telegrammed questions Bose wanted answered, Quaroni could answer back: 'I have been in touch with Rahmat Khan [Silver] about the content of your telegrams 77 78 79'.

Bose was by now well settled in Berlin, living in great comfort in the former residence of the US military attaché, provided with money by the Germans, which he considered as a loan to be repaid, and reunited with his Austrian wife. But in keeping with his secretive nature he did not let on he was married. Rommel, meanwhile, was sweeping through North Africa, and there was fighting in Iraq between the British and the Iraqis where Rashid Ali al-Gilani, a nationalist, pro-Axis politician, had led a coup toppling the pro-British Regent Prince Abdullah. Britain had granted Iraq independence in 1932 but had a treaty that maintained its hold, including Royal Air Force bases which secured its oil pipelines to Haifa. Britain's use of Indian troops, sent into Basra to make Rashid flee and win an important victory, confirmed to Bose how, for more than 200 years, Britain had always used Indian soldiers to maintain its worldwide empire. Two days after Silver's return to Kabul Bose was telling the Germans what they needed to do about India. In his memorandum, he wrote: 'I therefore request that an early pronouncement be made regarding the freedom of India and the Arab countries'. Germany, said Bose, must help revolts in these countries; attack India—the heart of the British Empire; overthrow the pro-British Afghan government, and help the Iraqi government. If all this was done Germany would have a string of friendly countries 'from North Africa on the one side and right up to Japan in the Far East'. This would become even more important if Germany were in conflict with Turkey or the Soviet Union, although Bose also argued that:

> For the success of the task of exterminating British power and influence from the countries of the Near and the Middle East, it is definitely desirable that the status quo between Germany and the Soviet Union should be maintained.

When Quaroni asked Silver how he felt about an Axis declaration on India he skilfully batted it away: 'He would prefer first to consult friends in India.' But when Quaroni asked who were the leaders supporting the Axis in India Silver was ready with his fiction, providing a host of names like Sardul Singh Caveeshar who Silver well knew wanted nothing to do with him. For good measure he transposed Caveeshar from Lahore to Calcutta. He also confidently lied that the Bose article he had taken back to India was now

... circulated throughout India as a clandestine pamphlet; he has heard that copies have arrived as far away as Peshawar. Propaganda has already been initiated among the Afridi in collaboration with us.

He promised to look into getting two duplicators and two small printers in to the tribal areas. He also advised 'radio transmissions from Rome and Berlin to be in English' and 'he will send a report [on how it is received] after his next journey'.

What really got Silver going was how much money the Italians would give. Quaroni reported to Rome:

> Meanwhile he thinks it is necessary, to make a contribution of at least 20,000 Indian rupees to the [Axis work in India] ... It is necessary to have the means as soon as possible because the [Kirti] organisation has only 1,500 rupees and there are 2,000 employees without work because of the lack of funds.[10]

Silver also told Quaroni how he should be paid, warning him that he:

> ... now seems less sure of being able to change sterling bank notes in India. To avoid having money that cannot be used, it would be preferable to send the funds necessary for the work to be done, both on the frontier and in India, in gold dollar bills. Gold is difficult to transport because of its weight, but is of course the safest form and can if necessary be changed in Kabul, also for Indian rupees. Rahmat has promised to consult the bankers in India who form part of Bose's organisation and to give us precise information about the possibility of changing sterling in India. He considers that for the work that Bose intends to carry out in India, but not repeat not for work on the frontier, counterfeit rupee bank notes would serve provided that they are well made.[11]

The problem for Quaroni was that the Axis powers were taking far too long to decide:

> I apologise for reverting so insistently to the subject of my telegram no. 6432, but it concerns the matter that is made of prime importance by the events that are unfolding. If we do not consider this with the necessary urgency and seriousness, we may one day find ourselves with all routes closed and unable to continue the tasks that seemed promising.[12]

By the time Quaroni sent this telegram on 5 June 1941 Silver had spent over a month in Kabul and was preparing to leave, and Quaroni warned Rome that while he '... will be back here in exactly one month ... next time he must not have to wait here for 25 days for instructions ... It costs us a lot, it is dangerous and it is a complete waste of our work in India'.

Silver had already got the Italians to pay for their stay in Kabul, having convinced the Italians that it was dangerous to stay for long in the *serai*. The Italians had agreed provided Silver's group lived with other Indians in Kabul as it would raise no suspicion, and a flat on the upper floors of the house Uttam Chand lived in was rented. However, even then Silver did not reveal to Sodhi and Ganguli that he had been meeting Quaroni. He would go away for several hours during the day and come back to tell his colleagues that the Italians were passing occasional messages back and forth via Uttam Chand about what Bose was up to in Berlin. When Bose asked for information about events and people in India, particularly Bengal, Silver got Ganguli to write it out, telling him he would give it to Uttam Chand to pass on to the Italians. In reality he was giving it personally to Quaroni.

He did this even when Sodhi heard a broadcast from Rome at Uttam Chand's shop on India, which sounded to him like the voice of a man he knew, Ajit Singh from his Ghadar party days. This inspired him to send a message to Rome to find out more about what the Ghadar party was doing and ask them if they would like Sodhi to come to Europe. Silver took the message to Quaroni but gave it his own twist, with the result Quaroni cabled Rome:

> Rahmat Khan asks to ask Bose if he has been in touch with the Gadar [*sic*] Party. If Nattan Singh alias Buddasingh [the Ghadar party link man in Europe] happens to be in Europe and if Bose could get in touch with him, he should ask him to send to Kabul the personal correspondence that would have a strong effect on the Kirti party. Ask him to consult Rattan concerning the Indians who are to be found in Russia. If he could send them to Kabul where they could go on to India, they would be very useful for working on Forward Block. Ask him also to consult him about Sodhi (my telegram no. 246), because we need a decision urgently about him. And ask him also to send him a telegram saying which personalities or representatives of the Indian parties have made contact in Europe so that he can perhaps take parallel action in India.[13]

It was not until 25 May 1941 almost a month since the trio had arrived in Kabul, that Silver finally told Sodhi and Ganguli the Italians had sent Uttam Chand a message that they were now ready to meet the Indians. He had a sort of an excuse: Ganguli had developed a sore on his foot and a high fever, had had several fainting fits and was hardly in a condition to move. He seemed to Sodhi a sickly youth, but Silver's behaviour reveals him to be very far from a team player, a trait that would come to the fore over the next few years. While he could follow the party line on policy, spying for him was essentially a very individual activity and one in which he had to be in sole control. The only man he shared information with in Kabul was Uttam Chand, who, as the contact man for the Italians, could not be avoided.

The meeting of 25 May between the Indians and the Italians was a historic one, as for the first time sabotage was discussed in detail. Quaroni had checked out Sodhi and Ganguli with Bose and now, while his wife and Anzilotti listened, he gave Ganguli an hour's instruction on how to apply dynamite sticks with a fuse for blowing up bridges, railway stations and buildings. He also told them that whenever possible castor oil should be mixed with petrol at RAF aerodromes to help ground planes. He suggested they target the great Attock Bridge that guarded the frontiers of British India.

The next day there was another meeting, at which for the first time Silver met a member of the German diplomatic staff, Carl Rudolf Rasmuss, a former German Trade Commissioner in Calcutta, who could speak broken Bengali. Rasmuss had a long chat with Silver:

> ... and explained that he had come to Kabul to develop Subhas Bose's plans. Rasmuss said Bose wanted him and Sodhi to continue to serve as contacts between Kabul and India, so as to pass on instructions to Bose's followers. They must also arrange to work in close co-operation with the tribal leaders, especially the Faqir of Ipi with whom Rasmuss was very anxious to establish close direct connections. Rasmuss wanted [Silver] on his return to India to tell Bose's party about their leaders' negotiations with the Axis powers and also prepare a monthly budget of expenditure ... He told Silver to bring back a detailed report on the situation in India, Bose's party organisation, its leading members, party strengths etc. He also handed Silver a photograph of himself in Nepal with the Nepalese Development Minister, whose name he gave as Ganja Ram Singh, saying he was his friend and against the Nepalese ruling family and the British, and that this photo would serve as a passport for anyone wanting help in Nepal.[14]

Sodhi had listened carefully to Rasmuss's demands that Silver bring back a full written report showing details of work province by province, military dispositions, aerodromes, maps of strategic positions etc. He and Silver agreed this would be something for Sainsra's skills at fictionalising to exaggerate as much as possible, as the Axis powers seemed willing to spend large sums of money. During the meeting Sodhi also interjected, saying the party in India badly needed money, and with it could achieve 'big results'.

What happened next was astonishing. At the end of the meeting Rasmuss handed Silver Rs 5,000 Afghanis and 'told him that a further Rs 20,000 Afghanis would be waiting for him at Crishini's home'. Clearly the Germans were contributing their share of the money the Axis were paying Silver, although the Italians were still his major paymasters. Interestingly, while all three Indians were present at this meeting Rasmuss took Silver to one side and paid Rs 5,000 in great secrecy to him, a payment Silver did not disclose either to Sodhi or Ganguli. Sodhi only knew of the Rs 20,000 from Crishini. As for the hapless Ganguli, who was not a member of the Kirti party but the only true Bose party member, he was told nothing. Nor are readers of Silver's memoir. Instead, they are told how useless the Italians were: 'The Italians never started the work of training our comrades for which they had come all the way to Kabul'.[15]

Quaroni was keen to stir up trouble in the tribal areas but Silver convinced him that, he and Ganguli should return to India given his helpful instructions in the arts of sabotage. But then what should Sodhi do? Quaroni thought the Indian could help him solve the problem of the Axis not being able to send Europeans to the tribal areas, and suggested to Sodhi that he would best serve India if he went there. Sodhi immediately scotched this: he did not speak a word of Pashto. Silver decided to reveal, presumably to Quaroni alone, that not only did Sodhi not know tribal languages, but he was also a Hindu—possibly the only time in all his conversations with Quaroni when he told the truth. Quaroni readily accepted Silver's advice, a man he trusted completely by now, and felt reassured that Silver and Ganguli would on their return to India make good use of what he had taught them.

Sodhi was in a curious position. Without going into details of his attempt to suborn Indian soldiers he had admitted to Ganguli that the reason he had come to Kabul was to avoid the Punjab police putting him on a murder charge. This had horrified the Bengali as for him anyone trying to escape being hanged after committing a revolutionary act was no true revolutionary.[16] As for the Italians Sodhi felt he could not give any hint that he was on the run from the Indian police and stressed that he was anxious to go to Russia to find out what had happened to Cheena and Ram Kishan. The Italians insisted that he must stay in Kabul, and Sodhi decided to use this enforced stay to get past the guards at the Soviet Embassy and talk to a Russian official.

On 14 June 1941 Silver and Ganguli left Kabul, arriving back in Mardan four days later.[17] Ganguli shed his Pathan clothes, became a Bengali again and headed for Calcutta, while Silver, after a brief stop in Mardan, set off for Lahore, reaching the Nawakot safe house on June 22. He immediately briefed his party leadership but even as they met Hitler was unleashing his army against their beloved Soviet Union and the world of Silver and that of his communist comrades was thrown into chaos. '... all our thinking and planning came up for a drastic change. Very long and serious discussions took place among us, and we had to revise our line of action ...'[18]

Moscow Calling

The German invasion of Russia meant that almost overnight the Communist view of the war changed dramatically. In Russia the war was now the great patriotic war. For Communists round the world it was transformed from the imperialists' war into the people's war. By the time Silver met his fellow Kirti party members in Nawakot, shortly after his return to Lahore, he found all his comrades were parroting this new line. But this posed the question: what should they do with Bose, now living in the capital of the enemy that was devastating the Communist homeland? Should they continue to work with the Nazis and the Italian fascists? Like all dutiful Communists they needed instructions from Moscow, and the Kirti leaders had no way of contacting them.

Had they been part of the mainstream Indian Communist party they would have had instructions from the British Communists, who acted as mentors for their Indian counterparts. Within weeks of the German invasion Harry Pollitt, the general secretary of the British Communist Party, had written to the CPI that now was not the time to talk of liberating India: Communists faced a 'fundamentally new situation' and there could not be 'any sectarian attitude of the Communist Party, any standing aside and not pulling our weight in the common effort to defeat Hitler, and putting forward impossible demands'.[1] By impossible demands he clearly meant asking for Britain to set India free.

However, these isolated Punjab Communists had in their grubby little hands the lovely money the Germans and Italians had given. More was on offer, and so they decided they would cut off all links with Bose's organisation in India and not pass on any messages from Bose to his followers in Bengal. Bose himself at this point was still under wraps in Berlin pretending to be the Italian diplomat Signor Orlando Mazotta—indeed, he had even told his Austrian wife that in any correspondence she should refer to him by that name. At the Nawakot meeting, therefore, Kirti leaders decided they would not tell anyone that Bose was in Berlin: it would be the great Kirti secret.

As for the Germans and the Italians in Kabul, they would maintain contact, and feed them duff information. Their fervent hope was that while they were doing this, Sodhi in Kabul would finally manage to get past the guards of the Soviet Embassy in Kabul and talk to a Russian diplomat.

Sodhi had by now made some headway with the Russians, although not quite as much as he wanted. He might have been living in a flat paid for by the Italians, but he was confident they could not keep a watch on what he was doing, so he went to the Soviet Embassy and spoke to the doorman in Russian, but was turned away, which made him realise that if even speaking Russian could not get him past the Afghan doorman, then the guard must have taken him for a local probably trying to pester the diplomats for a job. Sodhi could not, of course, bleach his brown skin white and look like a European but he could dress like one, instead of a Pathan. In the bazaar he purchased a second-hand suit, tie, collar and hat and a couple of days later, on 18 June, went back to the Embassy.

It is a reflection of the deep-seated racism of the times that, in the midst of a war meant to be between western democracies and a country that preached the supremacy of the white races, a brown man in a neutral Asian country made up of wholly brown people felt he had to dress like a white man to persuade his fellow browns to open the embassy door of an European country. Even more telling is that in June 1941 this was the embassy of the world's only Communist country, whose creed was the universal brotherhood of the world's workers, but whose officials were all white. It is hard to believe in the second decade of the twenty-first century, but that was the world in the fourth decade of the twentieth.

Sodhi was proved right in his assumption. Instead of sounding like a Pathan who knew a bit of Russian, now he spoke to the Afghan guard in English and said he had come from the British Legation. The guard had no hesitation in opening the door, and Sodhi finally managed to speak to a Soviet official. A short, fat, clean-shaven man who gave his name as Moradov, possibly one of the two Russian agents working for the local NKVD station, he listened as Sodhi, now speaking in Russian, told him that he had been in Moscow, where he was called 'Sherwan', and explained that he wanted to return to find out what had happened to Cheena and Ram Kishan.[2] By now the Soviets had had plenty of warnings that the Germans were about to attack, including a personal one from Churchill to Stalin. The Russian dictator had dismissed that as a British plot, and Moradov may have seen Sodhi as part of one too, just like Mikhailov, the Russian ambassador, a few months previously when Silver had pointed out Bose to him. While Mikhailov had wanted nothing to do with Silver, Moradov held out some hope, saying he would report to Moscow and let him know. He also dutifully noted down the Kabul address Sodhi gave him: C/O Uttam Chand. Sodhi had not told the Russians about working for Bose, or having any connection with the Axis Powers in Kabul, and could hardly tell him now that that the address he had given was a flat paid for by the Italians. It was not that he wanted to keep any secrets from the Russians: his reason for not being entirely transparent with them was his fear that any such disclosures might only feed Soviet paranoia. The time for full disclosure would come when Moscow responded favourably to his request.

Three days later Sodhi was in the flat when he heard on the wireless about Operation Barbarossa. He went straight back to the Soviet Embassy, now even more anxious to get to Russia, 'and uneasy about his entanglement with the Fascist representatives in Kabul. He still kept quiet about the latter, however, and the Soviet official said under war conditions it would be quite impossible for him to proceed to Russia, and advised him to go back to India'.[3] The Russians also told Sodhi that Cheena was on his way back from Moscow with a message from Russia to the Indian Communist Party to give their unqualified support to the Allied war effort.

Indeed Cheena was: his reaction to the news of the invasion, which he heard in Moscow, was to offer to fight for the Red Army. Kozloff's response showed how the Russians saw this as a patriotic war which would be won by Russians. Kozloff told Cheena the Comintern appreciated his offer, but wanted him to return to India and tell Indian Communists and other Soviet sympathisers that this was no longer an imperialist war. Britain was now allied to the Soviet Union, and it was the duty of all Socialists and Communists to support the war rather than obstruct it. Moral or verbal sympathy with Soviet Russia was not sufficient: Indian comrades should actively help by enlisting in the Indian Army and otherwise support the British and their war effort. The British and American Communists were now supporting the war, Kozloff explained, and Communists the world over should join the anti-fascist front. If Russia were defeated it would be the end of Britain and of communism. The verbal instructions were supplemented by written communications.

About the middle of July 1941, therefore, Cheena, accompanied by Kozloff, left Moscow for Stalinabad (now renamed Dushanbe , the capital and largest city of Tajikistan) by train and then flew to a Soviet frontier post near the Afghan border. With Ram Kishan still in a sanatorium it was decided to leave him behind, and we must presume that is where he eventually died. At Kharog Cheena was given Afghan clothing, Rs 300 in cash, and a Tajik guide to accompany him across the Afghan border and show him the route to India via the Boroghil Pass into Gilgit via Yashin. The guide left him at Darkot. Here Cheena's luck ran out. On 18 August 1941 he was arrested as a suspicious stranger and handed over by the Darkot Lambardar to the Gilgit authorities. At first Cheena tried to bluff his way out by claiming to be a Muslim, but then admitted who he was, and when questioned by the Punjab CID sang like the proverbial canary.[4]

At this stage the British in India were still trying to work out how Bose had fled the country and who had helped him. That Cheena, an ardent Communist, was involved, or that the Kirti party had played the leading role, came as a surprise. Of course, Cheena could not tell them anything about how Bose had finally made his getaway, as by then he was already in Moscow. However, his confession contained not only information about Kirti finances and its relations with the Indian Communist Party, but also fascinating details about undercover work by Silver, Sodhi and Abad Khan, who he referred to as Abbas Khan, for the Punjab police to act on. But for some reason they did not, and it was not until 17 December 1941, more than four months later, that Cheena's confession reached an official of IPI in London—the man whose real name was Mr Silver—with copies to SIS and MI2. And far from making London want to know more about the Indian codenamed Silver, the reaction of the real-life British Silver was merely that the Kirti connection was 'confirmed in a general way by quite independent information obtained in this country'.[5]

What worried London more was Bose's links with the Sikhs and how he might exploit these in Berlin, the fear being that he might try to suborn Sikh soldiers who were now German prisoners of war.[6] There was no attempt made to explore what Silver the agent, Sodhi or any of the others implicated in the confession had been doing, and certainly no surprise expressed that the Punjab had not followed this up further, all of which reflected the very distinct, compartmental divisions in the British and Indian administrations, and a certain amount of rivalry as well. So Silver's spying network was left untouched. In Kabul Sodhi, unaware of what had happened to Cheena, could only wait for Silver to arrive from India and in the meantime hope finally to persuade the Russians that they were genuine Indian Communists willing to help the Communist motherland fight the Germans.

Silver meanwhile had been quite busy shuttling between Ghalla Dher and Lahore and, while still needing to keep a look-out for the police when he met confidants, now felt free to talk more candidly about what he was getting up to in Kabul. On his return he had got in touch with Abad Khan via his brother, who worked as a manager in the cinema in Mardan. Silver gave him 200 Rupees for his expenses, candidly telling him of his contacts with the Axis, and also that Bose in Berlin was looking for an Indian secretary. The Axis success in North Africa meant the Germans now had many Indian prisoners of war of whom one was Abad Khan's brother Arab Khan. A fitter in the army he was being held in a camp in Berlin. Abad, sure that Arab would make a good secretary, urged Silver to recommend him to Bose, and promised to find out Arab's exact address. Before Silver left for Lahore the two men agreed that they would stay in contact by passing messages either through Silver's younger brother or through Waris Khan, a tea vendor outside Peshawar's Bajeri gate whom Abad always kept informed of his whereabouts.

In Lahore Silver was soon busy in the Nawakot hideout helping Sainsra concoct a two-page typed report to be presented to the Axis. This writer of Punjabi fiction had invented a new political organisation called the 'All-India National Revolutionary Committee'. As Silver later confessed to the British police, what Sainsra prepared in the name of this organisation 'was a completely fictitious report full of false and exaggerated claims on behalf of Bose's revolutionary following'.[7] Given that Kirti had cut off all links with Bose's followers, what Sainsra produced, for even such a master of fiction, was quite a leap of imagination.

However, preparing this report took time, and with the Germans devastating Russia both Sodhi and Uttam Chand grew very anxious, and started sending messages to Abad Khan that they wanted Silver back in Kabul, Sodhi sending a coded telegram that read: 'Send Rahmat Khan or allow me to sell the motor parts'. Abad took this to mean that Silver should be sent back to Kabul as soon as possible, and within days Silver was back in Peshawar with Sainsra in tow.[8]

Silver candidly disclosed to Abad that he had with him a written report from Kirti to the Germans in Kabul, but not what the report contained. Instead, he said it comprised a list of Kirti party members who were prisoners of war in Germany and Italy, a lie clearly designed to encourage Abad to provide him with Arab's details, his company number and where he was in Berlin, all of which Abad happily did. Giving the Germans a true fact about a British prisoner in their hands, Silver reasoned, would establish him as having good military contacts in India—significant credentials since the Germans were keen to subvert the Indian Army. Moreover, with Bose seeking to recruit British prisoners of war in Germany to form a Free India Army, Silver could throw a bone in his direction knowing it would not amount to much. The subsequent history of Bose's Indian Legion in Germany, which operated under German control in Europe, proves Silver, once again, right in his scheming.

On 7 July 1941 Silver finally reached Kabul. On this, his third trip, he had another companion, Modh Shah, with him, but with Shah a fellow Pathan this time he did not have to pretend his companion was deaf and dumb or watch his every step, as he had had to with Sodhi and Ganguli, and consequently this was much the most relaxed visit so far to the Afghan capital. At Uttam Chand's place Sodhi, with no little pride, briefed him on his meeting Moradov, and the news of Cheena's impending return.[9] Sodhi was confident he could easily get the Russians to meet Silver.

But first there were the Italians to deal with. Madame Quaroni was soon in touch, but before Silver could satisfy her request to see his report he had to deal with the consequences of an attempt by the Axis to contact the Faqir of Ipi. It would have a dramatic effect on Silver's relations with the Axis powers.

In the time Silver had been out of Kabul the Italians and the Germans had tried to contact the tribal pimpernel, with a view to encouraging him to turn his anti-British sentiments into a full-blown revolt that would spread throughout the tribal areas. Quaroni had finally persuaded Rome that 300,000 Afghanis could be paid to the Ipi, and on 12 June 1941 Anzilotti set out from the Afghan capital. With the Italians and the Germans supposedly acting in concert, Berlin had been very keen their man, an Abwehr agent called Lieutenant Dietrich Witzel, recently arrived in Kabul, should accompany him. He will figure more prominently in our story but for the moment what is significant is that, as his cover name of 'Pathan' indicated, he saw himself as an expert in the region and was in charge of German arrangements with the Faqir. Quaroni however took an immediate dislike to him and would not allow him to go on the trip occasioning a furious row with the Germans.

Anzilotti had prepared carefully for the journey. He had left the Legation dressed as he always did in a smart suit, then gone very surreptitiously to another house and emerged dressed in Pathan clothes. He had then walked out of town to a waiting lorry and headed for the Faqir's place. He had spent three days at the Faqir's hideout in Gorwekht, near Gardez, 100 kilometres south of Kabul.

The Faqir told Anzilotti that he was as ever ready to take on the British, but to do so he needed weapons, ammunition, a wireless transmitter with a trained operator and lots of cash. His cash demands were spelled out very precisely: £25,000 paid every other month. Should he succeed in extending the revolt to other tribal areas this would rise to £50,000 and if the entire Frontier rose in revolt then the Faqir wanted £75,000. The return journey was not easy. Anzilotti had to walk all the way back to Kabul and got back to the legation 22 days after he had left.[10]

Quaroni saw the mission as a great success and Anzilotti would have the distinction of becoming the only Axis diplomat to visit the Faqir during the war. The Germans had monitored Anzilotti's trip with great envy and were spurred to mount Operation *Feuerfresser* (Fire-eater). This was to lead to what the Germans called *Grossaufstand*, a full-scale tribal uprising, with Mohmands, Afridis and Wazirs going to war with the British, attacking the British fortifications on the Frontier passes and significant military installations in the north-west of India. The two agents deputed to journey to Gorwekht, along with a dozen tribesmen carrying ammunition and money, must rank as the most bizarre agents the Abwehr used in the entire war. One was a specialist in tropical medicine and the other a lepidopterist, their cover story was that they were carrying out research. But while the Afghans may have failed with Anzilotti, the Germans walked into a trap set up by an Afghan patrol just south of Kabul, the tropical medical specialist was killed, the lepidopterist arrested along with all the tribesmen, and the Afghans got hold of everything the Germans were carrying.

Silver had arrived back in Kabul just as news of the incident reached the city and became fevered talk among the diplomats, in particular the British and Soviet, now on the same side. The Afghan government, trying to play a delicate balancing act, put all the blame on the German Legation, although when the Afghan Prime Minister, Hashim Khan, met Pilger soon after his tone was different. In fact he apologised to Pilger, and with German troops going through Russia like a knife through butter—in the phrase of the then-British ambassador in Moscow Sir Stafford Cripps—Khan even told Pilger that should German troops be near Afghanistan then all of Afghanistan would take up arms to support the Germans, 'about 500,000 men including the tribes'. However, he did tell Pilger not to take part in such ridiculous plans because they did not know Afghanistan and had also underestimated how huge the British spy network in the country was.[11]

While the blunder proved that the Germans could not even mount a relatively minor operation, let alone set the frontier on fire, it actually helped Silver. The Germans still had half a million Reichsmarks available in hard currency. And gold from the money they had earmarked for sabotage and subversion in Afghanistan and India. This amounted to two-and-a-half million Afghan Rupees. With the British and the Soviets about to invade Iran there was all the more necessity to spend this money quickly. The Faqir of Ipi might be unreachable, but here was Silver in town promising to deliver, and indeed claiming to have delivered, all sorts of things in India. What was more he was able to journey back and forth between Kabul and India through tribal territory with ease, having done so three times already in the space of six months. Who could possibly doubt the value of such an agent?

Quaroni may have been the senior Axis diplomat in Kabul, but he simply did not have the money that the Germans could command, and the bungled German attempt to meet the Faqir would spur the Germans to take over from the Italians in dealing with Silver, although it would only be on his next visit that Silver would become aware of his transfer. So, for this trip, while Rasmuss was now present at his meetings with the Axis, he still reported to the Italians. And it was to Quaroni that he gave the two-page report Sainsra had typed up in Nawakot. Quaroni was quite overwhelmed, and his extensive telegram to Rome gives some idea of how inventive Sainsra had been.

> Work at the frontier continues ... They have sent people to Burma; They have sent people to Nepal in accordance with Rasmuss's instructions; They have put trustworthy personnel among the new recruits in the Indian army; They are preparing sabotage at schools; as soon as they are ready they will request European experts; They have not yet been able to organise supplies of petrol in the tribal territories on a sufficient scale ... Despite the government's efforts ... Gandhi's revolutionary movement is greatly

increasing, especially following the military defeat of the English. [British arrests has meant] the Forward Bloc apart from Bengal, the Punjab frontier province organisation, was almost destroyed. It was however possible to rebuild it with the despatch of an active squadron of experts and the engagement of new elements and work continues with the support and mass repatriation. We publish our newspapers at the frontier; many propaganda pamphlets; writings against the war, against England, against conscription are distributed everywhere in the Punjab [the main centre for recruitment] and our activity has a good effect on the army. Indian units have mutinied in both Lahore and Ambala, they refused to embark, hundreds of soldiers have deserted and are working with us, especially among Hindu soldiers. Punjab: we have inspected the peasant committees who have a strong influence on the soldiers: they serve as our cell and in the army both in India and outside it. We have strong influence on the trade unions, especially in the railway workshops and metallurgic industries; we have made progress on a student movement. Situation good [on the] frontier. We have a strong influence on the peasants and tribes. Work is now starting to organise them on a common platform. Bengal: we have predominant influence on young peasants and trade unionists: they have started to work for the army. Bihar: we work in Tatanagar [the steel city of India] and Asansol [main coal producing area]. In the [princely] States we work together with zamindars. Work has borne good fruit ... Practical results:

1. Government has not managed to suppress the movement;
2. Military production from India is very slow;
3. Recruitment is slow: for the most part fed by racial groups who are not volunteers;
4. Morale of the army is becoming very bad.

The committee will meet in the course of this month to adopt a plan of work for the whole of India, after which a detailed report will be sent out with facts and definitive solutions.[12]

Sainsra had judged it perfectly. He knew that the arrests that had hobbled Bose's party were something a diligent reader of Indian newspapers might have picked up on, and we know how avidly Quaroni read papers from India. But having enticed the Axis with this odd nugget of truth he overlaid it with many lies covering all of India, confident that Quaroni or Rasmuss had no means of checking them. They could only rely on Silver.

The sting was in an attachment to the report, which spelled out that the work of setting up an anti-British front in India was very difficult. After a province-by-province estimate of costs, the demand was for no less than

80,000 Indian rupees to cover the next three months, or at least that is what Silver and even Sodhi would later confess to the British. However, Quaroni telegrammed Rome that it was 90,000 rupees per month. Whether the pair deliberately underestimated the amount to cover up the fact that they may have pocketed the difference or their recollection was wrong is impossible to say.

Quaroni told Silver that their money demands would have to be referred to Berlin, and gave him in cash 5,750 American Dollars for Bose's party, and 5,000 Afghanis for Silver's own personal expenses. He also gave him a box of detonators for Ganguli and other sabotage agents in India. Given all the excitement caused by the shooting of the two Germans both Quaroni and Rasmuss strongly advised him to return to India immediately, prepare another report and then come back to Kabul, by which time Quaroni hoped the situation would have calmed down and Berlin and Rome would have given a response to their demands. Rasmuss listened quietly as Quaroni spoke, aware that the money Quaroni had handed over was German money. That meeting in the second week of July 1941 was a turning point in Silver's relations with the Axis. Quaroni carried on as the Italian Ambassador in Kabul but having, as it were, done his job by recruiting Silver, he was now considered redundant by the Germans. And on Silver's next visit to Kabul, the following month, he found the Germans had taken over.

The other major development on this Kabul visit was that Silver finally met the Russians. Sodhi's meeting with Moradov had meant that they, like Madame Quaroni, now regularly came to Uttam Chand's shop to find out when Silver would be back. Soon after his return there took place, possibly in the flat paid for by the Italians, a meeting between Silver and a Russian—possibly Moradov—with Sodhi acting as interpreter. This was the first time Silver had met anyone from Russia, and now he finally came clean about how his work for Bose had put him in touch with the Axis powers. On learning this the Russian returned to the Legation, and was back a short time afterwards saying he had informed his superior officers, who would report the whole matter to Moscow. Meanwhile there was no harm in continuing their contact with the Axis, provided they did not interfere with British war preparations. Like the Italians and the Germans they also advised Silver and Sodhi to leave Kabul and return to India. There had been more arrests by the Afghans in the wake of the failed German attempt to contact the Faqir, two of whom were friendly with Haji Subhan and his German wife. The Russians had observed that Subhan and his wife were frequent visitors to Uttam Chand's house. There was a risk the Afghan police might come calling to the shop, and if so Silver and Sodhi would be caught up in the net. At the same time the Russians told Silver to let them know as soon as he returned to Kabul, and that he should report first to them before seeing either Rasmuss or the Italians. They also instructed Silver to bring back with him a full written report from the Kirti Party which could be sent to Moscow.[13]

The superior officer consulted must have been Mikhail Andreyevich Allakhverdov, the 41-year-old Kabul head of the NKVD, codenamed Zaman, who controlled around 15 agents from several nationalities: seven Afghans, one ethnic Tajik, one Uzbek, two Indians, two Poles, one Frenchman, one Swiss and two Russians.[14]

The Soviet response showed they had calibrated Silver's worth accurately. Like the Axis they were worried about his safety in Kabul in the climate then prevailing in the Afghan capital, but unlike the Axis they knew they could rely on his Communist beliefs. The encounter also illustrates how dramatically Silver's career as a spy had progressed. In February 1941 he had arrived in Kabul for the first time escorting Bose, fulfilling his desire for adventure and an exploration of unknown, possibly even dangerous worlds. In March, through Bose, he had been recruited as a spy for the Italians. In April he had returned to find he was now spying for the Germans. Now, in late July, he was spying for the Soviets. What is more, while the third nation he was spying for, the Soviet Union, knew all about his connection with their enemy, his original spymasters were in the dark about his other roles, and would remain so throughout the war. In all the great and dramatic stories of Second World War spies it is doubtful if anyone developed such a relationship between sworn enemies, and in such a short time.

But while all this was going on, how did the British, who had for so long employed so many agents in Kabul, remain in the dark? The truth is that they knew something was afoot, but not the whole truth. In a memo dated 12 July 1941 the Department of Military Intelligence informed the War Office that:

> During the last three months, the Italians and the Germans—the Germans are now showing signs of taking over control—have been busily engaged in the formation of a somewhat grandiose organisation in Afghanistan for raising a revolt there and on the N.W. Frontier of India. This organisation was to be directed by the left wing Congress leader, Subhas Chandra Bose, from Rome through his agents in Kabul. These were instructed to get in touch with the Faqir of Ipi and other tribal leaders, raising a revolt on the Frontier and in the Punjab. Meanwhile others were to sow disaffection in Indian war factories and among the rank and file of the Indian Army. The most recent evidence is that the Faqir of Ipi is now regarded as the most profitable source of trouble.[15]

But, as this note shows, they knew nothing about Silver. Anglo-Soviet co-operation was growing at a rapid rate, as events in Iran the very next month, of which more later, would demonstrate. But it had not yet reached the point where the NKVD was ready to share Silver with the British. As for Sodhi, while the Indian police were hunting for him, they did not divulge this to anyone else, and were unaware that he had already left the country.

In mid-August Silver, Sodhi and Modh Shah set out for the journey back to India, this time having to take a detour around the Budkhak checkpoint where, unlike on all Silver's previous five crossings, the guards were very much awake, partly because both the British and the Russians had begun to exert pressure on the Afghan government about the activities of Germans in the country. Silver decided to circumvent the police check, a longer journey of seven to eight miles which brought them to a place from where they could catch a truck to Jalalabad. While Sodhi hurried on to India, Silver lingered in the tribal areas, visiting Kudakhel, an important centre of the Mohmands in the north, and Swal Qila, in the village of Bandagai.[16] He already knew the leaders there, Miran Jan and his younger brother Mulla Jan in the first and Sanobar Hussain in the second. In his memoir Silver emphasises that these visits were about fomenting anti-British activity among these tribes, but the real reason was that, aware he would be making frequent trips back and forth to Kabul, he wanted to cultivate new tribal areas as staging posts for his journeys. Miran Jan also solved the problem of what to do with the box of detonators Quaroni had given him—there was never any chance Silver would take them to Ganguli and his friends in Bengal. The tribals could always use them if not in their wars with the British then in inter-tribal clashes. And Silver knew by gifting them to Miran Jan he was proving to the tribal leader that he was a resourceful man.

On his return to India Silver attended a full-dress meeting of most of the top Kirti leaders at the Nawakot house back in Lahore, where, with Sodhi's help, he briefed the others on what had happened in Kabul. Sodhi mentions the odd voice arguing that all contact with the Axis should be ended. Silver later told the British:

> The Kirti leaders were pleased with the sight of further money and also relieved to know that the Russians were at last aware of their guilty secret and approved of the course they had followed.[17]

At this stage the Kirti leaders could simply have cut off links with Bose's party, but they decided to have one final meeting with Bose's men. Silver was sent to Calcutta to see Ganguli and Bakshi and other Bose contacts and get their views on the changed circumstances of the war. On no account, of course, was Silver to tell them that Kirti had started working with the Russians.

Unlike his previous visit, when he had just sauntered up to Sarat Bose's house, this time he was much more discreet. He had decided that when he was travelling in India he would now call himself Harbans Lal. Ganguli had given him the name of an employee of Nath Bank to contact, and through him a meeting was arranged. Surprisingly, given the precautions Silver was taking, this was at a house on Chowringee, the main thoroughfare of Calcutta, which at any time of day would be teeming with British civilians and, by the summer of 1941, quite a few military personnel. But the two supposedly anti-British revolutionaries were not detected, though a British spy would have found the conversation fascinating. We have two very different versions of what happened.

The first version is what Silver would later tell his British interrogators. He told Ganguli that Kirti was proposing to abandon its anti-war policy, and would only work with Bose's men if they agreed to sign the Communist Pledge. Ganguli's response was that Bose's followers had fundamental differences with the Communists, and after the two men failed to agree, Ganguli took Silver to meet Sarat Bose and Silver's confession to the British reads:

> Sarat explained that he was not concerned in any political differences between the communists and Bengal political groups. From this attitude it appeared that Ganguli had previously primed him of the Communists' changed attitude and hostility to Bose. Sarat questioned Silver as to Subhas's present whereabouts. He had apparently not heard previously of his arrival in Berlin. He told Silver he was sorry Subhas had not gone to Moscow, and then enquired what the Kirti group were proposing to do as regards the Kabul contact now that Subhas had joined the Axis. Sarat tried to convince Silver that the Axis had no inimical intentions toward India and their quarrel was only with the British. He was clearly hoping that Silver would continue to agree to act as Bose's Kabul contact. Sarat also wanted to know if the Punjab communists had any independent connection with Russia, to which Silver replied 'No'. The meeting ended inconclusively and Silver did not see Sarat Bose again.[18]

Ganguli's version of what happened in Calcutta between Silver and himself is very different. Sarat does not figure in it, and he says Silver told him that whatever Kirti decided, he would never give up the struggle against the British as he wanted to avenge the death of his brother. The two versions could not be more different but there is reason to doubt the Silver version. Silver does not repeat this story in his memoirs where he invents a fictitious second visit by Sodhi and then a visit by him to Calcutta, but nearly a year later, when he says he could not meet anybody because of 'wholesale arrests by everybody I had known before.' In contrast Ganguli's has the ring of truth. While the Communists' support for the British was public knowledge, Silver did not want to give any hint that he endorsed such a position and was no longer prepared to work for Bose. His fear was that, given Ganguli knew of his work in Kabul, he might suspect that as per communist party policy he had actually contacted the Russians and was now working for them. The more he pretended that nothing had changed for him, the greater the chance of making sure his secret would be safe.

Silver's action on leaving Calcutta reinforces this conclusion. He made sure that for the rest of the war he never saw Ganguli again and indeed, after this visit to Calcutta nor did he see anyone from Bose's camp either. Over the next six months Ganguli went to Lahore three times, but never met Silver, and when he asked for him was told he was working in the tribal areas, although at what was never specified. Ganguli did catch up with Silver, but that was 32 years later, in a world far removed from their meeting in 1941.

The meetings in Calcutta mark a very significant transformation in Silver's life as a spy. As we have seen, his spy career had started quite accidentally, being the right man in the right place. But now, established as a spy, he had completely severed his links with Bose, the man who had helped make him a spy leaving him free to feed Bose and his backers whatever lies he felt like concocting, confident that they would never find out the truth.

Did this arch deceiver feel a pang of guilt at this stage? Possibly, but if so he hid it well. As Silver saw it he had no choice. He had started off wanting to free his country and he mourned the brother he had lost in the struggle. But for him siding with the British was necessary: in the context of the war it was both morally right and also in the ultimate interest of India. Unlike his former leader he clearly saw a Nazi victory as infinitely worse for India. Ganguli, reflecting the view of Bose and other Indian revolutionaries, saw no reason to abandon the view that the war provided the great chance of removing the British from India. For them, judging what the Nazis were like was like asking a slave not to rebel against his existing slave master because he was receiving help from another man who might prove even worse. This never came into their consideration. In Silver's eyes, Ganguli and his ilk took the wrong, short-sighted, self-defeating route.

Not that Silver spent too much time debating these issues. There were practical concerns raised by the spy business. The Dollars the Axis had given him had to be changed into Rupees, which could not be done in Lahore, so Sodhi was sent to Bombay to cash the Dollar notes at an American bank, returning at the end of August 1941 with Rs 18,400. Silver was given Rs 2,000 to purchase two battery-powered wireless receiving sets for Mir Jan and his Mohmands, in recognition of the help they were giving him in crossing the tribal territories.

So, well-armed, he set off on his fourth visit for Kabul, either on 3 or 4 September.[19] Also in his knapsack, and even more important, was a few pages of report from the 'All-India National Revolutionary Committee'. This was another elaborate, wonderfully crafted, piece of fiction from Sainsra.

Taking the Nazis for a Ride

During Silver's absence from Kabul, Uttam Chand had become more involved with the foreign powers there. Rasmuss had asked his help in getting hold of gold sovereigns—Shankar Das, the Indian merchant helping the Italians, could not obtain enough—to pay bribes to Afghan officials and also the tribal leaders, and soon Uttam Chand was buying some 2,000 gold sovereigns [1] as well as Indian currency for the Germans from various brokers in Kabul. He also took to visiting the Russian Minister telling him more about Bose and Silver, passing on various titbits of information about how the Japanese were trying to bribe Afghan officials, and how the Kirti party was not happy about Silver maintaining relations with the Axis powers.

As Uttam Chand recounted to me when I asked him if Silver and he were playing a double game:

> In reality we—I myself—were anti-Germans. I had knowledge that if Hitler wins he will rule for 5,000 years. I had developed connections with the Russians through Sodhi. When Bhagat Ram [Silver] came I met the Assistant Ambassador in Kabul. I met him many times. We used to spend one night with the Russians and one night with the Germans. We were favouring Russia so that they should win the war. We were telling the Russians information about Germany.[2]

Like Silver Uttam Chand became adept at fooling the Germans. Rasmuss had given him four sticks of dynamite:

> I stored them in my house in a room and told the Germans that I had sent them to India. At that the time there was a big movement of Hurs in Sind. Bridges were blown up and we said 'there your dynamites are working'. They were happy.[3]

Uttam Chand and Silver were undeniably very close and the shopkeeper was always Silver's first port of call in Kabul. However, on his next visit in

September 1941, when he went to visit the Russians alone, Uttam Chand for the first time began to doubt his veracity.

Silver's appearance at Uttam Chand's shop on 14 September was soon followed by an NKVD agent eager to talk to him. The next day another Russian agent appeared, asking Silver to start at the beginning and relate everything that had happened since his very first visit to Kabul. This endless questioning revealed that, in contrast to the Italians and the Germans, who had instantly accepted Silver, the NKVD, reflecting the greater paranoia of Stalin and his security chief Beria, wanted to make sure his story stood up. Just as he had with the Axis powers, however, Silver proved persuasive—indeed, so pleased was the Russian agent by what he heard that Silver was asked to come back to the Embassy with him. So finally, on 15 September 1941, seven months after he had first started watching the Embassy hoping to catch the attention of a Russian in a Kabul street, the gates of the Embassy were opened for Silver, and he was ushered into to see Zaman.

Zaman heard how Rasmuss had asked Silver to collect industrial and military information for the Germans, and where members of Silver's party were working in India, Silver making it clear to the Russian that the Kirti party had decided that Moscow must decide whether he should continue to keep these Axis connections. Zaman, as Silver later told the British, had one question for him:

> … was [he] prepared to face the risks involved? Silver said he was, and that his party in India also wanted him to do so. The Russian told him there was always the danger of his being found out but the work he was doing was of great value, and that he should try to convince Rasmuss as much as possible of his value to the Axis and should also shed all Communist appearances.[4]

Russian sources say Silver in his response to Zaman was more fulsome in his protestations:

> I support the revolution in India and its liberation, and the Soviet Union. I know that Indian liberty depends on your victory and that Hitlerite Germany and her Allies are your and our enemies.[5]

Zaman reported all this back to the head of the NKVD foreign intelligence, Pavel Mikhailovich Fitin, a native of Siberia who had qualified as an agricultural engineer. Described as a man of 'high intellect and outstanding organizational ability' Fitin achieved rapid promotion in the NKVD, taking up his job in May 1939. This had come about as a result of Stalinist purges, leading to the execution of his predecessors and creating gaps in the NKVD hierarchy. In 1941 with Stalin, convinced his intelligence services were giving him false information, Fitin seemed destined for the same fate. But then came Hitler's invasion and, as one Russian historian puts it, 'Only the outbreak of war saved P. M. Fitin from the firing squad.' Now, ignoring Comintern warnings, he approved Silver. The Russians gave Silver a code name, Rom, clearly a variation of Ram, and his operation Marauders. Given how Silver would go on to fleece the Nazis this proved a very appropriate name.[6]

As if to suggest Silver's reliability was still being tested, after reading the report Sainsra had prepared for the Germans they did not return it to Silver to pass on to Rasmuss but retained it.[7] The morning after the meeting with Zaman, using Haji Subhan, who knew nothing about Silver's Russian connections, Silver arranged a meeting with Rasmuss. They met not at the German Legation but at a flat owned by a German businessman. The Italians were clearly out of the picture and, as if to emphasise this, at the very start of their meeting Rasmuss told Silver, as he later recalled, 'that I must break my relations with the Italians and in case I did not want to do so, then the Germans will have nothing to do with me.' Silver readily agreed but made a mental note that the much vaunted alliance of steel between Italy and Germany did not match reality. For a spy wanting to fool the Axis this was very useful information and which he would exploit when he was finally engaged in deceiving the third Axis power, the Japanese.

Apart from this stern warning about the Italians Rasmuss had greeted Silver cordially and asked him what he had brought from India. Silver explained that he had to leave Kabul at the end of his last visit hurriedly owing to all the excitement caused by the shooting of the two Germans, and for the same reason had not brought any written report back with him lest he was searched on his arrival in Kabul. Rasmuss appreciated this precaution and Silver then gave him a highly coloured account of how the Forward Bloc had started organising on an All-India scale with a view to starting an anti-British mass movement when the time came. He also told Rasmuss the British were trying to expand Indian war industries, but that the Forward Bloc were concentrating on anti-recruitment propaganda and planting cells inside the Indian Army. Contacts had been sent to Nepal with the photograph Rasmuss had given him [in reality the photograph had been left with Ganguli in Calcutta], and also to Burma to see the Dobama leaders as desired by Subhas Bose. In the labour field the Forward Bloc was energetically spreading propaganda and preparing the ground for large-scale strikes. They were also organising a big secret underground organisation in the name of 'The Indian National Revolutionary Committee' in which the Kisans [peasants], Bengal Volunteers, Trade Union Congress and other left wing groups were all enthusiastically co-operating. Forward Bloc influence was increasing by leaps and bounds but time and further preparation was necessary and they would also need money.[8]

As Silver boasted of these imaginary deeds, Rasmuss was busy taking notes barely able to contain his delight. Berlin, he assured Silver, would be informed immediately, but for the moment Silver would have to wait in Kabul. It is astonishing that Rasmuss could be so gullible, but at this stage he was very worried that British and Soviet pressure would lead to all Axis personnel having to leave Kabul. Consequently he was keen for Silver to establish a channel of communication with Bangkok. Silver was given the names of two of Bose's agents in Bangkok, Satyananda Puri and his assistant, Nandy and told to arrange for two of Bose's men in Bengal to be sent across Burma to Bangkok to establish contact with them using the password 'Elephant'. Puri would then arrange a meeting with a German agent called Von Plessen, who was also head of the German Mission. Plessen would give them money and further instructions. As for getting the money to India this would be through the manager of the Calcutta National Bank, which had a branch in Bangkok, so that money deposited in Bangkok could be drawn out by Bose's party workers in Calcutta:

> Rasmuss also instructed Silver to establish contact with Ipi, so that the Germans could be independent of the Italians, who were then the channel with Ipi, and so that instructions could be sent to Ipi through Silver if the Axis were forced to leave Afghanistan.[9]

Silver, of course, had no intention of going anywhere near the Faqir of Ipi, aware of how a few months earlier Sainsra trying to get to the Faqir had just escaped being exposed as a Hindu and forcibly converted.[10] Unlike Sainsra, Silver—a proper Pathan—was confident he could have fooled Ipi's people into believing he was a genuine Muslim but he had no desire to take any chances. And while it is not clear what lie he told Rasmuss he never went to Waziristan and never met the Faqir.

That Rasmuss still believed the Germans could contact the Faqir of Ipi, given the bungle they had made of their previous attempt, emphasised the incompetence of the Abwehr operation in Kabul. The only explanation for this may be that at this time Rasmuss was in such dread of what might happen to the Germans in Kabul that his thinking was muddled. And this fear was genuine enough for just then the British and the Russians were indeed hunting the Axis in Afghanistan, and Silver arrived in the Afghan capital to find it seething with rumour and hearsay as never before. Its bazaars had always been full of gossip, but in September 1941 he found the local conversations ranging from the British and the Soviets being on the point of marching into Afghanistan, to how long the present Yahya Khel regime could survive. Such febrile rumour-mongering stemmed from two events, one occurring just before he arrived and the other unfolding while he was there.

The first was the joint British and Soviet invasion of Iran, a neutral country, in August 1941.[11] For some years the Iranian king, Reza Shah, keen to modernise his country and make it less dependent on Britain and Russia, had allowed in German businessmen, technicians and industrialists. There was also German intelligence activity in Iran, and in July 1941 an Abwehr officer had been sent on a reconnaissance tour, in view of the planned operation into the Middle East and India. There were certainly not as many Germans in Iran as Allied propaganda put about. In July 1941 Stalin told Sir Stafford Cripps, then Britain's Ambassador to the Soviet Union, that there were between six to seven thousand Germans in the country ready to carry out a coup against the Baku oil fields, and he wanted urgent action.

The Soviets' decision that Iran must be occupied received strong support from Delhi, always more worried about security on India's northern border. Wavell, who had just taken over as Commander in Chief in India, on 17 July telegraphed the war office that it was 'essential to the defence of India that Germany should be cleared out of Iran now'. He felt failure to do so might lead to a repetition of events in Iraq, where the British had just about managed to defeat an anti-British revolt and followed this by occupying Syria, both operations succeeding by very narrow margins. Wavell was ready to send Indian troops to occupy Iran and for weeks leading up to the invasion the Shah was subjected to much abuse by BBC broadcasts in Persian from New Delhi.

There was another pressing factor. Two months on from the German invasion of the Soviet Union, it was obvious that sending British supplies through the Arctic route to north Russia was fraught with problems. A much better option was sending them through Iran, but the British and the Russians could hardly ask for such facilities and claim to be honouring Iranian neutrality.

Britain and Russia demanded Iran expel all Germans and, when Iran refused without any further warning, on 25 August 1941, British and Soviet forces invaded the country. As Russian troops entered Iran they proclaimed that they were 'guided by feelings of friendship for the Iranian people and by respect for the sovereignty of Iran'. The British dropped leaflets announcing that they came 'as friends to save Iran's freedom'. The British occupying forces consisted of three infantry divisions and part of an armoured division, which was a curious reversal of history. Iran had often invaded India, the last and most spectacular being the nineteenth century invasion of Nadir Shah who had butchered the inhabitants of Delhi and the loot he had returned with included the Peacock Throne of the Mughals. But these were not Indian soldiers conquering for an Indian King, their invasion of Iran was in the name of a foreign ruler, George VI, to help the war aims of their British conqueror.

Initially, Teheran was not occupied. But with the British press accusing the Government of pussy-footing, and despite the Iranians imprisoning all

Germans males of military age, on 17 September, Tehran was occupied. Reza Shah was forced to abdicate and his son took over.

Interestingly, the Soviets showed greater suspicion of the British during their joint occupation of Iran than they had done with the Germans during their joint occupation of Poland in 1939. They rejected Churchill's offer to send more Indian troops to Iran freeing Soviet forces to fight the Germans. Instead they asked for 25 to 30 British divisions to be sent to Russia to which Churchill responded: '... it would be silly to send two or three British or British–Indian divisions into the heart of Russia to be surrounded and cut to pieces as a symbolic sacrifice'.[12] And when weeks after the invasion, Wavell met Kozlov, the Soviet Commanding General in Transcaucasia in Tbilisi he was so unhelpful that Wavell wrote, 'The Russians would tell us nothing of any of their plans for meeting any German attack through the Caucasus....'[13]

In Kabul Silver found that the invasion had been badly received by almost everyone in Afghanistan with many expressing sadness that this had happened to a Muslim country. For all Silver's Soviet leanings he was made aware that for the great majority of Afghans the Russians were the godless enemy, and there was much talk that a number of persons suspected of being Soviet agents had recently been arrested in Herat. Soon Silver was hearing stories doing the rounds in the bazars of Kabul of the Great Game having changed to the Great Partnership. The new partners, the rumours said, would now insist that Afghanistan open up for free passage of supplies to Russia. The British and the Russians did not go quite that far but, as with Iran, they now demanded that the Afghan government expel all non-official Axis personnel from the country. When, initially, the Afghan government refused to give in to the Allies' demand Delhi imposed economic sanctions, reducing oil supplies and delaying the shipment of new lorries which Afghanistan had ordered. Silver could see that the British sanctions created significant hardship, although British agents reported that while many educated Afghans were hoping for a German victory, the poor blamed the Germans for the rising prices of many commodities.[14] The unrelenting pressure made the Afghan government wary that the British and the Soviets might jointly invade. And while this never happened, Churchill, overruling both the British ambassador Sir Francis Wylie and the Indian Military Intelligence department insisted that the Germans be expelled.

Silver, in the middle of shuttling between the Germans and the Russians, witnessed this drama being played out. Stories swept the city that the Germans, having been tipped off by the government, were burning their papers, selling or packing their personal effects, and preparing to damage roads and bridges before they left. The Germans from their side were also spreading stories of Soviet atrocities in Iran. The shrewd political operator in Silver sensed that the Afghans would eventually have to capitulate to their two powerful neighbours. The interesting question was: what concessions could they extract? And could there be a guarantee that this would be the last of the demands? The Afghan Prime Minister secured in writing an assurance from the British that they had no intention of developing transit routes to the Soviet Union through Afghanistan without Afghan co-operation. He also extracted an agreement to repatriate both Germans and Italians, at British expense, through India. Hashim Khan had been Minister in Moscow in 1925–26 just as Stalin was consolidating his power and disliked the Russians. As a consequence of this he was keen to make sure that none of the deportees would be allowed to fall into the hands of the Soviets. All this made him feel he would be entitled to 'claim to have kept the laws of Muslim hospitality inviolate'. It was very important to him for domestic reasons as there was much contempt in Afghanistan for the Iranians 'for their cowardly surrender to the Allies and the handing over of the Germans and the Italians who were their guests'. In the end 204 Germans and Italian nationals left Kabul for Peshawar in two batches at the end of October 1941.

While all this was going on Rasmuss feared he might be asked to leave. The British would have liked Rasmuss to be expelled as well, but that would have meant asking the Afghans to break off diplomatic relations and they realised this would be going too far and would not be accepted by Hashim Khan. Though Rasmuss himself could now relax, the whole affair had put the Germans on the back foot. Silver was now the only game in town and Rasmuss wanted to make the most of him. Blissfully unaware that he had become a double agent, Rasmuss passed on to him instructions from Bose.

Bose wanted Forward Bloc contacts in the Indian Army fighting for the British in Libya to be given the password 'Silver Moon': if captured by the Germans or the Italians they should give this password and would be treated as friends. Swallowing the misinformation Silver was feeding him that there were Forward Bloc sleeper cells in the Indian Army, Bose advised they should not risk being captured, but work at the Army bases and rather send as many soldiers to surrender using the 'Silver Moon' password as they could. Berlin was keen that Forward Bloc men be sent to the Persian Gulf, Ceylon and Burma, and for Silver to bring two selected men to Kabul, one for training in cipher work and the other in sabotage. Rasmuss laid great stress on the need for a landing ground and petrol store in Mohmand or Bajaur country: Silver agreed and on a later visit told him that with the help of Sanobar Hussain, one of his close tribal contacts, work was in hand and 3,000 gallons of petrol had been arranged for.[15]

Silver knew that in this instance Rasmuss could never find out he was lying. However his response was very different when the Germans wanted Silver's help in contacting tribal leaders to foment unrest to accompany German plans to attack India from the north-west once they had finished with Russia and the Caucasus. Then Silver scotched every suggestion the Germans made. Sometimes the German would give him a name—many had come from Ghulam Sadiq Khan, a former Afghan Foreign Minister who now lived in Berlin—and Silver would reply that the person was already under arrest. His favourite response was to say 'that it would be stupid for him' to make contact, as Khan 'was well known as an opponent of the present Afghan government', which could only cause problems for the Germans.

Silver was much more receptive to the idea of the Germans training him to transmit wireless messages for them, this having been an express instruction from Berlin. In July 1941 two more Abwehr agents, both wireless operators, Wilhelm Doh, codenamed Giessen and Zugenbühler, codenamed Rashad, had arrived to supplement the one already there. That the Germans had three wireless operators in their Legation was a revealing insight into their thinking about espionage work in the region. With Kabul having no Enigma machine the Abwehr personnel used the AA cipher and the traditional coding method based on a particular book and page. The two newcomers had brought with them portable transmitting and receiving wireless sets, along with two battery chargers, to enable short wave contact between the German embassy and anywhere in Afghanistan or even north-west India. Doh took charge as Silver's tutor initially instructing him on the use of the smaller portable transmitter, and later on a much bigger one with a greater range. He was also given English charts of Morse code to learn. Silver was an eager pupil, but Rasmuss felt he should bring a special agent from India to Kabul to be properly trained in sending and receiving messages. Silver never did bring such an agent although a year later he did have specialised help in sending wireless messages back and forth from India to Berlin. But by then, as we shall see, Silver had linked up with Peter Fleming with the Germans completely unaware of his Fleming connection.

With Rasmuss fully trusting Uttam Chand, he agreed that Silver could keep both transmitters in Uttam Chand's shop, but insisted that the smaller one had to be taken to the tribal areas. Uttam Chand told me:

> The Germans trained me how to use the transmitter. The code to begin the transmission was five letters: BERLIN, and it was broadcast just before the Hindustani News. I used the transmitter myself two or three times as did Bhagat Ram [Silver]. We used to transmit, (1) what is the condition of India, (2) what is happening in general, (3) whether Netaji [Subhas Bose] should open his mouth and reveal he is in Germany.[16]

Silver immediately told the Russians about the transmitters, and they asked Uttam Chand to place the smaller one in a box of crockery. A few days later one of Zaman's NKVD agents visited and, under the pretence of buying some

Above left: 1 Silver dressed like an Afghan while in Kabul during the war.

Above right: 2 Silver in tribal dress—as he moved between India and Afghanistan.

Above left: 3 Gurudasmal, Silver's father, looking suitably resplendent.

Above right: 4 Hari Kishan, Silver's brother, executed by the British.

5 Silver and his wife, Ram Kaur in their old age.

Above left: 6 Mathura Devi, Silver's mother, in her old age.

Above middle: 7 Ram Kishan, Silver's political mentor, who died in a Soviet sanatorium.

Above right: 8 Achhar Singh Cheena, Communist party official and close friend of Silver.

Above left: 9 Abad Khan, a transport contractor who helped with Silver's journeys to Kabul.

Above right: 10 Silver (in middle) talking to Abwehr agent Witzel (back to camera on the right in white suit) in Calcutta in 1973, their first meeting since their time Kabul during the war. (*picture by Milan Hauner*)

11 Silver in glasses in the front row in a rare suit, surrounded by historians and delegates at the International Netaji seminar in Calcutta. (*picture by Milan Hauner*)

12, 13 and 14: *Left:* Peter Fleming, brother of Ian, and head of D Division in Delhi that ran Silver. *Centre:* Faqir of Ipi, a redoubtable foe of the British, financed by the Germans. *Right:* George Alexander Hill, Head of SOE mission in Moscow, who liaised on Silver with the NKVD.

15 and 16: *Left:* William Magan with his wife Maxine. Magan worked with Silver in Delhi transmitting false messages to the Germans. *Right:* Pietro Quaroni, Italian minister in Kabul, who recruited Silver as a spy.

Above left: 17 *From left to right:* Mohammed Hashim Khan, Prime Minister of Afghanistan 1929–1946; HM Zahir Shah, 1914–2007, king 1933–1973; HRH Sirdar Shah Mahmud Khan, Field Marshal and War Minister of Afghanistan, uncle of the king.

Above right: 18 Kabul street scene, 9 June 1943.

Right: 19 A crude telephone system spans the major cities of the country. This man is a district official responsible for upkeep of about 75 miles of line, making a test call after repairing damaged wires. The extent to which Nazis had gained a foothold is best illustrated by the fact that Berlin is the only European capital with which Kabul is connected by a radio telephone. Photograph dated 1 September 1940.

20 Caravans in Afghanistan in the 1930s.

21 Attock Bridge, the gateway to British India across the River Indus as it looked 1931 and which the Axis powers wanted to demolish.

22 Afghan men relaxing at a bazaar. A photograph by Maynard Owen Williams. *National Geographic*

23 From 3 to 10 June Witzel rode a horse out of Kabul as far as Ghazni, 160 km south on the road to Kandahar. This photograph of the gateway at Ghazni was taken a few years before by Maynard Owen Williams. *National Geographic*

24 The main street of the 'Silk City' of Kandahar. A photograph from the 1930s by Maynard Owen Williams. *National Geographic*

25 One of the gateways into the old city of Kabul in the early 1930s.

26 A view of Kabul in 1938. The streets are narrow and tortuous and the buildings are mainly windowless and built of mud and wood.

27 A Kabul alleyway with open drain.

28 A market in Kabul, 1935.

29 An Afghan hillside village demonstrates well the nature of the terrain traversed by Silver on his numerous journeys.

30 A mixed horse and camel train in Kabul.

Above: 31 A glimpse of the edge of Paghman Gardens, with a rushing stream. Paghman was built in 1928 by King Amanullah. This was Quaroni's Italian retreat.

Right: 32 Pathan Pashtun tribesmen, 1947.

33 Subhas Chandra Bose shakes hands with Adolf Hitler on 27 May 1942, at the Wolfsschanze, the headquarters in East Prussia which Hitler had built for the start of his Russian campaign. The other person is Hitler's English interpreter, Dr Paul Schmidt. Hitler told Bose that the chances of an anti-British uprising in India would be better served with Japanese assistance, since German troops were still very far away. If 'Germany could gain access to the borders of India like Japan', which might take another one or two years, he 'would have requested Bose to stay with him, march to India with German troops and subsequently kindle the revolution against the British.' For his voyage to Japan, Hitler offered Bose the use of a German submarine.

34 Subhas Chandra Bose inspects a somewhat disorganised parade of unusual Wehrmacht soldiery in shorts and with backpacks.

35 Subhas Chandra Bose with Heinrich Himmler, 15 July 1942. The photo was taken at Hegewaldheim, Himmler's field headquarters in former German town of Angerburg in East Prussia, (now Poland).

36 King Amanullah with his beautiful, unveiled, wife Souriya walk in Berlin during an official visit to Germany, 24 February 1928. Afghans, opposed to his modernising ways, with the help of the British, deposed him in 1929. Bose, unsuccessfully, pressed the Nazis to bring him back to power.

Above left: 37 Subhas Chandra Bose reviewing his Azad Hind Waffen-SS volunteers, *c.* 1942. *Bundesarchiv*

Above right: 38 Subhas Chandra Bose making a speech to India.

Below left: 39 Subhas Chandra Bose and Fregattenkapitän Werner Musenberg on German submarine U-180, which sailed from Kiel on 8 February 1943. Ultra had told the British of Bose's plans to rendezvous with the Japanese submarine I-29, just east of Madagascar in the Indian Ocean. The Admiralty wanted to intercept Bose as the transfer was made but British Intelligence chiefs, after considering the likely impact on Silver's spying operation, overruled it.

Below right: 40 The crew of the Japanese submarine I-29 after a rendezvous with the German submarine U-180. Bose is sitting in the front row, second from left. Although the German-Japanese naval rendezvous had taken place on 26 April 1943, due to rough seas Bose was only hauled on to the Japanese boat on the morning of 28 April.

41 Subhas Chandra Bose and Lakshmi Sahgal, the Minister of Women's Affairs in the Azad Hind government, at the camp in Bras Basah Road. Bose is seen here reviewing an Indian National Army female combat regiment.

42 Subhas Chandra Bose with members of the *Azad Hind Fauj*, or the Indian National Army, Singapore, 21 October 1943.

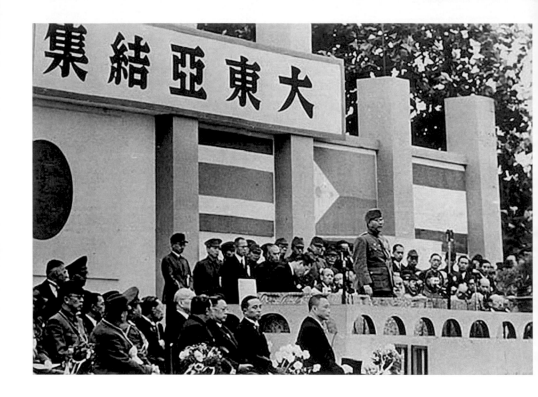

Above: 43 Bose making a speech at a Japanese venue.

Left: 44 Bose in a photograph inscribed while in Japan, November 1943.

crockery, took it away. The larger transmitter also found its way into the Russian Embassy, although Rasmuss subsequently demanded its return and Silver had to fetch it back.

And to Silver's great delight there was more money than he had ever received before: 800 gold sovereigns and £14,625 in English currency notes—in five, ten, even fifty-pound denominations. For Rasmuss this was no problem—he had only to open the Embassy safe and dip into the vast sum the Germans had brought to Kabul. As Quaroni would tell SOE's man in Kabul:

> Rasmuss and others had bought a lot of money to Kabul. At the best the German legation had in their safe, to the best of his belief, some three or four hundred thousand pounds' worth of sterling, notes, in denominations of from 5 to 50 pounds, 2000 sovereigns and 10,000 dollars. The Germans had not been able to dispose of more than a very little, if any, of the Sterling notes even when they had offered to sell at a rate as low as 13 Afghanis to the pound. But the dollars and the sovereigns had been disposed of and the Germans were therefore now short of usable funds [Quaroni was talking in October 1943]. Rasmuss had been buying a certain amount more sovereigns in the bazaar.[17]

Rasmuss also gave Silver 50 German automatic pistols, some ammunition, sticks of dynamite and four portable wireless transmitters, all for use by the Kirti party. What Rasmuss did not know was that, as soon as Silver had collected the swag, he headed not out of Kabul, as Rasmuss assumed, but left out of the German Legation, round the corner, and straight for the Russian Embassy.

There he showed the NKVD's Kabul head what the Germans had given him, with the weapons being proudly displayed as 'exhibits' looted from the Germans. The Russians decided to keep all the military equipment, and also some of the money: 302 gold sovereigns and £12,000 of the cash leaving Silver to return to India with 498 gold sovereigns and £2,625. With the Germans at the gates of Moscow a look at some of the weapons the Germans used was useful, and it was hardly surprising that the Russians also wanted some of the German money. What was odd was the portion they kept and here we have three sets of figures for what Rasmuss paid Silver.

The figures quoted are from Silver's confession to the British. Uttam Chand's confession gave very different figures. He said that Rasmuss had given Silver £13,000 and 750 sovereigns of which Silver gave the Russians £10,000 and 300 sovereigns. And when Sodhi made his confession he said that Silver on his return to Lahore told him Rasmuss had given him 500 gold sovereigns and £7,000 of which the Russians had kept two gold sovereigns and nearly £4,500 of the cash.

So did Silver pocket some of the money? Uttam Chand certainly thought so, telling his interrogators he had:

> … come to know that Bhagat Ram [Silver] had made material concealment from the Russians over the money he received from the Axis and did not disclose the whole truth to them about weapons or the number of wireless transmitters which Rasmuss gave him.[18]

It is certainly possible: Silver's memoir has a fascinating description of how on his return to India he enlisted his younger brother and a friend to help him dress up like a Muslim woman to travel back to his village, where his mother was delighted to discover that underneath the burkha was no woman but her own son. However, as Silver never disguised himself like this before or after, it is likely the burkha was meant to conceal the money and gold underneath. And certainly after leaving his village, he behaved like a man with money, in Lahore booking himself into 'a good hotel'[19] and around this time starting to brag about the money he was getting. Abad Khan got the impression:

> … that he had received a considerable amount of money from the Axis in Kabul and had supplied it to the party. He also told me that Germans were ready to give as much money as I needed but I refused to work for money. He also said that the Germans in Kabul were pressing him to buy a car which would be used between Kabul and Peshawar on urgent occasions but I did not agree, because I could easily send information through taxi drivers… I knew that Silver was visiting Axis Legations as well as the Russian Legation and was playing a double part. When I asked him he said he was not sincere to the Axis and that he was plundering them for the sake of the Russians.[20]

Crucially Silver also omitted both from his memoir and his full and frank confession to the British one visit he made to Kabul towards the end of 1941 when he also received substantial amounts of money and gold from Rasmuss; the details of this undisclosed visit was revealed to the British by Uttam Chand. He says Silver came to Kabul for a brief visit in November 1941, during which he gave Rasmuss a short report which he did not show to the Russians, to their great annoyance, telling them it contained:

> … nothing new. It showed general resentment against the British who refused to part with power. His party had stressed to him he should also make the Russians aware of Indian public feeling which was dangerous to the Allies so that Moscow could tender wise advice to the British Government.[21]

This time, according to Uttam Chand, Rasmuss gave Silver more money, with the two men having a discussion about the currency. Rasmuss would have preferred to give Silver Pound notes, but Silver told Rasmuss that, although Britain owned India, Sodhi had found it impossible, both in Bombay and Lahore, to convert Pound notes into Indian Rupees. Silver would later tell Uttam Chand that he knew a Sikh pilot who was making air mail flights to England and could convert them there. But whether this was another Silver tale or the truth is hard to say. Uttam Chand says the German on this secret trip gave Silver 50,000 in Afghan Rupees and 500 gold sovereigns. While Silver did not much like having gold he knew that, unlike the Pounds, there was a means of using them, for the previous consignment had been given by Sodhi to two trusted Kirti party workers to be sold through goldsmiths a few sovereigns at a time to fund party activity.

So what became of this cash? We do not know. It does not feature in the statement of Axis money Silver received which was prepared by the British following Silver's confession, nor is it mentioned by Sodhi. The implication that Silver kept the cash for himself is compelling. This trip was certainly very secret, indeed so secret that Quaroni did not know anything about it. This explains this curious telegram from Quaroni to his Foreign Office on 24 November 1941:

> Rahmat Khan has disappeared: it is feared that he has been arrested; the Lahore committee have not resumed contact with us.[22]

Silver on his return to India from this secret Kabul trip spent some time in the Nawakot safe house, watching Sainsra craft out more fiction to give to the Germans. The report drew on Indian newspapers and a publicly available Bombay handbook on the Indian Army, and, like any skilful fiction writer, Sainsra blended his invention with facts that were freely available to make it seem authentic. So the military appendix of the report included troop movements and dispositions at British cantonments like Rawalpindi and Lahore: what Sainsra invented were the numbers. This was supplemented by a great deal of Sainsra fiction: that the Kirti party was working within the Indian Army and had agents in units in Libya and the Far East, and that defeatism was spreading to the point where regiments would soon surrender without fighting. The report also gave industrial information and news about strikes culled from newspapers, with the party claiming credit for having organised them. Rasmuss's eagerness to hear about landing sites was fed with talk of petrol being stockpiled for the 'Mohmand aerodrome'. The report promised the collection of mica and zinc, despite the fact that there was government control of these commodities. It concluded with advice that Bose, who had still not told the world he was holed up in Berlin, should not come out of hiding unless he could get a Free India Declaration approved by the Axis powers. It took Sainsra five days of slaving over the typewriter to mix fact with fiction, and then early in January 1942 Silver was ready to hit the Kabul road for his fifth journey, all in the space of eleven months.

There is some confusion as to when he arrived in Kabul. He told the British it was 12 January 1942, but German records suggest a few days later, although since he always met the Russians first that would tally with what he told the British. This was the longest visit Silver made to Kabul during the war, five whole months from January to May 1942 and was his most important visit. Not only did he plunder more money from the gullible Nazis, but his relationship with his Russian spy masters reached new heights.[23]

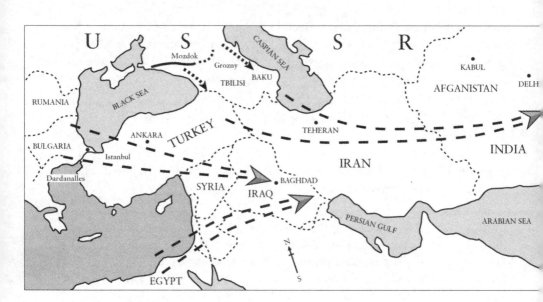

The route Hitler's armies would have taken to India had his plan to defeat Russia worked. Rommel's anticipated victory in the desert, he got to within 150 miles of Cairo before losing to Montgomery in El Alamein, would have provided an additional spur.

More Nazi Loot in Kabul

Silver's sixth visit to Kabul took place against a background of momentous developments in the war. Two weeks before he left for Kabul the Germans had been stopped at the gates of Moscow, marking the first defeat of Hitler's army; but in East Asia Japan seemed unstoppable. Before he had left Peshawar Japan had taken Hong Kong and Manila. As he crossed into the tribal areas, with large swathes of Malaya under its control, it was advancing towards Singapore. Three days after Silver reached Kabul, Japanese troops invaded Burma and moved ever nearer to India. Things were also changing in Kabul, as Silver found when on arrival he went straight to Uttam Chand's shop, as he always did.

To his great surprise he found Uttam Chand pulling down the shutters not just for that evening, but for good. The Afghan government had told him that, never having been an authorised retail trader, he could not run it any more. However, he assured Silver, he had rented spacious premises in new Kabul where he could carry on his business, to which he was moving the next day. But, friendly as the relationship was, the two men did keep secrets from each other, and Uttam Chand did not disclose that while Silver had been away in India, Rasmuss had approached him to hire a house to accommodate Sanobar Hussain, who was coming to Kabul to help the Germans with their plans in the tribal territory. These new premises would clearly serve that purpose, and were also near the German and other embassies.[1]

Silver's priority was to see the Russians. At the Embassy the Sainsra report was translated into Russian and read carefully by Zaman. The Russian had no problem with the political part but was horrified when he read the military appendix: to him the military details seemed to be conveying valuable information to the Axis, and he insisted the report be changed radically before it could be given to Rasmuss. Even when Silver revealed how fiction had been mixed with already-available fact Zaman was not convinced. Quick-thinking as usual, Silver pointed out that retyping the report at the Russian Embassy would mean differences in typeface and paper, and the signature on the report would no longer be that of the man who usually signed them—he meant Sainsra, although did not disclose his name. The Germans would surely smell a rat. Zaman eventually agreed that the report could be given to Rasmuss in its original form.

Silver also gave Zaman an application by Kirti to be officially recognised as the communist party of India—in effect a *quid pro quo* from the Russians in return for spying for them. Zaman gave the standard response that it would be passed on to Moscow, although he must have been aware that Moscow was unlikely to change its allegiance from the All-India communist party CPI to this regional, Punjab-based party.[2]

Silver appears to have spent a week with Uttam Chand and the Russians before contacting Rasmuss, meeting him on 20 January and being introduced to Dietrich Witzel, a man Silver would get to know very well and even meet after the war. A member of the special Brandenburg Regiment, trained for various subversive activities by OKW/Abwehr II for the forthcoming war against the USSR, Witzel had arrived in Kabul in May 1941. He never met Subhas Bose but he had a journey very similar to the Indian leader the other way round, travelling via Moscow, where he witnessed the May Day parade of 1941 on the Red Square, then taking the sleeping car in a special train right up to the Afghan border at Termez. Witzel had been selected for Kabul, apparently, by random. It is possible—says Hauner—he could have been a Nazi, without necessarily being a card-carrying party member and long after the war did not answer questions as to when he lost his belief in Endsieg—ultimate victory. Witzel had been assigned a very specific task in Kabul: preparing the ground through workable radio communication for the anticipated breakthrough of the Wehrmacht across the Caucasus. But on arrival and having discovered Silver this was downgraded to what was considered the more important task of organising sabotage and subversion with the help of anti-British organizations inside India, culminating in the specific plan of a German airborne operation (*Unternehmen Tiger*) to the tribal belt in the NWFP. This would become a Witzel obsession.[3]

In his memoir Silver misspells Witzel's name, as he does that of Rasmuss, but writes: 'At that very first meeting with him I guessed that he must be the chief of the German Secret Service in Kabul'.[4] Given the Abwehr officer's arrival the previous May it may seem surprising that it had taken him eight months to meet Silver but since his arrival he had had to put up with the hostility of Brinckmann, who had complained to his SS masters that the Abwehr man consulted Major Schenk—the half-Jew—more than him. Now, with Brinckmann deported, Witzel was taking over the military intelligence side of Silver's operation, while Rasmuss would deal with the political side.

Quaroni would later dismiss Witzel as worthless. In addition to his code name of 'Pathan' he had studied Persian for three years in Berlin and considered himself a Persian expert. But his Persian was so bad that no-one who did not know German as well could possibly understand it. Neither did Witzel speak Pashtu and was so ill-informed about Afghanistan that in one report he made much of the fact that Afghan men often had a harem, leading him to warn Berlin that, should German soldiers arrive as liberators, they would not expect to be accommodated in a private home. But in his favour Witzel was assiduous, sending back to Berlin three or four reports every month on the military and political situation in Afghanistan and India.[5] All of which meant that for Witzel Silver's input was invaluable. Declaring themselves delighted with the report, and not for a moment suspecting that they were being passed recycled newspaper stories, Witzel and Rasmuss now began to cross-examine Silver, not in an aggressive fashion, but rather in the manner of pupils learning at the feet of a master.

Witzel started off by talking about Ceylon, Iran and Burma, explaining that the British and Russian occupation of Iran meant Axis contacts had broken down and they badly needed news of military dispositions and ship movements in the Persian Gulf and the Middle East. No problem, said Silver. Zaman may have been horrified by the details of Silver's 'military report', but Witzel wanted more. Names of units and all troop movements completed or intended were, emphasised Witzel, very necessary, especially on the North West Frontier. To this end Witzel gave Silver a typewritten list of military commands, districts, brigades etc. in India, which he said was taken from a pre-war Indian Army list: Silver was to bring this up to date, including all the new regiments that had been formed and where they were stationed.[6]

When Witzel asked for recruiting figures Silver, who knew what had been published in the press, replied that 40,000 a month were joining the Army, and went on to say that Japan's entry into the war in December 1941 was likely to increase this figure considerably. This came as a surprise to Rasmuss and Witzel: Silver's explanation was that generally throughout India, even in extremist national circles, there was an antipathy for Japan, and India's fear of Japanese domination was greater than its dislike of British rule. In reality India's attitude to Japan was more complex. At the beginning of the twentieth century there had been much admiration for Japan following the 1905 victory over Russia, in particular the Battle of Tsushima when the Japanese fleet had vanquished the Russian one. This was seen as reversing the defeat four centuries earlier in the Battle of Lepanto when a fleet representing Catholic maritime states had defeated the Ottomans. For many in Asia Japan's victory represented the rise of Asia after a long period under the dominance of Europe. But in recent years its image had been tarnished by its brutal war of aggression on China—even Subhas Bose had criticised Japan for that; neither did Indian businessmen care for Japan dumping shoddy, cheap goods on the Indian market. But by now Silver had such a halo round him that everything he said was readily accepted by the Germans. The real reason Indians were joining the Army in large numbers was because it provided employment and more pay and benefits than any work they could get in civilian life.

Silver also lied skilfully when Witzel wanted to know why there were so many British troops still on the North West Frontier when Japan was threatening Malaya and Burma. The troops on the Frontier, he explained, were mainly forces from the princely states, hastily being trained up. There were in fact no princely forces at all on the North West Frontier.

Now it was Rasmuss's turn. What contact had developed, he inquired, with Burma? Men had been sent, lied Silver, but they had not yet returned. Having told Witzel that the British were recruiting more soldiers because the Indians hated the Japanese more than the British, he now told them that anti-British feeling was rapidly mounting, and that the Forward Bloc was growing apace in organisation and strength. In December, following the Japanese entry into the war, the British, aware that Subhas's brother, Sarat, was secretly meeting the Japanese consul in Calcutta, had arrested him, the first and only time the barrister saw the inside of a prison. Rasmuss wanted to know the reasons for this, and whether it was known outside Forward Bloc circles where Subhas was now. Had Rasmuss borrowed Quaroni's copy of the *Statesman* he would not have had to ask the question: two months earlier the paper had reported the Government of India's announcement that they thought Bose was either in Rome or Berlin, with the *Statesman* commenting that since Bose was a Nazi that was the best place for him. Silver's reply showed how he could invent almost any lie with impunity: unconcerned as to whether Rasmuss read Indian newspapers or not, he boldly stated that he did not think the police knew where Subhas was, as they were still looking for him in India. When the ever solicitous Rasmuss enquired whether he had managed to change the pound notes successfully, Silver replied that he had handed these over but up to the time of his departure not heard anything.

Even the fact that Silver had not brought along two selected party members with him for training in sabotage as agreed did not upset the Germans. Witzel accepted Silver's explanation that Kirti wanted him to be given the training so they would know what type of men to select. Witzel knew that Berlin was keen for such work. On 6 January, 1942—a week before Silver had returned to Kabul—Bose in Berlin had been introduced to Colonel Erwin Lahousen, an ex-Austrian head of Abwehr II, the military intelligence outfit to which Witzel reported. And on 27 January 1942, six days after Witzel's first meeting with Silver in Kabul, Bose, Lahousen and Colonel Yamamoto, the Japanese Military Attaché, met again in Berlin with the Indian leader presenting an extremely optimistic, indeed somewhat fantastic, picture of how the British Raj was on the brink of collapse, and all that was required was a push. But despite this Bose could not get the Germans and the Japanese to agree a declaration on Free India which he had set his heart on. He also could not get the Japanese, then steamrolling through European colonies in south Asia, to say when they might attack India. A few days later, on 6 February 1942, there had been a further meeting in Berlin between the Indian, the German and the Japanese with Yamamoto saying the Japanese could advance in a host of directions—Australia and even the Soviet Far East. But while this meant that the Axis had not worked out their wider plan for India, these meetings in Berlin did see agreement that in the meantime Bose's organisation should be used for extensive sabotage work to prepare the ground should the Japanese head for India.

Witzel decided he would train Silver in cipher work—not at the Legation, however, but the home of Dr Friescher. The training was spread over several weeks, and Silver was shown how to use one code in figures and another in letters, both intended for secret correspondence and for messages to be broadcast by Azad Hindustan Radio from Berlin to India. The key-book for the figure code was a small pamphlet in English published in Berlin called *The Miracle of Stable Prices in Germany*; Witzel gave Silver two copies. For the other code, the code-word was 'Motherland'.

Following the cipher training Witzel gave Silver a course in sabotage methods. This included the preparation of bombs and explosives; the use of detonators and inflammable substances made out of simple bazaar ingredients; sabotage of railway lines, machinery, and factories; and setting fire to cars, factories and houses. For this Witzel had twelve pamphlets printed in English, each bearing a different number and explaining the type of sabotage and what materials to use. According to the instructions there were three types of sabotage: hindrance; interruption; destruction. Witzel explained that Azad Hindustan Radio would give specific instructions in code as to which targets to attack, by referring to these pamphlets. Witzel impressed upon Silver that the instructions in the sabotage pamphlets were only to be shown to the secret Party headquarters, and said he was deliberately giving Silver only one copy of each pamphlet. It was clear that no one else in India was being given these codes and sabotage instructions.

The moment Witzel's tutorial had finished Silver went straight over to the Russians and spilled the beans. He gave them one copy of the stable primes code booklet, keeping the other to take back to India, and explained the full working of both codes to the Soviet Legation. He also handed over the original sabotage pamphlets to the Russians. They would then be able to listen in to Azad Hindustan Radio's cipher messages and also keep a check on any special targets in India the Axis were interested in.

A few days later at another meeting with the Germans Rasmuss explained that the real messages would start from 10 October 1942, a date chosen to coincide with Silver's eventual return to India. In fact, even while Silver was still in Kabul, Azad Hind radio had broadcast a number of coded messages, but during the sabotage training Witzel had explained that these broadcasts were meaningless and merely intended to spread excitement in India among Bose's followers.

The British, eager to know the plans Bose was hatching, carefully monitored these fake Azad Hind radio broadcasts from Berlin, the first of which was heard in London at 5.30 p.m. on 28 April 1942. The British record of it reads as follows:

You are now going to hear a very important announcement issued by our leader, Subhas Chandra Bose. Our Leader Subhas Chandra Bose has issued the following statement which we would beg our listeners to broadcast throughout India. The statement begins: 'After a great deal of careful preparation, we have decided to establish closer contact between our comrades living outside India and those comrades who are living at home. For this purpose we are going to use a modern and up-to-date instrument. We are going to make two experiments and watch the results. After these experiments we can decide our future plans. On Sunday 3rd May, the first batch of our comrades will be sent to India by plane and according to our calculations they will reach their destination in India in the early hours of the morning of 4th May, between two and three o'clock. After dropping the parachutists the aeroplane will return at once. We are purposely not giving out the exact place of arrival, because our enemies will then attempt to arrest our comrades. We know quite well that our comrades who are making this hazardous journey will be killed at once if they fall into the hands of our enemies. We request our co-workers, friends and sympathisers everywhere in India, to look out for aeroplanes and parachutes in the early hours of the morning of 4th May between two and three o'clock. As soon as they see the parachutes, they should kindly give all possible help to the parachutist comrades, give them shelter. Moreover, the article to be carried by the parachutist should be hidden in a safe place. When all this is done, the parachutes should be either buried under the earth or set fire to, so that there may not be any trace of them. In no case should they be burnt at night, because fire may attract enemy agents to the place. If all goes well on 4th May, then the second aeroplane will reach India on 8th May, in the early hours of the morning between two and three o'clock. It is not necessary for our comrades and friends in India to light any lamps as a signal, because that has already been arranged by our agents in India at the exact place where the aeroplane will arrive. Ordinarily it would not have been necessary to make an open announcement like this, which our enemies in India will naturally hear and note. It would have been enough to inform our agents secretly of the particular place where the parachutes will be dropped. But in such attempts one has always to provide against accidents, and since this is our fourth endeavour of this kind, we want to take all possible precautions that the comrades flying to India do not fall into enemy hands. That is why, after a great deal of hesitation, we have been forced to make a general appeal to our friends and sympathisers all over the country. We hope that, very soon, our technique will have so improved that it will not be necessary in future to make such an open statement, which our enemies can hear. We hope that, in future, it will be (possible?) to inform, by secret means, our confidential agents of the exact place where the parachutes will land. If anything goes wrong on 4th May, we may have to alter the next date, otherwise the second aeroplane will arrive in India on the morning of 8th May.

There was a second broadcast by Bose at 5 p.m. on 7 May 1942, which the British again monitored:

I announced on the 28th April and the 2nd May from this station that we wished to send some reliable co-workers to India by plane, with equipment. I announce to you now that the first batch landed safely at the appointed place, but owing to the mistake of some people in India they were not fully successful. The people of India warned the enemy agents by showing more light than was necessary. The agents immediately began to investigate and our members had to destroy their equipment. However, our members are safe and alive, as no agent was able to detect them. The parachutes, according to the instructions, were destroyed. The only regret is that we lost the equipment, which our members took with them. According to our plans our second plane will arrive in India on 8th May between 2 and 3 a.m. We ask our agent to show only the amount of light specified in our instructions. If they act according to the instructions given then we hope to succeed on 8th May. I ask our agent, friends and sympathisers to look out for the parachutists on 8th May between 2 and 3 a.m., and be prepared to help them in every way. They must be careful and must not make mistakes this time.

Finally, just after 8 p.m. on 22 May, Bose made a third broadcast on parachute landings in India.

We are glad to inform our countrymen that the second attempt made by Azad Hind on 8th May to establish contact with our comrades at home was successful. We are grateful to our noble friend (Kaysar?) whose assistance was of very great help. But for this assistance the experiment of 8th May might have ended in failure. However, the two aeroplane flights on 4th May and on 8th May have enabled our comrades to gain valuable experience, which will be of great use on subsequent occasions. We hope, in view of this experience, it will not be necessary in future to publicly announce any aeroplane flight to India, since such announcements give information to our enemies as well. We shall, however, make one further request of our friends and sympathisers in every part of India. It is possible that when our comrades fly to India in future they may not have time to dispose of the parachutes after landing, because they must hurriedly escape with their luggage. Consequently, if anybody comes across a parachute lying on the ground, he should not make any fuss ... but quietly burn or bury it.[7]

At this stage Bose, after fourteen months in Berlin, had still not emerged in public. He would only do so a week after this broadcast following his meeting with Hitler. For the British these broadcasts were significant to judge what their 'implacable foe' was preaching. If Silver heard these broadcasts he made no reference to them, either in his confession to the British or in his memoirs, as he knew they were fake. There is, not surprisingly, no evidence of any such landings ever taking place, for the simple reason that the Germans did not have any airfield in the area.

But they remained keen to land men in the tribal areas in their efforts to help the Faqir of Ipi. Indeed, after the fall of Singapore on 15 February 1942 Witzel had resumed preparations for Operation *Tiger*, the full-scale frontier uprising the Germans had originally planned for September 1941, by which time Hitler had been confident that Russia would be conquered and Operation *Barbarossa* complete. That had failed, Operation *Tiger* was postponed, but Witzel was still very optimistic of German success in Russia and on 11 March 1942 he asked permission to carry out his scheduled dash to the frontier to explore the terrain for the construction of a landing ground for the reception of commander units from Germany—the thinking being that Bose would be brought to India from Europe by an Axis aircraft. Witzel also wanted to see where he could erect a wireless station there to enable the direct transmission of intelligence information from India. The tribesmen, meanwhile, were to be given an intensive course in sabotage and other subversive activities. Witzel wanted to visit the frontier with Zugenbühler and Silver. But Berlin took two months to decide, by which time Silver had left Kabul and did not have to find an excuse not to get involved. As it happened, after Silver left Kabul Witzel on his own for a week, from 3 to 10 June 1942, rode a horse out of Kabul as far as Ghazni, 160 km south on the road to Kandahar. He never did get near the border or the tribal territory, claiming that the Afghan police were always watching him. For a man who did not know Pushtu it showed a certain sense of adventure and might have won him some medals in Berlin but, as Hauner writes: 'it epitomised the lack of knowledge about the country and its people, which was a common feature among German agents in this part of the world'.[8] Given the quality of this Abwehr agent Silver could hardly fail to dupe him.

In April 1942 Rasmuss informed Silver that the latest instructions had been received from Berlin, and gave him two typed pages of instructions. They were

- to form guerrilla bands of deserters from the Indian Army, who should be trained to operate behind the British lines when the Germans attacked from the north-west and the Japanese from the east;
- to persuade as many Indians as possible, meanwhile, to desert with their arms and carry out an intensive whispering campaign spreading defeatism and calling on Government officials to resign;
- to undermine confidence in the British currency, combined with a propaganda campaign enumerating Axis victories in Russia and the Far East;
- to encourage everyone to listen to Azad Hindustan Radio, especially serving troops;
- to encourage the formation of political volunteer groups among peasants, workers and students, who would be told secretly to join the guerrilla bands as soon as India was attacked;
- to send trusted workers from Chittagong to the Madras coastal area to prepare the local inhabitants to welcome the Japanese troops and act as their guides;
- to spread false propaganda about British troops raping Indian women;
- to encourage slowing-down tactics in factories, but not to sabotage any big industries;
- to prepare a parallel Forward Bloc administration to be set up in the name of Azad Hindustan in enemy-occupied areas as soon as India was invaded;
- All volunteer organisations to obtain secret arms and hold themselves in readiness meanwhile. They should be told that a large 'Indian Army' was being trained in Berlin from among prisoners of war and German internees who would come to liberate India;
- Simultaneous preparations were necessary among the tribes so that large-scale tribal risings would coincide with internal revolt and an Axis invasion. The Faqir of Ipi would give the lead to the Tribes;
- Meanwhile, stocks of secret petrol and bombs should be arranged in India and tribal territory. Landing grounds should be prepared in tribal territory where German parachute troops could be dropped from the air;
- Propaganda should be widely spread urging Indians to resign from the Army and from civil employment as the defeat of Britain was imminent, and adding that those who did not do so before India was attacked would be treated as enemies by the invading Axis troops. For this purpose

lists of pro-British Indians were to be prepared, and held in readiness. Intensive propaganda against the British scorched-earth policy was also very essential.

Meanwhile, Bose wanted

- numbers for military deserters and how many of them had deserted with their arms, and details of where they were now in hiding;
- also, what proportion of the Indian Army was likely to remain loyal when the Japanese invaded the east of India;
- Whether the Forward Bloc contacts in Burma and Ceylon had achieved any success yet.
- What was the position of Nehru and other Congress leaders following the breakdown of the Cripps negotiations?[Cripps now a Cabinet minister had made a fruitless attempt to bring the Congress and the British together]
- Any German or Italian Prisoners of War who escaped should be given refuge in tribal territory, though no special names were mentioned.

Bose also wanted to know the reactions in Bengal to the Forward Bloc Ministers, and the present whereabouts of a number of his political supporters in Bengal who were mentioned by name. Wherever there were Sikh troops Bose wanted Sikh agents to be used to infiltrate their ranks.

Rasmuss now told Silver to prepare to return to India to carry out the new programme. However, the Russians, having digested all that Silver had fed them, asked him to wait a few days as they were expecting an important official from Moscow.

The official—the Soviets did not reveal his name—turned out to be in charge of Soviet Asiatic Intelligence, or so both Silver and Uttam Chand were told, having directed Russian intelligence in Europe before the German invasion. He spoke German and several other European languages but no English or Hindustani. On his arrival three members of the Russian Legation—one to act as interpreter—accompanied Silver to what turned out to be a long meeting. The Russian officer wanted to hear the whole of Silver's story—his early Communist connections, how he helped Bose escape. The questioning began at 7 p.m. and continued until 5 a.m. the next morning, interrupted only for food and brandy.

Silver found the meeting exhausting, not merely because of the insistent questioning by the nameless Russian, but because over these ten hours he drank several glasses of brandy. The more he drank that night the more he wanted to go to the lavatory, but felt embarrassed about always excusing himself, and for the last three hours of the meeting could not summon up the courage to do so. The result was that back at Uttam Chand's house the next day he had severe difficulty in passing water and had to see a doctor. This was a revealing insight into Silver's character and, to an extent, a reflection of his cultural background where such intimate personal matters were not openly acknowledged. He could easily deceive the Italians and the Germans and parley with the Russians but was not able to mention the need to relieve himself.

Silver recovered sufficiently to have two more meetings with the Russian, and told him everything Rasmuss had told him. Uttam Chand was also present at one of the meetings, and the Russians impressed on him that he must keep Silver's role secret. Worried that Silver might overplay his hand, the Russians warned him to be on his guard against giving the Germans any cause to suspect he was betraying them, or not following the instructions Bose was sending from Berlin.

There was also one little doubt the Soviets had about Silver. They knew he would never betray the Soviet Union, but might he help the Japanese, who were not at war with them? There was no difference between the German and the Japanese war plans, his Russian minders told him: they were one and the same enemy.

But who was this mysterious Russian? Was he really the Head of Intelligence in the Asian Department of State Security as he claimed? Or was he Captain Raistev, whom British agents monitoring Europeans coming in and out of Kabul had noted arriving there on 10 April 1942, and who then posed as Secretary to the Military Attaché Major Karpov.[11] In recent years the Soviet scholar Iuri Tikhomirov, who has unearthed the few Soviet documents available on Silver, has asserted that the real name of Silver's interrogator was neither Raistev nor Karpov, but Andrei Makarevich Otroshchenko, head of the NKVD Middle Eastern Department, who had been ordered to go to Kabul in January 1942 and used the cover name Sasha.[12]

Raistev or Sasha, the Russian was delighted with Silver. It was clear that Silver had won the Germans' confidence and they completely trusted him. For the Soviets this was a priceless discovery: in Kabul, in the midst of war, they had an Indian with wonderful access to their enemy. Sasha's visit had been shrewdly timed, for the Soviets were keen to know where the Germans' forthcoming summer offensive of 1942 would be. They had stopped them at the gates of Moscow the previous winter, but in which direction had Hitler's army turned? Even some information as to how the Germans viewed any move further east, and India itself, would be valuable. They told Silver he must maintain his Axis contacts and obtain as much information as possible, particularly in relation to German plans in Afghanistan and the Middle East. After the third meeting the Russian told Silver to return to India, but not before seeing Rasmuss once more to 'comply' with the instructions he was given.

The other reason for meeting the German, as both the Soviets and Silver anticipated, was to collect more funds from them, and once again Rasmuss was generous: no pounds, again, but 500 gold sovereigns and 100,000 Afghani rupees. Straight afterwards Silver dutifully told the Soviets about the meeting, and for them it could not be sweeter: not only was their enemy paying their own agent, but they did not have to pay him any money, as he had more than enough from the Germans.

Silver in his memoir does not disclose any of this, except for this intriguing passage: 'Meanwhile I had met some other friends who were connected with us in our common cause. Through them I wanted to build some more contacts'. It is hard to resist the conclusion that the friends he was referring to were Sasha and his fellow Russians.[13]

There was a moment during Silver's four months in Kabul when Rasmuss might have smelt a rat. News came that Sodhi and two others had been arrested by the British. The police in India, having for almost two years been outfoxed by the Kirti party, were now catching up, although very slowly. Even then it was quite by chance that Sodhi fell into their hands—in fact he had been arrested the very day Silver reached Kabul. On the morning of 12 January 1942 he had been changing trains at Kishenganj Railway Station in Delhi to catch the Grand Trunk Express for Wardha, where he planned to meet CPI leaders and renew negotiations for a 'united front'. But as he waited at the station he was spotted by the police and, as the British note put it, 'He was completely taken by surprise, and within twenty-four hours of his capture began to talk freely'. As the British official also noted:

> I am informed he faces two serious charges, namely abetment of mutiny amongst Sikh troops, both before and during the war, and latterly taking part in a seditious conspiracy on behalf of foreign Powers to wage war against the King, and that his only anxiety is to save his neck.

Sodhi's statement at last revealed to the Allies what the India Office would later come to dub the 'Bose Conspiracy'. The note that winged its way to the real Mr Silver at IPI expressed pleasure at the Nazis being so easily deceived tinged with a touch of complacency:

> The main conclusions to be derived from Sodhi's disclosures regarding the Bose conspiracy are that, at any rate so far as Kabul, the North-West Frontier and the northern part of India are concerned, there is no cause for anxiety. Sodhi and the Kirti group joined Bose's proposed Axis scheming more or less by accident and soon found that they offered generous prospects for party funds. The proposals which they put forward to cause trouble in India found favour in Kabul beyond their intrinsic merits and were well paid for...

The statement of Harmindar Singh Sodhi has considerable propaganda value and I suggest this aspect of the matter be brought to the notice of the Government of India. The world at large, perhaps more than the Nazis themselves, should be interested to know that large sums of Nazi money had been paid to further the grandiose schemes of Subhas Bose which turned out to be nothing more than paper schemes drafted by Indian communists with their tongues in their cheeks who saw an easy way to make money.[14]

Back in Kabul Rasmuss had been very intrigued when he heard the news of Sodhi's arrest. Was this, he asked Silver, the same Sodhi he had met? Would he betray secrets? Silver knew he was in a tight corner but, feigning certainty as only he could, he presented Sodhi as the old revolutionary who had been through much in many countries and would never betray a thing.

Having neatly got out of that jam, and feeling very secure, Silver now, after four months, prepared to leave Kabul and, as he had always done since first coming to Kabul, bade Uttam Chand a fond farewell and, in particular, his devoted wife Ramo Devi. In Hindi the word *Devi* means goddess, and while Silver did not, of course, worship her, he had always appreciated the care she took of her visitors, living up to the legendary Indian tradition of *attiti grahan*. Westerners so unused to this, often find this custom impossible to understand, that you look after visitors better than you do your own family. For Ramo Devi it came naturally. Silver had come to respect her since his first stay in the company of Subhas Bose when, aware he was an important person on the run, she had balanced care for him with the need for secrecy. As Silver put it in his memoir: 'She managed the children so well we never had reason to suspect that they were ever talking. Under her control even the servant proved to be useful and reliable'.[15] Much had changed since then in the intelligence operation Silver and Uttam Chand were involved in, but not in how Ramo Devi managed both the home and Silver's frequent visits—with him staying this time for four long months that was no mean feat.

But for all the respect Silver felt for Ramo Devi, his relationship with her husband had begun to sour. Silver had never much liked the way Uttam Chand could be indiscreet, concluding that the shopkeeper was never really cut out for the true world of spies. On this trip he had reason to be very upset by what he felt were Uttam Chand's loose and personal remarks about him. Over tea one day with several fellow Indians in Kabul including Haji Subhan and some Indian professors, Uttam Chand taunted Silver as to why he did not accompany them when they visited certain brothels in Kabul—although all these men were married the occasional visit to a prostitute was still very much part of their lifestyle. Silver jokingly replied that he had lady friends of his own in India and, when Uttam Chand sneeringly asked who, gave the name of a film actress in Lahore and recounted the amorous adventures he had had with her in Delhi and on the train to Calcutta. In fact Silver had never met the actress but only seen her on the screen and had never even been to Delhi. Silver was not pleased when Uttam Chand gleefully spread the story around among the Indian community in Kabul.

Worse was to come after Silver's illness following the long drinking session with Sasha. Having organised medical treatment for Silver, Uttam Chand told mutual acquaintances that Silver was suffering from gonorrhoea, implying that Silver did visit prostitutes after all. In due course Uttam Chand repeated this allegation to his British interrogators, and when Silver was in turn questioned he was visibly upset and told the British he was prepared to be medically examined to prove it false.[16]

Nevertheless, he recognised how valuable Uttam Chand was, he knew he had to put up with him as the shopkeeper was his essential Kabul base and was not seeking to break with him and his wife. But Silver would never see them again. By the time he returned to Kabul for his next visit in August 1942 both were gone, and his whole spying operation had been revolutionised, with the Russians forced to share a spy with another country, the most unusual decision over intelligence they ever made during the war. It also meant Silver, already spying for three countries, became a quadruple agent, and this fourth country was one he would never have expected to work for. His spying career was no longer a partnership, with him as the main agent and Uttam Chand the sub-agent: from now on he would be the only agent in this fascinating Kabul intelligence game, a situation that would not change until Germany surrendered and Silver's spy career finally came to an end.

13

Russia's Gift to Britain

In February 1942, as Witzel had been tutoring Silver in sabotage, the Japanese had taken Singapore, inflicting, as Churchill put it, the worst defeat ever suffered by British arms, with the surrender of 120,000 British, Australian and Indian forces. The Indian troops were surrendered separately, which many Indians saw as evidence of racial segregation, and played into the hands of Bose later. The collapse had reverberated around the world. In April Admiral Nagumo's naval raid on Ceylon prompted speculation that it was a forerunner for an invasion of India.

That month Allied intelligence concluded that if Japan attacked there would be a complete collapse in India. In Whitehall some military planners had come to accept that India being conquered by Japan was a foregone conclusion. Interestingly, Hitler shared Churchill's distress about Japan's success, the only time the two men agreed on anything, and spoke of giving the British 20 divisions to 'help throw back the yellow men'. [1]

As Silver left Kabul in May 1942 the Japanese conquered Burma, the largest country on the south-east Asian mainland, panicking the British in Bengal and leading to their demand that fighter squadrons be sent out from Britain, a demand which Lord Beaverbrook contemptuously rejected. Many Indians too were terribly frightened, but what also upset them was that, despite all the talk of the war being a fight for freedom, the old racial barriers still remained. So in the panic retreat from Burma many of the Indians, of whom there were a million in the country, found that their brown skins were considered inferior to the whites when it came to getting on steamers and other transport to flee the Japanese. Many Indians died horrible deaths in the retreat, and the racial discrimination led to questions in the Commons, while members of the Muslim League spoke of 'the shameful discrimination against Indian nationals'. Gandhi told *Time* and *Life* magazine reporters, 'One route for the whites, another for the blacks! Provision of food and shelter for the whites, none for the blacks! And discrimination even on their arrival in India.'[2]

Japan's incredible overthrow of European colonial rule in Asia also had major consequences for the stability of British rule in India, and dramatically altered the whole political context of the intelligence operations in which Silver was involved. By the time Burma fell the last chance for the British in India and the Congress Party to co-exist during the war had gone. The fall of Singapore had prompted the British Cabinet, despite Churchill, to try and do a deal with the Indian nationalists, and in March 1942 Stafford Cripps had flown to Delhi with proposals that promised India the right to frame its constitution after the war in return for immediate co-operation during it.

Historians have continued to debate what caused the Cripps mission to fail. In the long historical view is it hard to disagree with Cripps that, while he could not go as far as the Congress wanted—Hamlet without the prince, as one Indian newspaper called it—once inside the British tent the Congress could use their elbows to get much more. The Congress, led by lawyers now intensely distrustful of the British, were pedantic and missed a historic chance to get the India they had so long been fighting for. It was Gandhi who orchestrated the Congress refusal, by this time convinced the Allies would lose the war. Ironically, this supreme pacifist was also impressed by Subhas Bose's courage and resourcefulness in making his escape from India, having been a keen listener to his broadcasts from Berlin. Linlithgow, the Viceroy, had been opposed to the mission from the start, and in a telegram to Amery made this historic assessment of British rule:

> Cabinet will agree with me that India and Burma have no natural association with the empire, from which they are alien by race, history and religion, and for which as such, neither of them have any natural affection, and both are in the empire because they are conquered countries which have been brought there by force, kept there by our controls, and which hitherto, it has suited to remain under our protection.[3]

The highest British representative in India was confessing that, after nearly two centuries of British rule, there was nothing that tied Indians to the British except British power. The failure of the Cripps mission fundamentally changed political India, with Gandhi breaking with the British and calling for them to 'Quit India'.

The British now needed political friends. They already had Jinnah's Muslim League, which from the beginning of the war had supported the British, but in the summer of 1942 a new ally emerged, the Indian communists. They publicly opposed Gandhi's Quit India plans, declared their support for the Allies, and P. C. Joshi, general secretary of the Communist Party of India, quickly did a deal with the Home Secretary of the Bombay Government whereby the party would make sure the factories kept running in return for party leaders being freed.

For much of the war British agents had infiltrated communist meetings and reported on their activities. Now some among the British could even see the communists as helping form a partisan army modelled on the one that was harrying the Nazis in Europe.

During his visit to India Cripps had suggested communists be recruited to help the war effort, with contact established between the communist branch of the All-India Student Federation, the Government and the Army. The students had come up with four plans: join the Army accepting Viceroy's and Emergency Commissions, form arson squads, carry out public relations to promote the Army with the general public and watch the coast for Japanese ships. But the Army got so enthusiastic on the public relations side of the plan that the IB, having fought the communists for three decades, was alarmed. It was left to Colin Mackenzie, who had arrived in India in July 1941 to set up the SOE India Mission, to develop this most unlikely war-time partnership.[4]

Mackenzie, the only SOE head of an overseas mission to last the entire duration of the war, had a first from Cambridge in economics and was known as Moriarty. This was because of his limp, having lost a leg in the First World War. He decided to retain the arson squad idea but hoped that after a Japanese occupation these squads could be a cover for sabotage work.[5] Joshi was keen for the communists to form part of a guerrilla force to fight the Japanese. But Mackenzie shied away from too close a co-operation between the communists, as he felt such training 'might have some sinister implication'. He wanted to use communists to deal with fifth columnists, with selected party workers given training in 'night work, stalking, camouflage, selected bits of silent killing and knife and rope work'. Joshi welcomed it, as he felt that if the Japanese landed 'all known communists would be rounded up and shot'. For him 'in taking action against fifth columnists they would be protecting their own lives'.[6]

Mackenzie had to fight the provincial police in India who were very dubious about the scheme, with Bengal, Orissa and Madras opposing it vigorously. Two years earlier the Bengal government had banned pamphlets calling on Hindu–Muslim unity simply because they were published by Communist students. To treat these students as allies now was very difficult. Mackenzie used his personal friendship with Linlithgow to force them and the IB to abandon their historic antipathy for the communists. Mackenzie's paramilitary training of the communists did not last long. By June 1943, with the Japanese no longer considered a threat to the east coast of India, the programme was closed, but Mackenzie bargained with 'Joshi for the services of particular communists for operations outside India for the rest of the war'.[7]

Silver arrived back in India with Zaman's instructions to keep the communist party leadership fully briefed with what he was doing ringing in his years and was immediately made aware of how the world had changed for his comrades while he had been away in Kabul. A few weeks after his return to Peshawar, in July 1942, the British legalised the Communist Party. And for good measure Kirti finally merged with its bigger brother the CPI. The impact of this on Silver was enormous. As we have seen, in the past Silver had crept into Lahore surreptitiously as he headed for the dingy, secretive Kirti hideout at Nawakot. Now Silver for the first time marched up Lahore's McLeod Road, one of the main thoroughfares, to the offices of the CPI to meet Teja Singh Swatantra, the Kirti leader, who had organised the merger. Swatantra would play an increasingly important role in Silver's life, almost replacing the guru he had lost: Ram Kishan. Swatantra having debriefed Silver decided that the CPI leadership must meet Silver and he took him to Bombay, to the CPI's headquarters. In the past year Silver had briefed any number of comrades about what he was doing. But now he was meeting a communist heavyweight, Gangadhar Adhikari whose staple diet were the speeches and writings of Marx, Lenin and Stalin and who, after Indian independence, edited the Documents on the History of the Communist Party of India. The spy and the party theoretician had several meetings spread over a week—Silver says he stayed in Bombay for eight days—with Silver narrating the full story of his Kabul adventure. The CPI's advice to Silver was the same as Kirti or, as Silver put it, not 'interfere in my activities'. However, there was one difference in the overall situation. By this time having formally allied with the British war effort the communists were publicly attacking Bose very viciously as a fascist stooge, a man who would sell India to Hitler and Tojo, the Japanese dictator. In June 1978, while researching my book on Subhas Bose, I interviewed Adhikari in Delhi. He admitted to me that the communists had 'played a double game', attacking Bose during the war because of his alliance with the fascists even as Silver retained his links with the Nazis. His justification was that at a moment of great crisis risks had to be taken, despite the ideological contradictions. It is what he said next that showed that like Silver this great party thinker could also doctor the truth. He told me that the connection was kept because they had a commitment to Bose and 'information was coming'. All they had to do was to send someone to collect it:

> Our plan was to do nothing with the information received. Silver was a courier, merely carrying information to Bose. We were keeping ourselves informed about what was happening, that's all.[8]

I was far from convinced of this portrayal of Silver as a mere courier and in my biography of Bose I wrote that:

> But was it so simple? Such a double game involves many risks and carries the charge that the information was eventually passed on to the British ...

till the end of the war he [Silver] remained free. Even when we have allowed for Talwar's [Silver's] extraordinary brilliance at deception we are left with some doubts. After Russia's entry into the war the Russian and British agents compared notes and Russia, presumably, informed Britain about its role in getting Bose through. Bhagat Ram Talwar [Silver] must have figured there yet he was allowed to operate freely.[9]

But when I wrote the British archives disclosing the truth about Silver and the Indian communist party had not been released. So, I was not aware of the communist cover up, or how economical with the truth Adhikari had been. In reality what Adhikari told Silver was carry on spying for the Russians and feed misinformation to the Germans. What is not clear is what the Indian communists told the British about Silver. Given the strong links Joshi had formed with Mackenzie you would expect something to be divulged but, probably, the communists thought they were doing enough to help the British war effort and the British with their extensive spy network in India could work out who Silver was. And indeed the British by now should have arrested Silver

It was now six months since Sodhi had made his confession and all the information needed was available to the British authorities. So why did they not arrest Silver? The British in India certainly did not lack manpower when it came to surveillance, having a vast network of informers estimated as no fewer than 'thirty thousand ... native police spies maintained by the Raj'.[10] The answer lies in the clumsy, inefficient, way the much-vaunted British security apparatus worked both in India and Britain. For a start IPI in London did not get Sodhi's statement until two months after he had confessed. The official in London reading it correctly surmised that:

> The full story of this scheming, however, is not likely to be known until Bhagat Ram [Silver] of Galladher (alias Rahmat Khan, Bose's so-called secretary) is arrested and discloses all he knows. It is possible that by this time the arrest has actually taken place, in which case he may have explained where he deposited the arms and money made over to him by Rasmuss, the German Commercial Attaché. His statement to Sodhi that these were deposited with the Soviet Legation in Kabul is far from convincing and not supported by any other evidence.[11]

But no such arrest had been made. It is clear Sodhi's confession had gone to London but had not been circulated round the agencies in India and Afghanistan. The result was that, while IPI in London knew the real name of Silver and his village, back in the subcontinent many in the British intelligence network did not know who Silver was and others kept getting confused over his various aliases. Even the Punjab police, who knew him well and had often arrested him had at this stage only heard 'unconfirmed reports of the subversive actions of a Muslim named Ramzan [a code name Silver had never used and appears to be an inversion of the one given to Ganguli] among the trans-frontier tribes in Afghanistan'.[12] In one case Silver was even mistaken for Uttam Chand. It was only three days after the note on Sodhi arrived on IPI's desk in London, on 27 March 1942, that there was the first mention of him in the Kabul weekly intelligence summary. This spoke of a certain 'British subject Bhagat Ram', 'a clever but suspicious character' who was often visiting Uttam Chand's place. The following week the name 'Rahmat Khan' appeared in the summary. But even then the British in Kabul had no clue he was the main man describing him as Uttam Chand's sub-agent. In London too there was not much co-ordination between IPI and the Foreign Office, with the result that when, in early April 1942, J. M. Pink at the Foreign Office read the Kabul summary he dismissed it as containing 'little of interest'.

It was another fortnight before the British in Kabul knew who Rahmat Khan really was, but they still did not know he was feeding false information to the Germans and the Italians on behalf of the Soviets.[13] The British in Kabul continued to see him not as an important spy but someone who worked for Uttam Chand, whom they saw as their main target. This blind spot is all the more curious because they had had access to the telegrams Quaroni was sending from Kabul. As we have seen, back in March 1941 these telegrams had made it clear how he had recruited Silver. On 2 April 1942, Quaroni, despite being frozen out by Rasmuss, had worked out the truth of who Silver worked for:

> Contrary to what I said in my telegram no. 659 of 24 November [1941], Rahmat Khan has not been arrested [by the British] but is in Kabul. It is said that he is one of the Indian Government's principal informers in Kabul. Given his history and his circle of friends, it would be more logical to think that he has decided to work for the Soviets. However it is certain that he has moved on to serve the enemy. He has made no attempt to resume contact with us. I think it would be opportune to warn Bose of the foregoing.[14]

Quaroni, of course, did not know Silver was keeping his links with Rasmuss and by this time his relationship with the Germans was so poor that he did not feel it was at all necessary to warn his ally. Rome, in turn, seeing Bose becoming more ensconced with the Germans in Berlin, also felt no need to warn Bose. But the really crucial thing is neither London nor Delhi took any notice of this cable. This was just one of those documents deciphered but either unread or just put to one side.

Silver, of course, had no clue the mess the British intelligence was making and he returned to Punjab from Bombay still worrying about being arrested.

His main concern was to find out what his old comrade, Sodhi, had told the police. The solution was simple. He used a thousand rupees of Nazi money to bribe someone in the Punjab CID and obtained Sodhi's confession.[15] Silver was shocked. Sodhi, fearing for his life, had revealed all the secrets. How would this affect him, Sainsra and even Abad?

Silver and Sainsra hurried to see Abad in Peshawar, who did not want to talk in his shop and took them to a park near the Fort. There the pair told Abad he was named in the Sodhi confession. The three discussed in the light of what Sodhi had told the police whether it would not be best to walk into the nearest police station. Silver made it very clear to Abad he and Sainsra were not prepared to give themselves up. Silver was still taking precautions to make sure he was not detected, staying in safe houses, getting a woman member of the party to dress up as a Pathan Muslim lady, complete with Burkha, to act as his courier.

The three then discussed various plans to keep out of police clutches, including a rather far-fetched Abad suggestion that the party start a hotel where a reliable party worker could take shelter. With Silver flush with cash from Rasmuss, Abad also arranged for him to hire a building owned by a retired deputy superintendent of police. For Silver this was almost pocket money, Rs 500. But before the hotel could be opened Abad was arrested and the hotel never materialised.

It was while they were sitting in the park that Silver heard from Abad news that made Sodhi's arrest seem a relatively minor affair. Uttam Chand had been arrested by the Afghans and deported to Peshawar where he was now in jail. The arrest had taken place a few days after Silver's departure from Kabul and, as Silver would soon realise, it would completely change the way he operated. As we shall see it would force the Russians to remodel their Kabul operations drastically, the British would finally arrest Silver and this would result in the historic intelligence partnership between Silver and Peter Fleming.

While Silver was the main man for the Soviets in Kabul—indeed, the only spy they had in this part of the world—the Russians also had much regard for Uttam Chand. He was their point of contact with Silver; he provided a home for him, and, when Silver was away, he visited the Embassy with information on what was happening in both Kabul and India, some of which came from lorry drivers plying the Kabul–Peshawar route and stopping by his shop. And they knew the Germans also valued Uttam Chand too, Witzel having given him the same instructions in how to use cipher code as he had Silver. But in the classic way the Russians operated their spy rings while they drew Uttam Chand into their intelligence operation, they did not tell him everything. So, for instance, when in April 1942 Sasha came to interrogate Silver, Uttam Chand was in on only one of the meetings.

Uttam Chand also acted as a check on Silver. Though Silver professed his communist beliefs, Zaman and the Soviets, like Rasmuss, had no means of verifying his bona fides. The Comintern knew about the Kirti party and some of its leaders, but it was a still fringe party, not the official Indian Communist Party controlled by the British Communist Party, whose loyalty to Stalin and the Soviet Union could never be doubted. The Soviets just did not have the same sort of control over the Kirti and from their experience in Spain they knew how dangerous fringe parties could be to the Soviet cause. And here Uttam Chand was enormously useful. He could confirm to the Russians whether Silver was telling them everything that passed between him and the Germans—and now and then he warned them that Silver was not telling the truth. He was, for example, able to tell them that during Silver's October 1941 visit he had shown Rasmuss the Sainsra report without showing it to them, something they were considerably annoyed to hear. During Silver's four-month stay in Kabul from January to April 1942, Uttam Chand began to grow more suspicious that Silver was not always telling the truth, that much of his time with the Germans was spent helping the Faqir of Ipi—something he had not told the Russians. Uttam Chand went so far as to tell the Russians that, in his opinion, Silver's conduct was 'unsatisfactory'.[16]

However what the Russians did not know was that, as we have seen, the relationship between their two agents had begun to sour. And what the Russians also did not know was that the Afghan government had had their eyes on Uttam Chand and were getting ready to strike. On 25 May, 1942, nine days after Silver had departed for Peshawar, the Afghan government served an order on Uttam Chand to leave the country. The arrest was made at the request of the British, who had known all about Uttam Chand from Sodhi's confession, although when the Russians protested they pretended it had nothing to do with them. His property was searched, yielding some compromising items, sealed and confiscated. Uttam Chand was transported by the Afghan police to the border and deported. They knew the British would know what to do with him, and soon enough he was being interrogated by the frontier police and confessed everything.

This was obviously alarming news to both the Germans and the Russians, although their reactions were very different, the one showing naivety, the other incredible cleverness. On hearing the news Rasmuss and Witzel had rushed to Uttam Chand's shop and remonstrated with the Afghan police that Uttam Chand was their friend. When the Afghans brushed them aside and took Uttam Chand away they followed them back to the police station and tried to secure his release, all of which did a good job of revealing to the Afghans that Uttam Chand was connected to the Germans. Silver would later tell the British police that it was 'typical of Rasmuss and Witzel's heedlessness and overbearing confidence'.[17]

The Russians, meanwhile, watched the Germans make fools of themselves. Not only had they no interest in telling the Afghans that Uttam Chand was actually their man; they also decided that, as the British were their allies, had engineered the arrest and now had their man in custody, they would approach them to release him and, in exchange, they would offer up Silver to the British as a spy they could share. This was the only time in the war the Soviets made such an offer, and in the intelligence saga of the Second World War it remains unique.

Strictly speaking, just over a year later, in September 1943, there was another joint Anglo-Soviet intelligence operation, the 'KISS operation', in which the British used the transmitter of an Iranian sent back to Teheran by the Abwehr to feed the Germans misinformation on matters such as Soviet troop movements. But KISS was a phantom spy: now the Russians were offering a real-life agent who had been fooling the Germans and the Italians for over a year already and was ready to do much more. The way the Russians made their offer was also unique. In September 1941 the two countries had come to an arrangement whereby the NKVD and SOE were each allowed to station an intelligence mission in the other nation's capital. Now the Russians used this unique war-time link to tell the British about Silver.

On 27 June 1942, three weeks after the British had arrested Uttam Chand, the official assigned by the NKVD to liaise with the British, General Alexander Ossipov, met SOE's man in Moscow, George Hill. Ossipov opened the conversation by asserting that the nineteenth-century Great Game was officially over: 'As you know, Soviet Union has no interest, repeat no interest, in India'. He then went on to say:

> NKVD have information Germans and Italians directed efforts [in] Kabul against British interests in India. Information included names of principal agents, sub agents and documentary evidence of those engaged in subversive activities ... He is only aware that little time ago frank opinions were exchanged between British and Soviet ministers in Kabul. Suggested better results could be obtained from collaboration of our respective organisations in this field. If we agreed to exchange in principle NKVD will supply available information forthwith. Please reply urgently.[18]

In return the NKVD wanted information from the British about 'similar activities along Soviet ambush territory i.e. along Southern Siberian border'.[19] London interpreted the Southern Siberian border as meaning the far-eastern Chinese–Soviet border, about which, as London cabled back, 'the information at our disposal is scanty'. Curious about this unprecedented Soviet offer, London told Hill, 'We are making enquiries and will reply soonest.'

On 4 July Hill met Ossipov again and this is when the Russian gave details of Silver (G) and Uttam Chand (H) and what they were doing in Afghanistan (I):

> NKVD consider G and H to be highly reliable sympathisers who have been operating under NKVD orders to contact German and Italians at I.

Pretending to work against British India or Soviet Union on behalf of Axis. Fairly recently both given funds by German organisation and 19 pages of written operational instructions in English for activities against our and Russian interests. Instructions are held to be by NKVD as genuine and copy to be passed to us in the next few days. G is now somewhere in India and expected to return to I shortly. H is British subject at present under arrest at I. Reasons said to be (a) Failure to get his British passport renewed. (b) Trading in K without a licence. NKVD will welcome any assistance H can be given to recover liberty. NKVD suggest G and H should operate for us jointly, outwardly appearing to work for Axis, and should be allowed to have some success in order to get their would-be employers marked confidence.[20]

Hill was, of course, very keen to take up this offer but warned: 'Utmost secrecy essential and no, repeat no, contact should be made between British and Soviet organisations at I'.[21]

The IPI, while initially puzzled by the Russian offer saying, 'The Russians' appeal to the English isn't clear', soon came to the conclusion that, 'Uttam Chand's arrest influenced them. They aimed at setting him free'.[22] Interestingly at this stage the Russians believed Uttam Chand was still held in Kabul when in fact he was in a Peshawar jail. They were clearly working on the assumption that as the British had instigated this arrest they should now intervene with the Afghans to free their man. There were also other factors that explain the Russian decision to approach the British. With Sodhi also arrested they feared the British might also arrest Silver and destroy their precious direct link to the Abwehr. They were also worried what Silver under interrogation might reveal to the British. In the summer of 1942, with the British, having fallen out so spectacularly with the Congress Party and becoming increasingly panicky about their hold on India, the Soviets had reason to fear that depending on what Silver told them the British might divert more troops or supplies to India, which could have seriously affected the help they were giving the Russians. In this fight for survival the Russian dictator did not care that he was helping the British retain their colony: what mattered was not India's freedom but the Soviet Union's very existence.

The Soviet interest in the Sino-Soviet border was also genuine, as in July 1942 Stalin and the Soviet generals were in disagreement as to whether the Germans might link up with the Japanese, forcing the Russians to fight on two fronts. The previous winter, freedom from worry about a Japanese attack on their eastern front had enabled the Soviets to stop Hitler's army at the gates of Moscow by bringing reinforcements from Siberia. But a section of the Japanese army, known as the Strike North faction, had long been insisting on fighting the Soviet Union. With Japan having conquered Burma and destroyed all the European colonial powers in south Asia, and with Hitler's army once again on the march in Russia, would they listen again to their 'Strike North' generals and use their Chinese bases to invade Russia? Yet having received such an unprecedented offer from the Soviets, the British took months to respond. There is no simple explanation as to why the British took so long to act. And while the British pondered Silver swung into action in Peshawar.

He did not know what Uttam Chand would tell the British but concluded that like Sodhi he would reveal all and decided he could not linger in Peshawar, but would be safer in Kabul. He quickly sent a message to Rasmuss through a courier and then left for the Afghan capital on 16 August 1942, taking two other colleagues with him. Having by now made the route to Kabul almost his own he had no reason to think the journey would be different, but this time he did encounter a problem at the border checkpoint. On his previous six crossings the guards had been asleep; now there was a border guard who was wide awake with the rank of Tehsildar, commander. It could have been tricky but, noticing the Tehsildar had a revolver, Silver asked him what cartridges he used. The Tehsildar confessed he was finding it very difficult to get any cartridges—could Silver perhaps help him get some in Kabul, for which he would be prepared to pay immediately? Silver assured him that on his return from Kabul he would bring cartridges for the Tehsildar, and then, with the show of a commander in charge of his troops, turned to one of his companions and said, 'Make sure you get these cartridges and deliver them to Tehsildar Sahib [the term of respect used for white men] on your return journey.' The result was that the officer was satisfied with their 'bona fides' and allowed Silver and his companions to proceed.[23]

Arriving in the Afghan capital at about 3 a.m. on the morning of 26 August, and without Uttam Chand's shop to use as a post box, Silver was forced to fall back on his original method of wandering round the bazaars until he chanced on two Russians. This took two days which explains why in their memo on Silver's travel the Russians gave the date of Silver's arrival as 28 August. At a subsequent meeting Silver showed the Soviets the further report he had brought back from India for the Axis, a copy of which the British found among his papers when they finally arrested him.

On Silver's January visit Zaman had been horrified by the detail of the military information: now the Russian said that it should show Indian troops in greater numbers to impress the Axis with the strength of Indian defences. They also wanted higher figures shown for aircraft, tanks and mechanised equipment, to convince the Axis that, whatever may have been the case when Burma and Malaya had fallen earlier in the year, India was a different proposition. Silver altered his figures accordingly.

But Silver confessed that it was impossible to keep generating such fiction. The political side of his reports was simple—he could easily invent such details—but to go on providing the Germans with convincing military information, given that he knew nothing of military matters, was very difficult, and he suggested the Russians should ask the British authorities to furnish him with the required military information so his contact with Axis could continue without risk. In effect Silver was requesting the Russians to turn him over to the British. Zaman did not let on that they had already told Hill about him, merely saying that they had been considering this.

The Silver-Russian meetings took some time, and it was a week before Silver was ready to meet the Germans. For most people this would have been tricky, for in Uttam Chand's absence his contact with the Germans had to be with Subhan's wife. On his previous visit to Kabul Silver had incriminated her husband leading to the Afghans arresting him, shortly before they had arrested Uttam Chand. However, by now, he was such a practised dissembler that when he saw her he feigned surprised that Subhan had been arrested and made all the right sympathetic noises. And he betrayed no reaction when the German woman threatened reprisals on the Afghans, telling Silver that within six months German troops would be in Kabul, 'And then we will see how they can escape from the sins they have committed against the Germans by helping the British and the Russians here.'[24] The poor lady, having no idea who Silver really was, readily passed on his message to Rasmuss that he was coming, and she promised to inform the German that he had arrived. The next evening, 24 August 1942, Silver handed over his report to Rasmuss and Witzel.

Rasmuss confessed he had tried to get Uttam Chand freed but failed, and suspected the British were behind his arrest. Silver could see that Rasmuss was very nervous and the German revealed that, along with Subhan, an Uzbek spying for the Germans had also been arrested and he feared Silver might be in danger. 'Because of serious developments in the city,' he told Silver, 'we would like to keep you here [in the Legation] safe for some days, though it would be somewhat troublesome for you.'[25]

Silver was appalled. He would be confined to a room in the Legation and, to make sure he was not noticed by the Afghan staff, food would have to be brought to him secretly. But what, asked Silver, would happen if the staff heard a noise from his room, like a cough? Surely they would grow suspicious, keep a watch on the room and notice him while he left the room to go to the bathroom? Nevertheless, Silver stayed there for the next three days while they cross-examined him on his report. It was then sent by wireless to Berlin. During his concealment in the German Legation Silver heard Quaroni arrive one day and confess to Rasmuss that contact with Rahmat Khan [Silver] had broken down. Quaroni, of course, did not pass on that Silver was working for the Russians. The result was that after Quaroni had departed Rasmuss came to Silver's room and the two men had a good laugh at the expense of the pompous Italian. Quaroni may have jump-started his spying career, and indeed saved it by not revealing all to Rasmuss, but by the time Silver was interrogated by the British he could recount the story with relish as evidence of Axis stupidity.

It was obvious that Silver could not hole up for long at the Legation. Rasmuss agreed he should find his own accommodation, with the Germans readily paying for it. Silver rented a flat in Baber on the outskirts of Kabul and promptly contacted the Russians. Such was his confidence in his own ability that he had no fears Rasmuss would shadow him, reasoning that he knew all the Germans very well and would spot them before they spotted him.

Delighted as the Russians were to hear that his fictitious doctored report had been well received by the Germans, they wanted more. The message from Moscow was that, with the approach of autumn, Axis war plans would change. The previous month Germany had launched its attack on Stalingrad, to the considerable surprise of Stalin, who had told his generals that in 1942 Hitler would again target Moscow. So what were the Germans' plans? Where were they heading? Silver must try and probe Rasmuss and Witzel and stay in Kabul as long as he could.

Through September 1942, therefore, staying in a flat paid for by the Germans, Silver passed on to the Russians everything the Germans told him. We do not have any details of what they were as Russian records on this subject have not been opened, but they must have been useful as the Russians kept asking him to go back and see Rasmuss and Witzel.

His self-taught spying skills had grown so much that he told Rasmuss he was sending a tribal man back to India and asked Rasmuss if there was any specific information he wanted. There was, of course, no such man, but the deluded German by now had such faith in Silver that he never asked Silver who this tribal messenger was or asked to see him. It was only after more than two weeks of German hospitality in Kabul, Silver was finally asked to do some work. A messenger had come from Waziristan with four letters from the Faqir of Ipi. With Subhan in jail the Germans had lost their translator. Could Silver, Rasmuss asked, help out? Three of them were in Urdu, one Pashtu, and all badly written. Two were addressed to Rashid Ali Gallani and the Grand Mufti of Jerusalem, both then in Berlin, with the Faqir declaring:

> I am at present maintaining friendly relations with the German government and I am prepared to accept their assistance in my fight against England. I am extremely glad that you are in touch with them and may God keep you. If I receive the necessary help I shall be able to fight against England for seven years.[26]

The important letter in Urdu was addressed to Rasmuss, acknowledging the receipt of 7,500 gold sovereigns and 50,000 Afghani rupees, one German automatic rifle, five revolvers and one wireless transmitter with generator.

Ipi was getting very short of ammunition and wanted more money and ammunition dropped by plane at night. Ipi went on to tell Rasmuss:

> At the present time the English are recruiting for the Army and it is impossible for me to stop this as there seems to be desire to serve them amongst the poor. If you send me sufficient money, I could interfere with this recruiting. The English have already called up the first drafts of 2,000 Mohmands and a small number of Afridis. I have sent my agents to Baluchistan and Tirah (Afridi districts) for the purposes of organising against the English.[27]

The Pushtu letter gave an account of the Faqir's latest fight with the British in Datta Khel. The Faqir's men had surrounded the fort there, foiling several British attempts to break out and killing or capturing 150 men. In one attack 22 British lorries were routed, some of the occupants killed or captured. Seven escort tanks and three planes were also destroyed. But with the help of 90 tanks and reinforcing aircraft the British managed to get 3,000 soldiers and 10,000 scouts into the fort, although it was still surrounded. The Faqir then gave estimates of the strength of the British forces employed on the Afghan–Indian border to deal with the fighting: Peshawar, 4 Brigades; Bani 16,000 scouts and 20,000 troops; Vane 1 Brigade and 1,000 scouts; Kazmuck 1 division; Kohat 20,000 men; Khyber 1 division; Thal 2 Brigades.[28]

Fomenting more trouble in the tribal areas excited Berlin, and Witzel wanted Silver to accompany him to the tribal areas. As Silver later told the British: '[I] succeeded with some difficulty in persuading him against this, by saying the tribesmen would kill any European and that if he accompanied them he would be exposed and unable to do his work'.[29] But Witzel would not give up, and started coming up with increasingly bizarre ideas of how to get to the Faqir, every one of which Silver shot down.

Witzel's first suggestion was that one night they would get on horses and ride along the mountain tracks to the Faqir. Silver rebuffed this by saying that if the Afghans discovered the absence of Witzel and Zugenbühler they would institute a search and arrest them. How about going at night on foot along the mountain tracks, Witzel responded. Silver's reply was that Zugenbühler was not physically capable of such a journey. Witzel's final plan was the most bizarre: that the two Germans would hide in Silver's flat, during which time they would grow beards, dress as natives, and then leave Kabul. Silver rejected this by saying that in event of failure he ran the risk of being arrested by the Afghan government.[30] Ridiculous as Witzel was, it is easy to understand why he was so keen. As Rasmuss had told Silver, the Germans had sent a portable wireless transmitter to the Faqir, but he clearly lacked anyone who could operate it.

Several days later Rasmuss had more letters for Silver to translate. One was from Quaroni to the Faqir, another from the Germans. The letters had already been translated from Italian and German to English, the only European language Silver knew. He now had to translate both of them into Dari, the only language the Faqir knew. Quaroni admitted arms could not be supplied to the Faqir at present, and 'this situation will continue until we can establish air or other communications with you'. Until then his advice to the Faqir was to be less active and concentrate on trying to unite the tribes under his leadership:

You must preserve your forces until the moment comes for us to give you real assistance. That will not be until we can advance our front, and if you dissipate your strength before this you will be unable to assist your Afghan friends. It is most essential for you to undertake large-scale operations so that when the time arrives a united attack can be made on the British, who, with God's help, will be routed.

Rasmuss's letter to the Faqir admitted Germans could not help until Hitler's armies 'captured the Caucasus', but offered hope on airlifts:

Clearly at first, aircraft will not land, but will only drop certain things and ammunition by parachute. Already it is time to find a suitable place for this, far from high mountains essentially level, two and a half miles in length and one mile in breadth. Should you succeed in finding level space that will be even better as aircraft later on will be able to land. We will let you know when your aircraft will arrive. You must arrange following on this landing ground: bonfires per side on each border along length of selected ground. By day they must give off the smoke, by night burn brightly without smoke. In addition there must be a bonfire marking each corner of ground. Furthermore, the halfway line of ground must be marked with two bonfires placed opposite each other. As a preliminary you should send a map of district when landing ground has been selected.

And while Rasmuss was grateful to the Faqir for information about British troops he wanted not only numbers 'but also name of military units. The report should appear as follows: 10th Sikh Regiment 2 Battalions 11/402 Gurkhas are now at Razmuk'. He also wanted to know how many 'first-rate soldiers' the Faqir needed and how much he would have to pay each soldier, the ammunition he considered essential and what this would cost. Instructing a wireless operator, as the Faqir had requested, was not a problem, but he asked the Faqir, 'Have you a man with a little experience in this matter and can you send him to us?' The letter concluded by saying the Germans were sending with the letter 100,000 Afghanis and £300 in gold by special messenger.

Silver immediately showed all the letters to the Russians, who photographed them. They were particularly keen on the Faqir's letters and Silver, working in the flat the Germans had paid for, translated them into English for the Russians before handing back the originals to Rasmuss. The only information he could not give the Russians was who had brought the Faqir's letters from Waziristan and who would take back the Italian and German responses.

In later conversations with the Germans Silver was told to prepare a landing place in the tribal territory, where a small number of German parachutists could be dropped by night, an order reinforced by a telegram from Berlin in which Bose emphasised its necessity. Witzel estimated that the Germans would need to send a group of seven including a doctor, a W/T engineer and electrician, a mechanic, a topographic specialist, military instructor, W/T telegraphist and photographer. They should be equipped with arms, ammunition, money, topographic sets, maps, instruments and medical stores, disguises and make-up. Members of the field party must be selected with a view to their bearing a resemblance to local inhabitants. Landing grounds must be marked by bonfire. Silver was asked to report on the preparations for the reception of the parachutists, and their subsequent concealment in safe places, perhaps a house in tribal territory. Yes, he replied, such arrangements could be made, but it would be impossible to keep the presence of Europeans secret in tribal territory, and the British authorities would soon come to hear of it. But he did tell the Germans that a possible site for an airfield would be the flat land in Banjaur between the inhabited parts of Bandagal and Djar, or between Khora and Ramakaya, a district he personally knew well.

From Bose came special orders that the Forward Bloc must co-operate with the Faqir of Ipi and other tribal leaders, with Bose's followers sent out to the tribal areas to promise aid, defence from attack, and tribal freedom on independence—Bose also wanted feedback on which tribes would be ready to fight the British. Propaganda stressing the material gains of an Axis victory was necessary. It was also most important to establish immediate contact with the Japanese via Rangoon. Bose was, particularly, keen to know what contacts had been sent to Ceylon, and what the Forward Bloc was doing there. His message added that two Indian Legions had been formed in Berlin from Indian prisoners of war and other internees, and that he himself had been assisting in instructing them.

Bose was keen too for Silver to monitor the radio broadcasts he was making from Berlin, one in the name of Congress, another in the name of the Muslim League, both pretending to be from India. He further told Silver that from 10 October 1942 he would broadcast signals for commencing sabotage, as specified in the booklets Witzel had already given Silver. His other task for Silver was to check on Germans still in India who had escaped arrest and try use them against the English authorities.

By the middle of September Berlin had sent Rasmuss a questionnaire for Silver. It ran to two pages and listed 27 points. They provide a fascinating picture of what the Germans were looking for, how much they relied on Silver, and how Silver would need more help to satisfy them than Sainsra could provide:

(1) Numbers, designations, armaments also dispositions of English military units;

(2) Numbers, designations, armaments also dispositions of garrisons of [the] government of India troops [the troops in provinces and states ruled by the Princes];

(3) Information about the arrival [and] despatch of troops from India, point of assembly, actual numbers and whence they come;

(4) Designations and names of regiments, designations and disposition of divisions into which these regiments are grouped;

(5) Information [about] transfer of goods to India from Iraq and Syria and Iran;

(6) Designation, armaments race [note: word 'race' not clear from Russian text, possibly 'negro' and 'white'] and disposition in India of American troops which have arrived there, where they are stationed and numbers of [their] garrisons;

(7) Number, armament, designation and composition of garrisons and dispositions of Indian army;

(8) Political and military position in Sinkiang;

(9) Are there any Indian divisions whose staffs consist entirely of Indian units?

(10) Designations of newly-created Indian units;

(11) What Indian divisions consist of English and Indian units?

(12) Number of artillery regiment in any one Indian infantry division;

(13) Are there any special divisions [created] among [the arriving] English forces [when] they join Indian divisions?

(14) General number of Indians and English troops in the North West Frontier Province; size of each detachment;

(15) To check whether there is any semblance of truth that at the beginning of August there arrived in Calcutta, a powerful military force, perhaps a motor school division;

(16) What was the selection board of the American Economic and Technical Mission now in India under Dr Grady? Does [the] Mission intend to construct assembly shops for armoured vehicles and lorries? If so, give production capacity;

(17) Where are the Indian shipbuilding and dockyards situated?

(18) What is the number of [men in a] mountain artillery regiment [when an] Indian infantry division [is established].

(19) Have battalions of Indian Territorial Army, [which have been] retained, agreed to have Indian Field Brigade R.A. merged with [the] Regular Army? If battalions have been merged find out their numbers?

(20) It is well known that there are units of mountain artillery consisting of Indians. Are there also artillery units composed of Indians?

(21) What is [the] proportionate number of British and Indian officers? How are they classified [by] rank?

(22) In event of showing the number and name of military formations, it is essential to point out the number of battalions;

(23) What quantity and what type of war material is being produced by the factories of [the] Eastern Supply Board? What is [the] production capacity (actual and potential) of railway workshops? Is it possible to build armoured fighting vehicles or only assemble them?

(24) Report position of all factories known to you to be engaged on war work;

(25) Is aluminium, formerly imported, being manufactured at Aluminium Rolling Mill, built by America and where is the factory situated?

(26) Is there confirmation of the fact that in Bangalore at the end of 1941, work began on an aircraft factory managed by India Air Grassi Co? What [is its] capacity? Does this factory only manufacture fuselage or engines as well?

(27) [Has] the production programme for steel increased at Tata Works? Ascertain whether they produce guns, machine guns and automatic weapons. By how much has production of war material increased in relation to total production?[31]

With Silver passing this on to the Russians immediately the NKVD in Kabul was reading this German questionnaire within hours of Berlin sending it to Rasmuss and Witzel.

The Germans also told Silver, as he would later inform the British, that there must be an intensified and year-round programme of damaging railway lines and other communications under the cover of the Congress movement. Berlin also wanted to know what the immediate reactions in India would be to Rommel's successful capture of Egypt. Was the Quetta–Kandahar–Tarmiz railway open to military transport? What supplies were being sent from India to Russia along the Quetta–Zahidan railway? Sabotage of this rail link was a matter of great importance, said the Germans, especially the tunnels. However, this was not in the detailed eight-page memorandum of information from Kabul that the NKVD gave to Hill in Moscow.

In the nearly two months Silver spent in Kabul he had a chance to explore how the Abwehr regarded the progress of the war, and was interested to hear that, while the Germans spoke glowingly about their advance towards their main objective, Stalingrad, they expected stiff resistance. Witzel even declared that they did not intend to occupy all of Russia, rather their objective was to defeat the Soviets in the south, then enter Iran and Iraq and join up with their forces in the Middle East and, 'if they succeeded in achieving this target there was no power in the world to stop them from achieving their final mission'.[32] And Witzel was confident the Germans would reach the Indian border, a confidence Rasmuss shared.

During one of their many meetings Rasmuss had come to the flat with cuttings from Indian-language newspapers he said he had been given by Najibullah, the Afghan Foreign Minister. Despite the British arresting Gandhi and the entire leadership of the Congress within hours of Gandhi giving the call for the British to Quit India, the Raj had not nipped in the bud what Silver would accurately describe to Rasmuss as 'a real mass upsurge', and a remarkable testimony to the strength of Indian nationalist feeling. Leaders no-one had heard of before had emerged to direct a major rebellion against colonial rule.

Silver now deftly guided Rasmuss on the radio propaganda the Germans were planning. Rasmuss had suggested that, with Jinnah's Muslim League collaborating with the British, the Azad Hind, Free India, radio broadcasts from Berlin should attack Jinnah. Silver, well aware that the communists were opposed to Quit India and would soon support the creation of Pakistan, counselled caution. Rasmuss then suggested systematic sabotage of the big industrial plants; Silver countered that:

> As we are heading towards the independence of our country it will be harmful to destroy industries which are likely to help build our national economy.

Realising he might have overstepped the mark, he suggested that Rasmuss refer back to Berlin and Bose 'without mentioning my opinion on this'.

By August 1942 the British were faced with their worst crisis since the 1857 Revolt. 318 police stations had been burnt, 945 post offices raided and 59 trains derailed. It required all the armed might of the British in India, fifty seven and a half infantry battalions and 35,000 men, to crush it—although, as Linlithgow wrote to Churchill, for reasons of military security the gravity of the situation was being concealed. The Whipping Act, first passed in 1933, was reintroduced, with a British diplomat in Washington telling the Office of War Information that:

> ... it is felt in London that whipping is a very much less severe punishment than shooting ... already there has been some major interference with the railway lines round Patna ... it may be necessary to resort to the most drastic measures to prevent the interference of military communications, including the machine gunning of saboteurs from the air.[33]

There are no estimates of how many were whipped; it was discussed by the War Cabinet and, when questioned about in the Commons, Amery justified it by saying that whipping in India was 'administered by a light rattan cane and not by the "cat"'.

By the time the rebellion was put down over 66,000 people had been arrested. In 538 instances the troops had to open fire, on six occasions rebel territories were bombed from the air, Tiger Moths were used to keep communications open, and at one stage Bihar was cut off from Bengal and Assam. By November 1942, 1,028 people had been killed and 3,215 injured. Despite this, the situation remained so grave that in March 1943, in the secret note sent by Major General Rob Lockhart, which we have already quoted, he said: 'For the duration of the war, and probably for some time after, India must be considered as an occupied and hostile country'.[34]

How, asked Rasmuss, could the Germans help to stop the British using the army to suppress the Quit-India movement? Silver's response was interesting:

> I suppose you do not want the army which is engaged in suppressing the quit-India movement should instead go to fight against your armies somewhere in the Middle East?[35]

In his autobiography Silver adds 'this was, of course in a lighter vein', although whether he said it with a smile to the Germans is debatable. Writing thirty years after Indian Independence, where the Quit-India movement is seen as the one that brought India freedom, he clearly had to qualify his remark.

Rasmuss had told Silver he must be in the tribal territories by 2 October 1942 but, having no intention of going, he played for time, and meanwhile discussed with the Russians what he should do. They had, of course, no interest in him being marooned in the tribal areas: they needed him to shuttle between Kabul and India and carry on deceiving the Germans. Silver came up with a clever ruse. He would tell Rasmuss that since they had requested such a great deal of information on India—no fewer than 27 points in their memorandum—he could only pass through the tribal areas on his way back to India, not linger there for any length of time. Rasmuss agreed.

The Soviets had instructions for Silver as well. These were to contact the Communist Party on his return to India. Its leaders in Bombay were already in touch with the British GHQ and the Russians had a message they wanted Silver to give to Joshi. They wanted the CPI to arrange for two reliable contacts to be sent to Burma to play the same double game with the Japanese that Silver had successfully been doing with the Germans. These agents were to use the password 'Silver Moon'—the password, of course, that Bose had given Silver for the two men he wanted sent to Burma. Matters became complicated when Rasmuss told him that Berlin had changed the password to 'Rising Moon'. Silver's solution was to invent another lie. He told Rasmuss the old password had already been given to the two men, who were now in Burma. Of course no such men had been sent, but such was his hold over Rasmuss that it was seen by the German as just the sort of thing a shrewd agent would say. And at Rasmuss's insistence Berlin agreed that the old password, 'Silver Moon' should be retained.[36]

Silver was by now getting ready to leave Kabul. However before that he had one task to perform: check with the Russians regarding his status with the British. The ruthless operative Silver had become would not have shed many tears for Sodhi, Uttam Chand and Abad Khan, all of whom had been arrested, Abad being arrested in Peshawar on 1 October and, like Sodhi and Uttam Chand, telling all to the British. [Silver learnt of his arrest only on his return to India]. These three had played a huge part in making Silver the spy he now was. All three were now in jail would, probably, remain there for the rest of the war (as would prove to be the case) but all that mattered to Silver was that he should not suffer the same fate. He had every reason to fear that as he crossed back into India the police well briefed on him would be waiting. So, just before leaving Kabul on 25 October 1942, he had one final meeting with the Soviets. It was here that the Soviets told Silver his position had been discussed with the British authorities in Moscow and gave him specific instructions about what he should do. If he was arrested on his return to India, 'he should at once explain matters to a British officer and ask that General Headquarters Delhi be informed of his arrest but that it should otherwise be kept strictly secret'.[37]

The emphasis on a British officer was significant. The Russians knew that the arrest would be made by the Indians who worked for the British, and in the febrile climate of India Silver telling the truth to an Indian policeman could be dangerous, as there was no guarantee some had not switched their allegiance to the Quit-India movement.

The assurance from the Soviets meant so much that Silver left Kabul in a style not matched by his previous six visits. Having purchased two horses, one of them for his companion Murtaza, and loaded on his luggage, he rode out of Kabul more like one of the heroes in the Hindi films he loved, a man who had come to a city, got what he wanted and was returning to his homeland content.

He might have felt less relaxed had he known that the Russians had not been completely honest with him. The arrangement with the British was not quite the done deal they had implied. Although it was now four months since the Soviets had approached the British with their remarkable offer, the British had still not agreed to the three Russian conditions: release Uttam Chand, provide information on the Southern Siberian border, and agree that collaboration over Silver would be through the British-Soviet intelligence links in Moscow. This last Soviet condition, on which the Russians were quite inflexible, would prove a major headache for the British and have a big impact on Silver. We need to look at the extraordinary wartime NKVD–SOE partnership to understand why.

Silver's Moscow Centre

Silver's spying career brought him into contact with a whole cast of characters far removed from the world in which he had grown up in Ghalla Dher. Had he met the Englishman who acted as his contact with the Russians in Moscow, however, Silver would have accepted that, despite the differences between their two worlds, they had much in common. That this unlikely Englishman featured in the Silver story adds another twist, and shows how complex this spy saga was.

This was the only time when the NKVD, the Soviet foreign intelligence, shared information provided by a spy with a foreign government. Britain's Special Operations Executive allowed the Soviet 'devils' to control the spy and drive this part of the amazing alliance.

The NKVD could not have been more different to the SOE. The Russian name stood for People's Commissariat for Interior Affairs, its officials had blue stripes on their uniforms and, as O'Sullivan says, 'was an institution unlike any other in the twentieth century'.[1] Created by Lenin in 1917 as the Cheka, it had been renamed GPU and then OGPU, which Stalin in the 30s took personal control of, becoming the unofficial Commissar. It was seen as the 'sword and shield' of the party to report and deal with anyone seen as party enemy, with Stalin describing the People's Commissar Lavrenti Beria as 'our Himmler'. The SOE was the reaction of a democratic state—at least at home—to a Europe now under the Nazi jackboot.

Well before the war the British had already had well-established, highly regarded intelligence outfits, such as the Secret Intelligence Service (SIS) and the Security Service MI5. The SOE was set up by Hugh Dalton, the Labour politician, who felt that, with Europe enslaved by Hitler, there was a strong need for organised subversive activities—political subversion and economic sabotage without resorting to open warfare. Such operations were 'too serious to be left to soldiers'. Dalton's vision had contradictions. 'What is needed, he said, 'is a new organisation to co-ordinate, inspire, control and assist the nationals of the oppressed countries who must themselves be the direct participants'. He did not, however, see India or the colonies as 'oppressed'.[2] Dalton may not have shared Churchill's vision of the Empire, but he did not believe in giving Indians freedom, and would suggest that the answer to the Congress demand for independence was to 'organise, indirectly and discreetly, some alternative political party to the Congress, and prevent the latter from winning so many elections'.[3] He wanted to recruit British working-class trade unionists and socialists but, as Philip Knightley says, in practice:

> The top ranks of the SOE were quickly filled by public school–Oxbridge men and women, … Stockbrokers, businessmen, Lloyds underwriters and merchant bankers made up the bulk of SOE's recruits [The British also used American journalists to spread propaganda, particularly to counter calls to set India free]. All were conservative by birth and upbringing … [resistance groups in Europe] regarded SOE as a secret army of imperialism and the average SOE officer as a would-be Lawrence of Arabia, 'the perfidious, arrogant champion of an Empire'… They had been brought up on the assumption that the British were a superior race, natural owners of an Empire on which the sun never set. They took it for granted that one Englishman was worth five Germans, 10 Italians, and an incalculable number of lesser breeds.[4]

George Alexander 'Pop' Hill, SOE's man in Moscow, fitted this description to a 'T'. Hill had much in common with Silver, and in some ways his life story remains an even greater mystery, with several blanks that just cannot be filled. There is doubt about when and where he was born: in 1892 in Estonia, or in 1893 in London. We know more about Silver's family and upbringing than Hill's. He was said to have come from a family of freemasons, been in Russia as a child, and had a Russian nanny hired by his father, who did business in Persia and Russia; but nobody knows for sure. Like Silver, Hill wrote his memoirs. Two books dealt with his experiences during the First World War and the inter-war years, but a memoir of his life in the Soviet Union during the Second World War was never published, and is lodged in the Hoover Institution Library and Archives at Stanford University. One thing it has in common with Silver's memoir is that it did not disclose the entire truth: Hill does not go into the operations in which he was involved. Silver does not even get a mention. The theory that there may still be secrets about Hill's life gains credence from the fact that his personnel file, which by now should have formed part of the British Archives in Kew, remains closed. Given how much wartime material the British have released, and that much of what Hill did after moving to Moscow is fairly well known, this is surprising.[5]

Hill, wounded at Ypres, became part of the British Intelligence Service in 1917. He worked in Russia, along with British spies such as Sydney Reilly, Paul Dukes and Somerset Maugham. He was a member of the Bruce Lockhart British mission to Russia to fight the Bolsheviks and impressed Lockhart, who described him as 'beyond suspicion. Hill was bold and brave'.[6] Hill later claimed that, while he rescued the Romanian crown jewels from the control of the communists, he also assisted Trotsky in setting up the Red Air Force, which helped the communists to defeat White Russians, whose generals he was assisting in their fight with the reds. All this prompted one Hill biographer, Martin Kitchen, to dismiss Hill's memoirs as heavily 'embroidered' and written more in the style of John Buchan; spying as a wonderful adventure rather than the real nitty-gritty. In 1918 the Cheka issued a warrant for his arrest.[7] The Russians killed all 14 of Hill's agents, but he survived and was awarded the Distinguished Service Order.

Between the wars Hill worked for Royal Dutch Shell and the Globe Theatre but, if some of his biographers are to be believed, he was sacked by the SIS when he threatened to reveal secrets and, desperately short of money, sold British secrets to German intelligence. Life was difficult.

As the Nazis advanced into Prague in April, 1939 the SIS turned to Hill. It seems Churchill persuaded the SIS to help him out as he had been Churchill's 'unofficial adviser' when Churchill was urging the White Russians to fight the Bolsheviks. Clearly the British knew nothing of Hill's alleged work for the Germans, as he was brought back into intelligence work as if he had never been away. He instructed Kim Philby in intelligence work; in his memoir, written after he had finally defected to the Soviet Union, Philby called him 'Jolly' George Hill.[8]

Hill was deemed 'perfectly capable' of maintaining 'confident relations' with the Soviets.[9] The Soviets knew what he had done in 1917, read his book and valued his technical knowledge. Philby endorsed him, and Philby's defection in 1963 raised questions as to whether Hill was a double agent.

Despite objections by some in the SOE, in September 1941 Hill arrived in Moscow, having been made Lieutenant-Colonel, to be its liaison officer with the NKVD. Officially it was known as the British Liaison Mission to the Russian Defence Department. M. R. D. Foot, in his history of the SOE, was to write that Hill was 'an odd choice' and that he 'seems to have been quietly nobbled by the NKVD; he gave them, and they gave him, no trouble'.[10] If Hill was a Soviet spy he certainly showed no love for Russia or communism in his memoirs.

With the British penchant for fancy nicknames, the Moscow mission was called SAM, with the NKVD given the nickname YMCA. Hill, occasionally angered by the Russians, and aware he was being closely monitored, referred to those who watched him as his YMCA boys. He was not impressed, either, with the people SIS had sent to Moscow. Whether the Russians considered Hill one of their own or just a good-time guy who saw spying as a bit of fun, they certainly treated him well. He was given good living quarters in wartime Moscow and, despite the privation, had the best food and drink available. Hill lived in what had been the apartment of the Italian military attaché and had a full complement of servants. One of them reported back to her Soviet masters on what Hill was up to.

These reports would have been full of Hill's parties, for he frequently used his apartment to entertain. Drink flowed freely, and the Soviets suspected that Hill made people drunk to get information from them. They also noted that he liked Russian people and wanted post-war collaboration between Britain and the Soviet Union.

Unlike Hill's NKVD counterpart in London, Ivan Andreyevich Chichaev, who took his wife to London to work as his secretary, Hill had left Dorothy, his third wife, at home. The NKVD quickly sensed that would leave Hill open to seduction. It was standard NKVD policy to use selected women who were well trained linguists to mix with foreign officials and report back to them. In foreign intelligence circles they were called 'pigeons'; Hill's pigeon was a 40-year-old, Luba Alexeevna Polik, manager of the Hotel National overlooking the Kremlin.

The contrast between SOE and NKVD was vividly brought out in the man to whom NKVD assigned the Silver operation. He was Gaik Badalovich Ovakimyan, a chemical engineer who had been a Soviet intelligence official for a long time and was known to the British by another name, General Alexander Ossipov. Before he returned to Moscow and took charge of the Silver operation his remit had been extraordinary. He had gathered a lot of technological information, supervised the assassination of Trotsky that Stalin had ordered, and as his supervisors were liquidated he was awarded a medal which denoted he was an 'honoured chekist [intelligence official]'. The FBI, who called him the 'wily Armenian', arrested him in New York where, from 1933, under the cover of working as an engineer for a Soviet trade mission, he ran a huge spying operation. By April 1941 he had 221 agents, while at the same time coping with several attempts by officials in Moscow, who suspected his allegiance, to recall him. This would have certainly meant the Gulag. As for many in the Soviet Union, the Nazi invasion changed his life, and Stalin was said to have personally intervened with Roosevelt to secure his release and bring him back to Moscow. There, instead of facing execution, he was, in the autumn of 1941, given the tile of 'Colonel Ossipov' and the job of liaising with the SOE mission in Moscow. In 1943 he also acted as liaison to OSS.[11]

Hill developed quite an intimate relationship with Ossipov, who tried to woo Hill to work for the Soviets. The two became such good friends that the Russian took the Englishman to a special NKVD tailor for a fitted fur coat.

You get some idea of how much Hill liked Colonel Ossipov when you read his description of the Russian:

> ... about forty, of stocky build, strong-limbed, and of pleasant countenance, quite well dressed. He speaks excellent English, fair German and no French. Very quick on the uptake.[12]

But he did occasionally get irritated with Ossipov's behaviour:

> A queer devil that. Leaves me stewing for ages, then telephones at 4 a.m. and enquires if I'd like to go down to the front.

But Hill, unlike the head of the US Military Mission to Moscow, was not frightened by Ossipov who, on meeting the Russian, thought, 'one could easily picture him as a boon companion of Boris Karloff'.[13]

As Hill did not mention Silver in his memoirs, we know nothing about how he and Ossipov liaised over Silver. All we can be certain about is that Ossipov was the only NKVD man who handled Silver, as Hill rarely dealt with any other Soviet official. And it is indicative of how highly the Russians valued their Indian agent that, apart from Silver, Ossipov's other major war concern was to head up Enormoz, the ambitious Soviet spying operation that discovered the Americans were making the atom bomb.

Hill's praise of Russians did make the British in London feel he had 'gone native', and there was talk of recalling him. But he had a good relationship with the British ambassador, Clark Kerr, and this meant he stayed. Guy Liddell suggested in his diaries that one reason for Kerr's fondness for Hill could have been that the two men had some sort of sexual relationship:

> There are rather unpleasant rumours about the reasons for this association. It is thought that Hill may be rendering certain services which, if known to the Soviet authorities, would place the ambassador in an extremely embarrassing position. This may be all idle gossip, but there is no doubt that Hill sees a great many papers in Moscow.[14]

While we will never know what Hill's relationship with Kerr was, we do know that the main problem with the Silver operation was that the Soviets wanted more than the British were willing to give them, such as information on the Siberian–Chinese frontier. The British claimed they did not have any such information, as it was outside their sphere of influence. The Russians refused to believe that, and Hill was constantly caught between trying to keep up with the Russians, aware of how much Silver meant, and trying to convince London to be more co-operative. While he was in Moscow, Hill had sleepless nights about how London were denying the release of information to the Soviets. He wrote to London:

> We have disappointed them particularly in our ability to respond in exchanging information ... our action regarding [Uttam Chand] and long delays in replies from India.

On 28 November, 1942, six months after Ossipov had told him about Silver, Hill wrote to London that he 'had a nightmare in which a jealous young Indian policeman covered himself in glory by apprehending Bhagat Ram'.[15] As it happens, the very next day in Lahore a whole posse of Punjab police officers called on Silver, and his life in India changed dramatically.

Britain's Man

Russia's promise to warn the British who Silver was should have made his return from Afghanistan a carefree one—surely now he would not see the inside of a British jail again? Nevertheless, he claims he crossed the border into Peshawar taking his usual precautions: wearing disguises, travelling sometimes on a bus, sometimes on a tonga. But he did visit his brother Jamnadas, who as a member of the banned Congress party was expecting to be arrested any day, and Jamnadas even escorted his brother back to his village.

The boost the Russians had given him was best displayed when he got to Lahore and checked in at the Terminus Hotel, then one of the best in the city, taking care nevertheless to sign the register as Harbans Lal, the alias he had often used in India. There, following meetings with Sainsra at the Nawakot house, he spent some days reading three months' copies of the *Tribune*, an English-language paper Sainsra had collected for him, to bring him up to date with the latest political developments. On 11 November, as per Russian instructions, he left for Bombay to see the Communist Party hierarchy. Despite the ban on the communists being lifted Silver was still worried the office might be under surveillance, and hung outside it hoping to catch P. C. Joshi. But after four futile days standing by the kerbside, having given up on the idea of meeting Joshi, he returned to Lahore on 23 November 1942 to help Sainsra concoct another fictitious report on political and military matters for Rasmuss and Witzel.

It was then, at the house in Nawakot, the British finally came calling. The Punjab CID arrested both Silver and Sainsra, unearthing during the raid the various documents and codes Rasmuss and Witzel had given him, including one of the English copies of *The Miracle of Stable Prices in Germany* along with handwritten notes he had kept of Rasmuss's instructions, the originals of which he had given to the Russians. There were also copies of various reports he and Sainsra had concocted for the Axis, 12 pamphlets of German sabotage instructions, rough notes Silver had made of instructions from Bose in April and October 1942, and a set of diametrically opposite instructions Silver had drafted to give to the communists in India as a programme to adopt against the pro-Fascists in India.

Silver was certainly not expecting the visit, for he had done nothing to warn the two women in the house, Sainsra's sister and niece. One was the wife of a British Indian soldier who was a prisoner of war in Italy and might have been in Bose's Indian Legion; the other was a young girl of 16. Neither knew what was happening, nor did they know Silver's true identity and what was more, they were not interested in politics. The CID officers having quickly established this had no further interest in them.

These CID officers were the Raj's Indian policemen. That they were fellow Indians was no surprise to Silver and he responded just as Zaman had instructed him to, demanding to see a British officer and refusing to say anything until they produced their white superior. Silver was taken to the Lahore Fort where, as we have seen, twelve years earlier his brother Hari Kishan had been taken and 'tortured'. But now, as soon as he was faced with the white British officer, Silver needed no encouragement, let alone torture, to talk. The statement recorded:

> He then disclosed his identity and asked that his arrest should be kept strictly secret and GHQ should be informed. He also said that his arrest should not be mentioned in the press.[1]

The statement went on:

> Since his arrest Bhagat Ram [Silver] had explained all the papers recovered from his possession and from Sainsra, and also given a detailed explanation of the two German codes and of the money received from the Germans. He has also given the above statement [which ran to 29 typed pages] voluntarily and without hesitation. He is prepared to go back [underlined in the original] to Kabul and continue his contact with the Axis, reporting details to the Russians in Kabul and to the British if and when he returns to India.[2]

After his lengthy statement the British cross-examined him, and now he revealed his true feelings about Bose. Long after Indian independence he would speak eloquently at a seminar held by Bose's supporters about Bose's patriotism. Throughout he, like everyone else at the seminar, referred to Bose not by his name but as Netaji, leader, the reverential term given to him by his followers. In December 1942 this is what he told the British:

> He now regards Subhas Bose as a traitor to his cause and having deliberately betrayed those who helped him. He is thoroughly glad therefore that he has

been able to pay him back in the same coin. He has no sympathy with the present Congress movement which he regards as only serving enemy interests. From his conversations with Rasmuss and company, he does not believe the Congress Party in India has any direct connections with the Axis, or that at any specific item of the Civil Disobedience campaign has Axis inspiration behind it except indirectly. He admits that his own contacts with the Axis in Kabul developed purely fortuitously as a result of Bose's journey, and Bose having subsequently nominated him as his link with India. He is absolutely confident the Axis in Kabul has no other Indian agent working for them in India, and no independent means from Kabul of checking up on his completely non-existent contacts with Bose's organisation in India. The Germans, Italians and Japanese all have their own Afghan, Turki and Uzbek informants, but they are casual informants and not agents in the real sense of the word.[3]

Here it must be emphasised that, while Silver was betraying the great cause of Indian freedom to which he claimed to be committed, he was not being malicious. He could have done immense damage to the Congress had he lied and told his British interrogators that the Axis powers were in league with the Congress and its Quit-India campaign. Churchill, driven by his hatred for what he saw as the Hindu Congress party, was convinced the Congress was acting at the behest of the Japanese, a quite ridiculous claim. Churchill was also eager to prove that Gandhi was a fraud who survived his fasts by mixing glucose with his water, another baseless charge he would repeat in his war memoirs before being forced to withdraw. A Silver lie about the Congress connection with the Axis would have been seized on by the British and delighted Churchill. The fact that he did not does not mean Silver was a man of honour but that he wanted to emphasise how unique he was. This emerged when the British worried about Afghans visiting India asked: might one of them not rumble him? Silver's response was none of them had or were likely to obtain access to Bose's 'real following'.[4]

The British could not believe they had such a jewel in their possession. Silver argued that it had come about thanks to three exceptional circumstances: Bose persuading Berlin they could trust Silver; what the Germans had read into events in India, particularly the Quit-India movement; and 'thirdly the fact that in the atmosphere of Kabul, and with the Germans' keen interest in Tribal Territory, Bhagat Ram [Silver] exactly fitted to the role he is supposed to have filled. It would in fact have been very difficult to find a substitute with the same qualifications'.[5]

But, asked the British, what about the Russians? Silver replied confidently:

The Russians themselves have taken good care to see that this is not disclosed to the Afghans or anyone else, and their movements and meetings with them have been decided accordingly.

While many Indians, and Haji Subhan and his wife, knew of his associations with the Germans:

> ... none of them either knew or suspect he had been playing a double game. His contact with the Russians is also unknown in the Tribal territory, but the top Kirti and CPI leaders in the Punjab know all about it.[6]

Outside this circle only Uttam Chand knew of his connection with the Russians and everything that had gone on in Kabul before his arrest.

With the Russians pestering the British to release Uttam Chand, they were keen to find out what Silver thought of his fellow Indian, and here the answers he gave were fascinating. Yes, he trusted him, but Uttam Chand was indiscreet, and Silver admitted that he had not always told Uttam Chand 'all that passed between him and the Germans on one hand or the Russians on the other'.[7] This confession confirmed Uttam Chand was right to suspect him. Silver acknowledged his debt to Uttam Chand and his wife for providing him safe refuge, food and warm shelter in the cold of Kabul. Without Uttam Chand he would have had to cook, perhaps rent a flat, even hire servants. And Uttam Chand's shop selling crockery and other wares had been such a valuable cover for meeting the Russians. It could not have appeared more normal: they had just come to buy cups and saucers—and there was Silver, another customer, there. But, he told his British captors:

> Despite those considerations it would be quite impossible for Uttam Chand to return to Kabul without endangering his [Silver's] position ... Uttam Chand's German connection is an open secret with the Afghans. Likewise his externment to Peshawar and the fact that he has been in custody in India are also known. Hence if he returned to Kabul he would be suspected by the Afghans if not by the Germans and it would be impossible for Silver to continue his connection with the Russians anywhere near Uttam Chand. The latter's usefulness has thus gone.[8]

Nothing better illustrates Silver's ruthlessness. He had long discarded Bose who had given him the opportunity to become a spy. Now he was ready to discard the man without whose help it is extremely doubtful he could have developed such an amazing spy career. As far as Silver was concerned Uttam Chand could languish in jail (an attitude which would cause no end of problems in the intelligence alliance between the British and the Russians).

The British now had to make a judgement call on which spy to believe and there was, they concluded, just no choice:

> [Uttam Chand had] tried to make out that he was the prime mover in establishing this Russian connection and alleged that [Silver] was attempting

to double-cross the Russians in certain material respects. We had reason to doubt this and hence regarded the whole U.C. statement with suspicion.[9]

With Japan still a threat, the British were keen to find out if Silver had had any dealings with the Japanese. Silver's view was that, while Berlin was keen to establish contacts between Bose's followers in Bengal and the Japanese, nothing of the sort had happened. Silver exuded confidence that he had the complete confidence of the Axis, and was 'glad to take back any military or political information GHQ would supply him with to bolster up his position and mislead the Axis'. However, he reminded the British that 'the Russians would have to be informed first and have repeatedly said they do not wish any information of value given to the Germans'.[10]

The only worry Silver had of being exposed was the German insistence on parachute landings in the Tribal Territories and his visiting the Faqir of Ipi. Witzel and others might want to accompany him to help the Faqir store wireless transmitters, especially if it looked like the Afghans might expel the Axis Diplomatic Mission. There was the further risk that the Axis in Kabul might contact Bose's group either in India or outside it, through one of the Axis agents absconding across the frontier. While he was confident that no such independent contact existed, he mentioned something odd that had happened during his last trip as he went through Mohmand territory. A certain Khushal Khan, the leader of one of the tribes, he was told, had received a typewritten letter 'from someone in GHQ Delhi, enclosing certain military information which the sender wanted to send to the Axis in Kabul. There were some rough maps and charts enclosed with red markings said to have been made by General Wavell himself:

> He had not seen the papers himself, but his informant had, and the sender had said he would supply better information than 'Mukherji' and suggested money should be paid through the Spanish Consulate in Bombay via the Vijya Bahrti Bank and also gave a Bombay house address.[11]

Silver offered to find out more if he was allowed to return to Kabul.

How much of this story is true is debatable. It is clear Silver feared that, despite the Soviets having spoken to Britain, he could suffer the same fate as Uttam Chand and again see the inside of a Peshawar jail. He wanted to impress on his British captors that he was too important not to be allowed to continue what he had been doing. However, as though to emphasise the danger Silver went on to say that he was not sure how much longer he could carry on: 'He does not expect to be able to continue double-crossing the Axis more than one or two times more at the most'. But he promised the British that if it looked as if they were about to rumble him and were preparing to leave Kabul in a hurry, he could entice them to 'an agreed place in Tribal Territory where they could be arrested under British arrangements. Before this happens he wants to exploit his Axis connections for the defeat of the Fascist powers'. And if this was not convincing enough, Silver asked for no money or other consideration in return, 'and leaves it to the British and Russian authorities to decide in the light of the statement he has given. He says he understands there is full and complete understanding between the British and Russian governments. He does not believe there is any possibility of the Russians concluding an independent peace'. (It is interesting Silver should mention this for it shows his awareness of how delicate the British-Soviet alliance was. Indeed at this stage in the war with Churchill ruling out a second front as the Russians were demanding—and which would ignite a major debate—Stalin feared the British might want a separate peace with the Nazis). He was keen to leave for Kabul before the middle of December, visiting Mardan on his way via Mohmand Tribal Territory, promised that in Kabul he would report to the Russians, and 'on his return to India make a full report either in Lahore or Delhi in person',[12]

The British could not have been happier with the confession and cross-examination. They now had a detailed account of the money the Axis in Kabul had paid Silver, and IPI would soon have the fictitious report he and Sainsra had prepared. Having got all they wanted, the British did not see any need to detain him, and Silver was released. After a detour to his village just before Christmas 1942 he headed for the tribal areas on his way to Kabul.

Silver arrived in Kabul on 2 January 1943, Ossipov later telling Hill that 'before meeting Rasmuss he informed the Russians of what had happened to him in India and how he had spent 15 days in prison'.[13] The British arrest was unexpected for the Russians and also for Hill, who informed London: 'we told you in good time of A's [Silver's] journey to M [India] and we were convinced that no such events would ever take place'. Delhi disputed this claiming that the arrest was 'owing to the fact that YM [NKVD] had not warned us in advance. Once it was made clear who he was, (he had been given precise instructions by YM in I [Kabul] to be allowed to ask to speak to the military authorities in the event of trouble), he was at once released'.[14]

But while the British and the Russians squabbled over the handling of Silver the long absence of Silver from Kabul had also had an effect on the Germans as Hill recorded:

B [Rasmuss] was very concerned at long delay in A's return and sent some people to him with a note. (Copy of this note is attached, it has no address or signature). A told B ...of his arrest and B took this to be true. He was also given your information which satisfied him. During A's absence B received letters from Faqir in reply to letters sent in October 1942.[15]

It may seem very surprising that Silver should have told the Germans that he was arrested by the British. His arrest was a secret known to very few even in British intelligence—why tell the Germans? That he did shows the enormous confidence Silver now had in his own ability to fool the Germans. But it was also to cope with an issue that suddenly emerged when he met the Germans, a situation he felt he had to defuse. The German concern that Silver was taking so long to return had turned to alarm when, during his absence, the two companions he had left behind in the Kabul flat the Germans had provided suddenly disappeared.

The presence of the two was meant to reassure the Germans that while Silver had to go to India he would be back. They were, in a sense, his human security. Now the Germans, in particular Witzel, got so panicky that Witzel decided to visit the flat and see what was happening. By then Silver had been back for a few days but had not yet contacted the Germans as he was busy briefing the Russians and taking instructions from them before meeting Rasmuss and Witzel. Witzel arrived one evening just as Silver and two of his companions, who had returned with him to Kabul, were preparing to sit down for a meal. It was quite a moment. Witzel knocked on the door and there was Silver opening the door himself. Witzel tried to conceal his anxiety by telling Silver that since he had been passing through the street where the flat was, having seen the window open, and judging Silver was in, he had knocked on the door. However, Silver quickly judged how anxious Witzel was when he asked what had kept Silver in India. This is when Silver decided he would admit that he had been arrested in India.

Silver could see he had shocked Witzel and this meant there was no alternative but to spin another lie. It is impossible to say whether Silver had rehearsed this lie or it just came to his head. What is not in doubt is that it was quite an extraordinary falsehood. He told Witzel how he had been rounded up with 60 people in Peshawar while carrying out a diversion during a demonstration.[16] However, because of 'some negligence' by the police, and exploiting the chaos and confusion, he had managed to escape. Witzel, who by now saw Silver as a personal friend, readily believed the story, did not ask for any details and Silver knew he had once again got away with his lies. IPI was later to comment this was an 'unreal version'.[17] However, the British were impressed by the ease with which Silver had fooled Witzel and Rasmuss and this was further proof of his hold over the Germans.

Silver followed this by presenting the report Sainsra had concocted, full of fiction about the military situation in India. Rasmuss and Witzel were dazzled by what they thought were authentic details of Allied strength. After reading the report Rasmuss went on to hope that, should the Japanese launch their campaign to conquer India, and the Quit-India movement be intensified, the 'big Anglo-American armed forces would be in a bog'.[18]

A few days later there was more drama. Witzel and Silver had agreed to meet at a spot where Silver would hand the German his report on the political situation in India. Silver in his memoir stated: 'This contact place was located near the Russian legation'.[19] But when Silver got there he found not Witzel but the wireless operator, Doh. The next day, when Silver went again to meet Witzel at the same location, there were a large number of plain-clothes policemen around, and when Witzel arrived he hurriedly passed him a typed slip of paper and left. Silver waited until he had returned to his flat before he read what was on the slip. It said that Doh had misplaced the letter Silver had given him, and Witzel feared it might now be with either the police or the Russians. There followed a further meeting, at which Silver admonished the Germans and suggested that they change their meeting place lest they be noticed. Witzel could only apologise profusely, and Silver made a careful note thinking that sometime in the future this evidence of German incompetence could come in useful. Within a year he was to be proved right.

After the drama that had marked the start of this trip, what followed was for Silver almost anti-climactic. On 10 January 1943, as the Russians later reported to the British, Witzel took Silver to the German legation 'where he spent the next six days being interrogated on his report with which Rasmuss and Witzel were very pleased'.[20]

During this stay in the Legation Witzel also sketched out what the Germans expected from Silver and his organisation. The Germans, said Witzel, plan to land an aeroplane in the tribal area, for which there would be a coded message from Azad Hind radio (there was such a message but no plane landed), and also land men on Indian soil by submarine. The Germans also asked Silver for help blowing up tunnels in Iran that were used for supplies from India to the Soviet Union, and also 'draw up a concrete plan for the uprising'. Silver quickly dealt with the Iran idea by telling Witzel it was impossible for his organisation to do anything in Iran as they had no contacts there.

Witzel gave him a large map which showed the German dominion reaching all the way to the Indian border and even extending into parts of India. 'The map was a patchwork of many pieces': Russian, Iranian, Afghan and tribal regions were depicted by means of aerial photography, while the European part was properly surveyed. Only the southern part of Russia was included, which convinced Silver that once the Germans had over-run southern Russia they would reach the Indian border through the tribal areas and then enter the Indian subcontinent, 'presumably with our help'. Silver had no doubts the Germans would come to occupy the country not liberate it.[21] All these German plans were, of course, passed to the Russians the same day.

There was one other important task Witzel had for Silver, establishing direct radio transmissions from India to Kabul. This was something Witzel had been keen on for some time. Silver had told the British about it and this solved a huge problem for them. One of the most intriguing aspects of the Silver story was that in order to operate as a spy he always had to make long journeys on foot from Peshawar to Kabul during which he was not in contact with anyone. No other spy the British operated carried such a burden. It is doubtful if any other spy in the Second World War of whatever nation had such a work load. Yet, as Silver had told them, the Germans had given him several radio sets all of which had been left behind in Kabul, either with Uttam Chand or the Russians. The British could see this was a great opportunity that had been missed. If only Silver could get one of the sets to India then he could transmit from India to the Germans in Kabul. It would mean, instead of Silver having to become a courier in order to spy, he could become more like other double agents run by the British. With the British now turning their attention to the war with Japan they were also keen to develop communications in the East. So before leaving India Silver had been told to suggest that what was needed was a radio link in Calcutta for transmission to Burma. But while Berlin was keen to develop direct transmission they had no interest in Burma, and instructed Witzel that the transmitter should be set up in Delhi for direct communications between the German Legation in Kabul and India.

Now in Kabul Witzel gave Silver detailed plans about the transmission. The Delhi station would be called Mary, the Kabul station Oliver. Transmissions from Delhi would be on Tuesdays, Thursdays, Saturdays and Sundays, four transmissions each day, starting at 4.30 in the afternoon and ending at 00.40 at night, with different wavelengths, or kilocycles, for each transmission. However, Mary should be ready to receive from Oliver at any hour. There would be different call signs for the daytime and night-time transmissions. The communications between Mary and Oliver were to be in English and in Morse code. Silver dutifully reported this to the Russians, and they in turn informed Hill for passing it on to London.[22]

While Silver was in Kabul the British in London were also weighing up how important Silver was, and how to factor him in to strategic decisions. These deliberations assumed an urgency when the British discovered that in March 1943 their great enemy Subhas Bose was on a U-boat making his way from Germany to Japan. On the 12th, as the U-boat, having made its wide sweep of the Atlantic, headed for the Cape of Good Hope and its rendezvous with the Japanese, there was a meeting at Bletchley Park, the wartime centre of British intelligence and the headquarters of Ultra, the remarkable machine used by the British to break German codes and read all their messages. Gathered in the Nissen huts clustered around Bletchley Park's Victorian mansion that day were officials of IPI, SIS and MI5.[23]

The meeting had been called to evaluate the intelligence the British had about Bose thanks to Ultra. The intelligence chiefs had to decide what should be done about him now that he was on his way back to the East, and the likely effect his return to Asia would have on the Silver operation. No documents regarding this meeting have ever been released by the British, but some years ago a Russian author discovered in the Soviet archives a document summarising its proceedings. A Top Secret document, it was numbered 9 in the Soviet archives and had the heading, 'Soviet agent Report on the British intelligence'. In the upper left corner of the document one of the handwritten notes read 'Summary of English counterintelligence, received by our agents'. The report began by saying it was a 'Summary received about Bhagat Ram [Silver] at a meeting of representatives of the I.P.I, S.I.S and M.I5 in Oxford 12th of March 1943'.[24]

The importance of this document cannot be emphasised enough. This was a report about an internal British meeting. No foreign power was supposed to know about the meeting or see a report of it. It had reached Moscow because the Soviets had a high-powered mole at the heart of British intelligence. That mole, the Soviet agent referred to above, was Kim Philby, Russia's most famous spy working in the heart of British intelligence. Although Philby was not at the meeting he had got hold of what had happened at it and, as he did almost every night, reported to his masters in Moscow what the British were secretly plotting. And this is what Philby told his Soviet bosses about what the British chiefs discussed about Bose and Silver on that March day:

> The most serious fact in our situation is that Bose is on the way to Japan in the German submarine. They suppose if he gets to Japan he'll be able to contact his own Indian party, Forward Bloc, and first of all he'll find out that the colossal organisation of Bhagat Ram Talwar [Silver] doesn't exist—the whole thing is pure blackmail. The Admiralty wants to withdraw him when the Japanese boat takes him from the [German] submarine. It's a very good plan, especially if it comes into being, because Bhagat Ram Talwar's [Silver's] organisation will be safe and the Germans will be able to boss the latter without Bose.

If Philby had accurately reported to Moscow then this means the British were confident they not only knew how Bose planned to get from Germany to Japan but where the transfer would take place, and that if they had so chosen they could have picked him up while he was on the high seas. The fact that they were considering this highlights the value they played on Silver. As we have seen, when back in 1941 Bose had escaped from India the British considered assassinating him, but did not know the route he was taking from India to Europe. Now, as he planned to return to Asia, they knew his route. However, unlike 1941, their reason to kill Bose was not so much about what he might or might not do, but rather what effect Bose's return to Asia might have on the Silver operation. The British were worried that a Bose return might blow Silver's cover. In order to prevent this they were prepared to consider a major naval operation on the high seas in the middle of the war to pick up Bose and ensure Silver's secret was not discovered. Through the war various countries carried out amazing operations to protect their spies, but that such an operation was considered to protect a single Indian spy and his double-crossing operation shows how unique Silver was.

However, in the end when the German U-boat linked up with a Japanese submarine in the Mozambique Channel near neutral Portuguese territory, the British did not intervene. Why? Since British files on this have never been opened we do not know. One reason could be that just then the Americans were also planning a major assassination.

The Americans had been consistently breaking the Japanese codes using their counterpart of Ultra, Magic, and had discovered the route of an air journey Admiral Yamamoto, the great Japanese naval commander who had plotted the Pearl Harbor attack, was about to take. Roosevelt had approved of the planned assassination, and it seems the Americans and the British did not want to jeopardise this. The fear was that by picking up Bose they might reveal the secret of Ultra, or Magic, or both, to the Germans and the Japanese. Killing Yamamoto was a much higher priority, in terms of winning the war in the Pacific, than exterminating Bose in order to protect Silver. Silver was important but Yamamoto was even more so. As Commander Edwin Layton, urging Yamamoto's assassination, told Admiral Nimitz, US Pacific Fleet Commander, 'He's the one Jap who thinks in bold strategic terms ... Aside from the Emperor, probably no man is so important to civilian morale.'[25]

Yamamoto was killed on 18 April 1943. On the morning of 26 April the British, in effect, allowed Bose's German submarine in very rough seas to link up with the Japanese submarine. The next day Silver, who had left Kabul on 2 April, arrived back in India. But with Silver's former leader now nearer home, Silver had a new challenge.

A Very Special Sahib

Silver arrived back in India from his eighth visit to Kabul very aware that life for him in India would change. There was no longer any question of dodging the police at Mardan, visiting Ghalla Dher wearing a burkha, or slipping into Peshawar and then secretly making his way to Lahore and the Nawakot house. Not surprisingly, as he made his way back through the tribal territory in April 1943, he felt on top of the world; as he later told the British, 'he was in good health and spirits and very pleased with the success of his mission'. He reached Swal Qila on the 21st, where 'we had our own conveyance arrangements made'[1] to take him to a secluded place in the Punjab. What he does not say, but SOE files reveal, is that the transport was laid on by the government of India. In the past he had worried about travelling to Rawalpindi, lest he was recognised by any police informers. Now he was the most important agent the British had ever had and virtually escorted to the city. And this time there was no need to get on the train at wayside stations to avoid detection. Now he was taken to the main Rawalpindi station and put on the train to Delhi, reaching the Indian capital on the 29th.

The choice of Delhi was interesting. It would have been ironic had Silver been taken to the SOE India Mission which was based in Meerut, 45 miles away. This was, as we have seen, the very place Sodhi had moved to when the police in Punjab had closed down the Kirti newspaper printing presses for subversion. Now, of course, communists were not enemies to be hunted but allies to be cultivated, and Silver was the most special of communists. But while SOE was involved in handling Silver in Moscow, Delhi was where the British had the man ideally suited to provide him with his deception material: Peter Fleming.

Peter Fleming was undoubtedly quite the most extraordinary man Silver met during the war. A well-travelled man, an established author and a former correspondent for *The Times*, such was his search for adventure that in the 1930s he had explored the rivers of Central Brazil in search of a missing

English colonel, an expedition that had produced a bestselling book. This had been followed by a 3,500 mile trek, walking and riding, from Peking to Srinagar, ignited by the romance of crossing Tartary. Such was his stature that even British Generals would stand up when he came into the room.

But since the start of the war Fleming had been frustrated by lack of adventure. Then in January 1942 he had been summoned to India by Archibald Wavell, Commander in Chief of the Allied Forces in the South-West Pacific. Wavell's message was succinct: 'Should be glad of Peter Fleming as early as possible for appointment my staff.'[2] The two men had met in Cairo and liked one another immediately. According to a friend who knew them both, their conversations would be punctuated with long silences, which both of them found 'intensely satisfying'. Wavell found Fleming an attractive character and liked his ideas on enemy deception, a subject of interest to him too. In India Fleming reported to Brigadier Walter(Bill) Cawthorn, the Director of Military Intelligence and some months after Fleming's arrival a certain Enoch Powell joined Cawthorn's staff although there is no evidence that Powell ever met Fleming, let alone Silver. Had he met Silver he could have spoken to him in Urdu, a language Powell was then learning. The chat between the two might have been interesting. Powell fell in love with India, the love of the conqueror for his conquest, wanted to administer the country and saw India free of British control as a personal catastrophe, confessing that he had spent a whole night walking the streets of London and occasionally sitting down in a doorway with his head in his hands.

By the time of Fleming's arrival in Delhi in March Java had fallen and Wavell was back as Commander-in-Chief in India. Fleming had initially stayed at the bungalow of the Adjutant of the Viceregal Bodyguard in the gardens of the resplendent Viceregal Palace, but subsequently moved somewhere even grander: the house of Colonel Jack Tweed, Commander of the Viceregal Bodyguard, and his wife. This is how the Sahibs had always lived in India during British rule, and Fleming was no exception. For all the changes and privation the war had brought to Britain, in India life for the British continued as before, as Wavell himself had found out on his return to India in 1941. Talking of his accommodation in Simla he wrote:

> I am his Excellency the C-in-C and Defence Minister and have two houses and as far as I can make out nearly 100 servants of all sorts, including a very good cook with several assistants, very bad for my figure.[3]

Had his fellow Britons, struggling under rationing known about this, they would not have been amused.

From an upper-class, essentially aristocratic background, Fleming was, he confessed to a friend, shy and naturally fastidious, and wished he could cross social boundaries more easily. He had difficulty socialising with people who were not from his class. The language used by working-class Englishmen, for example, he found difficult to accept: on his way to Freetown a sailor watching the pilot of an aircraft being rescued cried out, 'There's the bastard's fucking head!' Fleming, by then 34, was so shocked that he wrote:

> If foul language is used as a kind of quaint and amiable patois it loses all its force as invective: for if the wretched boy in the sea had been a German, the sailor could have said nothing more.[4]

He could also be puritanical. Once on a deception mission he found his medical adviser, Ran Antrim, reading some girlie magazines and was very shocked. Antrim was amused: 'Really, Peter, you sound almost like a bishop.'[5] And he made no secret that he did not like India or Indians. He preferred the Chinese (who would later give him the Order of the Cloud), visited Chungking repeatedly during the war and after the war drew this sharp distinction between the Chinese and the Indians:

> During the war I sometimes had to fly from Calcutta to Chungking. This took a day. The streets of the two cities provided as vivid a contrast as you can find in Asia. Garbage, corruption, poverty, crowds, noise and a steamy climate were common to both. But it was hard, almost, to believe that the Bengalis and the Chinese were members of the same race. The brown men dressed in white looked listless, sullen, foolish, ineffective, miserable: the yellow men dressed in blue, swarming up and down the tortuous dark grey alleys clinging to the scarred bluffs above the Yangtse and the Kialing, looked exactly the opposite of all those epithets. You felt as if you had landed on another planet—more inconvenient, more expensive, if anything slightly smellier planet than the one you had left that morning, but a planet (and this was what struck you more forcibly than anything) with a sense of humour.[6]

Fleming does not mention that his visits to Calcutta took place amidst the Great Bengal famine which, as we have seen, killed three and a half million in the province and saw the streets of this former British capital of India clogged with skeletal men and women. Indeed there were so many dead bodies that the local corporation formed the Corpse Disposal Squad. Indeed in 1943 Fleming devised a deception plan based on using one of the dead bodies but, as his biographer writes, because of the famine 'almost every corpse was far too emaciated to pass muster as that of a well-nourished secret agent'. In the end D division found one dead victim of the famine whose body was not skeletal but the deception plan did not fool the Japanese.

After three years in India the country had made such a poor impression on Fleming that as he prepared to leave after the war he had come to the conclusion that Indians could not even be considered mature people. Turning down a return to *The Times* after the war he wrote to the editor:

Four or five years of exile in the rather childish atmosphere of this subcontinent doesn't improve one's qualifications for helping to guide British public opinion through the sort of problems which will confront it when I return to civilian life.[7]

It is not hard to imagine how this Englishman must have felt condemned to spend the war in a country where the people were foolish, sullen, without a sense of humour and immature. He also shared many of the superior attitudes of his fellow British towards Indians, and not surprisingly he compensated for this by living in India like a classic British sojourner who saw little reason to make any concession to the country, least of all the Indian climate. He would ride out early every morning. Lunch would be sandwiches lying out in the blazing sun beside the swimming pool in the grounds of the Viceroy's house. He had a dog called Blondie, a black mongrel, and an Indian bearer his fellow British officers were convinced cheated him. In the evening he liked to play squash, and would try and go duck-flighting, borrowing an impounded shotgun. This often involved driving out of Delhi to some nearby jeel, and if necessary sleeping on the ground to catch the morning flight of the ducks.

Fleming had been put in charge of GSI (D), created to devise and implement programmes of strategic deception, 'to make your enemy take—or refrain from taking—a particular course of action', he would later write, 'and thereby to improve your chances of defeating him. Merely to gull him—to implant in his mind a false picture of the true situation—is only half the battle: it is not enough, even, that he should "do something about it". He must do what you want him to do'.[8] At his office 'on the ground floor of one of Lutyens' great red sandstone government buildings',[9] his attempts to deceive the Japanese intelligence services ranged from getting one of the secretaries to pose as a Wren and write passionate love letters to an imaginary boyfriend in Ceylon containing apparently indiscreet revelations about military affairs in Delhi, to Operation *Error*, a variation on Colonel Richard Meinertzhagen's famous ruse in Palestine in 1917, letting fall a haversack whose contents suggested to the Turks that Allenby's main assault was to be directed at Gaza. This time a briefcase of Wavell's was left in a crashed Ford car in Burma in the path of the advancing Japanese army to give the impression Wavell himself was injured. It had misleading information and some items to make it look genuine, such as private letters and a photograph of his daughter Pamela. In Fleming papers there is a lengthy description of Operation *Error* along with a diagram.

Fleming came up with other deception plans, like Pintails, dummy parachutists that on landing fired off a Very light to give the impression a signal was being given, and Purple Whales, a fictitious meeting of the Joint Military Council to be sold to Japanese intelligence agents using the Chinese. In May 1942 he had even been to Kabul, to meet Cornelius Van. H. Engert, who had recently opened the first US mission there, and establish a channel of communication with the Japanese. Unlike Silver, who walked the whole way from Peshawar, Fleming chartered a taxi for the 360-mile round trip.

The question we are faced with is why Fleming, given his well-expressed dislike for India and Indians, made an exception for Silver and took to the man? The only conceivable answer is that Silver came into Fleming's life at just the right time. In 1943, with the war entering its fourth year, Fleming felt stale and frustrated. Throughout the conflict he never got over not being able to take part in the shooting war and emulate his father, with his friends saying he had a 'DSO wish'. At the end of 1942 he would record that the highlight of the year's end was a tiger shoot in Bastar state. Its head and skin adorned the floor of his study.[10]

It would have been fascinating to know what Silver made of this singular Englishman. But, of course, there is no mention of Fleming in his memoir. Silver only says he went to Delhi to meet Swatantra and Cheena, who like most of the leading communists had also been released, without explaining why Silver should suddenly go to Delhi, a city he had never visited. Delhi was also not the natural habitat of Swatantra and Cheena, but by bringing them here the British had clearly decided that the entire Silver operation should be concentrated in the capital: Silver would no longer have to run to Bombay to talk to communist party leaders, something, given how much time he spent commuting between India and Kabul, he could certainly do without.

Kabul and its closed world had thrown disparate men and women together. Silver had met Quaroni in the Italian retreat in Pagham, broken bread with Witzel in the flat the Germans provided in Kabul, spent many hours drinking with Zaman and Otroshckenko in the Russian Embassy, and had meals with the German wife of Haji Subhan. However the British in India could not be more different. They maintained themselves as a separate caste in India, the highest in the land and with minimum social contact with the natives. By the time Silver took up residence in Delhi it was barely a decade since the British had shifted there from Calcutta. Peter Fleming was based in New Delhi: not the historic old Delhi of the Mughals where most of the Indians lived, but a city designed by Edwin Lutyens to be the capital of an Empire expected to last for another thousand years. Lutyens had been determined to impress on Indians British architectural splendour—but it impressed British visitors too. Hugh Trevor-Roper, on his wartime visit to India, found nothing much to like in the two great rivers of the subcontinent—'the Ganges, a brown and wretched water … the Indus … a colourless channel fringed with scrub'—but Lutyens'

New Delhi reminded him of Gibbon's words on Roman constructions, 'not afraid to show that they had the spirit to conceive, and the wealth to execute the most grandiose designs'.[11] For Lutyens this was all the more important given his feelings for Indians:

> The very low intellect of the natives spoils much. I do not think it possible for Indians and whites to mix freely; mixed marriage is filthy and beastly and they ought to get the sanitary office to interfere.

In one of the great ironies of our story Silver arrived in Delhi very aware that he knew Kabul better than he knew the capital of his own country. And, in a world specially created to serve the wider purpose of the conquerors of his land, he also knew he would have to step carefully.

In a little over two years Silver had met more Europeans than he had ever met before in his life, and they were, as we have seen, a remarkable bunch: Italian diplomats, Germans of all kinds from diplomats and Abwehr officers to businessmen and civilians, and Russian NKVD agents—and with some of them he had even struck up a friendship. But the nature of British rule in India meant that he had not really met anyone from Britain. Before his trip to Delhi the longest time he had spent with an Englishman was with a police officer in Lahore jail, and then under interrogation.

He was now working for the British, but outside the small, secretive, world of espionage he was part of the horde of Indians in the city, and against a background of much unrest in India had to be sure not to show too much affinity for the British rulers. He had arrived in Delhi when the revolt against the British was still at its height, and he was made aware of how even in the capital of the British Raj Indians working for the British could be harassed on their way to work. An office memorandum by the Secretary to the Government of India home department a copy of which was sent to the Private Secretary of the Viceroy, the Military Secretary of the Viceroy, the Political Department and the Chief Commissioner, Delhi, went as follows:

> The Government of India wish to assure Government servants working in Delhi and New Delhi that it is their intention to take all possible steps during the present disturbances to protect them from molestation when proceeding to and from office and on any other occasion. So far as their safety when to and from office is concerned, the Delhi administration have taken steps to guard during the rush hours the roads through which government servants have to pass and further measures will be taken if they are necessary.[12]

Government servants were told that if they were 'molested' they should make a report to the New Delhi police station.

The Fleming-Silver relationship was also shaped by the brand of apartheid the British imposed on India—never as rigid as the one in South Africa—but still drawing a sharp distinction between Europeans and the Indians. So, Fleming and Silver would never have socialised in Delhi. And the Englishman could not have established with Silver the intimacy he developed with other members of his staff, like the team of British girls drawn from the families of the headquarters staff, including Wavell's daughter Joan, who did the secretarial work. When the Japanese surrender in August 1945 saw Fleming winding up his operation he presented the girls with a copy of one of his books, saying that even his worst critics would admit that 'an early Fleming (there are, perhaps fortunately, no late ones) will often make an acceptable Christmas present to an old governess or an important aunt'. Such a present would have meant nothing to Silver.

As we have seen Silver spoke what can at best be described as broken English, and his first language was Urdu. Urdu was not a language Fleming knew or had any reason to learn. We do not even know how they addressed each other. Would Silver have called Fleming Peter? Doubtful: more likely Fleming Sahib. With Silver having so many names, he would soon get a new code name, Fleming was faced with quite a choice as what to call Silver and, it seems, settled on Kishen Chand. But while they socially lived in two very different and distinct worlds over the next two years the two men would get to know one another well, and become close colleagues who worked very harmoniously to deceive first the Germans and then the Japanese.

Fleming, for all his antipathy to Indians in general, developed great admiration for Silver. And for all that Silver's father had drummed into him that Indians were living under '*Angress ki Ghulami*', the slavery of the British, and that Hari Kishan was a martyr in the fight against British rule, when it came to Fleming there is nothing in the records to suggest Silver felt he was serving a member of the race that had conquered his people; or if he did then, like his spying for the Russians and the British, he hid it very well.

Indeed, for all the gulf in race, class and cultural background between the two men, there were many personal characteristics they had in common. Both had come into the world of espionage completely unexpectedly because of the war—in Fleming's case as one of that extraordinary collection of British academics, journalists and amateurs who proved gifted at intelligence, in Silver's through the desperate desire of an Indian revolutionary to free his country. And just as Silver had become a spy because he craved adventure, so skilfully deceiving your enemies in war provided Fleming with the adventure he had always sought. And the two men had one other common characteristic. Silver was a loner; Fleming saw himself as 'too much of an individualist' to command men.

It would be a gross overstatement to say that Silver's arrival directly contributed to GSI (D) growing in strength. But grow it did quite dramatically between 1943 and 1945. Both Wavell and Mountbatten, who at the end of 1943 took over as Supreme Allied Commander in South East Asia with Wavell becoming Viceroy, ensured the division expanded both in its activities and the range of its influence. In March 1944 Fleming's unit came under the headquarters of the Supreme Allied Commander, and acquired the name D Division, 'D' standing for deception. In 1945 there was a further change, with Mountbatten moving his headquarters to Kandy in Ceylon. But, D Division did not move south, remaining in Delhi and acquiring a new name, Force 456. However, the name D Division remained in use and many people thought it still existed, which created a wonderful situation for Fleming so that, as technically still head of D Division, he would sometimes write orders to the Commander of Force 456 and then, as Commander of Force 456, accept them.

Fleming in fact took his time to expand D Division. He had been directed to expand his office to nine officers, and he could have a clerk. In March 1943 Major Peter Thorne of the Grenadier Guards joined, like Fleming an Etonian and graduate of Oxford, tasked with giving the impression of a larger order of battle than was actually the case. Another recruit both an old Etonian, and wealthy as well, was Major Lucas Railli, a W/T expert, while Major André Bicat developed what has been described as a veritable factory of contraptions to deceive the Japanese. During 1943 D Division also opened a tactical headquarters in Calcutta, where Colonel Frank Wilson of the 19th Lancers, a skilful caricaturist, was asked by Fleming to produce a sketch book of members of various regiments in Calcutta, generally fictitious, which was then sold in Kabul for a handsome sum to fool the Japanese.

Fleming's D Division also had another group of British officials working for it. These were men of the Intelligence Bureau which, as we have seen, was the Intelligence Bureau of the Government of India's Home Department. Based in India most of their working lives, they were often referred to by the British as 'Indians', implying they had gone native. The relationship between the British who had come to India during the war and the British who had become part of India was never a happy one, and after the war it generated highly dubious stories of how Silver became a British spy.

Silver's memoir provides a glimpse of how his life changed once he started working with the British. He could not have shared the accommodation Fleming had in the Vice-regal complex, since this was reserved for the British, but the British clearly provided him with somewhere to stay, probably in old Delhi, where most Indians lived and that was comfortable enough for him to ask his wife and his mother to join him—the first time the family were reunited since he had started his spying mission. He was also paid to go and have a holiday in the hill station at Nainital.

His wife joined him in Delhi just before he left for Nainital. Having signed up for the British, he felt reassured that he had no further reason for the

CID knocking on his door. He recalled in his memoir: 'It was risky to live underground all alone, so it was good she arrived at Delhi before I had left'.[13] It is not exactly clear whether Silver left his wife behind in Delhi and went off on holiday on his own, living up to his image as a loner, or took Ram Kaur with him. It is charitable to assume he did, the first time since their marriage three years ago the couple would have gone on a holiday.

Nainital was not as grand as Simla, the great hill station the British in India would decamp to during the summer to escape the heat of the plains, but Silver spent a very comfortable ten days there during which 'I lived a carefree life, with good home cooked food and a lot of gossip and chitchat. This improved my health considerably'.[14] And as you would expect from the arch dissembler, Silver, instead of admitting that the British arranged this holiday, says that Swatantra and Cheena 'advised me to go to Nainital for a while for rest'.[15] He does not explain how the Indian communists who had long scoured for finance and found Nazi gold so useful, and most of whom had just come out of jail, found the money to finance his holiday. If the British did not pay then it was probably from a bit of the Nazi gold Silver had been allowed to keep, with his communist comrades giving him a holiday as a thank-you for the sterling work he had done for them.

Having had his well-deserved holiday in the hill station, the man who was now a quadruple agent returned to Delhi, his new base, ready for yet more adventure, which would see him become a quintuple agent, and acquire a new name. This was when he got the name Silver because of the fact, as we have seen, that in London there was a real Mr Silver, a high official of the IPI. What we do not know is who came up with this rather amusing code name. It is tempting to think it was Fleming. It would certainly have been just the type of joke he would have loved.

The Problem with Mary and Oliver

Silver returned to Delhi to find that Fleming and D Division were all ready to operate Mary and Oliver. A direct radio link meant Fleming could now recreate in Delhi what the great Garbo was doing in London. By this time Garbo lived in a house in north London, worked from an office near the Piccadilly Arcade in Jermyn Street, and in March 1943 had begun transmitting directly to Abwehr officers based in the German Embassy in Madrid. Here it is worth stressing that Garbo had to work hard to get Karl-Erich Kühlenthal, head of the Abwehr station in Madrid, to agree to such transmission. In contrast, it was Witzel who had been so taken in by Silver that he had convinced Berlin of his uniqueness, and had been pushing for it even with Silver not able to work out how this would operate. Now that he was under the wing of the British such transmissions made complete sense.

Fleming had—to an extent—made Silver very like Garbo, providing him accommodation in Delhi, but, unlike Garbo, Silver was not an agent wholly under British control. It was the Soviets who ran Silver, and the British had to get Soviet approval for any change in the operational arrangements. Aware of how difficult this would be, Fleming's D Division set about getting round this obstacle with great skill. And here events in Afghanistan would come in very handy, in particular the Tirazi plot hatched by the Germans in which Silver acted as a deep throat for the British. More of that later, but the net effect of this conspiracy was that it left Kabul in a state of some considerable unrest, with the British fearful of allowing Silver to go there.[1] The Tirazi plot also saw the British and the Soviets wanting the German and Italian Legations to be drastically reduced. This put Rasmuss in great fear that he might not only lose Witzel but also be deported himself. The German was desperate to warn Silver, but there was no sign of him in Kabul, and the essentially freelance and fiercely independent nature of the Silver operation meant that Rasmuss could never tell when Silver would reappear. He could only communicate with Silver when the Indian finally set foot in the Afghan capital, and his dread was that by the time he did the whole German intelligence operation in Kabul might have been liquidated, with Witzel, Doh and even he forced to leave the Afghan capital. He decided to do something the Germans had never done before in this spy relationship.

On 6 May Azad Hind radio broadcast from Berlin a call sign giving time and frequencies, asking for immediate contact to be made between Silver and Rasmuss. D Division immediately saw this as a great opportunity. They could argue that if they did not respond Rasmuss might think Silver was no longer operating, or his organisation had been rumbled by the British. To maintain credit with the Germans Silver had to get in touch with Rasmuss. However, in strict theory, Silver communicated with Rasmuss only under NKVD control through Kabul. So the next day Sir Stewart Menzies, 'C', head of MI6, sent a telegram from London to Hill asking the following message to be given to Ossipov in Moscow.

M [Indian] authorities are anxious lest the widespread arrests in I [Kabul, following the Tirazi plot] may result in exposure of A [Silver] to K [Afghan] police. They consider that until matters have calmed down it would be wiser for A [Silver] not to return to K [Afghanistan]. We should like views of YMCA [NKVD] on this point. As however it is obviously necessary that A [Silver] should reassure VE-IG [German legation] that he is safe and still functioning it is thought desirable that a brief report should be sent by him to them at once. Suggestion has been made and has met with A [Silver]'s complete approval that an interim report should be prepared in GP [Delhi] which he will send to I [Kabul] by a tribal messenger. A [Silver] states that this can easily be arranged. He himself will pretend to be in tribal territory. Suggested report which will deal with India affairs only will state that the committee in M [India] has suffered reverses and government forces have met with successes. It will contain some information relating to military matters on line desired by the ZD [Axis] but will say that committee is not entrusting everything to the messenger as he is not so experienced as A [Silver]. It will explain that A [Silver] has received information regarding the committee's difficulties from a representative called to tribal territory to meet him. He has not himself returned to I [Kabul] because he considers that affairs in India demand his presence. Some technical details regarding a wireless set purporting to be in the possession of the committee in M [India] will be given to enable the VE-IG [German legation] to establish contact with M [India] (this wireless set will be under our control).[2]

London had been careful to say the report would mainly deal with Indian affairs, and promised that a copy of the report proposed to be sent by Silver's substitute would be made available to them. But the Russians were taken aback by this British request. For a start they did not believe Silver would be in any danger in Kabul: 'We know of no facts which would cause us to fear exposure of A [Silver] to K [Afghan] police'. Not wishing to antagonise the British too much, however, they agreed that after the arrests conditions in the Afghan capital were probably not suitable for his return. They also agreed that the courier could be sent to Kabul with the report:

> Nevertheless we consider it essential that A [Silver] should return to I [Kabul] as soon as circumstances permit and continue work which he has so successfully executed up to the present.[3]

London had also asked Hill for an urgent reply as to whether the NKVD agreed on Silver making the broadcast. But it took three days before the NKVD let Hill know that they had no objection, and by this time Silver had already communicated with Rasmuss. The result was an almost grovelling British apology to the Russians, admitting that Silver 'has exceeded their [NKVD's] instructions'. But, reassured London, this did not mean he had 'sabotaged W/T communications' with the Germans. And in an effort to further calm Russian fears the British stated:

> ... owing to recent arrests and trouble in I [Kabul] fears are entertained by VEs [Germans] that their mission may be expelled and they have opened up on W/T set on off chance [of] contacting A [Silver] before they leave [Kabul].

Hill was told that Menzies, 'C', was 'most anxious to utilise this communication whilst available'.[4] Aware, nevertheless, that the Soviets might be feeling that the British were taking over full control of Silver, on 13 May 1943 London telegraphed Hill asking him to reassure Moscow that 'this will not interfere with Silver's return to Kabul as soon as this is safe'.[5]

But while the Soviets had agreed to the broadcasts, and also sending a messenger rather than Silver to Kabul, they were puzzled by the way the British choose his replacement. The man was Sayyed Mortas, a person the Russians had never heard of before. The British may also have misspelled his name, for the friend Silver was later to take to Kabul was called Murtaza. [It is very possible that to British ears Murtuza, a very subcontinental Muslim name, sounded like Mortas and they anglicised the original]. The Russians could not understand why the British had not sent Uttam Chand. As far as the Russians were concerned he was clearly the logical choice, a man they trusted and saw almost on a par with Silver. The British had him in custody—surely the simplest thing would be to release him and send him back with whatever report the British had prepared.

Matters were compounded by the inept British handling of Mortas. Given the code AD, he had left India in June, arriving in Kabul on 5 July 1943, and had his first meeting with the Germans on the 7th, giving Rasmuss a letter from Silver and another from Silver's fictitious 'revolutionary committee'. There followed a further short meeting on the 15th, at which Rasmuss gave Mortas a parcel to take back to India, containing a film with photographs of letters in code for Silver, 50,000 Afghan rupees and £250 in gold. Mortas, who left Kabul on the 16th, was told he should not remain long in India but come back quickly with information. The problem was that during his stay in the Afghan capital the Soviets never got to see Mortas. Far from making the Soviet Embassy his first stop in Kabul on arrival, as Silver always did, during his entire eleven-day stay in Kabul Mortas made no attempt to meet the Russians. The Soviets only learnt he was even in Kabul on the 14th, two days before he left. The Russians saw this as the British cutting them out of the spy ring they controlled, protested vehemently, and London could only plead that they did not know why. Mortas, they tried to reassure the Russians, had been given precise instructions to go to see Zaman. Not surprisingly the Soviets did not believe them.

Even now the tension that was building up could have been defused, had the British accepted the incessant Soviet requests for the release of Uttam Chand. But they did not and, through much of 1943 and even 1944, the Russians kept renewing their request, unable to understand why their ally and partner in this spy arrangement could not accept it. Surely this was one issue over which Delhi had full control? The more they pressed the British on it, and the more the British said they could not, the more upset the Russians got. In order to mollify them the British in India assured them that Uttam Chand was 'being given "A" class treatment and special medical attention in Peshawar jail'.[6] Years later when I spoke to Uttam Chand he told me that he had kidney trouble in jail, 'I was sent to MYO hospital in Lahore when I was in part coma.'[7]

Arrangements had also been made to hold his property in Kabul until the end of the war, to be returned to him on his release. To further placate the Russians they were also told that Uttam Chand 'had been informed of this'. The Russians found all this hard to accept, the more so as the British insisted that the Afghans had deported Uttam Chand 'entirely independently' of them.[8] The Russians knew from their own paid contacts in the Afghan government that the Afghans had only done so at the explicit request of the British.

The whole issue was complicated by the British not being entirely honest with the Russians about the Uttam Chand affair. They never disclosed the chief reason they still detained Uttam Chand: that he was indiscreet. As Sir Dennis Pilditch, director of the Indian Intelligence Bureau, stressed to Hill, he could not be released as he 'would jeopardise the Bhagat Ram [Silver] link'.[9]

The fact is, the British in India had by now developed very contrasting views about Silver and Uttam Chand. The British rated Silver very highly with Pilditch telling Hill 'that he was an extremely capable man, unattractive of appearance but a master of deception and disguise'. Such was the British regard for Silver that when he proposed Mortas as his substitute, although none of the British knew him or checked him out, they had no hesitation in accepting Silver's recommendation. Pilditch went on to draw a sharp distinction between Silver and Uttam Chand: 'Bhagat Ram [Silver] is not mercenary, and usually hands over all the money received by him [from the Germans], but Uttam Chand is prompted entirely by avarice'. However, Pilditch was also sure 'that Bhagat Ram [Silver] hides nothing from the Soviets, whereas he does not always give the government of India the whole picture'.[10] But this was a minor blemish in a man the British considered the greater prize. And given that Silver himself, as the British well knew, did not want Uttam Chand free, why upset their one great agent for another agent they did not trust or even much like?

Interestingly, while Pilditch thought Silver told the Russians everything, he did keep one secret from the Russians. Silver never told them he had told the British not to free Uttam Chand. The result was that the NKVD in Kabul harboured the impression that Silver must also be wanting his old Indian colleague back with him in Kabul, further encouraging them to keep pressing Hill to ask the British in India to release him. Like the NKVD in Kabul, the British in London also found it difficult to understand why Uttam Chand could not be released, attributing it to incompetence on the part of the Indian authorities.

The incessant Russian demands for Uttam Chand's release clearly rattled Pilditch, and some months later he came up with an extraordinary solution:

> If ... the Soviet authorities desired it, they [the British in India] had absolutely no objection to Uttam Chand's being released and conducted over the Soviet frontier, and they would themselves undertake to deliver him to the NKVD but they would not consider any request for his employment in Kabul, since he is quite unreliable and might well blow the whole matter.[11]

Such tensions between allies in war are understandable, but one major problem was that the British did not understand how the Soviet state worked. And this was vividly illustrated when, just as Mortas was setting off from India from Kabul, Wylie in Kabul stepped into the Silver operation for the first time, further infuriating the Russians. The Russians had always kept the knowledge of Silver's existence confined to very few people even within their legation, but in a conversation with the Soviet chargé d'affaires, Samylouski, Wylie mentioned that Silver was in the tribal area, would be coming to Kabul in the next ten days and was keen to meet someone from the Soviet mission. As we can see, Wylie had confused Silver with Mortas, but the fact that he had revealed Silver's name, and to a mere Soviet chargé d'affaires, 'appalled' the NKVD. What made this Wylie intervention all the more curious was that ever since his arrival as British Minister he had opposed any intelligence activity conducted from the Embassy in Kabul, managed to make sure the intelligence operative he had inherited was sent back and kept his distance from Connor-Green. Wylie's faux pas led to Ossipov summoning Hill and telling him:

> We consider that expansion of circle of people who know about A's [Silver's] role can only lead to undesirable consequences in sense of failure of whole business which has been so well organised. This case deserves attention also because there was no special need or urgency to transmit communication which was made by British Minister as we already knew about A's safe arrival in M [India] from your letter of May 8th and from your proposals [about the broadcast and Mortas coming instead] to which we agreed. Apart from all this you had the opportunity of handing this communication to us here in Moscow. We request you to bear in mind our point of view on this particular question.[12]

Hill advised London that in the Russian system the NKVD and the Soviet Foreign Office did not have much confidence in each other, 'so common between all our services', and also that the Russians would not understand that Wylie could be discreet and that such actions would not gain the British any benefit. London concluded:

> The whole trouble seems to be the lack of appreciation of the fact that NKVD and NKID play different roles and hide their works from one another. It appears that the Soviet Foreign Office was not entirely in the [Silver] picture and they are furious that our minister in Kabul should have put their local man wise to the story.[13]

But if the Soviet system reflected the intense paranoia of the Stalin regime, with one branch of the government being kept in the dark about what the other was doing, the Russians refused to believe that the Government of India was an independent organisation—to them this was just another ruse by the clever British. As it happened, at that very moment the Indian government, as if keen to advertise it was not London's bag carrier, was kicking up a fuss as to who controlled Silver, and Pilditch in Delhi was telling everyone that Silver was a British agent who had been turned over to the Russians. Fortunately this lie did not reach the Russians, but they soon became very aware that he wanted to muscle in on the operation. Hill had warned London about Russian feelings on this issue but, nevertheless, London felt Pilditch's case deserved a hearing. On 19 May London had told Hill that:

The authorities in India are exceedingly anxious that their officer who interviews [Silver] should have a very early opportunity to meet the Russian officer who handles him in Kabul, to discuss how best he can assist Russians in their plan for making most advantageous use of this agent. Such a meeting tends to reduce the risk of exposure which might result from inadequately co-ordinated action.[14]

Six weeks later, on 1 July, London was back, forwarding to Hill a telegram from India:

... [the] present roundabout method of communication ... unnecessary, foolish and inefficient, and from what they have seen of AE [Almazov or Zaman]'s handling of A [Silver] they regard him as a strictly practical person. If however YMCA [NKVD] do not trust him to act directly with M [India], M suggests YMCA should send somebody to I [Kabul] from ZR [Moscow] with whom M [India] can deal.

Delhi wanted to meet the NKVD representative in Kabul or India 'to discuss details of future handling of A [Silver]'.

London, aware of Moscow's feelings, left it to Hill to decide how much of India's view to convey to Ossipov. But they agreed with India that the arrangements had to be modified:

If this is not done there is grave danger of whole business breaking down. We are convinced that direct relations will be to the ultimate benefit of YMCA as they will facilitate a general exchange of intelligence about areas which are too remote to be dealt with here in detail. In effect DIB and AE [Almazov] are both acting as YMCA agents in this affair. It therefore seems obvious that they should communicate locally on day-to-day problems. No opportunity on your part to bring about this result should be lost.[15]

But Moscow would not budge, and Hill was soon back saying that the NKVD did not feel the meeting proposed was a good idea. They wanted more detailed reciprocal information on intelligence from the British, and as far as handling Silver was concerned that seemed to be going smoothly. Hill said his impression was that the NKVD were not prepared to disclose their 'real genius' in Kabul, and that they had not got a sufficiently 'good dummy' to put in his place. IPI, he suggested, should make no attempt to press the NKVD. Within days Ossipov handed Hill a letter explaining that, since they did not have an experienced worker in Kabul who could decide what action to take on his own account, they did not want to duplicate contact there. As it happens, about this time SOE's man in Moscow, Connor-Green, was speaking to Almazov, and would later say he felt 'he was [the] most communicative and intelligent member of Soviet staff'.

But if all this was frustrating for the British, by this time Fleming had fulfilled one objective: the Mary–Oliver wireless operation had started, and this was a great coup. In Kabul Oliver was being operated in the German Legation by Doh under Witzel's supervision, while in Delhi, Mary was coming from a hide-out in the Viceroy's garden in Delhi, with three British officers working under D Division's supervision. They were Silver's 'committee', and could not have been more dedicated to preserving the Empire. The three were William Magan, Malcolm Johnston, a former officer of the Indian police, and signaller Corporal Lappin of the Royal Corps of Signals who, says Magan, was 'a very discreet, likeable and efficient technician'.[16]

Magan, by far the most interesting of the three, was the only one in D Division to have left us a picture of how this trio deceived the Germans. An Anglo-Irish cavalry officer of the Indian Army's Cavalry Regiment (Hodson's Horse), he was known as 'Mullah Magan', as he never drank alcohol, and became a case officer for the Silver operation. Although Silver never got to know it, Magan had a prior connection with him, as he had investigated the mutiny that Sodhi had instigated in the Sikh squadron of the Central India Horse (CIH). Indeed, his write-up of the interrogation of the Sikh soldier who had led the mutiny so impressed Maxine Mitchell, then working as a secretary to the Director of Military Intelligence, that she fell in love with Magan and the two got married. Magan—briefed by Pilditch, who was anxious to get more credit for Silver than he was due—did eventually form a ridiculous impression of how Silver became a spy, and went to his death believing his version. But that can be easily dismissed.[17] What is more interesting is what the Magan trio did night after night when, by July 1943, the Mary–Oliver operation was in full swing:

> ... from our hideout in the Viceroy's garden in Delhi ... on which we sent a mass of false and misleading information. For the sake of notional security we kept changing our schedules, but there was always one in the middle of the night and our wives wondered what we were doing when we got up at two or three o'clock in the morning and went out to some undisclosed place on some undisclosed mission ... We [Magan, Johnston and Lappin] attended every wireless schedule so that we could answer any difficult questions that might be asked ... The two main purposes of this operation were first to put across false order of battle information, and secondly for counter-intelligence purposes. We could provide what to the enemy would seem to be a safe rendezvous to which we send any other agents whom they might wish to despatch.[18]

Soon a link was also established with Abwehr headquarters in Berlin via a station at Burg, near Magdeburg, called Tom. And so, thanks to Silver, for the rest of the war the British in India were broadcasting fictitious, misleading messages directly to the heart of Hitler's Secret Service, where Germans furiously translated messages from English to German thinking they were precious military information. This operation from Delhi also meant that, while Silver remained an agent the Russians were sharing with the British, the Russians had no control over the broadcasts from the Viceroy's garden (and if Magan's version is to be believed then they had no knowledge either). Fleming had engineered a marvellous coup at the expense of the Russians.

But relations between Magan and Fleming were not easy. There was deep distrust between the various British agencies, reflecting those like the DIB, composed of old India hands who were sure they knew India, and newcomers like SOE and Fleming. Magan had no love for Fleming, whom he later described as irresponsible and ambitious. The problems between the various British organisations got so serious that John Marriott of MI5, who controlled Garbo in London, spent some time in India in 1943 and reported back to London on 'quarrels between DIB and the army and [how] nobody had a very clear picture of precisely what he wanted or how the job should be carried out'. Of Magan's boss he told Liddell that he did not 'think much of Denys Pilditch of the Delhi Intelligence Bureau'.[19] Marriott's only satisfaction was that by the time he returned from India in August he had 'finally succeeded in knocking the heads of the military and the police together'.[20]

However, the situation that had resulted was very curious. D Division had direct access between Delhi and the Germans in Kabul and Berlin: what they did not have was direct access in Kabul to their allies the Russians. Here the old situation pertained: NKVD Kabul debriefed Silver in Kabul, then passed it on to NKVD in Moscow, who then passed it on to Hill, and eventually London and Delhi. Pilditch, his request to establish a direct link between Kabul and Delhi having been refused by the Russians, now set about trying to convince London that there was increasing worry about the way Silver was being managed. The result was a classic British solution: a meeting to discuss how to tackle the Russians. On Saturday 2 October 1943, therefore, a high-powered meeting of all the British intelligence organisations was held at MI6's headquarters in London's Broadway, in the offices of Colonel Vivian. Hill flew in from Moscow, Pilditch from Delhi, and also present were Major Seddon and an unnamed MI5 representative.[21]

Pilditch felt the present system posed a danger to Silver, as a result of the direct wireless communication through the Oliver–Mary connection linking Fleming's Delhi operation with the Germans in Kabul. The scenario he presented was as follows. Silver is in Kabul, meeting the Germans, and being asked all sorts of questions about the situation in India, on both military and political issues. At the same time, though, having swallowed his lie that he had a committee in Delhi, Rasmuss and Witzel are also putting questions over the wireless direct to this 'committee'—Fleming's D Division, of course—which have to be answered within 24 or 48 hours. But with Delhi not having direct contact with Silver in Kabul, this means an elaborate rigmarole to make sure Silver and Fleming's D Division do not give contradictory answers that will give the game away. Before Silver's first journey back to Kabul, after Mary and Oliver had got going, Fleming and his team did instruct him that when he was asked direct questions on which he was unable to stall he should pass them to the NKVD, which would then pass them back to Delhi via Moscow and London with all possible speed. But surely Moscow could see this was too cumbersome? Clearly direct communication between Silver in Kabul and Delhi would be quicker and make more sense, and would also enable Delhi to send warnings to Silver when he was in Kabul, 'in order to prevent him making any false step'. And anyway, asked Pilditch, did the NKVD not realise India did not always act under orders from London? London could not dictate, but was 'acting merely as a post box', and would rather prefer the whole business be handled in India. Hill was asked to clarify that India did not want the NKVD representative in Kabul to 'act any more on his own initiative than he does already', but merely make everything quicker.

Pilditch was so keen to change the arrangements and be at the centre of things that he was prepared to go to Moscow, and Hill was asked whether Ossipov would meet Pilditch in Moscow. Pilditch was willing to fly to Moscow from Delhi via Tehran and spend a few days in the Soviet capital talking to the NKVD bosses before flying back to Delhi. He was sure 'that conversations could be satisfactorily concluded in a matter of forty-eight hours and there would be no necessity for him to prolong his stay in Moscow and thus awaken NKVD suspicions'.[22]

Hill felt that direct communications could be established and the NKVD would have no objection, but cautioned that it would be 'injudicious to alter the present arrangements'. Seeing how keen Pilditch was, he warned he should not think of rushing to Moscow, certainly not before Hill, who had come to London for a brief visit, had himself returned to Moscow. London had no objection to Delhi being more involved, and some in London were getting worried that all this Hill support for NKVD suggested he might be going native. However, on this occasion SIS and IPI backed Hill, saying they 'were most anxious' that SOE should handle this:

> SOE Moscow mission was better placed than any other to work with the NKVD. Furthermore, since the SOE branch of [Moscow and] NKVD regarded this matter as their own special pigeon, it would be a mistake to suggest taking it away from them and making it a matter of exchange between the representative SIS organisations.

To further bolster Hill's status, mention was also made that Hill 'had the entire confidence of the Soviet colleagues'.[23]

Such problems between two countries co-operating in such a sensitive area were to be expected, especially given how different these two Allies were. The essential problem over the Silver relationship was that the Soviets felt that in Silver they had given a huge present to the British, and the British were now being very miserly in return. The British had passed on no information about the Siberian front, which had been the first intelligence request the NKVD had made when Ossipov informed Hill about Silver. The British had since given the Russians some information, such as about German agents in Tashkent, but so unspecific that the Russians could not even find out the names of these agents.[24] The Soviets also realised that, while they controlled how Silver was briefed and debriefed through the NKVD in Kabul, for long periods of time he was in India and under British control. The British could, if they liked, suddenly send him to Kabul, and in September 1943 this happened in a way that again made the Russians furious.

It had been decided that Silver would go to the tribal areas in August 1943 to meet Mortas as he came back from Kabul. Soon after this decision was reached Rasmuss conveyed through the Oliver–Mary traffic that Silver should immediately return to Kabul. However, Delhi decided to ignore the request and told Silver that after meeting Mortas he should return to Delhi. No sooner had he got back on the 11th then the Oliver–Mary traffic brought another urgent demand from Kabul that Silver be at once despatched to Kabul with his companion, to take over a second wireless set with codes before certain Germans left Kabul. Having only a few days earlier decided to ignore Rasmuss, Fleming and his team now changed their mind and agreed that Silver and his messenger should immediately head back to Kabul. As per the spy-sharing arrangement the British had with the Soviets, they should have first secured NKVD approval. But D Division decided there was no time for this, and so Silver, accompanied by a new messenger called Kassim, set off. Only then were the Russians told he was on his way and would arrive on the 27th.

Ossipov tersely told Hill the Russians wanted to be consulted

> ... in advance about all Bhagat Ram's [Silver's] activities, in order to avoid one-sided decisions which carry threat of bringing failure to work. Our department [is] concerned owing to fact that Bhagat Ram [Silver] left Delhi for Kabul as a result of a one-sided decision whilst we were only informed today August 27th (i.e. the day on which it is presumed that he will arrive in Kabul). And in effect will make contact with Germans.

Delhi's explanation was that:

> It was at the express wish of Witzel (who wished to hand over a wireless set and additional instructions) communicated by wireless to the Central

Committee that the decision had been taken to send Bhagat Ram [Silver] to meet him before his departure. Had Bhagat Ram [Silver] waited until the approval of the NKVD had been received, Witzel, as it then appeared, would almost certainly have left Kabul for Europe before he arrived. The actual decision was taken on 20.8.43. It was communicated on the 21st and reached London on the following day. It was passed on from London to Moscow on 25.8.43. Had direct contact existed in Kabul between the local representative of the NKVD and the Indian authorities there would have been ample time to inform the NKVD in Moscow of the action proposed and obtain the latter's concurrence.[25]

This explanation, not surprisingly, did not convince Moscow. In the aftermath of the Tirazi affair there had, as we shall see, been a general British and Soviet demand for the German and Italian legations to be reduced, and Witzel was leaving. But as the Russians saw it, Witzel's safe passage was being organised through British territory in India. The British could always delay the arrangements to make sure Silver got to Kabul before he left.

Hill sympathised with Moscow, and complained to London about the Government of India's behaviour, saying IPI

... should fully appreciate that NKVD feels strongly that they are not repeat getting a square deal in this matter and are most sensitive on subject. In their opinion we are behaving in a dictatorial manner and are not treating them as an equal partner in handling their agent.

Hill acknowledged that IPI wanted to establish a close liaison with NKVD either in Delhi or Kabul or by sending a specialist to Moscow, but said 'unfortunately NKVD will not play on these. Submit therefore it is most important that we should do our best to keep existing liaison working as satisfactorily as possible'. He went on to say, 'we should endeavour to consult Russians on all matters concerning A [Silver]. This will undoubtedly cause considerable time delays, which is regrettable, but I fear unless we do so NKVD will suddenly close down on A [Silver]'.[26]

The British decision to rush Silver back to Kabul appeared all the more curious to Moscow, as the British were still saying they were worried about the risk of Silver going to Kabul—indeed, to ensure the Germans did not detain Silver for a long period the report he carried for Rasmuss was asking for his immediate return to India for urgent party work. And if he faced an emergency in Kabul he was told to inform the NKVD, so that India might be informed via Moscow and London. The NKVD agreed but, Hill felt, 'were unappeased'.

Hill summed up the whole situation:

I consider that their amour propre would have been saved had M [India] telegrammed to Moscow action they propose to take and waited for NKVD's concurrence before doing so. It is desirable for M to appreciate that they must expect time lag of at least 24 hours from the time when we have deciphered message to time when it is collected by NKVD. This is inevitable owing to the way our liaison works under Russian cut-out system. It is clear to us that our Soviet colleague in turn passes on such messages to yet another department. Actually in passing your telegram over 40 hours elapsed before NKVD collected this message.[27]

What Hill did not know, and the NKVD never learnt, was that, as with Uttam Chand, the British in India were not being completely transparent with the Russians as to why Silver had been sent back to Kabul in such haste. Much more than what might or might not happen to Witzel, Fleming and his colleagues had got worried when they read Rasmuss's coded message Silver had brought back. It was in several parts, but it was the second part that Fleming found fascinating and which had made him change his mind.

This related to what Subhas Bose was hatching with the Japanese. It spoke of subversive activities to synchronise with military operations the Axis powers were planning, which could see Bose leading an army into India from Burma. For Fleming, Bose and the Japanese were of now of greater interest than anything the Germans were doing. *The Times*, noting Bose's arrival in Tokyo, had commented that

The transference is more than the transference of a single man: it implies a shift of emphasis in Axis propaganda. A year ago Germany and Italy were promising the few listeners in India that their troops would soon be entering India from the west. Now they say action will come from the east, from Japan.[28]

The IPI in London was confident that, having failed to arrive back in the east in 1942, Bose had missed the boat in mounting a major revolt in India. In 1942 he could have exploited the near-revolution that broke out in August during the Quit India movement, but now 'his chances of stirring up a major revolt appear to be small'. Nevertheless this IPI note, whose top-secret status was emphasised by its headline, 'Not to be Reproduced or Quoted', also warned:

Bose's great drive and political acumen, his prestige in Indian revolutionary circles, his understanding of both Indian and English character, will be of great value to the Japanese whose propaganda against India has hitherto lacked imagination ... there is no doubt that under Bose's direction subversive activities and espionage in India will be greatly intensified.[29]

As it happened, at that very moment Bose was holding meetings with the Japanese, pressing them to invade India, and also meeting a Japanese intelligence officer who two years earlier, as Japan advanced through Malaya, had played a key role in suborning Indian troops fighting for the British to switch to the Japanese, with the promise that Japan would help liberate India. While Fleming was not privy to Bose's activities in detail, he sensed something was up and was keen for Silver to find out more, for which it was essential that Silver link up with the Japanese in Kabul.

This was the real reason he was being hurried back to Kabul—so that before the Germans disappeared he could use Rasmuss and Witzel to put him in touch with the Japanese Legation in Kabul. In effect this meant Fleming had set the quadruple spy the mission of using the Afghan capital, where he had begun his spying career three years earlier, to become a quintuple spy, the only one of the Second World War.

Silver and the new Great Game

We have seen how the Tirazi plot and its ramifications affected Silver. This anti-Soviet plan by Afghans who were sympathetic to the Germans was one of the most bizarre episodes of the war and led to the only time during it when London joined Moscow to take on Washington. Here the historic, and much romanticised, Great Game was stood on its head. But, even as the British threw in their lot with the Soviets, they were concerned that nothing should be done to endanger Silver. So, while the British urged Afghans to expel Axis diplomats like Witzel and Doh from Kabul, having identified them as spies with the help of Silver, they were very keen to make sure that Rasmuss remained; without him, Silver could not continue to feed the Nazis duff information. And for all the anti-German feelings stoked up by Wylie, the British worried of the danger this might pose to Silver's life when he came to Kabul.

The affair centred around a German attempt to exploit anti-Russian feeling in Afghanistan, where the plotters gave the impression that they been reading John Buchan's *Greenmantle*, a First World War adventure story. These Germans worked on the theory that anti-Soviet feeling could be aroused among the non-Russian people of the Soviet republics of central Asia, to the benefit of the Nazis. As a secret British note put it:

> The German Legation maintain an organisation of cells throughout northern Afghanistan with a view to collecting information from and spreading disaffection in Russian Turkestan and organising guerrilla bands which, at a suitable moment during a Russian collapse, would cross the Russo-Afghan frontier and 'liberate' Russian Turkestan.[1]

In Saiyed Mubashir Tirazi, who worked for the Royal Secretariat in Kabul, the Germans found the ideal Afghan. He devised a scheme whereby 10,000 Uzbek exiles in northern Afghanistan would mount horses and, like some modern-day Mongol army, sweep over the Soviet border into Bokhara and Tashkent. The scheme was dreamt up in the summer of 1942, just as the German offensive was reaching its peak. Tirazi envisaged that his Uzbek horsemen, driven by the incentive to liberate their lands from the 'godless' communists, would ride their steeds into Soviet territory just as the Germans—having captured Stalingrad, Hitler's supreme objective in 1942—made the breakthrough in the Caucasus. Although the British described it as an Axis conspiracy, the Italians had no part in it. Indeed, Quaroni would later inform the British that he had told Pilger that this plot was 'not only dangerous but futile'.[2]

While Tirazi was the overall leader he had in Kabul a man called Sher Mohamed Beg, whom British agents described as 'leader in Kabul' and head of the military section of the plot. Tirazi was keen to cast his net wide, and India was an ideal place to seek support for his plan.

In September 1942 he fired off a letter to the Bukhara Mujahir Association in Delhi, asking for its help in liberating Russian Turkestan from the communists. His timing was dictated by the fact that the Axis looked to be winning on all fronts and India was in open revolt against the British. Two months later, Tirazi contacted the president and secretary of the Jamait Ulema, a Muslim organisation that supported the Congress-led revolt. Tirazi wanted Jamait's help to organise intelligence and subversive operations in Soviet Turkestan. The British in Kabul were soon aware of what Tirazi was up to. SOE's man in the Kabul Embassy, W. R. Connor-Green, who could speak Russian, had intercepted these communications, securing 'photostats of correspondence between Tirazi and Bokharan emigrés and other malcontents in India regarding activities by them against us in India in return for German help in liberating Bokhara'.

The British had also gathered new evidence about their old enemy the Faqir of Ipi. The agents run by Connor-Green in Afghanistan reported that on 16 February 1943 the Germans had written to the Faqir to say they were sending him money. (The Germans had originally written the letter in English, then got Silver to translate the letter into Dari, the Faqir's language, soon after his arrival in Kabul in January 1943, before despatching it to the Faqir). In their letter the Germans suggested to the Faqir that he summon leaders of the tribes so he could distribute the money to them, and to learn about Germany's propaganda plans. The money, as the British Foreign Office put it, was 'for the creation of disturbances in Indian tribal areas ... we have a list of 36 Afghan subjects engaged in this plot of whom two are dead and one is in prison. They are mostly Afghan tribesmen'.

Tirazi's plot did not begin to unravel until the early summer of 1943. On 26 April Wylie wired London:

During the last three weeks the Afghan Government have arrested both here and in the north of the country large numbers of émigrés from Russian

Turkestan who have been engaged in anti-Soviet conspiracy organised and directed by the German legation in Kabul.[3]

Those arrested included Tirazi and his son. To make sure London took the conspiracy seriously, Wylie added: 'Tirazi has also been in touch with Bokhara emigres in Delhi, and this part of the organisation is clearly directed against us'.[4] In addition to this intelligence, authorities in India had

> ... collected a mass of evidence which proves German intrigue on an intensified scale on the Indian frontier [a reference to the German offer to the Faqir of Ipi]. This also is confirmed by information from very secret sources. These matters raise issues of serious importance.

In the previous four months Connor-Green had been supplying the Director of the Intelligence Bureau with 'with fairly complete details of this whole plan'. As it happened, as Wylie was cabling London, Pilditch was visiting Kabul, giving Wylie an opportunity to discuss it with him. For Wylie this was very useful, for he worried that 'excessive and undesirable telegrams' between Kabul, London and Delhi might fall into German hands; he suggested that Delhi and London wait till Pilditch returned to Delhi to pass on what the British in Kabul had discovered.

Wylie's telegram shows how the Great Game had changed as a result of the Second World War. Now it was no longer Britain *v.* Tsarist Russia, but Britain allied to Stalin's Russia against Hitler's Germany. To emphasise how important the Russians now were, London instructed Wylie that, while he should keep the Soviet ambassador informed at every step, 'it seems unnecessary for you to say anything to the US minister at this stage'.[5]

During his years in Kabul, Wylie had developed a reputation for being a cautious diplomat who did not like confronting the Afghan ministers. But now he was fairly straining at the leash. This change in attitude may have been prompted by the fact that a British agent reported that the Germans were offering a reward to any Afghan who would be prepared to assassinate Wylie or any member of the British Legation. Quaroni would later tell the British that this was a piece of fiction, possibly dreamt up by one of the Afghan agents employed by Connor-Green, but this revelation came long after Wylie had left Kabul. Wylie wanted London to allow him to give the Afghan Prime Minister a dressing-down for allowing such anti-British and anti-Soviet activity, and to repeat the dose he had administered to the Foreign Minister two months previously. In March, just weeks before Tirazi's arrest, Wylie had met Ali Mohammed Khan, the Foreign Minister, and 'had a go' at him about the Afghans for having done nothing about some Germans allegedly operating in Afghanistan's southern Province.[6]

At that meeting Wylie, behaving like a headmaster admonishing a naughty child, had told Ali that just because the Germans were on the retreat on the eastern front and in North Africa, it did not reduce the German menace.

> It was in fact arguable that they were all the more interested in inducing chaos in this part of Central Asia ... they might think a revolution in Afghanistan a very cheap way of damaging the Allies because the retention of strong British forces on the North West Frontier of India would be a considerable aid to the Japanese.

The Foreign Minister's reaction had been so 'bland' that Wylie decided to 'give his pretended complacency some more jolt'. This jolt was to remind the minister of a German intrigue involving the Faqir of Ipi, which Wylie presented as an attempt to 'overthrow the existing regime in Afghanistan itself'. When the minister pointed out that he had met Pilger but the German had denied doing anything improper Wylie, growing into his role as headmaster, said, 'Tut-tut!' Then, after a short history lesson about relations between Britain and Afghanistan, Wylie told the minister that 'it was their duty both to themselves and to us to keep the closest possible control over the Germans, the Italians and the Japanese in Kabul'.[7]

Wylie now proposed to give a similar headmasterly dressing down to Hashim Khan. As we have seen, back in September 1941 Wylie had resisted Churchill's demand that the Afghan government should be made to expel Axis civilians. Then he had not wanted to see the British join hands with the Russians in bullying the Afghans. But, having been overruled by the British Prime Minister, and aware of how successful Churchill's approach had proved, it was Wylie who was now the hawk. He wanted the Afghan government to arrest a list of the Faqir's co-conspirators, compiled by Connor-Green. And he saw the Tirazi affair as an 'opportunity of clipping the wings of Axis legations here—perhaps for good'. And when Delhi and London took their time he complained that they had missed the 'psychological moment'.[8] Wylie went on to say:

> ... overdoing the waiting game in Kabul during the next month may prove to be very dangerous. If German [spring offensive of 1943] happens and if it succeeds at the outset you may find that Afghans have [only] scotched the northern plot and not killed it. If on the other hand the offensive fails from the outset there is the consideration ... that Axis legations here—with their organisation only dispersed and not destroyed—may cause very considerable trouble on the India frontier and possibly in Afghanistan itself.[9]

Wylie had worked out in detail what he wanted to do when he met the Afghan Prime Minister. He would hand over a list of Afghans who must immediately be arrested, and detained 'till the war is over'. If he refused Wylie would threaten him with the Russians. The British 'will place information we have at our disposal with our Russian Ally and discuss the whole situation with them'. For good measure he wanted to tell the Afghan leader that the only reason the British had not so far shared the information with the Russians was 'because we have no desire to embroil Afghanistan with Russians, though we must at the same time protect our Ally's interest, which is gravely threatened by this conspiracy'.

If this threat failed, Wylie would tell Hashim Khan this would 'compel us to take into consideration at once the whole question of Axis legation in Kabul', a clear message that the British would ask the Afghans to expel all Axis diplomats. Even if the Prime Minister gave in he wanted to advise the Afghans to cut back the staff at all three Axis legations to just two each: a Minister and a Secretary; and 'the Secretary ... should be in each case a person known to us and comparatively innocuous'. As a sweetener, Wylie was prepared to guarantee safe conduct to neutral territory for those Axis staff whom the British wanted the Afghans to throw out. They would include the four Japanese engineers who were then working in Kandahar. The demands, Wylie told London, must be backed by threat of economic sanction. With the Afghan economy dependent on its supply routes through India, this was a huge threat, one which Wylie was sure would work, and 'render the Axis prestige here impotent for harm till the end of the war. [The] blow to Axis prestige in all this part of the world, including Persia, will also be practically irretrievable'.

London reined back Wylie, rejecting his suggestion that the British demand the right to vet the secretary of Axis Ministers in Kabul, and also toning down the language used for getting the Afghans to reduce the staffs of all three Axis legations. Even so, the wording Wylie used was such that, while the British would later claim they had made no more than a request, the Americans, and even the Russians, got the impression that the British were demanding the Afghans reduce the staff to two immediately.

It was significant that in this new version of the Great Game, Britain could not act without Russian co-operation. In a telegram dated 12 May the Secretary of State Foreign Affairs India Office told Wylie:

> Our relations with the Soviet Government require that we should not only inform them but also obtain their concurrence in our action. They may wish to support our representation from the outset and if so we cannot object ... you should now urgently inform the Soviet chargé d'affaires [the Soviet ambassador was away] of the action which, subject to agreement of the Soviet Government, we propose to take and to give Connor-Green's information [of the persons to be arrested]. You should make it clear to

him exactly what you intend to pass to the Afghan government, including photostats of letters and list of individuals. A copy of what you give him should be sent to me by air mail.[10]

The same day the Foreign Office sent a secret telegram to its embassy in Moscow, which neatly sums up how much London wanted to work with the Soviets on this issue:

Please explain the situation to Soviet Government. Before His Majesty's Minister [in] Kabul is authorised to approach [the] Afghan Government, we would like to be certain that Soviet Government see no objection from their point of view to information regarding the [anti-Soviet] plot ... being given to Afghan Government or to any other part of our plan. You should emphasise that we would value a very early reply, and the more time elapses between Tirazi's arrest and our own démarche the less effective the latter will be ... We recognise that Soviet Government may wish to make a parallel representation at the outset in respect of German and Italian legations although not of course the Japanese. If so, you might suggest that from tactical point of view it might be better from them to remain in reserve at this stage while we use them as a bogey. But if they press this point you should agree, provided that this does not mean delay. In any case we hope that they will see no objection to His Majesty's Minister, Kabul acting as soon as possible in the expectation that his Soviet colleague will get his instructions at about the same time. But we consider it important that Soviet representations should be separate from our own and not joint as latter would be too heavy a weapon at any rate at this stage. If the Russians make parallel representations we can both demand arrest of individuals [of the Tirazi network] ... if Soviet Government so desire, although many of them are probably already under arrest.[11]

By this time the British had already given 'some of our information about this plot' to the 'Soviet authorities through secret channels', clearly the NKVD–SOE link that also serviced Silver. The Foreign Office also made it clear to its embassy that 'for your own information secret channels referred to in para 2 (b) were through Soviet embassy in Kabul and through Hill in Moscow' [in other words Hill talking to Ossipov].[12]

But while this telegram made it clear that, in dealing with the Tirazi plot, the system being used was the one set up with the Soviets to run Silver for the British, there was also a worry. How would all this affect Silver? Ossipov and Hill discussed this and London informed the British Embassy that it was 'agreed by NKVD [that] BR [Silver] lies low in India until trouble dies down'. This made London confident that 'Special arrangements concerning BR

[Silver] should not in our opinion be upset by the proposed action in Kabul'. The last thing the British wanted was that, in all the arrests they wanted the Afghan government to make, Silver should by some chance get caught. That London made such a specific reference to Silver showed his value and importance to the British–Soviet intelligence partnership.

Although nothing in the documents available so far shows that Silver helped the British to compile a list of anti-Soviet Bokharan émigrés, or of those tribesmen helping the Faqir of Ipi that the British wanted the Afghans to arrest, there is enough circumstantial evidence to suggest that his contacts provided the British with the intelligence in this affair. In his telegram to London asking for authority to give Hashim Khan a dressing-down, Wylie had said with some confidence: 'very secret information available to me from other sources confirm accuracy of C Green's reports'. This appears to refer to Silver, and was very likely based on what Silver was now telling Fleming's team in Delhi about what was going on in the tribal areas.

Britain's cosiness with Moscow worried Delhi, where memories of the Great Game still lingered. Delhi was still not convinced that the old Russian bear could really be trusted. But Wylie was calling the shots, and from Moscow came further evidence of Anglo-Soviet co-operation. On 21 May, London heard from Kerr in Moscow that he had seen the Soviet Foreign Minister and that:

> M Molotov has replied that Soviet govt investigated proposed representation to the Afghan govt which they consider most useful. As soon as His Majesty's Minister has approached the Afghan govt Soviet minister will be instructed to make similar representations making use of information about plot 'C'.[13]

'C' was the code word to describe what Wylie and others were calling Axis conspiracies in Afghanistan. But in order not to let on to the Afghans that the British and the Soviets were collaborating, it had also been agreed that the list of Afghans the two governments wanted arrested should not be exactly the same. So the British would not demand the arrest of Afghans engaged in the Tirazi-orchestrated northern plot against the Soviet Union, while the Soviet Union would not demand the arrest of Afghans engaged in anti-British activity with the Faqir of Ipi.

With the British and the Russians singing from the same hymn sheet, London let Wylie loose, and at 4 p.m. on 27 May 1943 he met the Afghan Prime Minister. It was not quite the encounter Wylie had hoped for, and did not go at all well. When Wylie mentioned names of three men the British wanted arrested, Hashim Khan responded by saying that the persons named were 'of no importance and could not possibly be dangerous and [he] could not arrest them without endangering peace at the border, which in the long run would do us more harm than good'. Hashim Khan had, in any case, only heard of one of these men. Moreover, he emphasised, they could not possibly be arrested while they were on the border. Perhaps, suggested the Prime Minister, they could be arrested if they came to Kabul? This made Wylie snort in some exasperation that 'if it was left like that [he] knew perfectly well that these men would not come to Kabul, at any rate for a long time'. When Wylie persisted in demanding the arrest of the three, the Prime Minister got 'rather aggressive', which made Wylie make the threats that London had agreed he should make. In the end it was agreed the Prime Minister would come back in a week. This brought to a close a meeting which Wylie summed up as follows: 'Tone of conversation throughout was unfriendly but Prime Minister controlled his temper—sometimes apparently with difficulty—and attempted no fireworks'.[14]

Wylie left the Prime Minister all the more convinced 'that it was high time the Government here was pulled up short. Whether it is their hatred of Russians, or indeed ourselves, whatever the cause may be their present relations with Axis seem to me to constitute real danger to the Allied cause in this part of the world'.

Two days later, on 30 May, Wylie could report that all this British bluster had worked. He had been summoned by the Foreign Minister that morning and 'he was friendliness personified'. Two of the three on the British list were being arrested, though the Afghans had doubts whether the British information was all correct. Wylie accepted the arrests were not easy for the Afghan government.

Keen to calm Wylie down, the minister mentioned that he had summoned Pilger about the Tirazi conspiracy: 'He was very contrite, he had had severe reprimand from his Government and [said] that on his personal honour nothing of the sort would ever happen again'. Wylie did not say tut-tut this time, but observed that the German promise meant 'not till the next time, and Minister of Foreign Affairs did not disagree'. The Foreign Minister also agreed they had exercised little control over the foreign exchange the Axis diplomatic staff received, 'but they would now reinforce that control on the lines suggested by His Majesty's Government'.[15] Although neither men knew this, the knock-on effect on Silver was immediate. With the Afghan government limiting the amount of Afghan and Indian rupees Rasmuss could get, he would have to pay Silver even more in gold, dollars and pounds.

By 2 June the Soviet ambassador, Mikhailov, had returned to Kabul. The next afternoon he met Wylie, who reported:

He [Mikhailov] has instructions to see Prime Minister as soon as possible and say (a) that Soviet Govt have already more than once drawn attention of Afghan Govt to hostile activities of German and Italian legations, in

particular their intrigues with Bokharan refugees; (b) that Soviet Govt
have now obtained proof of organised conspiracy not only in Kabul but in
Northern Afghanistan; (c) that leader in Kabul is one Kursh Ahmad, who is
in close contact with Rassmuss; (d) that through the last-named, refugees
have sent letter to German Govt offering to [embarrass] Soviet Govt in
every way possible during spring and summer of 1943; (e) that in pursuance
of this suggestion Germans and Italians are organising revolt against
Bashachas and intend to send rebels arms and money by aircraft; (f) that
Soviet Govt have evidence that German and Italian legations are engaged
in plot to damage their British Ally; (g) arrests made by Afghan Govt are
entirely inadequate to put end to these hostile intrigues against Soviet Govt
and their British Ally; (h) that the attention of Afghan Govt is invited to the
provisions of Soviet-Afghan Treaty of 1931; (i) that Soviet govt insist refugee
organisations be immediately liquidated, all leaders—of whom list is to be
handed over—being arrested and removed from Soviet Afghan frontier; (j)
that Afghan Govt must in their own interest reduce the staffs of German and
Italian legations as soon as possible to Minister and one Secretary each.[16]

Apart from the joint British–Soviet invasion of Persia in 1941, the war would
feature no joint action of the two countries against a neutral power on quite
such a scale. However, even this did not quite satisfy Wylie, who wanted to
know whether the Russians were demanding the Axis legations be reduced
or merely advising. The ambassador's answer was that he saw no difference
between 'advice' and 'demand', an answer that was a wonderful insight into
how Stalin's Russia operated. The Soviet ambassador's 'manner', reported
Wylie, 'was extremely cordial', and he told the British that the Russians were
'gratified at our co-operation over this whole affair'. Wylie assured Delhi and
London that the two would maintain 'closest possible contact with each other
till business is settled'.[17]

Everything seemed to be going well for this new version of the Great Game
when suddenly a nation that had no previous interest in Afghanistan, and was
barely a nation in its present form when the original Great Game was played,
intervened.

Before seeing the Prime Minister, Wylie had also met the US Minister in
Kabul, Cornelius Van Engert. The American who, as we have seen, Fleming had
driven out to Kabul from Peshawar to meet just over a year ago, had written a
book on Afghanistan and was, in many ways, the most knowledgeable of the
foreign diplomats in the Afghan capital. All the evidence suggested that he was
sympathetic to what the British were doing. The British did not see Americans
as having any interest in Afghanistan apart from dealing with incessant Afghan
government requests to increase the sale of *Karakuli* [sheep wool], its main
export, to the US. Indeed, the fact that Engert was a scholar of Afghanistan

was seen as a sign that the Americans merely wanted to know more about the country rather than really get involved in Afghan affairs. But Engert soon learnt details of Wylie's meeting with the Prime Minister and informed the State Department that the two had had 'a stormy exchange of views', and that 'the Soviet Government had been provided by the British authorities with names of some sixty (60) agents of the Axis in Northern Afghanistan and that the British minister at Kabul had been given authorization to support the Soviet Embassy there in case the latter should request the arrest of these agents'. Engert also reported that some of these Axis agents 'hold position in the Government of Afghanistan', although only Tirazi could be said to be part of the royal establishment. Wylie, he told Washington, was said to have warned the Afghans that if they did not agree to reduce the Axis Legation then the British and Soviets would join forces to take further steps, which he thought would be 'a demand to expel the Axis Legation'.

The State Department were alarmed, and told Engert:

> State Department is ... convinced that any [attempt] to force Afghan Government to expel Axis legation or even to forcing them to compel legations to reduce their staff drastically would be inexpedient and might be considered by Afghan Government as unjustified infringement upon their sovereignty and result in feelings of bitterness towards all Allied Governments which might outweigh benefits for Allies including USA. Therefore if further [representations] are made on this subject it is desired that with cognisance of British Minister you make known to Afghan Government our position which is as follows. USA Government actually considers as prejudicial to its interests any activities on the part of Axis ... which might hamper British or Soviet war efforts by creating disturbances in vicinity of Indian or Russian frontiers. It would therefore be glad to see Axis legations in Kabul either closed or drastically [reduced] as to their staff. However this Government realises that maintenance of Axis legation should be question left to decision of Afghan Government and although we feel Afghanistan's best interests are not served by continuing friendly relations with Axis Powers—whose disregard for justice and right have been amply proved throughout the world—this Government does not associate itself with any effort which is now being made to prevail upon Afghan Government either to sever relations with Axis countries or any reduction of personnel of their legations. USA Government's attitude is based on conviction that Afghan Government will naturally wish to act in its own self-interest [and also] on firm confidence in friendship of Afghanistan.[18]

Interestingly Engert did not, as he should have done, go and see Hashim Khan first, and a 'shocked' Wylie wired London on the 8 June that:

American ambassador has just been to see me. Following is practically the exact text of the telegram dated 5 June which he has had from State department and which he read out to me.

Wylie could not wait for Engert to leave and cable to London the State Department telegram above. Engert had confessed to Wylie he did not know why the State Department had taken this attitude. All he could do was speculate that Washington was upset that the British and the Soviets had not informed the Americans. However, he felt the most likely reason was it had come from Roosevelt himself. Just previous to this, the Soviets had broken off diplomatic relations with the Polish government in exile. Soviet troops were about to reach the Polish frontier and Stalin had his own plans to install a communist government which, much to the anger of both Roosevelt and Churchill, he eventually did. Roosevelt, Engert told Wylie, was 'said to be incensed at this action on the part of Soviet Government'. Engert thought that the President felt that if the British in India were collaborating with the Soviets, 'given the latter's methods nobody knew what heavy-handedness [we might] not resort to [before] it is all finished'.

Engert reassured Wylie that 'he had made no recommendations of any sort to State Department'. But he did it 'rather too frequently', which had the opposite effect of making Wylie very suspicious of the American. Wylie in turn told the American that British actions had been misinterpreted. There had been no demand for expelling the Axis legation, the reduction in staff was not a 'demand' and the British were 'seized of delicacy of the whole situation in Afghanistan and had devised their demarche accordingly'. Then, carefully concealing how closely the British had co-ordinated their actions with the Russians, he robustly said that Engert must know 'well enough that His Majesty's Government had not the slightest intention of letting Soviet Government take control of their policy in Afghanistan'.[19]

By this time alarm bells were also ringing in London. On 7 June an American diplomat, Gallman, had written to Hankey, head of the Eastern department of the foreign office:

With reference to these developments the State Department points out that while the government of the United States appreciates how desirable or material reduction of the Axis legation staffs would be it is believed that any show of compulsion by the British or the Russians would cause so much bitterness throughout Afghanistan that any benefits that might otherwise accrue would be outweighed and that should the demand be acceded too by the Afghan government under duress, the very stability of the present regime might be endangered by the resultant resentment among the tribes. Then, too, it is felt that unless the United States government clearly disassociated itself from a course of action so obviously offensive to the Afghans, the United States might also become the object of hostility and the present good will of the Afghans enjoyed by the United States could not be made use of in the interests of all the Allies.[20]

The Americans made it clear that if the British carried on bullying the Afghans they would tell the Afghans that the British and the Soviet action did not represent all the Allies and, while the Americans also wanted the Afghans to break relations with the Axis, this was 'entirely a matter for the government of Afghanistan to decide'.

The Foreign Office in London, appalled by the letter, immediately summoned the American ambassador, John Winant, to the Foreign Office; the only time in the war such a summons was issued.

On the afternoon of 11 June Winant met Anthony Eden in Whitehall. Eden's officials had prepared a closely typed two-page *aide-mémoire* on the subject.[21] This spoke of the 'proof positive' the British and Soviet government had about Axis agents 'organised and financed by Axis legations in Kabul'. Wylie's less-than-friendly meeting with the Afghan Prime Minister was presented as very reasonable requests by the British, not any kind of bullying of a neutral, landlocked country surrounded by two big powers. The Americans, said Eden, were under 'a misapprehension'. The British were not demanding the Axis legations be reduced, they were merely requesting it, and these 'very moderate requests' were in the interests of the Afghan government. The British were, of course, being deceitful, for Wylie had taken great pride in the fact that he had been more robust in his meeting with the Afghan prime minister than the Soviet ambassador had been, informing London, 'I do not gather that the Soviet government's démarche as put by ambassador had an edge on it at all.'

The note Eden handed to the Winant conceded that the British representations in Kabul 'were carefully concerted with the Soviet Government' but this was 'based on the imperative necessity of safeguarding security on the frontiers of India and of the Soviet Union'. In the best Foreign Office tradition of lecturing nations that did not know what they were doing, the American ambassador was told:

> As the threat to the security of these frontiers did not appear to affect the interests of the United State of America, His Majesty's Government did not seek the support of the United States government for their representations to the Afghan government ... In these circumstances His Majesty's Government were surprised to learn the United States Minister at Kabul had been instructed that if further representations were made he should make to the Afghan government a communication which could not fail to encourage

them to refuse the entirely reasonable requests which His Majesty's Government and the Soviet Government have made. In view of their special responsibilities in Afghanistan as a neighbour of India, His Majesty's Government would naturally have expected to be consulted before any such demarche was decided upon ... if the United States Minister in Kabul acts on the instructions which have been sent to him, the only effect will be to convince the Afghan Government that, far from agreeing in principle with the Anglo-Soviet requests, the United States Government entirely disapproves of them and the Afghan Government may very well draw the conclusion that the United States Government is prepared to support them if they should decide to refuse. As the United States Government is not directly concerned with this question of security it may be doubted whether the Afghan Government would expect the United States Government to express its views on this matter; or again whether the latter would incur Afghan hostility unless they disassociate themselves from the Anglo-Soviet approach, especially as the negotiations are proceeding quite satisfactorily. In these circumstances His Majesty's Government entertain the very strong hope that the United States Government will refrain from a démarche which would not fail to prejudice representations essential for the British and Soviet war effort and that fresh instructions may be issued as a matter of urgency to the United States Minister at Kabul.[22]

There was no sharper rebuke that the British delivered to the Americans during the entire course of the war. Winant certainly got the message, telling Eden the *aide mémoire* was 'a very fair and restrained statement of the position'. Winant's attitude was so encouraging that the Foreign Office told Wylie, 'He then made it quite plain that ... he was not in sympathy with his Government's position. I think we can be sure that he will support our representations strongly.'[23]

All this high-powered activity by Eden certainly paid off, and by 19 June Wylie could report that the State Department had first of all apologised for not informing Engert that they were simultaneously informing London of their concerns, and that having read Eden's *aide-mémoire* they had instructed Engert not take any action along the lines of the memo that had caused the rift with the British. Wylie and Engert would have further meetings to clear the air, at the end of which Wylie would conclude that, for all his academic learning, the American was a fool: 'Only possible explanation seems to me that at some stage in his communications with State Department he completely lost his bearings.'[24]

The Russians were amused by the spat between the British and the Americans. Mikhailov did not get on at all with Engert and felt that the American Government were 'having far too happy a time *tertius gaudens* [benefiting from the conflict of the other two allies] and that they should be brought in and made to pull their weight as Allies'. Wylie did not agree with Mikhailov; he did not think Engert was that sophisticated.

During all this, Silver remained the elephant in the room, although Wylie had a hint of his role when, in his meeting with the Foreign Minister, he was told the Afghans 'had definite evidence against two Germans only. Witzel and Doh'. The British had not heard their names and were intrigued as to who these two Germans were. Five days later Silver revealed the truth about them.

> Information received from a most secret source and dated 15 June indicated that the Afghan Government is trying to persuade the German Minister voluntarily to agree to the removal of Witzel and Doh, both of whom are known by the Afghans to be occupied in espionage.

Silver was clearly was the 'most secret source'. And he kept feeding the British information. A Foreign Office memo of 15 July noted:

> The decision to renew our 'advice' for a reduction in the Axis Legation staffs was influenced by our possession of information from *a most secret source* [my emphasis] that the Afghans are now pressing the German and Italian legations voluntarily and in their own interests to curtail anti-British activities and to send home compromised members of their staff, including Witzel, Doh and Anzilotti. This manoeuvre is likely to be successful. The German minister is in favour of dispensing with the services of Witzel and Doh, whose activities have been an embarrassment to him. Their work has already been taken over by Rassmuss, and certain contacts have been handed over to the Japanese. The Italian minister seems prepared to get rid of his chief intriguer, Anzilotti.[25]

As the affair drew to a conclusion, however, London got worried that it might all backfire and jeopardise Silver's operations: 'The chief danger is that [at] a latter date the Afghan government may move too fast for us and close the legations, thereby jeopardising the link in which we are interested'. This link was, of course the Silver link with Rasmuss. For all the bluster about cutting back Axis diplomatic staff this was one Axis diplomat the British did not want forced out of Kabul. On 29 July the Afghan government, 'having discovered intrigues of Witzel and Doh told the German minister that they must leave Afghanistan;' they had also told the Italians that Anzilotti should go, and agreed to 'repatriate' a total of six Japanese, the four engineers plus a Japanese woman working in Kabul and Kamamyami, Chancellor of Legation. At the request of the Axis legations it was agreed that the departure of those being sent home would be presented as 'recall' by their own governments. The Afghans wanted the British to make the arrangements and to ensure there was no publicity about the departures, which the British agreed to do.

All that remained to be worked out was the route Witzel and the others would take to get home. Delhi initially wanted all the Europeans to go round the Cape to Lisbon and with the 'degree of surveillance when in British hands' very precisely defined. London thought that the 'simplest course from security angle would be to fly them to Iraq', and then on to Turkey. They would have to pay their own expenses, their baggage would be searched for 'contraband' and they would be kept under surveillance. And, of course, Moscow had to be kept informed. If the Afghans objected to searching the baggage, they were to be told that this was regular British practice whenever Axis diplomats had been repatriated, and that the British would do what they could to prevent publicity. It was finally agreed that they would travel through India, sail from Karachi to Basra on or about 28 August, with the Japanese leaving via Russia at the beginning of September.

Suddenly, the British were confronted by a new Afghan demand. The Afghans had no time for the Germans but they were diplomats, and therefore they wanted their 'honoured guests' treated well on their journey home. They knew how the Iranians, after the Anglo-Soviet invasion, had not cared to look after the Axis diplomats. They were determined that nobody would accuse the Afghans of that. For all the mischief the Germans might have got up to, for the Afghans extending hospitality to guests mattered. So before Witzel and the others could leave, the Afghans demanded from the British cast-iron guarantees about how they would be treated. It was, said the Afghans, a matter of prestige for them to ensure the diplomats were escorted home safely through British territory and not searched. All the British were prepared to give was a letter the diplomats could carry that would 'simply state that HMG have agreed to allow their passage to Germany/Italy'. London made it very clear that 'no more comprehensive assurances entitling the travellers to any form of immunity can be considered'. The British were prepared to give oral assurance that 'personal search would only be carried out if we had serious grounds to suspect articles not on the list were being carried'.

This led to another fraught meeting between the British—now represented, after Wylie's term as minister had ended, by Giles Squire, who had taken his place—and the Foreign Minister. With Afghan Independence Day celebrations coming it was not until September that they were ready to leave: then another major event intervened.

On 8 September 1943 the Italian armistice was signed, which meant that Italy was no longer an enemy but one of the Allies, and this transformed the positions of both Anzilotti and Quaroni, and cast a very different light on this extraordinary affair. Within days of the official announcement of the armistice, Squire was told by the Afghans that Anzilotti had said he could not possibly travel with Germans, as he now regarded them as enemies. To make matters worse, the poor Italian diplomat did not know where the Italian Government was, or the route he should take to reach Italy. The Afghan Government advised delay, and the British quickly saw how they could profit from this. Squire was told to get in touch with the Italian, find out what he wanted to do and what his movements after Kabul would be; he also agreed to postpone Anzilotti's departure. London told Squire that 'if he proves co-operative by providing useful information you might do what you can to prolong delay as much as possible'. But now the Afghans intervened, and rejected the Italian suggestion that, given Italy was now part of the Allies, Anzilotti should not go at all. His offence, they argued, was against the Afghan Government, and he had to go. In any event Anzilotti did not provide Squire with much information. It was Quaroni who did. He talked at such great length about what the Axis had done in Kabul that he demolished the picture Connor-Green and his agents had so assiduously built over the previous two years.

But as Quaroni filled up Connor-Green's notebooks, more of which later, the arrangements for the Axis were worked out. The Japanese left via Russia; Witzel, his wife, Doh and Anzilotti made it back to Europe through the same route via Peshawar, the boat to Iraq and then Turkey. The only interesting point about all these Axis departures was that when Witzel and company arrived in India, Delhi discovered they were expected to pay £300 to the Germans, the sum the Afghans had told them they would arrange with the Indians as part of what they saw as hospitality due to guests. A stunned Delhi asked Kabul to check before making the payment.

However, this journey of the repatriated agents did have a sting in its tail. Five weeks after Witzel left Kabul Najibullah Khan, the Afghan Director-General of Police, told the Counsellor at the British Embassy that they had long been anxious to get rid of Rasmuss and asked His Majesty's Government to 'kindly make arrangements for his return to Germany similar to those made for Witzel and Doh'. Squire informed London and Delhi, 'They [the Afghans] believe that his departure will be as welcome to us as it is to them.'[26] Nothing could have been further from the truth.

The British wanted Rasmuss in Kabul to enable Silver to continue deceiving the Germans; they could not work out why Rassmuss should be removed. They got a whiff of an answer during the war, but not the full story. It was only long after the war, when the Soviets were occupying Afghanistan, that it emerged that this had come about because the Russians had decided, much as they valued Silver, why stop with him? What about his German spymaster, Rasmuss? Surely they could now also make Rasmuss a double agent, and get him to spy against his country? But this time they were not going to work with the British, but go solo. It was to prove yet another amazing twist to the Silver story.

Silver had arrived in Kabul two days before the Italian armistice, with Witzel frantically preparing for his departure but at this stage blissfully unaware that the man he considered his greatest spy had helped engineer his expulsion. This formed the backdrop to the final wartime meeting in Kabul between the Indian and the German, and much the most fascinating.

Now We Have Five

One reason why Fleming was so interested in what Subhas Bose was up to was because he was fascinated by Bose himself. 'Brilliant, audacious, overweening, shrewd', Fleming wrote after the war:

> Bose in the years before the war had led a career of what might be described as calculated turbulence ... He had ... acquired something of an international reputation as the standard bearer of Indian independence ... With the possible exception of Gandhi, there was not one of the King-Emperor's subjects on whom the British authorities were less anxious to bestow a martyr's crown ... [after his arrival in East Asia Bose] got control of the Japanese-run 'spy schools' at Rangoon and Penang, he put in hand vigorous measures to improve the quantity and quality of clandestine intelligence activities to the Japanese High Command.

Fleming had something of the Arthurian warrior about him: he wanted to fight enemies who were a match for him, not weaklings, and in Bose he saw the worthy adversary he had always been looking for. After a year of dealing with the Japanese themselves Fleming had got fed up with trying to deceive them, concluding that they were not really up to the game of deception. Japanese intelligence staff—he was convinced—were very incompetent: they believed the most 'outrageous and implausible fabrications' and were too slow-witted to make the correct deductions. He was frustrated by the 'ignorance and folly that prevailed on the receiving end'. It did not help that local Japanese commanders also had little time for their intelligence staff, which only encouraged Fleming to combine serious messages with abuse meant to annoy them. One of his agents called Brass repeatedly told his Japanese contact that his commanding officer was living with a prostitute, and that the ruling family of Japan had short furry tails of which they were inordinately proud.[1]

Lt-General Fujiwara Iwachi, at this time the intelligence officer to Major General Kunomura, Chief of Staff of the 15th Japanese Army, was an exception to Fleming's rule, but would later confirm that when it came to the societies in South Asia the Japanese were invading, 'the gathering of information and preparation of such special operations in the South [Asian region] were simply inadequate'. Such information, he emphasised, was 'indispensable for any special operations involving political and psychological aspects, and espionage and counter-espionage activities [special operations, literally secret wars]. It was also essential for any political manoeuvring after the areas came to be occupied'.[2]

Bose, however, the head of D Division was sure, would provide a challenge to his powers of deception. In Fleming's archive there is a five-page handwritten note on Bose, clearly written after the war, labelled, 'Battle of Wits—Bullfighter':

> His friends are always pleased when a man who is rather deaf acquires a hearing-aid; and the arrival of Bose in the Japanese camp was for analogous reasons welcomed by the small Deception Staff in Delhi. They were already—or had been until he left Germany—in touch with Bose through a high-grade channel to the Abwehr, and they had good reason to hope that his quick wits, his dynamic personality and his long experience of under-cover activities would before long widen the front, hitherto disappointingly narrow, on which they were in contact with the enemy's Intelligence; they looked forward, also, to dealing with a sophisticated adversary who could be relied on—as the Japanese could not—to see the point of the information they gave him. These hopes were only partly fulfilled.[3]

Another sheet of paper in Fleming's archives marked 28 July 71 suggests he was collecting material for a book on D Division's work. However, 17 days later Fleming, while grouse shooting in Scotland, had a sudden, massive heart attack and died instantly, and the book was never written, which is a great pity. But his assessment of Bose remains remarkable, in stark contrast to what the British said about Bose during the war, and many still think—and also, of course, to what Silver now thought of Bose.

Throughout the war the British loudly proclaimed that Bose was a 'traitor' or, as the *Sunday Express* headline of 4 June 1942 describing his meeting with Hitler put it, 'India's Quisling'. A secret IPI note on him declared:

> Weak-minded, suffering from an inferiority complex, lacking in all the qualities of leadership, he shrank from the all-India position thrust on him and sank into a provincial leader whose one absorbing interest apparently was to mould the affairs, not even of the Bengal Congress, but of the Calcutta

Corporation ... his mental equipment is not generally regarded as being in the same class as that of Gandhi and Nehru.[4]

But Fleming had correctly divined that Bose liked playing the deception game. 'Propaganda,' Bose had told his associates, 'must be bumptious to be really effective. We must always be thinking up new things to hold the interest of the people.' For him these new things meant also exaggerating his own military strength: 'In India, the British Army boasts of its military strength ten times more than its actual strength. Indians believe this and are being influenced by it. Now, I follow the British Army's example, and would like to propagate that the Provisional Government of India has more than 30 divisions.'[5] Soon after his arrival in Singapore he had met Fujiwara, and while Bose would probably have agreed with Fleming that Japanese intelligence was not much good, he knew Fujiwara was an exception. Bose was very aware of how, in December 1941, the Japanese had suborned Indian soldiers fighting for the British in Malaya as Japan advanced. It was Fujiwara who in December 1941, had formed a friendship with Captain Mohan Singh of the 1/14 Punjab Regiment and, in a historic meeting at the village of Alor Star in north Malaya, persuaded the Sikh and his fellow Indian soldiers that with the British having been defeated the Japanese could help them remove India's 'shackles of slavery' and make 'Asia for the Asiatics'. This had led to the setting-up of the first Indian National Army under Japanese auspices. But while that had collapsed as the Indians realised that Japanese were guilty of racism, arrogance and mistreating people under its rule even more so than the British, Bose had taken charge of the second INA and was busy trying to attract local Indians to supplement its core component formed from Indian prisoners of war.

Bose had settled in the Kallang area of Singapore, in a beach-fronted house with spacious gardens. He had discarded his flowing silk suits, in one of which he had arrived in Singapore, for an imposing military uniform: khaki tunic, forage cap and knee-length military boots. And, having almost overnight converted himself from a middle-aged politician into one who looked like a general, he had given the clarion call of *Delhi Chalo*—Let us go, Delhi—calling on Indians, '*tum mujhe khoon do, main tume azadi doonga*': You give me blood; I will give you your freedom. Now that Bose was in Singapore there was much gossip amongst the British in India as to whether he might suddenly return to India, and Ian Stephens, editor of the *Statesman*, shocked a Calcutta dinner party by saying that were the Japanese to parachute Bose on to the city's Maidan, the huge green area in the centre of the city, some 90 per cent of the city's inhabitants would rush to join him.

So now Fleming had the chance to take Bose on. Much taken by that section in Rasmuss's message that spoke of just such a planned march to India by

Bose and the Japanese, he had inserted into the report Silver carried a passage saying why such a thing would not work: Silver's 'central committee', Rasmuss was told, was struggling against many difficulties and setbacks. The report also contained a good deal of misleading military information exaggerating the strength of Allied forces in India.

Fleming had also tutored Silver carefully in how to respond to Rasmuss if he asked what the British were planning in Burma. In December 1942, after almost two years of doing nothing since its fall, the British finally reappeared in their former colony, and three British-Indian divisions attempted to seize Akyab Island on the Arakan coast, but were easily rebuffed by the Japanese. Then in February 1943 Orde Wingate launched *Operation Loincloth*. The title of the operation, a mocking reference to what Gandhi wore, saw a British infantry brigade, lightly equipped and specially trained, penetrating the Chindwin river area to operate behind Japanese lines for two months and temporarily cut the Mandalay–Myitkyina railway line, killing many Japanese. In military terms it meant little, but psychologically it was very significant. For the first time, British troops had taken the offensive against the Japanese and shown they could fight them in the jungle, and the British press soon built Wingate up as a great 'man of destiny'. Although Wingate's Chindit activities were not meant to be a prelude to an invasion of Burma, when Rasmuss asked Silver if this was so Silver was to reply: Yes. Training in jungle warfare to fight in Arakan was also in progress, he would go on to tell the German, and the British could go on the offensive quite soon.

But eager as Fleming had been for Silver to hurry back to Kabul in August 1943 as Silver set off for his ninth visit to Kabul, he had his fears. Just before Silver left he bumped into an Afghan contact from Kabul seemingly quite by chance in a Delhi street. When he told Fleming the Englishman got very worried. Could he be a government agent? If he was, and the Afghan saw Silver in Kabul, wouldn't he immediately suspect that Silver was working with the British? Not only would it blow his cover: it could also put his life in danger. Despite his eagerness to fool the Germans yet again, Fleming wondered whether he should go back, but Silver, bitten by the spy bug, could not imagine not going. To try and protect him Fleming made sure a letter sent via Hill to Ossipov asked the NKVD to warn Silver to exercise great care 'in order not to appear within field of vision of Afghan police'.

The Russians had readily agreed to protect their treasure but this trip once again showed the growing tension between the allies over the management of Silver. This time the Russians angst was about what they saw as lack of adequate information from the British about Silver's movements. As we have seen they had been told by the British that Silver would arrive in Kabul on 27 August 1943 when in fact he and his messenger Kassim arrived on the evening of September 1st. Given that Silver was going through tribal territories on foot, the five day delay was very understandable but it did nothing to allay Russian suspicion of the British manipulating Silver. The Russian response was for Zaman to spend two whole days exhaustively quizzing Silver, and only then was he allowed to meet the Germans. Witzel dutifully came round in his car and drove him to Rasmuss's house. The Germans were 'very pleased' with the report that Fleming and his D Division had invented—so pleased that they took Silver to the Legation, where he spent the next five days.

There, Doh told him that a spare transmitter would be sent with Silver to Delhi, Rasmuss using the *Oliver–Mary* communication system a few days later to inform 'the committee' [D Division] this was to be kept in reserve in case the police seized the 'existing transmitter with the central committee'. With the Germans' situation becoming increasingly difficult, Berlin had instructed Rasmuss to close down all secret work in Kabul, except with Silver. The Abwehr was insistent that Silver's 'central committee' connection should be maintained, and what better way than by a direct wireless link between Abwehr headquarters and Silver's 'central committee'? Witzel now gave Silver details of a German station at Burg, near Magdeburg, that went by the name of *Tom*. Back in Delhi the real central committee of Fleming, Magan and the rest of D Division could hardly believe what they were hearing, even though by now they well aware of Silver's ability to convince these gullible Nazis in Kabul of almost anything. On Silver's return to Delhi Magan and company were soon using *Mary* to send messages to *Tom*, directly to the heart of Hitler's Secret Service, and, says Magan, 'we had three wireless schedules daily to Berlin'.

Such was the trust the Germans had in Silver they also gave him the choice of choosing his own transmitter. Witzel and Doh took Silver to the room in the Legation where three sets of transmitters were stored and reassured him that they had been tested in Berlin and were in working order. He choose one that was packed in two heavy suitcases weighing 80 pounds and, given the spell he had over the Germans, it is very possible he got Witzel to drive him back to his Kabul flat with them. They did not stay there long, as that very day he deposited them at the Russian embassy. He would later tell the British the reason he did not bring the set with him was because lugging two such heavy cases through the tribal territory would have aroused suspicion. The Russians, of course, were only too happy to look after this important Abwehr kit. But storing it at the Soviet Embassy in Kabul would, as we shall see, cause D Division some headaches, and put further strain on the Anglo-Soviet intelligence co-operation over Silver.

Oblivious of this, meanwhile, Witzel then spent nearly two days giving Silver detailed instructions on a new book of codes for the *Oliver–Mary–Tom* traffic. Fascinated as ever by the tribal areas, he also handed over three large maps of the whole area from Berlin to Kabul, instructing that they be kept concealed in the tribal territory. Witzel also had plenty of questions for Silver. He wanted to know the organisational strength of the 'central committee'; about the special services corps Jai Prakash Narain, a rebel Congress leader, had been training on the Nepal border at the time of his arrest; and about the various revolutionary groups that had sprung up since the launch of the Quit-India movement. Silver was not prepared for such questions, and knew little about any of events Witzel was referring to, but made up answers so successfully that Witzel was convinced he was fully in charge of what was happening in India. But when Witzel wanted hard information such as reliable addresses in Eastern India to be communicated to Bose, Silver gave nothing away, instead turning the tables to get information out of Witzel. Since many secret addresses had been exposed by carelessness, he told the German, it would be unwise to divulge any such information until Bose's messengers had been contacted and their reliability established—a sly way of getting Witzel to disclose the names of the agents Bose was sending to India so that Silver could then pass them on to his 'committee'. Skilful as Silver now was at dissembling, it says little for Witzel that he did not for a moment suspect he was being duped. The conversation ended with a classic Silver touch. As Witzel pressed him for at least one address they could forward to Bose in the Far East, Silver provided the name and address of a friend of his in Lahore, Ram Parshad, a bookseller at Lahori Gate in Lahore city. This poor man had no idea Silver was using his name in such a way, and in any case was nearly 2,000 miles away from eastern India, where a Bose agent was likely to arrive.

The Germans were eager for such information because they had fresh instructions for Silver from Bose. These included plans to land men by plane in the tribal areas, establish a provisional government in India before Witzel left Kabul, and intensify propaganda among the British-Indian army, which Bose complained was 'not very effective'. Rasmuss and Witzel also told Silver that Bose would begin the march on India along with the Japanese at the end of October or the beginning of November, 1943. For Silver this was very interesting news.

Bose was now far down the road on his march on India. He was reinforcing the army of Indian prisoners of war with recruits from Indians living in East Asia, and had also formed a women's regiment, arguing that giving Indian women military training would make them more disciplined and in turn produce better-disciplined children. And, seeing himself as no different from the leaders of countries occupied by Nazis who had formed exile governments, Bose had set about forming the Provisional Government of India. Bose, with great fanfare, proclaimed the establishment of the government in October 1943, a month after Silver left Kabul. The government's first act was to declare war on Britain, but also, rather bizarrely, on the USA. For good measure Bose also demanded all the rights and privileges of a head of state, with the Japanese even giving him his own special plane, but staffing it with a Japanese crew, two of whom spoke Hindustani and were clearly meant to monitor what the Indian leader said and did.

Bose was also pressing the Japanese to launch an attack on India. Despite the myth that has grown up since, the Japanese High Command, as Sir John Figgess told the Historical Section of the Cabinet Office on 26 June 1948 after consulting the surviving Japanese commanders:

> ... did not seriously contemplate an invasion of India by land in 1944. They did, however, hope to inflict such serious defeat on the British Indian forces that Subhas Chandra Bose would be able to lead his Indian National Army unopposed into India and thus achieve a virtually bloodless conquest.[6]

Even Bose did not visualize a swift march to the Viceroy's Palace in Delhi. His plan was, with Japanese help, for his INA to establish a foothold in India from where his revolutionary army could steadily advance further, or at least create such a position that, whatever the outcome of the war, a free Indian state of some size would survive—the same sort of entity that Sukarno was able to establish in 1945 in Indonesia. In a meeting with the Japanese Foreign Minister in June 1943, soon after his arrival in south-east Asia, Bose had urged an attack through Chittagong, seeing the fall of this East Bengal port as the catalyst for the INA: the British would be thrown into disorder, and Bengal would form a ready and welcome base for revolutionary activities. For the Japanese, however, Chittagong was strategically impossible: the supply problems would be horrendous. Being a port, it would also be exposed to attacks from both air and sea—two sectors in which Japanese strength was rapidly waning.

By August 1943 Japanese had finally formulated their plans for India and Bose was informed that the INA would be actively involved in an offensive the Japanese Army was preparing on Imphal in the mountainous regions of the Burma–India frontier. Brushing aside Wingate's Chindits as of no consequence, and confident they could rout the British as they had done in Malaya, the Japanese were sure it would all be over in three weeks.

On this trip to Kabul Rasmuss was eager to know from Silver what the reaction would be to such an attack. Well briefed by Fleming, Silver responded that the committee would be only half prepared, prompting Witzel to assure Silver that due warning of the attack would be given, followed by instructions of what to do, and arms and technical experts would be landed by submarine. He wanted Silver's committee to select suitable landing places between Madras and Calcutta on the Orissa coast, and discussed using light coastal aircraft to establish contact with submarines and to take personnel and cargo ashore. There was again talk from Witzel about dropping men by parachutes in tribal territory, which he felt could profitably be synchronised with the Japanese invasion. Rasmuss and Witzel were also keen for an indication of the internal disorder likely in India in the event of an invasion. And what plans had his committee made for guerrilla warfare behind Allied lines? Silver promised to discuss the matter with the committee, but emphasised that it could not make a programme of subversive action unless Bose took them more into his confidence as to his own plans for the future.

So far the Japanese in Kabul had been the great other in this story. Despite the much-talked-about Axis alliance, the Japanese were almost detached from the Germans and the Italians, one reason being that they felt they had established all the necessary sources of information in India with one Japanese *chargé d'affaires* in Kabul, using a 1941 visit to India to scatter the ashes of a prominent Japanese, to fix up secret communications between Japanese underground agents in India and the legation in Kabul. We do not know what these connections were, but Quaroni, who thought the Japanese were cleverer then the dim-witted Germans, gathered that what interested the Japanese legation most was information about shipping, which the Japanese diplomat had collected very satisfactorily.[7] The Japanese and the Germans, Quaroni would also advise Connor-Green, just did not get on— and in 1942, when the Germans were still hoping to capture Stalingrad, there was much ill-feeling between them as to who was to have India. Quaroni would also tell the SOE man that Russo–Japanese relations were a good deal more intimate than the outside world would suggest: the German legation in Kabul had received orders to the effect that in talking business to the Japanese they were to reveal nothing about German anti-Soviet plans, since Berlin had discovered that the Japanese were passing on all such information to the Russians. What the Germans and Quaroni did not know was that this was because the cables of Baron Oshima, the Japanese ambassador in Berlin were being read by the Americans. He was, as Max Hastings puts it, 'the Allies' best secret agent of the war'.

Despite all this, Rasmuss was quite happy, when pressed by Silver, to introduce him to the Japanese representative in Kabul. Amazingly, one reason was that, for all the money the Germans had given Silver, Rasmuss and Witzel felt guilty they had not been able to give him even more. The restrictions put on the Germans by the Afghan government in the aftermath of the Tirazi affair meant very limited access to Afghanis and Indian rupees and Rasmuss could not apologise enough for the 'obstructive attitude' of the Afghan government. However, he assured Silver, the Japanese were in negotiation with the Russians for a courier to come to Kabul from Japan, and if this succeeded he might bring money in the diplomatic bag. Rasmuss also held out the hope that by putting Silver and his committee in direct contact with the Far East it would not only provide his committee with adequate funds but also ensure a supply of arms, equipment and technical assistance. But while the German was ready to act as a go-between for Silver and the Japanese, he warned Silver that Berlin did not want the Japanese to know the plans for wireless contact between 'the central committee' and Germany, which was why he insisted that the report he had brought from Delhi could not be shown to the Japanese in its entirety. This resulted in one of the more comical aspects of Silver's spy saga.

The report Silver carried had two parts, a military one and a political one. Rasmuss had no problems showing the Japanese the full military part. However, he could not let the Japanese know of Oliver, Mary and Tom so he prepared an abbreviated political report excluding references to them. He then attached it to the military part. So, a fictitious report prepared in Delhi by Fleming and his D division had now, in effect, been further embellished by the Germans. The meeting between Silver and Inouye, the Japanese attaché in Kabul, was arranged at the German legation. Rasmuss and Witzel worked out a careful plan as to how they would go about it. Just before Silver met Inouye Rasmuss gave the Japanese the report he had doctored, emphasising its priceless quality. Then Witzel brought Silver in and introduced him formally to Ionuye. The date of this meeting, 8 September 1943, is worth noting, as it marks a landmark moment in Silver's spy career. This is when he officially became a quintuple agent.

Just as when he had met Quaroni and Rasmuss, Silver quickly impressed Inouye. Their meeting lasted an hour with the Japanese, fairly early in their conversation, telling him his government had instructed him to establish close contact with Silver and his 'committee' through Rasmuss. The meeting convinced Silver that here was yet another Axis diplomat-cum-intelligence chief who was ready to be deceived. Inouye was eager for answers, but Silver, a veteran in pretending to say something without actually doing so, nearly always referred him to the latest report he had given Rasmuss. Well briefed by D Division, Silver also told the Japanese that the 'Anglo-Americans' had a very powerful air force in India, and that he thought they would land by air in south Burma and north Malaya to cut Japanese supply lines to Burma.

Inouye, of course, had no message from Bose, and Silver, immediately sensing a chance to get the upper hand, told him that as his 'committee' worked for Bose, Bose should keep them closely informed of his plans so they could 'march in step with him on a common enterprise'. Eager as his 'committee' was to work with the Japanese they could hardly do so if they did not know enough of what Japan was planning. So convincing was he that Inouye sympathised, and said he would convey the committee's sentiments to Tokyo.

Important as meeting with Inouye was, Silver spent much of his time in Kabul, with the Germans, as he had since 1941, and once again demonstrated his great skill in misleading them. This was most evident when the Germans started quizzing him on a subject he knew nothing about: Mussolini's recent downfall and the King of Italy's appointment of Pietro Badoglio to take over. With Italy's fate hanging in the balance after Allied military successes, Berlin was very anxious to know how this affected Silver and India, and Rasmuss handed Silver a list of 24 questions about what would happen should Italy defect from Axis to Allies, as it did within weeks. Though Silver had not been briefed by D Division, or had any reason to anticipate such an event, and knew nothing about the political situation in Europe, he improvised such brilliant answers that Rasmuss was 'highly delighted'.

In some ways the most bizarre moment of Silver's talks with the Germans concerned what could be done in Teheran. As an alternative to the direct *Oliver–Mary* wireless channel, Witzel had suggested during Silver's earlier visit, between January and March 1943, that contact between India and Berlin could be established via Iran. Silver had immediately invented an imaginary relative in Tehran by the name of Purshottam Das, who he said would be ready to act as a courier. The Russians in Kabul approved Silver's ruse, so did Moscow, and 'Das' had been given a coded symbol, AC. Delighted with the discovery of an agent in an Allied-occupied country, Rasmuss and Witzel had passed on his name to Berlin, which asked for the new agent's address so that someone might be sent to contact him.

As can be imagined, Fleming and D Division had much fun with this latest fiction of Silver's, and began to spin more fantasy for the Germans. In June 1943 Berlin had been told that one of Silver's agents had gone to Tehran and found 'Das' seriously ill and keen to return to India. The Germans were further told the two men had discussed the possibility of a substitute, with 'Das' suggesting a Muslim who had been in Tehran for some time and was bitterly anti-British. Another agent with a suitable Muslim name was found. As opposed to the fictitious Das, this man was in fact genuine, and given the code name NT. Assured he was a real Muslim and reliable, the NKVD gave its assent to using him. Now in Kabul in September Witzel wanted to activate this agent and told Silver that when the German agent contacted NT in Teheran he would give the code name 'JQ' (Hattiph). Silver agreed to communicate the secret password, but warned that he must consult with his 'committee' before anything could be done. We do not whether NT ever met JQ resulting in the Allies capturing a German agent in Iran. But even if this did not happen it shows the sort of games the nonchalant Silver could play with Rasmuss and Witzel.

However amidst all this deception there was a very serious moment which provides a revealing insight into Silver's character. It concerned Bose's offer, broadcast from Singapore, to send rice to famine-stricken Bengal. For Bose, the reports of corpses strewn around the streets of his beloved Calcutta he knew so well were truly heart-breaking. And his offer was in stark contrast to the reluctance of Churchill and the war cabinet to divert war-time shipping so that food could be brought to alleviate the starvation in Bengal. But when Rasmuss asked what had been the reaction in India to the offer he did not get quite the answer he expected. Silver said that:

> ... a man in the street would certainly like to grab the offer, but the shrewd people would say that it was a propaganda move on the part of Subhas Chandra Bose, because it was clear that neither the British would allow it nor was it possible to send it when the bloodiest war was going on.[8]

Thousands of his fellow Indians may have been dying, but for Silver what mattered was what he saw as the bigger picture: winning the war for the Soviet Union and the British. As we have seen, the reasons for not diverting food supplies leaves no doubt the British administration should have been in the dock of world opinion for this very preventable tragedy. Yet Silver wanted to give no encouragement to the Axis to believe they could—on this issue at least—claim the moral high ground. And by using the word 'propaganda' in relation to the Bose offer he wanted to make sure of that.

This ninth visit ended much as the previous ones. A few days before his departure Witzel gave him three Leica negatives, coded messages containing wireless communications between *Oliver* and *Tom* and also suggesting landings sites from submarines. And as always the Germans gave him money: 500 gold sovereigns 10,000 American dollars for the 'committee's' expenses, and 3,000 rupees for his personal use.

But even the flint-hearted Silver, who had fleeced the Germans so much, noticed that this visit was different. Rasmuss and Witzel were no longer the confident Germans certain of ultimate victory they had always been. Rasmuss's morale was very poor, and he was haunted by the fear of impending defeat, admitting Germany was on the defensive in Russia, but still hoping the Russian army could not maintain its offensive. Even Witzel, who had always been the more ebullient of the two, was very downcast, and one evening, as he drove Silver to Rasmuss's flat, confessed that his days in Kabul were coming to an end. Arrangements had been made for him and Doh to be granted a safe passage by the British so they could leave via India and head home. Their only consolation was that with direct wireless contact between Berlin and Silver's 'central committee' their most valuable contact could still feed them information, even if both of them were no longer in Kabul. Silver was now so adept at deceiving the Germans that he made all the right sympathetic noises without, even for a moment, betraying that it was he who had told the British that Witzel and Doh were spies and engineered their departure. In stark contrast Witzel, who saw Silver as a dear friend was inconsolable. The German who so wanted to be a Pathan was bidding goodbye to the one real Pathan he knew and determined to make the parting memorable.

It was during this visit that Silver was given the Iron Cross for his services to the Reich. And almost as a personal parting present, Witzel gave Silver a Minox miniature camera and an automatic pistol. Rasmuss concerned about his safety urged him not to delay his stay in Kabul warning him there was increased Afghan police surveillance. He did want him to return to Kabul around the end of October 1943 but if he could not come, said Rasmuss, a courier would do and promised to transmit further tasks to him by wireless. Even for such a calculating person as Silver, it is possible he felt a little pang as he bade them goodbye.

Silver would never see Rasmuss again, although many decades later, he would meet up with Witzel. But by then the world both had known had changed dramatically. That meeting would take place many thousands of miles from Kabul, although ironically in a city, Calcutta, that will always be associated with the man who had played such a huge part in both their lives: Subhas Bose. And, as we shall see, it would involve the final deception Silver would perpetrate. But this time not on the Germans but on his fellow countrymen.

Silver left Kabul well aware how life as spy had changed, although he was not aware quite what a special spy he was. The first Axis power he had deceived, Italy, was about to switch sides and join the Allies—indeed, as Rasmuss and Witzel had been grilling Silver, not far away in the Italian Embassy, Quaroni was getting ready to talk to the British. Within days of Silver leaving Kabul, Italy having signed the armistice with Eisenhower's invading forces, Quaroni began to talk so volubly to Connor-Green that, one British official noted, 'it would be laborious to send you the full story of the examination of his statements, for that would involve a long cyphered telegram'.[9]

Silver spent little time thinking of the Italian. His concern now was how to make sure he could manipulate Inouye as he had Quaroni and Witzel. And he realised that he had his work cut out when, just as he was getting ready to leave Kabul, he received a coded message via Witzel. The message asked him to delay his departure for a few days, as Inouye would be sending some military questions for him to answer. However, when Silver turned up at the pre-arranged spot outside Kabul where he always met Witzel, the German confessed that no message had come from the Japanese. Silver expressed his annoyance and immediately began to think of ways of making Inouye as pliant as Witzel.

Of course, Silver could not leave without seeing the Russians, and he spent six days between 9 and 14 September 1943 briefing them on everything Rasmuss and Witzel had said, as well as handing over the wireless set and the gold sovereigns and dollar notes. And the Iron Cross for which he had no use and felt total contempt. What he carried back to Fleming's D Division were new cyphers and instructions from Germans.

But what about that troublesome Afghan he had met in Delhi? According to Silver he did meet him in Kabul and, instead of panicking, invited him for a meal to his flat. It turned out to be the last meal the Afghan ever had. This was because, Silver told Fleming, into the curry he prepared for his host he had mixed tiger's whiskers, these being a deadly poison. How far the story is true is impossible to say, but Fleming, nowhere as gullible as Rasmuss or Witzel, believed it, seeing it as further proof of Silver's remarkable prowess as a spy. Whether Silver told the Russians of this Afghan is not known, and it is very possible his safe return from Kabul was due to Russian protection rather than anything to do with tiger's whiskers in a curry.

Silver returned to India to hear more good news and more goodies from the British. Jamuna Das had been released from prison to visit his sick wife. In Delhi the home provided for him by the British where he lived with his wife and child now had a *chowkidar*, guard. Silver demanded more help and the British readily agreed to another assistant who during his absence in Kabul would 'look after my household' and act as a sort of major domo, helping him in his work and acting on any message he received from Kabul. Later in the month the British also organised trips to Bombay for him to brief the communist party leadership on what he was doing, and then holidays in the Naronna barrage in Aligarh district and then the Banbassa barrage in Nainital district, necessary, Silver writes:

> ... to recoup my health which was badly affected by the irregularities of an underground life. This period of my life in which I recovered my lost health and vigour will always remain in my memory. And the credit for all this goes to my wife. Though non-political she helped me loyally as a real Indian wife and it was actually because of her selflessness and devotion that I regained my health to a great extent.[10]

It is difficult to be sure about Silver's half-truths, but this passage suggests that she looked after their child in Delhi while he went on a holiday on his own round India, confident that the extra help the British had provided meant his wife and child would be well looked after. For Silver, the essential loner, life could not be sweeter.

The only cloud on his horizon was learning that Uttam Chand had been talking freely in prison, with the result was that it had become well known in certain political circles that following Bose's escape to Europe contact had been established with both the Germans and the Russians. What is more, in jail Uttam Chand had learnt from a Punjab CID officer that Silver was working for the British.[11] As Uttam Chand told me:

In 1944 I was in Lahore Fort and an Englishman, a CID officer told me that 'Bhagat Ram is working for us.'[12]

But at least Silver could be confident the British would not release Uttam Chand, which would have made life even more difficult for him. More worrying was that the friction between the British and the Russians that had marked his journey to Kabul soon resurfaced after his return. Moscow was now beginning to realise the consequences of sharing Silver with the British. When he had been their exclusive agent between 1941 and 1943, he had been footloose, going back to India to concoct fiction with Sainsra and then returning to Kabul. They knew when he would be back and felt in control. Now Fleming's D Division decided when he would return to Kabul, which the Russians resented. On 14 October 1943 Hill telegraphed London that Ossipov had informed him it had come to their knowledge that the Germans wanted Silver back in Kabul towards 20 October. The British, however, had not informed the Russians either about Silver's arrival in India or when he was likely to return.

> It is in the interests in the business that we should be informed not only of movements of A [Silver] but also of his position in M [India]. In case A [Silver] will be returning to I [Afghanistan] we hope that you will be good enough to inform us of his mission.[13]

India, via London and Hill, responded that it was not possible for Silver to go back to Kabul immediately, and that the 20 October date was not to be interpreted literally but merely a request. The Russians were told that, given that Silver was a member of a 'committee' it was 'unreasonable ... to spend all his time travelling as a messenger between Kabul and his colleagues in India'. He had been summoned back to India by the committee 'for important work'. Moreover, in the meantime Jai Prakash Narain had been arrested, which Delhi felt:

> ... must be interpreted by the Germans as a serious blow to the committee. Making still more necessary Silver's presence in India for some time to come. When time comes for Silver's return you will be given warning in advance for communication to NKVD.[14]

The British, of course, were lying, since this 'committee' was D Division, but they wanted to make sure Fleming's team had got all they wanted out of Silver and briefed him fully before sending him back.

The British also had their own problems, as a result of the wireless set Silver had left behind with the Russians. The German set Delhi already had was not working well, and after good contact with Berlin at the outset the tests had been unsatisfactory. With Witzel having given Silver a new set, Delhi knew it would be required to acknowledge receipt of this new transmitter and almost certainly be instructed to carry out tests with it. But with the set at the Russian Embassy in Kabul this was not possible, while to substitute another transmitter would be risky as it would be spotted by the receiving station. Delhi therefore asked the NKVD in Kabul to hand over the big transmitter to the British Legation in Kabul so it could be brought to Delhi—'The matter is one of great urgency.' Delhi also wanted the transmitter key to be sent, promising to send the name of the person in the British Legation the Russians should contact. However, the complicated communication arrangements of this unique spy-share arrangement meant DIB in Delhi had to telegraph London, which forwarded it on to Hill in Moscow, who was asked to approach NKVD 'forthwith' and make 'the requisite arrangements'.

As this was being sorted out in October 1943 there was another amazing development in Kabul, initiated by the Russians, which quite shocked the British, the details of which only emerged long after the war was over. This was the Russians' attempt to blackmail Rasmuss to become their agent. There is some dispute as to when the Russians dreamt up this plan, with one Russian historian claiming it dates back to May 1943.[15] That is debatable, but what is certain is that the idea originated not in Kabul but in the highest reaches of the NKVD in Moscow, Pavel Fitin himself and Vsevolod Merkulov, a member of the so-called 'Georgian mafia' of Beria and seen as his deputy.

Alexander M. Korotkov, given the code name Colonel Mikhailov, was sent to Kabul to trap Rasmuss, and met Rasmuss in a safe house in Kabul on 24 October along with Allakhverdov. The Russians had decided they would now tell the Germans that Silver had been deceiving them all along. Korotkov told Rasmuss that the money the Germans were giving Silver was now part of the Defence Fund of the USSR; Rasmuss was shown the codes and ciphers of the Abwehr. Korotkov also showed him the German General Staff's instructions that had been given to Silver to organise insurrection in India. Korotkov's message to Rasmuss was that his position was bleak and he had no choice: the only way out was to defect to the Russians. If he did not, his superiors in Berlin would be told, and he knew what would happen to someone who had helped the enemies of the Reich. If he survived, then after Germany had lost he would stand trial for carrying out espionage against the Allies. But if he came to work for the Russians he was guaranteed 'true friendship' and a position in post-war Germany. Rasmuss asked for time to think it over; Korotkov refused: he had to decide before the meeting ended. Placed in an impossible situation, Rasmuss agreed. But, as soon became clear, he had agreed only to give himself time to plan his escape.

The moment he was out of the safe house he applied for a safe-conduct passage through India as Witzel had done, and by February 1944 he was gone, reaching Berlin in March 1944. What we do not know is whether, in the four months between October 1943 and March 1944, he worked for the Russians. After the war the Russians were not able to find him in the POW camps, and speculated that, following his return to Berlin, he had gone over to the British at the end of the war.

The Germans were devastated, and while they suspected Silver they could not disown him. It was far too late for that. Their careers were linked with Silver, and any exposure of him would have meant their ruination. 'Their own double game with Berlin was less risky', writes Milan Hauner:

> … since nobody there was in a position to question and verify their reports. As the tide of war was definitely turning against their own country, the survival instinct of the bureaucracy proved more powerful than professional honesty, the latter considerably eroded by thirteen years of Nazi rule in any case.[16]

So why did the Russians want to trap Rasmuss? The view of some historians is that this goes back to Quaroni and his voluble conversations with Connor-Green in September 1943. At the end of November 1943 Quaroni also talked to the Russians, but refused to give any valuable information. The Russians, so the argument runs, wanted to get Rasmuss to work for them before he found out what Quaroni had told the British. This may be valid, although it is hard to know how Rasmuss would have found out. What is more, Quaroni, despite filling up many pages of Connor-Green's notebooks about Axis intrigue in Kabul, did not reveal anything about Silver. This is what Connor-Green recorded of their conversation:

> The only relations which the Germans had succeeded in establishing—and that was not anything to do with Ipi—was with some other agent, whose name Quaroni did not know, who apparently brought news from India. Quaroni had been shown some information that had been brought and was himself convinced that this was all bogus and the man was a British agent. The Germans however did not accept his opinion and had paid very large sums of money to him.[17]

In the file there is a pencil marking along this para along with the letters RK, a clear reference to Rahmat Khan. That even now Quaroni made no reference to Silver's name, despite being very aware that with Italy's changed circumstances he had to be co-operative with the British to establish his bona fides with the Allies, is quite astonishing. It may be a reflection of the spell Silver had cast even over the man who considered himself a cut above any other diplomat in Kabul.

Or else, having by then been frozen out by Rasmuss and the Germans, he just did not want to admit he had lost this amazing spy he helped create.

The British were aware that to press Quaroni on Silver might expose their own involvement. In a telegram to Squire in Kabul Weightman in Delhi summed this up well:

> ... one of the most significant features is his avoidance of any but the most indirect reference to the Silver business. Certainly in the earlier days he had knowledge of this link and in fact suspected [Silver] of working for the Russians [the British, as we have seen, had read Quaroni's dispatches to Rome], Quaroni's attitude on this point is so curious that, though the point will have been evident to you from the outset, we feel we must refer to the supreme importance of ensuring that Quaroni should receive no indication of our information and particularly that from our special sources or of our knowledge of Silver. It is no simple task to put questions designed to elicit information about Axis espionage in India without permitting any hint to escape of special knowledge in our possession but we know you will use all possible care.[18]

Whatever the reason for Korotokov blackmailing Rasmuss, the attempt did have a collateral impact on Silver, with the British and the Russians having a major disagreement over whether he could risk another journey to Kabul. By December 1943 Silver was still in Delhi, with the British feeling that now that Rasmuss and Witzel had left Kabul this had 'entirely altered the situation' and Pilger would not be able to handle Silver 'without risk to his [Silver's] safety'. India proposed to send a messenger instead, although the message he would carry would be a significant one and designed to correct the impression which might have been created in Berlin that Silver's 'committee' was ready to bring about a general revolt in India in the near future.[19]

This prompted a sharp response from NKVD. Hill was emphatically told that Moscow disagreed and felt it was important that Silver visits Kabul, as 'he alone is in a position to absorb plans for future and measures which German intelligence organisation is going to adopt'. Messengers, reminded the NKVD, are only couriers. And with Pilditch still keen to visit Moscow, the NKVD made it clear that unless Silver's future activities were approved that visit would be 'without purpose'.[20] Pilditch had not relented on his desire to share Silver directly between the NKVD in Kabul and the British in Delhi, but on this issue Moscow would not budge.

All this was a great strain for the British, with some in the intelligence agencies questioning what the Russian intelligence co-operation was bringing in hard practical terms. There had been co-operation in the Balkans and Bulgaria, but this was dubbed 'only pinpoints and contacts'. Silver was different, but even with him Menzies, Pilditch and IPI felt that the British had served the NKVD well, and the only problem with regard to Silver was the long lines of communication, for which the NKVD were 'themselves to blame'.

For the next three months telegrams flew between Delhi, London and Moscow, with Hill flying back from Moscow to London for another meeting to try and sort things out. This meeting, on 15 March 1944, also attended by IPI and Menzies, saw Hill make the point that Moscow were unhappy with Delhi's handling, and:

> … seemed to suspect that Silver had been adopted as a British agent. It was pointed out by IPI that without the Government of India's assistance Silver would be of no use to the Russians, since all the information which he had obtained had resulted directly from his briefing by the DIB and the C-in-C. [Wavell].[21]

By this time the British knew the Germans were aware Silver had been in touch with the Russians, but not how. And at this London meeting it was made clear that DIB was particularly upset by the Russians' demand for Silver's return to Kabul when there was 'great danger', with the partial liquidation of the German network in Kabul as a result of the Germans learning that Silver was in touch with the Russians. In the end, the British agreed to send him back 'purely as our desire to carry out Soviet wishes'.[22]

But even as Silver, in the middle of March 1944, prepared to leave for Kabul on his tenth visit in three years, Hill was told to tell Moscow that his mission now should be to renew and develop acquaintance with Japanese to establish contact with Bose. This was considered all the more necessary as there had been a comparative failure of wireless transmission between India and Kabul and India and Berlin. While technically the communications were satisfactory:

> … the Germans have evinced a curious unwillingness to co-operate. Nor have they shown any desire that Silver should return to Kabul. It would thus appear that they have lost their interest in him and hence there is not much point in his visiting Kabul unless he can establish relations with the Japanese.

India and London hoped the NKVD would co-operate, and maybe the German interest in Silver could be revived.[23] Furthermore, since he had now been put in touch with the Japanese, his importance to the Government of India had increased on account of the information he could give them on Bose's revolutionary plans for India. Pilditch was very keen to use Silver to work his magic on the Japanese and find out what these plans were. He was confident the Russians knew about the Japanese, and:

… since the India problem is largely linked to the war with Japan he presumes that it might be best to obtain their co-operation in penetrating the Japanese intelligence.

Moscow was told Silver was expected to leave on 13 April 1944 and arrive in Kabul on the 22nd. But even as they allowed Silver to go back to Kabul the British feared he would be arrested in the Afghan capital because 'of his dual role', meaning working with the Russians.

M [India] was averse to send him back and only agreed out of desire to accommodate NKVD. A's [Silver's] contact with ZA [Japan] of great importance to M who would not be justified in jeopardising this link merely to please NKVD and delay of departure seems due to M's desire to be reasonably sure that he had good chance of survival.

How much Silver was told about this is not clear, but his great Kabul adventure was entering its final phase, although even he could not have suspected that his amazing spy career was now turning full circle, and ending much as it had begun back in January 1941 when he had arrived in Kabul for the first time.

Back to the Beginning

Almost from the start Silver could sense that things had changed in Kabul, where he arrived at the beginning of May 1944 on his eleventh visit after a 'hazardous' journey through rain and hailstorms with a new companion, Ghulam Ulrehman, as Murtaza had fallen ill and had to be left behind. Rasmuss and Witzel had gone, and when he gave the D-Division report to Pilger, the hapless German minister told him he did not want to pass it on to the Japanese.

Silver could not escape from Witzel, however, for the German sent him a message from Berlin that must be one of the most remarkable a spy controller ever sent to a spy. Much of it reads like a love letter. Witzel's desire to pass off as a Pathan may explain some of this love. But there was also the fact that, despite serving the Nazis, he saw himself as helping oppressed people seek freedom and for him Silver was above all a freedom fighter. Silver passed on the message to the Russians, and through them the British, who made a summary of Witzel's sentiments:

> Difficulties had arisen for continued co-operation between Bhagat Ram [Silver] and the Germans because of the former allowing a third party to know the innermost secrets of the whole connection. This third party was not hostile to India and Witzel understood that some of Bhagat Ram's [Silver]'s countrymen were thinking it might help them to liberate India. [*Comment: This refers to the leakage of information to the Russians in Kabul*].[1] In this case, however, it had threatened to betray these innermost secrets to the British. This was the reason why Subhas Chandra Bose could not give Bhagat Ram [Silver] instructions. Only by returning to complete secrecy could the plans of Bhagat Ram's [Silver]'s leader be carried out. If Bhagat Ram [Silver] fulfilled this condition Witzel trusted that they could still co-operate for the liberation of India. They were both enemies of the imperialist powers which were oppressing the Indian people. Witzel therefore

promised Bhagat Ram [Silver] once more to fight them until India got her freedom, even if Germany's struggle finished earlier. Bhagat Ram [Silver] was not only Witzel's political comrade but his personal friend, who, as Bhagat Ram [Silver] told him, would do everything in his power to protect Witzel's life and his work in helping Bhagat Ram [Silver]. Bhagat Ram [Silver] was to consider the matter carefully and tell Witzel quite frankly if he could keep everything connected with this particular plan secret. If he could not do it Witzel asked him not to endanger his old friend for nothing and tell him openly the reason.[2]

Then, having behaved like a scorned lover, Witzel was back on his delusion of ending British rule in India, and told Silver that he would establish a wireless station in the middle of India for direct connection with Burma, known only to Silver through whom, as a 'Keyman', all information and instructions would pass. If Silver confirmed he would maintain the secret, the Germans would land a month later in the early morning, sometime after 3 o'clock, on the Bagaur airfield in the tribal areas. Silver should wait for them with:

a) 2000 gallons of flying petrol
b) Indian clothes for four men
c) The latest report
d) Ten men for unloading the goods
e) The arranged signals
while:
   f) Four men would be brought in two different ways to prepare hidings in the middle of India[3]

Witzel wanted Silver to tell him frankly if he was unable to provide all that was required, especially the petrol and airfield. The plan was so secret he could not even inform the 'Central Committee'. Silver would be informed of the exact date by broadcasts from Azad Hind Radio:

Fourteen days before, Azad Hind would start to send numbers again. Two evenings before, Azad would send '50/A/1 Bengal two days', and the evening before, '50/A/1 Assam one day'. This time the plane would fly back. Next time the plane would land again to fly on to Burma taking Bhagat Ram [Silver], or somebody else there.[4]

That Witzel could send this message from the Abwehr headquarters in Berlin when the Soviets were about to drive the Germans from Russian soil showed what an unreal world the Nazis now inhabited. However, Berlin did accept some reality, and informed the German Legation in Kabul that as the arrival of Silver had to be communicated via the Japanese it did not seem feasible to keep him entirely away from with the Japanese. In any case, the Legation had to make certain that for reasons of essential all-round security nothing leaked out about the intended enterprise. If Silver was counting on passing on his report to the Japanese, the Legation was requested to make sure he handed over a shortened version which the Legation would draw up.[5]

The British still feared for Silver's safety in Kabul, and had anxiously telegraphed Hill in Moscow to find out from the NKVD if everything was all right with him, and when he was likely to return to India. To the relief of the British the Russians did not seem as belligerent as they had been recently, and confirmed Silver had arrived in Kabul safely, Hill reporting that Ossipov had volunteered information.

It is fascinating to see how Silver presents this Kabul visit in his memoir. For a start he does not mention he met Pilger, describing him only as 'our German friend'. Witzel's message becomes one from 'Mazotta', when by this time Bose had long discarded that name and had left Berlin more than a year earlier. But his crowning moment of deception came when Witzel asked him about the 'leakage'. Witzel's fourth question was the deadliest:

> We have every reason to say that the Russians know about our relations with Indians and some of the reports which were given to us by you have also reached them. It is very likely that they might have passed them on to the British.[6]

It would have been understandable if Silver had been knocked back by this unexpected assault. Instead he turned the tables quite brilliantly:

> My answer to question No. 4 cannot be given unless and until you give me a convincing proof or a rational explanation for your assumption of leakage. I am not going to believe that while Mr Rusmus [*sic*] was passing through India someone had contacted him and told him this story of leakage. Firstly, the question of some pro-Russian person in our organization meeting Mr Rusmus [*sic*] while he was passing through India is absurd. Because nobody from our organization knew about his passage through India. I also did not know this though I was in India at that time. Secondly, the British government knew that Mr Rusmus[*sic*] had been in India for many years before the outbreak of the war and possibly he might be having some contacts in India. Naturally the British intelligence service was keeping a very close watch on him to find out who were his contacts. So the possibility of leakage in this manner must be ruled out. But there is another possibility—the possibility of the British secret service playing a hoax on Mr Rusmus [*sic*] cannot be ruled out. A man properly tutored by the secret service might have met Mr

Rusmus [*sic*] and given him this story. The British government knew that Subhas Chandra Bose had gone to Berlin with the active help of the Germans. They also might be suspecting that the German government might still be keeping contact with Subhas Chandra Bose's followers and anti-British revolutionaries in India. So the intention of the British secret service in giving this concocted story must be to create mistrust among ourselves.[7]

His final touch showed how accomplished he was in using unrelated incidents to weave a fictitious explanation. He now recalled an incident that had taken place more than a year earlier, on 9 February 1943, when he had given Doh a packet containing a report on 'secret military and technical matters and plans of our works etc.' The meeting had taken place 'in close vicinity of the Russian legation'. But Doh had misplaced it:

> The packet was most likely lost in the vicinity of the spot itself. Now it does not require much imagination to work out what might have happened to the packet if it had not gone to the dustbin. It was quite plausible that either a Russian or a pro-Russian passer-by happened to pick it up and having read its contents must have passed it on to the Russians. Or it might have fallen in the hands of the Afghan police and through them it must have reached Russian hands. This presumption is much more rational and plausible than the theory of leakage. And this also explains the later demand made by the Afghan government for the expulsion of Mr Rusmus [*sic*] and Mr Witzal [*sic*] from Kabul. I admit there might be a leakage, but certainly not from our side and I will not accept such stories without any valid proof. Therefore, the blame must be put squarely on Mr Hans Dow [*sic*] for his negligence. [8]

Just in case the Germans had still not got the point he went on:

> If you have got the least suspicion about me then it is not advisable for me to carry on relations with you any longer. You may inform Berlin and Mazotta about my views because I neither want to mislead others nor do I want to be misled myself. You have created a very serious position for me. I again repeat that if the leakage is there it is due to the carelessness of Mr Hans Dow [*sic*] and its consequences will be disastrous, much more to us than to you. This whole episode was most unfortunate as it has disrupted harmonious relations existing between us for the last three and a half years.[9]

Surely no spy in history could have so brilliantly presented himself as the victim of a deception rather than the perpetrator of it.

As always, Silver passed on everything the Germans told him to the NKVD. Moscow, of course, could not tell the British that they had tried to blackmail

Rasmuss but, worried the affair might leak out, decided to put their own spin on it to put the British on the back foot. So the story they gave Hill was this: the Germans had told Silver that, as Rasmuss was passing through India, he had been informed that all the German secrets, including W/T communications, were known to the Russians, who also had copies of his reports, and the Germans had assumed that codes and cyphers in use were also known to the Soviets. This was the first the British knew of the Germans being aware that Silver was working for the Russians, and wondered whether this was true or the Germans were just trying to mislead him. India felt that while:

> ... some leakage has taken place, Bhagat Ram [Silver] can be ruled out as well as the very few officers in India who are cognisant of the facts. But no guarantee can be given regarding any of his confidants in India or on the frontier. We would be grateful if you could ascertain from NKVD what they think of this curious business.

The British response delighted the Russians, now reassured that the truth about what they had done would never emerge.

The British confusion lasted some months, and it was only in June 1944 that they worked it all out, or at least some sections of the British intelligence community did, though not Hill who remained in the dark. Over dinner with Philip Vickery, Guy Liddell was given details of the Rasmuss affair:

> It appears that the Russians have been playing rather a dirty game.... They ... arranged a meeting with Rasmuss, the First Secretary of the German Legation, told him that they knew of SILVER'S code and that unless he was prepared to work for them, they would expose him. This, of course, had led to considerable suspicion by the Germans of SILVER.... he was [on his return to Kabul] cross-questioned about the code but apparently put up a good story and so far seems to have got away with it. Rasmuss, of course, refused to work for the Russians.... the whole matter could not be taken up with the Russians as the information about the meeting between the Russians and Rasmuss was obtained from a German BJ. The matter, however, is further complicated by the fact that George Hill, the SOE representative in Moscow, who is in touch with the NKVD, does not know about this piece of Russian duplicity and merely thinks the Government of India is being sticky.[10]

Despite all the problems Pilger was having with Silver he was still willing to arrange a meeting with the Japanese, but the Indian decided he would meet Inouye on his own. The Japanese was keen to find out why Rasmuss had suddenly left: 'My government suspects something behind this move'. This was too good an opportunity to miss, so Silver recounted the story of

Doh's incompetence and suggested that his 'departure might have been in consequence of that'. Inouye also knew about the leakage, and when he raised the question Silver in some indignation asked, 'Do you suspect me?' When the Japanese immediately replied, 'No,' Silver declared:

> The leakage, if there was at all, was not intentional. The Germans are making too much noise about this leakage, but they know very well about the loss of package which I gave to Mr Hans Dow [sic] and which contained very important secret information. I am not prepared to take any blame for this incident, nor are any of my men involved in it. This is how the Germans are trying to shirk responsibility for their own mistake.[11]

Like Quaroni, Inouye had no high opinion of the Germans in Kabul and readily believed Silver. He did, though, have one concern: 'Are there no pro-Russian or communists in your organisation?' Silver's response showed how well he had understood that as a spy you should not lie all the time: admit some truth in order to make the lie look more convincing. So he readily admitted that he was a member of the Communist Party of India. But this was something Bose knew before he had left India, and despite this had asked for his help to escape the country:

> I myself and my comrades feel very strongly that our main enemy is British imperialism and we have to liberate our country from their domination. And that is why we co-operated with Subhas Chandra Bose and helped him and have been co-operating with the Axis powers. From the beginning the Germans and the Italians knew everything about me and about the comrades who are working with me. I know very well what kind of people are working with us and I am quite satisfied with them. Now it looks very strange that our German friends are thinking this way at this stage.[12]

As he had done with Pilger, he threatened Inouye that he was quite prepared to walk away—that if the Japanese had 'even a shadow of doubt, it is quite fruitless to continue our relations'.[13] Far from wanting to end the relationship, by the end of the conversation it was Inouye who was grovelling. 'I am very sorry to put all these questions to you. We have no reason to suspect you personally. Nor has Subhas Chandra Bose any misunderstanding about you.'[14]

Had Inouye been reading the publications of the Indian Communist Party he would have realised Silver was lying. At that very moment the Communist journals, echoing what the British press was saying, were describing Bose as a stooge of the Axis, accompanied by cartoons mocking the idea that Bose could use the Axis to help free India. One showed him as a donkey being ridden by a bloodthirsty Japanese general, another as a rat being held up by

Goebbels while Hitler smirked and Bose declared, 'I am bringing freedom to India', and a third as a fat, tame 'Marshal' Bose being led by an evilly grinning General Tojo, the Japanese Premier.[15] But, like the Germans, Inouye did not follow the Indian press and was clueless about what was happening in the country. And as with the Germans, all this created the ideal pretext for Silver to raise the question of money.

His monthly expenses in the tribal area, he told Inouye, were between Rs 9,000 and Rs 11,000. The Japanese replied that their financial position was weak as they could not communicate properly with Tokyo, prompting the instantaneous response from Silver that since the Japanese had tried to land men on the east coast of India they should make sure these men contacted Silver: this would improve the communication facilities between his organisation and Japan. What Silver did not tell Inouye was at that very moment Fleming's D Division was dealing with the agents Bose had been sending to India.

Bose had brought over his spymaster from Germany to East Asia, N. G. Swami, who had managed to land quite a few agents in India, most of whom D Division quickly picked up and turned into double agents. Their best success came with an Indian peasant in his late twenties called Adjudya Das, a private in the British Indian infantry who had been taken prisoner by the Japanese and joined Bose's INA merely in order to get back to India. Having been parachuted into India with a Japanese radio set he immediately on landing reported to the nearest police station and became a D Division double agent. But despite such successes Silver knew that Fleming could do with all the help he could get and information about agents from the Japanese would prove very useful. Inouye promised that Silver would be kept informed.

Silver left Kabul feeling very satisfied with what he had achieved. He had lain to rest any question of being a double agent for the Russians or the British. The continuing trust of the Germans was demonstrated by his having been given new cipher communications codes for use between Berlin and India: *Flying Boat* and *Flower* instead of *Rice*. And just as his first stop in Kabul was the Soviet Embassy, so his first stop in Delhi was D Division, where he confidently told Fleming that with the Abwehr operation in Kabul having collapsed he could now concentrate on the Japanese. As Fleming saw the Japanese as the only enemy now worth bothering about, this was just what he wanted to hear.

As it happened, at that very moment the British were for the first time since being driven out of Burma engaged in a land war with Japan—the battle for Imphal. In February 1944 the Japanese had launched a masking operation in the Arakan, a coastal plain outside the Chin Hills mountain range that forms the Indo-Burmese border, hoping to divert British troops there. Although the British had won that battle it had come at a price, taking five divisions and an enormous airlift to hold off 12,000 Japanese men, with the British suffering 8,500 casualties and Lt-Gen. William Slim, the British commander, even having to commit his reserves. On receiving news of this Lt-Gen. Renya Mutaguchi, the Japanese commander, who back in 1937 had engineered the Marco Polo Bridge incident to start the war with China, gave the order for the advance on Imphal. He was so confident of victory that he told Japanese war correspondents:

> I am firmly convinced that my three divisions will reduce Imphal in one month. In order that they can march fast, they carry the lightest possible equipment and food enough for three weeks. Ah, they will get everything from British supplies and dumps. Boys! See you again in Imphal at the celebration of the Emperor's birthday on 29 April.[16]

Initially, the Japanese looked like repeating the success they had had when they had run through Malaya and Singapore. On 6 April Japanese radio confidently claimed that Kohima had fallen. (Japanese and British military records do not agree about the fate of Kohima. Japanese historians assert that Kohima did fall to their army; the British admit only that Kohima underwent a severe siege and that, after ferocious fighting, certain parts were occupied). By April the Japanese seemed certain of capturing Imphal too, but they made some strategic errors. This included failing to finish off the British 17th Indian division, which had been successfully bottled up in a narrow valley surrounded by towering mountains. The Japanese also decided not to go for Dimapur, the only railway connection between Assam and Bengal, which at the beginning of April was virtually undefended, as Slim, though dreading an attack, did not have enough men to protect it properly. Slim would later thank Mutaguchi for not being imaginative, a quality a great commander needs and which Slim, as he demonstrated during the Burma campaign, had in abundance. Perhaps, even if Mutaguchi had been more imaginative, defeat for the Japanese was inevitable as the tide of war had turned. The Japanese just could not match what Slim commanded, the British forces outnumbering them by more than 50,000 and they were also overwhelmingly supreme in the air.

The Imphal defeat meant Bose's plans were in ruins. His idea was that, as Japan advanced into India, his provisional government would take over administration of the areas captured. Special Indian currency notes and Provisional Government stamps were printed, detailed instructions given for the reception of British Indian Army soldiers who had been captured, and a 'Chief Administrator of Occupied Territories' was appointed. The INA carried a proclamation addressed to the brothers and sisters of India that the 'Provisional Government of Azad Hind (Free India) is the only lawful government of the Indian people' and calling for their co-operation, though it also listed 10 hostile acts meriting execution or severe punishment. The Japanese defeat meant all this was now a pipe dream, though Bose would refuse to accept it.

And for all the propaganda of the forces of Nippon fighting for India's freedom the Japanese did not allow Bose's INA much part in the fighting, with one of his officers complaining that the frontline duties consisted of:

(a) road making or preparing.
(b) repairing bridges.
(c) extinguishing jungle fires.
(d) driving bullock carts carrying rations for the Japanese troops ... duties of a labour battalion.[17]

However, the British were still some months away from deciding how they would evict the Japanese from Burma and Malaya: it would not be until December 1944 that the British crossed the Chindwin and the Japanese retired to the Irrawaddy. This meant that for very different reasons Silver was still a key player for both Inouye and Fleming, and even as Slim was proclaiming that this first land victory by British arms over the Japanese meant that 'the Japanese army has suffered the greatest defeat in its history', Fleming was planning to send Silver back to Kabul with messages to mislead the Japanese about British plans.

Fleming did later complain that his problem was British plans frequently changed: 'It is impossible, or at any rate, highly dangerous, to tell a lie until you know what the truth is going to be.'[18] This proved to be the case with regard to one of his deception plans. This involved telling the Japanese that the British planned to land on the coast and launch a drive towards Prome. However when the Army heard of it they were alarmed and rushed to stop Fleming, because that was exactly what they were planning. It would have been interesting, as in Burmese history Prome was the site of the famous battle in the First Anglo-Burmese war in the nineteenth century that saw the British eventually occupy Burma.

By July 1944 Silver was ready to visit Kabul, and for this, his eleventh, trip he had with him a D Division masterpiece for the Germans and Japanese that included the names of three individuals and their addresses in Calcutta, Dacca and Chittagong. Except that by the time he left Delhi on the 18th the information was not complete: he had the addresses, but D Division had not yet come up with the names, which he was told he would be given before he met the Germans and the Japanese. Then, to add to the complications, while Silver was in the tribal areas London informed Hill that the Calcutta address had to be changed since the house selected had since been destroyed by fire. The telegram did give the names of the three individuals in the three cities, and informed Hill that the occupants of the three houses had been instructed that Bose's agents would use the password 'Bengal tiger', which should be acknowledged with the password 'King Cobra'. The choice of tiger was interesting, as The Springing Tiger was the emblem Bose was using for his Indian National Army.

With the German flat no longer available Silver might have had accommodation problems, but he had struck up such a friendship with Inouye that he stayed at his house until 3 September. There were meetings with the Germans, not Pilger but the wireless operator, Zugenbühler. And he readily revealed to Silver it was the Russians who had approached Rasmuss and tried to blackmail him, which was why communications between Berlin and Delhi had had to stop. However, Zugenbühler assured him, this was just a blip. 'He again reminded me that we should try to investigate into the matter of leakage. I promised to do so.'[19] The Germans had new codes, *Orient* and *Importance*, between Berlin and India, and *Orient* and *Manuscript* between India and Bose. Berlin, he was told, would transmit the wireless plan to *Mary* when Silver arrived back in India. There was also a plan to have wireless *Tom–Mary* transmissions between India and Japan. However the German still wanted the *Mary–Tom* wireless communications maintained and Zugenbühler told Silver, 'I should contact Berlin by WT with the new code after I had reached Delhi.'[20]

Just before Silver had arrived in Kabul there had been an attempt to assassinate Hitler, in what has come to be known as the July bomb plot, and when Silver raised this Zugenbühler, revealing himself to be a true Nazi, brushed this aside, stating that 'the attempt on Hitler's life did not mean that his influence on the people had waned'.[21] What neither men knew was that Adam von Trott was involved in the plot and even as they spoke he was being tried in a mock trial and would be cruelly executed.

Zugenbühler did confirm that the Japanese had now formally taken over from the Germans, 'all instructions would be given now by the Japanese and Subhas Chandra Bose'.[22] This meant that in many ways his conversations with Inouye were more interesting. From them he gleaned a great deal of information as to how the Japanese saw the Russians. 'We do not expect Russia to declare war against us,' he was told. 'Even if Russia makes some demands we shall try our best to satisfy her.' Inouye's further comment that 'We have a very big naval force' showed he was just as deluded as Witzel.[23]

Silver for his part, well briefed by Fleming, tried to mislead Inouye by telling him that there would be no major land offensive on the India–Burma front. Instead, the Allies would make strong naval attacks supported by the air force. But they would finish the European war first, and only then try to capture the Andaman Islands and attempt landings to the south of Moulmein and perhaps north Malaya to cut off Bangkok, in a south Asian version of the second front in Europe. Capturing the Andamans, Silver told the Japanese, would cut the supply line to Burma by sea, and capturing Bangkok the supply line to Burma by land. This so impressed Inouye that he rushed to his office to communicate it all to Tokyo.

Silver then prepared Inouye for the revelation that the Allies might know about his dealings with the Germans and the Italians, by pointing out that Italy had surrendered and probably disclosed all her secrets to the British and the Soviets and, given the Germans' situation, should they surrender they would be expected to do the same. He advised the Japanese not to disclose the relationship they had with Silver, and in particular the new wireless contacts they were building. The Japanese readily agreed. Silver so impressed Inouye that he gave Silver 100,000 Afghanis.

There followed a final debrief with Zaman, and Silver set off back to India. What he did not know as he bade Zaman goodbye and left the Soviet Legation was that this would be the last time he would be welcome there. And what he was never to know was this had nothing to do with how the Soviets felt about him. They still valued him. Their anger was with the British who the Russians felt had cheated them over this unique spy-sharing arrangement. The hurt was all the more as the Russians had offered their spy to the British in the first place.

This visit had provided some clues that the Russians were getting very fed up with how the British were treating them. Ossipov had complained to Hill that the British had not informed the Russians about Silver's return to Kabul.[24] Since there had been complaints of this nature in the past the British were not too worried. The first sign that there was a fundamental shift in the Soviet attitude came when Hill on London's instructions told Ossipov that they proposed sending Silver back to Kabul. The NKVD told Hill that Silver's contact there was seriously ill and unable to keep the rendezvous, and Moscow could not send a substitute. Hill thought the contact was actually in Moscow, and due to remain there for five or six weeks.

By January 1945 London was getting very anxious that it had not been able to send Silver to Kabul, and telegraphed Hill to tell Moscow that it regretted the continued absence of Silver's Russian contact, and could not understand why the Soviets had no NKVD man there—they had received an account of Silver's last visit and knew he had to return. What was more, 'His organisation', as London described Fleming's D Division, had failed to establish W/T contact with Japan, which made the British and Silver 'suspect that somebody had altered the schedules'. Silver's 'organisation' had received a W/T enquiry from Berlin as to the cause of the failure, which according to Berlin was because of the frequencies used, and efforts were being made to establish contact. Hill was told to tell Ossipov that the British proposed to send Silver back to Kabul later that month, and hoped the NKVD would contact him 'and direct his activities while there'.[25]

The NKVD was told Silver would be taking a written report for Inouye, and:

If only for the purpose of sending such written reports we regard the continuance of A's [Silver's] visit to I [Kabul] as of extreme importance, whether we do or do not succeed in establishing direct W/T contact with the ZA [Japanese].[26]

With nothing forthcoming from the Russians the British decided they had to send Silver, and the Russians were informed that he had left Delhi for Kabul on 5 March 1945 and was expected to arrive by the end of the month. Silver set off not knowing whether Zaman was still there and seriously worried about heading for Kabul without NKVD approval. To avoid the risk of failing to meet the NKVD representative in Kabul he asked Fleming just before he left to pass the following message on to the NKVD:

Your man should cross Harthun Bridge every Monday and Thursday at 3, repeat 3 p.m. Kabul time, and go towards Barbar side or come from Barbar side. [Silver] or any of his other men will have orange-coloured handkerchief wrapped on his left hand and your man should have white handkerchief wrapped on his right hand. Whenever they would see each other then at the same evening at 6.45, repeat 6.45 p.m. Kabul time, they will meet again on the road which goes from Allalabad to Darul Ammon road and they will keep same handkerchiefs on same hands at that time also. And your man will question him, 'From where are you coming?' The answer will be, 'I am coming from Pagham'. Then you can trust him. Please inform your man there urgently in Kabul lest Bhagat Ram [Silver] may not put himself into danger for [trying to establish] contact with you.[27]

It was only after this message was sent that on 5 March 1945 Silver bade goodbye to Fleming and D Division and set off for his twelfth visit to Kabul, confident everything would work out. But even as he was negotiating the tribal territory on the night of 14 March, Ossipov met Hill and told him that the NKVD were 'not any longer interested in A [Silver] and unable to co-operate with us in his future activities'. Nothing had prepared Hill for such a response. He expressed his 'astonishment' at such a decision, and at such a moment, but it made no impression on Ossipov. Hill had often warned London about how sensitive the NKVD were, and now he expressed the 'fear that as far as NKVD are concerned matter is a closed subject'.[28]

Silver reached Kabul towards the end of the month blissfully unaware of what had happened in Moscow. As on his previous trip he found Inouye a welcome host, and dutifully he went to the bridge. But there was no one with a coloured handkerchief, and now history, as Marx had said, repeated itself as a farce. On his first visit, back in 1941, he had tried and failed to contact the Russians, even trying to waylay their ambassador. Now he decided he would go up to the Embassy as he had so often done in the last four years. The Russians were at the gates of Berlin, within weeks Hitler would commit suicide and the Red Flag would be flying over his Chancellery—his communist comrades ought to have much to celebrate. But to his shock the doors of the Embassy were firmly shut, and to make matters worse his attempt to get past the guards led to a furious protest by the Russians.

As far as the outside world was concerned, the war in Europe was coming to an end, and this was a moment of celebration for the Allies, but not with the NKVD in Moscow. In an extraordinary message to the SOE on 6 May, two days before Germany surrendered, the NKVD expressed astonishment that Silver had tried to contact Russian officials in Kabul.

That same day Colonel Graur of the NKVD met Hill and they discussed Silver's visit, after which Hill, signing himself as Brigadier G. A. Hill, DSO, OBE, MC, wrote a 'Dear Colonel Gaur' letter to the Russian that could not have been more plaintive:

I have taken note of, and reported to London—for transmission to India— the statement made by Major Panov on your behalf to Major Graham and Captain Wild on the 4th May to the effect that [Silver] had made attempts to contact the Soviet Ambassador and members of the NKID at the Soviet Embassy in Kabul. Further, that Major Panov was instructed to reiterate the statement you had made on March 14th to the effect that your organization was no longer interested in Bhagat Ram's [Silver's] activities and wished to have nothing further to do with him: and finally that your organization was surprised that Bhagat Ram [Silver] should have tried to make such an approach to the Soviet authorities in Kabul.

In order that there should be no misunderstanding between our various organizations, I think it is important that I should set forth the following facts:–

a) In a letter dated as far back as January 1945, I informed you that it was proposed by the authorities in India to send [Silver] back to Kabul at the end of that month. Bhagat Ram [Silver] left India for Kabul on March 5th, and I notified you of his departure in a letter signed on my behalf by Major McLaughlin, dated March 10th. Up to that date your organization had not informed us of any change in your attitude towards Bhagat Ram [Silver].

b) You will see, therefore, that Bhagat Ram [Silver] had already been en route for some nine days when you made the statement on behalf of your organization on March 14th, and, as has been explained to you before, we have no means of entering into contact with him except in India.

It was, in fact, impossible then to contact Bhagat Ram [Silver], to brief him regarding your attitude, and to inform him that you were no longer interested in this old and trusted agent, and that your organization was unable to collaborate with us in his future activities.

Until he returns to India we have no means either of finding out why he sought to approach the Soviet Embassy in Kabul (though you will appreciate that in the absence of any information as to the changed attitude of your authorities towards him, this was possibly quite a natural step for him to take) nor can we tell him not to approach the Soviet authorities again. But he will, of course, be informed of your organization's attitude towards him as soon as he returns to India, and I am confident that he will make no further attempts to approach the Soviet authorities in Kabul.[29]

It would be fascinating to know what Silver made of all this. His story had come full circle. His first attempt at a spying career had begun in February 1941 trying to attract the attention of the Russians in Kabul and failing. It was ending the same way. But since he never admitted he had spied for the Russians there is no mention of this in his memoir. Instead he regales us with the story of how, as he left Kabul for the last time, he was very nearly arrested at the main checkpoint out of the city for not having a permit to travel. He got out of it by paying, some *baksheesh* to the guards with some of the Japanese money, before reaching Delhi on 17 May 1945.[30]

The rest of his memoir is only another seven paragraphs, and describes how, Germany having surrendered and Japan clearly unable to carry on much longer, it was agreed with Swatantra that Silver would stay in his British provided house in Delhi to:

> ... 'watch the military situation in the east' while Swatantra would try to establish radio contact with Bose and suggest that he 'disappear from the scene of war', and that after the war Silver would go back to the tribal areas and 'mobilise all resources for anti-British activities.'[31]

Strip away the Silver lies and what this amounts to is that on his return to Delhi he reported to Fleming and D Division, who sent some messages to the Japanese, although, unlike the Delhi–Berlin wireless link, the one with Japan never worked.

D Division did have five radio links with the enemy through double agents, Indians whom the Japanese had sent to India where everyone without exception had finished up working under D Division control. A major problem with these links was that their radio channels had to course through Indian National Army headquarters in Rangoon ... Messages passed through inexperienced Indian and Japanese cipher officers, then had to be translated—a tortured process that meant it was almost invariably a garbled version of the original that finally reached its destination. This was a constant irritant to D Division. It must have been exasperating to have a double agent send off your perfectly coded prize story, wait weeks for the enemy response, then finally discover from it that your original message must have become so corrupt in passage that the response was useless nonsense.[32]

Fleming could not send Silver to Rangoon. His mission was therefore over. He was allowed to enjoy the accommodation the British had provided for him in Delhi until Japan surrendered, and the British paid him 'a lump sum of money for his services'.[33] We shall never know how much the lump sum was as the IB files were destroyed as the British prepared to leave India, but we may be sure it was not as much as he had fleeced from the Italians, the Germans and the Japanese. It also meant that this quintuple spy received money from four of the five countries he worked for; the only one who never paid him anything was Russia. Indeed the Russians kept a fair amount of the money he got from the Germans and the Japanese. Whatever sum the British paid it must have been enough for him to go back to Ghalla Dher and live there in some comfort. Whether he used the time to spread communism among the tribes is hard to say. It is more likely that, after an amazing hectic four years, he relaxed at home, a mere spectator as an extraordinary series of events unfolded in India, with one of them suggesting that, like Hamlet's ghost, the ghost of his former mentor Bose could cast a spell on India.

Bose had hoped that if he raised an army, then the Mercenary Army, as he called the one the British had built, would defect and become the army of liberation. But his belief that he had only to appear at India's borders and the walls of Jericho would fall proved illusory. However, in death as a result of a plane crash three days after Japan surrendered, he did have a revenge on the British.

During the war the British had kept secret the formation of the INA and what it had done from the Indian public. Field Marshal Claude Auchinleck, the Commander-in-Chief in India, was convinced that when the full story emerged the Indian public would be horrified. 25,000 INA prisoners were repatriated to India at the end of the war, and of those classified as 'black', who had fervently believed in the cause, three, a Muslim, a Hindu and a Sikh, representing all the major communities of India, were selected for trial. Auchinleck was confident that the trial would reveal the real nature of the JIFS, Japanese-Inspired Fifth Columnists that the British called the army Bose had commanded. It proved a colossal misjudgement.

Auckinleck, based on his knowledge of Indian soldiers, thought Indians would see these men as namak haram, the Indian term for those who had broken their word to serve the King Emperor. But Indians saw these men as patriots fighting for freedom. For them it was not a court martial but a trial of men whose only crime was they wanted to free their country. And the choice of venue for the trial—Delhi's Red Fort had been selected as it was considered ideal for press and media coverage—reminded the Indians of their struggle to be free of the British. Red Fort was where the last Mughal emperor, Bahadur Shah, had been tried after the revolt of 1857, and where Bose had promised to unfurl the Indian tricolour after defeating the British.[34]

Auchinleck's choice of the three 'blacks' to be tried also backfired. For Indians, this demonstrated that the INA was indeed a national army: that Bose had indeed succeeded in getting Muslims, Hindus and Sikhs to unite for a common cause. The result was that Congress, including Nehru, who had promised to fight Bose if he arrived with the Japanese, now rallied to the INA. The trial, as he put it, was a dramatic version of that old contest, England versus India. Even Jinnah, who had had no time for Bose and supported the British in the war, now sounded like an INA sympathiser.

The court martial accepted that all three officers were guilty of waging war against the King and sentenced them to transportation for life. But for the Indian public at large the men were heroes. Even as the trial was going on there were protests. The day the proceedings started, the police had to open fire on a protesting crowd at Madurai in south India. The Red Fort was besieged, and more than a hundred were killed or injured by police firing. In Calcutta, in a rare gesture of communal amity, Hindus and Muslims, their trucks flying both Congress and Muslim League flags, jointly took over the city, attacking American and British military establishments and shouting the slogans of freedom and nationalism coined by Bose: 32 Indians lost their lives and 200 were wounded. The violence soon spread along the Gangetic plain to Patna, Allahabad and Benares, and eventually, places as far apart as Karachi and Bombay were affected. Auchinleck, no longer confident he knew India and in particular Indian soldiers wrote to Wavell, the Viceroy:

> I do not think any senior British officer today knows what is the real feeling among the Indian ranks regarding the 'INA'. I myself feel, from my own instinct largely, but also from the information I have had from various sources, that there is a growing feeling of sympathy for the 'INA' and an increasing tendency to disregard the brutalities committed by some of its members as well as the forswearing by all of them of their original allegiance. It is impossible to apply our standards of ethics to this problem or to shape our policy as we would, had the 'INA' been of our own race.[35]

Auchinleck's lament summed up the vast gulf between the conqueror and the conquered with his reference to race and 'our standards of ethics' further emphasising this. Later Philip Mason, Joint Secretary in the War Department of the Government of India, declared that the INA's 'patriotic motive would be taken at its face value and its members would be treated as though prisoners of war'.[36] The three men were released and welcomed like the heroes of a conquering army, and for a time the INA seemed to have become India. However, selective trials continued, drawing more protests. In Calcutta there were four days of strict martial law which saw 50 dead and 500 injured.

To the bewilderment and horror of the British the protests infected the one section of India they thought would always be secure: the armed forces. 5,200 Royal Indian Air Force personnel went on strike, and a revolt began on a training ship of the Indian Navy moored at Bombay, sparking off a whole revolt by the Royal Indian Navy. In Bombay even the British-owned *Times of India* was forced to call the 'mass uprising in sympathy with the naval mutiny unparalleled in the city's history'. For a few days, some of Bombay's teeming working-class slums became 'no-go areas', and the British had to call in white troops to quell the uprising. In the end, 270 died and 1,300 were injured (the government's official figures were lower: 187 and 1,002).

The rebellious anti-British mood even surfaced when the British decided that the Allied victory would be celebrated on 7 March 1946 by military marches. In the capital the soldiers were first to march through New Delhi, then come into the old city and finish the procession in front of the Red Fort. As the Indian writer Nirad Chaudhuri recorded:

> ... the Indians were determined to prevent [that] ... There were serious disturbances in the old city. Its town hall was set on fire and partly gutted. Men in European dress were set upon, and the violence was so great that the police were compelled to open fire. Some of the rioters were killed. In New Delhi the military procession was jeered at and black flags waved at it. The soldiers, both British and Indian, were booed, and the procession into the old city was abandoned. Two field marshals who had fought the Germans victoriously, went home, admitting defeat at the hands of an Indian rabble.[37]

By this time Britain's newly elected Labour Government had begun to understand how much the war had changed India and loosened Britain's hold on its crown jewel. The February disturbances convinced the Prime Minister, Clement Attlee that the imperial tide had ebbed for ever. On his only trip to India, as a backbench MP back in 1928, he had called Indian nationalism 'the illegitimate offspring of patriotism out of inferiority complex' and fretted about the prospect of more 'jobbery and corruption' as self-government advanced. Now he recognised that India could be held by force of arms for a few years more, but the cost for a Britain devastated by war would be too high. In his speech to the House of Commons on 20 February 1947, he pledged that the British Government would transfer power to Indian hands, if necessary as two separate nations, 'not later than June 1948'. This finally led to the emergence of the two nations of India and Pakistan on 15 August 1947.

And this is where Silver re-enters the story. But the conclusion to his long campaign to free India was truly tragic. He was the Hindu Pathan, who saw himself as no different to a Muslim Pathan, apart from his religion, who had been born and lived happily in an overwhelming Muslim land. As we have seen, he had taken up Muslim names, convincingly posed as a Muslim, travelling through Muslim tribal areas between India and Afghanistan, and practically camping in Kabul for months. But his historic homeland had now become part of Pakistan, the new confessional state created on the basis, as Jinnah had declared, that the Muslims were a separate nation and had to have a country of their own. The Muslims, Jinnah had argued, could not be a minority in a Hindu-dominated India.

Had there been an ordered handover of power to the two states of India and Pakistan Silver might have been able to stay on in Ghalla Dher. But there was not. The partition of the subcontinent produced a murderous chaos in which a million were killed and several millions forced to leave their homeland. In this, one of the biggest population exchanges in history, Silver found himself on the wrong side of the fence. His Pathan land went to Pakistan, and now he could no longer live in the land of his birth, where his ancestors had lived for generations next to Muslims. Silver says he was in the tribal areas at that midnight hour when India got freedom and quickly decided 'it was not possible to do any useful work here'. He returned to Ghalla Dher and found, 'My family and other relatives had already reached India and there was nobody left in our ancestral place which I loved so dearly. I passed through that area with a heavy heart, in gloom and despair.' The family's departure also pained those Muslims who stayed behind and the historian Dr Sayed Wiqar Ali Shah says that:

> Warris Khan [Abad Khan's tea vendor friend] mentioned to me in a very emotional manner his last meeting with the mother of Bhagat Ram [Silver] before her departure to India. She was crying to leave the ancestral home and was not ready to move to an alien land.[38]

Silver had no option but to follow his family. 'The journey was irksome, hazardous and a long one'.[39] The final leg, from Karachi to Bombay, was by sea, and he arrived in India on 26 February 1948.

Silver ends his memoir there as if that was the end of his tale. But it was not. We know nothing of what he did between 1948 and 1973. This so confused some British officials like Wace that he concluded erroneously, 'When Partition came he was picked up by the Pakistan Government and disappeared'.[40] In fact he had not, and his 1973 reappearance provided the final twist to his story. This proved to be his last great deception, except this time he was cheating not the Italians, the Germans or the Japanese, the villains of the war, but his own people. As with all his previous deceptions this showed a great deal of invention and no little daring. And the manner in which he pulled it off, and in the process tried to mask what he had really done during the war, showed he had not lost all the skills he had acquired while shuttling between Kabul and Delhi. If anything, he had developed into an even more skilful liar, one willing to take on even those who had had well authenticated evidence to the contrary to prove that he had been one of the greatest deceivers in history.

Epilogue
The Unsolved Mystery

In January 1973 what was described as 'the first International Netaji Seminar' was held in Calcutta over four days. The dates chosen were significant: the 23rd, when it began, marked Subhas Bose's birthday; the 26th, its close, the day India became a republic. Twenty-six years after India had won freedom Bose's admirers wanted to celebrate his life and emphasise the great contribution he had made to removing the British. The conference was organised by Sisir Bose, Subhas's nephew, who had helped Bose escape, and brought together scholars who had written about Bose, sprinkled with men who had worked with him, such as Alexander Werth, a colleague of Adam Von Trott, and Silver. One of the participants in the seminar was Milan Hauner, a young Czech historian working on his thesis *India in the Axis Strategy*, a ground-breaking study that has since become the standard book on the subject.

'The conference was very big', Hauner recalls:

> ... bigger than any conference I had experienced in England or in Europe. There were hundreds of people, they couldn't get inside the Netaji Bhavan. There were processions leading up to the house because this was the anniversary of Bose's birth and that is a holiday in Bengal. He is a great hero, so there were thousands of people on the streets marching up and down in front of Netaji Bhavan. I was very impressed. The seminar was held in a marquee in the garden of the house covered with awnings. Among the hundreds of people from all walks of Indian life sitting on the ground there were ministers of the local Bengal government in the first row including the chief minister and many foreign guests. It was a very great Indian occasion. I was very impressed.[1]

For Silver the return to Calcutta must have brought back many memories. The conference was being held in the very house where Subhas Bose had lived and where Silver, on his return from Kabul, had seen Sarat and Sisir Bose. He could see how Sisir Bose had displayed the German Wanderer car in which he had

spirited away his uncle on that January night in 1941. With the conference
delegates having no knowledge of Silver betraying Bose and spying for the
Russians and the British, Silver was very much an honoured delegate. And,
despite the fact that he was not, like most of the participants, an academic
historian, or even able to speak English fluently, he showed the same confidence
that he had done when dealing with Quaroni, Rasmuss and Fleming. Before the
conference Silver had tested the waters with a series of articles about helping
Bose escape for *Blitz*, a magazine started just as Silver reached Kabul for the first
time and designed to help the war effort,which had since become India's leading
left-wing weekly. Now, in a paper entitled 'My Fifty-Five Days with Netaji
Subhas Chandra Bose', he took the story up to his third visit to Kabul just after
Hitler's attack on the Soviet Union.

Silver's use of the term Netaji was significant. Netaji means Leader, and was the
title given by his followers in East Asia. Western historians have interpreted this as
a sign of Bose seeing himself as an Indian Führer, but it really followed the Indian
tradition of calling a venerated man not by his name but by a title. So Gandhi is
always called either Mahatma, Great Souled One, or Bapu, father, and Rabindranath
Tagore, the first Asian to win the Nobel Prize for Literature, Gurudev, which means
great teacher. Silver was aware that in the eyes of Bose's followers those who did not
use that term were insulting their great leader and not acknowledging his great role
in the freedom movement. Silver had no desire to be accused of that.

Silver's paper was followed by a presentation from Ganguli. This was the first
time the two had met since their meeting in Calcutta in the middle of the war and
Silver was clearly keen to hear what Ganguli who, as we have seen, he had also
deceived, would say. Ganguli decided he would not hold back and disputed some of
Silver's claims. While he suspected Silver he had no evidence and contended himself
with hinting that Silver had double-crossed Bose and helped the British identify and
arrest many of the senior officials of Bose's movement.[2] With the British archives
not yet open no one knew the real Silver story and Ganguli's intervention was just a
moment in the seminar and not followed up by any of the other participants.

At first Milan Hauner, like many others, could not square what he had read of
this spy with the man before him.

> To look at him you would not be impressed at all. He was an elderly man,
> short, wearing glasses, entirely unpretentious. He was not wearing a suit but a
> loose shirt, like the ones Pathans wear, and a Gandhi cap. When pictures were
> taken he did wear suits. He spoke average Indian English and came over as
> semi-educated, but I noticed he understood perfectly what I was saying.

What struck Hauner, however, was that:

> I could see he was very popular and much sought-after. He was constantly
> speaking to people who apparently knew him very well and were close to the

Bose family. In 1973 I did not have any suspicion Silver was lying.[3]

There was one participant at this seminar who was particularly interested in what Silver said. Indeed, having played a huge part in Silver's spy career, he was very keen to meet him. This was Lieutenant Dieter Witzel. Hauner recalls:

> Witzel didn't speak at all. He of, course, didn't know me, and as we met at the reception of the hotel where we stayed Witzel said, 'Who are you, what are you doing in connection with this conference?' I said, 'I am studying in England and I am reading your reports from the German embassy.' That was the end of our conversation. He obviously got a bit alarmed and didn't speak to me at all for the rest of the conference.[4]

But while he shied away from Hauner he could not miss this chance to meet Silver, their first meeting since they had parted in Kabul. Hauner even managed to photograph the meeting between the spy and his German spymaster although Witzel was careful not to show his face. It was at that meeting with Silver that Witzel learnt that Silver had spied for the Soviets and the British. However, as though to compensate, Silver told Witzel how he had helped 'Indian freedom fighters' arrested by the British during the war as Axis agents, apparently claiming that in many cases he had arranged their release.

As Hauner told me:

> If Silver really told Witzel this story then this was an outrageous claim. These agents were executed by the British—unless they agreed to be turned round and work with the British against the Germans. When I met Witzel in 2008 in his home in Munich I confronted him with the testimony of Ganguli that he, along with many of his comrades, were arrested by the British because of Silver's treachery. I suspect Witzel told me this story in order to soften the impact of his 'late discovery' of the true story of Silver. He could not have discovered in Calcutta in 1973 that Silver worked for the Soviets. He must have suspected that when he and Doh were forced to leave Afghanistan in September 1943. They left under British and Soviet pressure, and Witzel must have realised Silver was feeding information about them to these two Allies. And while he was back in Germany by the time the Soviets tried to blackmail Rasmuss and revealed to him that Silver was their agent, in Berlin he must have heard what had happened.[5]

Witzel's very presence in Calcutta was testament to how good the post-war years had been to him, in contrast to many others who served the Nazis, including his Kabul boss Hans Pilger. At the end of the war the Russians had insisted that Pilger be handed over to them and he never returned home, presumably perishing in some Soviet gulag. Witzel, having had the good fortune to return home under British auspices, was never going to disappear. By 1952 he was again working for the German Government, the *Bundesstelle für Auslandsinformation*, a branch of the German Foreign Office (AA). Between 1952 and 1973 he visited India regularly, preparing each year a comprehensive annual report of statistical data about the country.

When Hauner met Witzel in 2008 he found him living in a nice villa with an even nicer garden in Graefelfing, a little suburb of Munich, and consoling himself with the notion that Silver was a freedom fighter. How this meeting between the spy and the historian came about is itself fascinating:

> He had felt offended by my comments in my book on his amateurish behaviour and naivety as the head of the German spy ring in Kabul 1941 to 1943, and suddenly emailed me in August 2008 asking me to come and see him. He told me to come at 3.15 precisely, not a minute later or earlier. As we sat down to talk he insisted that he wanted to make a 'declaration'. This was that R.K. (using Silver's Muslim code name of Rahmat Khan) was not an agent but India's *Freiheitskämpfer*—Freedom Fighter—who also happened to be a Communist working for the victory of the Soviet Union. That was normal, he said, in Third World countries in those days, not an exception. He warned me that I was not to argue about this. I must say I considered the 'Freedom Fighter' epithet for Silver a curious misjudgement on the part of a former intelligence officer.[6]

By this time, however, Witzel had little reason to remember the past accurately or accept what a fool he had been. For Silver the 1973 conference was more important. After long years of silence he was coming out, and it provided him with a very good opportunity to judge how the Indian public would receive his lies. Despite what Ganguli had said, with the razor-sharp observation that had served him so well during his spying career he could quickly see that the way he had spun the story of his war years had gone down very well with Bose's followers. Silver had little reason to fear he would be rumbled. Fleming had died two years earlier. The British, before leaving, had destroyed the records of the IB and other intelligence work. One man in India could have proved him to be a liar. However, here Silver was in luck.

That man was Uttam Chand. On his release in 1945 he had written a book called *When Bose was Ziauddin* which, given that the British were still in power, dealt mainly with how he had acted as a host for Bose in Kabul and told nowhere near the full truth. After Indian independence he could have done. For although he had worked for the Russians he had certainly not worked for the British, indeed had been jailed by them where, as we have seen, the CID had told him that Silver worked for the British. But then his career had taken a strange path. One group of delusional Bose followers, encouraged by some members of the family, have always refused to believe Bose had died in the air crash. Uttam Chand joined them, and in 1962 formed an organisation to welcome Bose's return. Exactly two years after the 1973 Calcutta conference he announced that a certain holy man called 'Tulsibaba of Mathia' would appear and reveal himself to be Bose. Since the day chosen would have been Bose's 79th birthday it could not have been sweeter, and 100,000 people gathered at a park in Kanpur. But Bose failed to appear. Uttam Chand was beaten up by the incensed crowd and had to be rescued by the police.[7] Sometime later when I interviewed Uttam Chand he refused to accept he was playing his own deception game, and insisted Bose was still alive—'But he is Krishna.' Then, having identified Bose with one of Hinduism's greatest gods, Uttam Chand went on to say, 'He could live to be a hundred and fifty. He is immortal.'[8] Uttam Chand had become so delusional that when I interviewed him at his home in New Delhi in October 1977 looking at me straight he said·

I was with Netaji on 24, 25, 26 December 1976 in India in Dehradun. He came to the shop of my brother-in-law at Dehradun. They informed me. I went there. Between December 1974 and 1976 I stayed with him for 10–15 days right up to December 1976 at 12 o'clock at night. Once I was called to Shaulmari Ashram by express telegram [Some of Bose's delusional followers believed he took shelter there after the war and lived as a holy man called Shaulmari Baba]. I was with him for two days. He was roaming hither and thither. Sometime he was in Benares. He went to Sadhana [meditation] on 2 January 1977. Before he went for Sadhana he said, 'Like Christ and Muhammad when I come out crores [1 crore = 10 million] of people will be with me.' About the air crash there was nothing. All is humbug. I don't accept his marriage.[9]

Whether Uttam Chand was spouting all this nonsense to remain in the public eye is difficult to say. But the effect was it reassured Silver that he had nothing to fear from the only man who could prove him to be a liar.

In June 1976 Silver published his memoir, from which I have quoted. An official publication of the Communist Party, it had a fulsome introduction by Chinmohan Sehanavis which praised the book for being 'an authentic account of the subsequent contact maintained with Subhas Chandra Bose after he had left Kabul. And all this comes from one who happened to be throughout Subhas Chandra Bose's sole companion and guide—Bhagat Ram Talwar'.[10]

The book was very carefully constructed, the first part setting out how Silver's family had always fought for India's freedom and even sacrificed a son for a cause, making it a 'family of martyrs'. The second part contained detailed descriptions of the journey with Bose, with Silver's actual spying career confined to 80 pages out of a 267 page book. The book also emphasised that the Germans would have come not as liberators but as conquerors and to make sure the reader understood Nazi plans there was a map captioned 'Hitler's plan for the invasion of India'. Silver went on to say that during the war he had wondered:

> ... if they at all reach the Indian border, will they come in as friends and liberators of Indian people or as invaders of India? The answer to this question became absolutely clear to me where I recalled to my mind the past experience of my dealings with them and their behaviour, as Germans. The intention was only *one* and that was if an opportunity comes to *invade India and occupy it* [italicized in the original].[11]

The editor of Silver's book, who may also have been the ghost writer as Silver was not proficient enough in English to write such a book, in a footnote acknowledged that Bose's view of 'our enemy's enemy is our friend' was not the view of the CPI, more so after Hitler's attack on the Soviet Union:

> ... the question of continuing to help Subhas was a very complex one. Ultimately it was decided to continue the contact with him on the ground that, if handled cautiously, the step would help strengthen us politically, organisationally and technically when the time came for our inevitable post-war uprising against the British master. Thus Bhagat Ram [Silver] had a delicate and extremely hazardous role to play which he did successfully till the end as the unfolding narrative here will amply bear out.[12]

The editorial comment was fascinating because in order to protect Silver's deception the party was now also lying about its own role as India became independent. Then, far from celebrating the departure of 'the British master', the communists refused to accept independent India as genuine, and launched a violent struggle to destroy it. It was only after this failed that it changed tack, and decided to take part in democratic politics and became the first Communist party in the world to win power through the ballot box. But, as a result of the schism between the Soviets and Chinese communists, the party itself had split, and Silver's book had been brought out by the original Communist Party, which was gradually losing support to the Chinese-influenced newer party and was keen to draw a veil over its wartime collaboration with the British and its denunciation of Bose. By the time the book was published some of the Communists were even admitting that their portrayal of Bose was wrong, and Silver was a wonderful tool for proving that not all Communists worked against Bose. Why, here was a man who had helped him escape, and throughout the war worked for him in league with the Italians, the Germans and the Japanese!

Silver was not the only one who lied in this book. So did highly placed Communists, in particular, Cheena. We have seen what happened to Cheena and

Ram Kishan when they went to the Soviet Union, and how Cheena left Ram Kishan behind in a Soviet sanatorium. An appendix to Silver's book had what was called 'Interview with Achhar Singh Cheena' where Silver questioned him about his journey to the Soviet Union. But, instead of admitting he had abandoned his comrade to the Soviets to die a lonely death far from home, Cheena brazenly lied. He told Silver, 'We started towards the Russia-Afghan border and there we had to cross the river Amu (Oxus), and while crossing the river Amu, Ram Kishan was washed away by the fast current of the river and got drowned while I succeeded in crossing the river.'[13]

We cannot say whether Silver knew Cheena was lying. Given that he considered Ram Kishan his political guru it is reasonable to assume that in this case it was Silver who was deceived by Cheena. We have examined many of the lies Silver told, but this lie by Cheena was quite the most callous. Like Silver, though, Cheena was confident he could get away with it, as he was sure the file that contained his confession, telling the truth of what happened to Ram Kishan, would never emerge.

Silver's final word of what he did during the war came when, between 13th and 15th May 1980, he was interviewed by the Oral History Project of the Nehru Memorial Museum Library, with the interview conducted in a blend of Urdu and Hindi, the two languages he was most familiar with. After repeating the story he had told in his memoir of how he merely collected information from the Axis and gave it to his communist party leaders the interviewer suggested to him that, given the Indian communists were then in an alliance with the British, some of his answers sounded 'very contradictory'. Was it not possible that the communist party shared the information with the British? Silver's response was so outrageous as to almost beggar belief. He now presented Teja Singh Swatantra, whom he very respectfully in the Indian way called Swatantraji, as the joint author of the reports Silver had presented to the party. Indeed he claimed that 'primarily he used to collect the material…at times he himself made the reports'. And that as 'I had very strong anti-imperialist and anti-British sentiments' there was no question of working for the British. Then he went on to emphasise to the researcher that he had had a conversation with the party about what they were doing with this information.

> I told them that you are supporting them [the British] in their war efforts, you do propaganda and publicise them, you have called this the People's War Policy … Now if you tell this [my information] to the British then in my opinion this would leave us crippled in the post-war period. We should be very cautious about this. That is why as far as I can think of they did not share details of my role with the British.

Of course, unlike us, the researcher conducting the interview did not know of his links with Fleming and the British so the poor man could not expose Silver's lies. As it happens it was soon after this that I also came in contact with him. He was living in Uttar Pradesh, in northern India, the country's most populous state. When I published the first edition of my biography of Subhas Bose he wrote to me, a letter that summed up the man rather well both in his use of English and also the way he upbraided me saying, 'You might have presented some copies to some of your friends. But you have forgotten me.' So having made me guilty he asked me to send him a copy of my book which I did.

I did not hear from him again. Then, as if he had made sure his version of history would prevail, he disappeared from view just as he had done after 1945 and died sometime in 1983. We do not know how and where he died.

For Silver this was clearly his last service for the Communist party. He had served it during the war, and now with India free he was keen to reclaim its reputation and prove that it was not the anti-national party its opponents claimed it was. It can be argued that he succeeded in his mission. The Indian Communist Party has never owned up to his role during the war, communist historians have not revealed what exactly happened between the party and the British in any convincing detail, and Silver's story remains a mythicized Communist contribution to the Indian struggle for freedom. But while this narrative may be necessary for the Communists, and is even understandable, it has meant that the many-layered story of how India won freedom, of the war's place in that quest, and what Silver really did, has been obscured. And will remain so.

It is, of course, not easy to come to terms with wars. Western Europe has, thanks to Germany acknowledging what the Nazis did. But in the eastern half of the continent the war is still a live issue, as the struggles between Russia and Ukraine and the problems in several other parts of the former Communist-ruled Eastern Europe show. In Asia the war is more contentious still, and casts a huge shadow over the relations between Japan, Korea and China, with the latter two nations feeling that unlike Germany, Japan has never acknowledged its war crimes, many of which were truly monstrous. Indeed, Japan tries to present itself as a victim because it was the only country to be devastated by the atom bomb. India, by contrast, should be able to do so.

For all its repressive nature, inherent in a colonial rule of whites over browns, British occupation of India does not compare with Japan's brutalities in Korea and China. As to how India secured its freedom, there is increasing evidence that many Indians no longer believe Gandhi just waved his magic wand of non-violence and the British fled. It was much more complicated than that. But for the Indian Communists to come clean and admit the role Silver and the party played is clearly impossible.

But just like the Indian communists the British too have huge problems with their war history, particularly when it comes to dealing with those from the brown and black empire who fought for them. Now much is made of the Indians who fought for the British in the two wars with British politicians fond of talking of 'our shared history', words that imply there was equality between the Indians and their white rulers. At no time is any attempt made to accept that these Indians were not fighting to preserve their freedom for the simple reason they were themselves not free. They were fighting to preserve the right of their white rulers to continue to run an empire which denied them freedom. This refusal to accept facts can make celebrations of how Indians and the British fought together for freedom in the two wars somewhat absurd and I was made very aware of this when in March 2016 I went to a ceremony held in London to honour the Indian soldiers who had fought in the First World War. The event at the Memorial for the Indians at Constitution Hill was moving. And to look at the faces of the white Chelsea pensioners hesitatingly munching their first onion bhaji and other Indian snacks was rather sweet. What jarred were the speeches and, in particular, that of John Whittingdale, the then Culture Secretary. Having emphasised that this was a fight for freedom he described how the Australians soldiers in Gallipoli welcomed the Indians and ate Indian food. In fact the white Australians found it difficult to tell the Indians from the Turks and in one case an Australian officer mistaking a Turkish soldier for an Indian paid for it with his life.

But Whittingdale ignored such well documented facts and painted a picture of one happy family where everyone was equal. Nothing could be further from the truth. As we have seen Australia was then a self-governing dominion while the British cabinet felt it would take Indians 500 years to rule themselves. And in any case the ministers felt brown people could not aspire to the sort of parliamentary democracy the British had granted their white Australian brethren. I would not expect the minister to be familiar with old Cabinet minutes but for one of his advisers who, I suspect, drafted the speech, not to know the difference in the status between the Indians and the Australians during the First World War indicates an astonishing lack of knowledge. A start in coming to terms with history as it happened rather than how we think it happened would be to acknowledge what Silver did, maybe even give him a posthumous medal. He would certainly deserve such an honour much more than the German Iron Cross Rasmuss and Witzel gave him in Kabul. It would be a gesture to understand this extremely complicated strand of British war history and how the non-white empire fitted into the story. However, even as I make this suggestion I realise that it is extremely unlikely that either the Indian communists or the British can face the truth. For both myths, rather than historical facts, are more comforting.

The result is that, 75 years after Silver first started shuttling back and forth between Peshawar and Kabul, spying for the Russians and the British in what was for him the larger cause of securing Allied victory over the Nazis, this story has had no closure. In fictional spy stories that is acceptable. In real life it distorts history and prevents an understanding of the past. But then, if Silver were alive today, he would say that is how even genuine spy stories should end. He remains a real life Kim and proof that truth can often be stranger than fiction, even fiction created by such a master of the art as Kipling.

APPENDIX 1

Chronology

Year	Date	World and Indian background	Events concerning Silver
1908	November		Silver born in the village of Ghalla Dher in the North-West Frontier Province of India.
1930	5 April	Gandhi picks up salt by the seaside and launches his non-violent campaign to free India from British rule.	
	April		Silver joins Gandhi's campaign and is jailed.
1931	9 June		Hari Kishan, Silver's brother is executed by the British after a botched attempt to assassinate the Governor of Punjab.
1933	30 January	Hitler comes to power.	In March 1933 Silver, jailed for his part in the freedom struggle against British rule, is released. He resumes political activity organising the non-violent protest against British rule in Ghalla Dher and surrounding areas.

1936			Silver helps the Congress in elections for the NWPF Assembly.
1936	25 November	German and Japan sign Anti-Comintern pact.	
1936–37		Military campaign against the Faqir of Ipi following tribal disturbances in Waziristan.	Silver masterminds the election of his oldest brother, Jamuna Das, to NWPF Assembly.
1937	7 July	Japan invades China.	
	8 July	The Saadabad Pact is signed by Afghanistan, Iran, Iraq and Turkey.	
1938			Silver starts agitation for land reform, is arrested and only released after Gandhi's intervention.
	13 March	Anschluss, Germany annexes Austria.	
	13 June	The Shami Pir proclaims Amanullah the lawful King of Afghanistan and marches on Kabul.	
1939			Silver becomes member of Kirti, the Punjab based communist party.
	July	Afghanistan proposes a joint defence scheme with Britain against Soviet aggression.	
	23 August	Nazi–Soviet Pact of Non-Aggression.	

26 August	Anglo-Afghan discussion in Kabul on joint intelligence measures against Germans.	
1 September	Germany invades Poland.	
3 September	Britain and France declare war on Germany.	
6 September	Afghanistan proclaims neutrality.	Silver in Chitral, exploring the tribal areas between India and Afghanistan, hears of the start of the Second World War.
17 September	Soviet troops invade Poland.	
30 November	Soviet invasion of Finland.	
12–16 December	Anglo-Afghan military negotiation in Kabul. Mutual Assistance Agreement.	
1940 February		Silver is asked by party to develop contacts in the tribal areas and organise anti-British sabotage. Meets Sodhi for the first time.
24 March	Pakistan Resolution proclaimed by Jinnah in Lahore.	
May		Silver gets married and a fortnight later is asked to get ready to escort an important person to Kabul.
10 May	British occupy Iceland.	
10 June	Italy declares war on France and Britain.	

	2 July	Subhas Bose arrested in Calcutta for anti-British activities.	
	1 August	Greater East Asia Co-Prosperity Sphere proclaimed in Tokyo.	
	13 August	Start of the Battle of Britain.	
	2 December	Bose is released from prison.	
1941	17 January	Bose leaves his Calcutta home disguised as a Muslim in the dead of the night, the first step of a journey which will end in Berlin.	
	21 January		Silver meets Bose for the first time in Peshawar.
	25 January		Silver leaves Peshawar for Kabul on his first trip, accompanied by Bose.
	1 February		Silver and Bose reach Kabul.
	17 February	Hitler orders a study be prepared for a military advance from Afghanistan to India.	
	23 February		Silver meets Quaroni, Italian ambassador in Kabul for the first time.
	18 March	Bose leaves Kabul for Moscow and Berlin.	
	19 March		Silver leaves Kabul for Peshawar at the end of his first trip.

23 March		Silver reaches Peshawar from Kabul after first trip.
31 March	Rommel starts Axis offensive in Libya. Pro-Axis coup in Iraq.	Silver goes to Calcutta and meets Sarat Bose, brother of Subhas.
2 April	Bose arrives in Berlin.	
20 April		Silver leaves Peshawar for his second trip to Kabul accompanied by Sodhi and Ganguli.
May		Silver reaches Kabul, his second visit.
2 May	British, using Indian troops, commence hostilities in Iraq and by the end of the month force coup leaders to flee.	
26 May		Silver meets Karl Rasmuss, German Abwehr agent for the first time.
8 June	British invade Syria.	
11 June	Hitler's directive no. 32 (Post-*Barbarossa* operations).	
14 June		Silver leaves Kabul for Peshawar at the end of his second visit
22 June	Operation *Barbarossa*, Hitler's invasion of Russia.	Silver reaches Lahore.
7 July		Silver reaches Kabul for his third visit.

14 July	Allied forces complete conquest of Syria and Lebanon.	
Sometime in July		Silver meets Mikhail Andreyvich Allakhverdov. NKVD chief in Kabul, for first time.
Sometime in July		Two more Abwehr agents, Wilhelm Doh (codename Giessen) and Zugenbuhler (codename Rashad) arrive in Kabul.
27 July	Japanese troops land in Indochina.	
11 August	The Atlantic Charter is signed, promising freedom for all but Churchill says it does not apply to India.	
Mid-August		Silver leaves Kabul at end of third visit. On his return to India visits Calcutta for the last time and deceives Bose's followers about his intentions.
25 August	Anglo-Soviet occupation of Iran, a neutral country.	
3 or 4 September		Silver leaves India for Kabul for fourth visit.
14 September		Silver arrives in Kabul for fourth visit.
15 September		Silver finally enters Russian embassy in Kabul declaring his allegiance to the Communist cause.

	Beginning October	Silver reaches India after fourth visit to Kabul.
	29 October	Expulsion of non-diplomatic Germans from Afghanistan.
	5 November	Imperial Conference in Tokyo decides on Pacific War.
	Early November	Silver returns for a secret fifth visit to Kabul.
	28 November	Hitler meets the Grand Mufti of Jerusalem.
	7 December	Japan attacks Pearl Harbor, launching the Pacific War.
	14 December	Germans retreat from Moscow marking the first defeat for Hitler's Army.
1942	12 January	Silver arrives in Kabul for sixth visit.
	12 January	Sodhi arrested by British police in Delhi.
	15 February	Fall of Singapore.
	27 February	Bose's first broadcast on Azad Hind Radio.
	18 March	Fall of Rangoon.
	5 April	Hitler's directive no. 41 (advance to the Caucasus).
	5–9 April	Japanese raid on Ceylon.

Around 10 April		Silver exhaustively questioned by Russians in Kabul.
1 May	Japanese take Mandalay; The Congress call on Britain to set India free.	
16 May		Silver leaves Kabul for India at end of sixth visit.
25 May		Afghan government expel Uttam Chand from Kabul.
27 May	Hitler receives Bose.	
4 June	Battle of Midway, the turning point in the Pacific war.	
21 June	Tobruk surrenders to Rommel.	
27 June		General Alexander Ossipov (NKVD agent) tells George Hill in Moscow about Silver and offers to share him with the British.
28 June	German offensive in southern Russia opens.	
24 July	The British lift the ban on the Communist party of India.	
8 August	The Congress passes its historic resolution calling on the British to Quit India. Within hours Gandhi and all the Congress leaders are arrested.	
16 August		Silver leaves India for Kabul.

26 or 28 August		Silver arrives in Kabul for seventh visit.
10 September	Some Indian prisoners of war in Japanese hands set up the First Indian National Army.	
9 October	Mutiny of Indian volunteers in Italy.	
23 October	Battle of El Alamein opens.	
25 October		Silver leaves Kabul after seventh visit. Russians tell him that they have agreed to share him with the British and instruct him on what to do when he sees the British.
28 October		Silver arrives in Lahore.
29 November		Silver arrested by Punjab police, provides a detailed confession and agrees to work for the British.
21 December	INA dissolved by its founder Mohan Singh.	
Late December		Silver leaves India for his eighth visit to Kabul.
1943	January	German Army withdraws from the Caucasus.	
	2 January		Silver arrives in Kabul.
	February– May	The first Chindit expedition .	
	2 February	Germans surrender in Stalingrad, the turning point of the war in Europe.	

9 February	Bose leaves Germany for Japan by submarine.	
12 March		Meeting in Bletchley Park about Silver, attended by all branches of British intelligence. Kim Philby sends report on the meeting to the Soviets.
20 March	British use repressive measures to quell unrest in India and Major General Lockhart, the India Office military secretary says that India is now 'an occupied and hostile country.'	
2 April		Silver leaves Kabul at end of eighth visit.
27 April		Silver arrives back in India.
29 April		Silver arrives in Delhi to meet Peter Fleming. The British provide Silver with accommodation and money in Delhi.
27 May	British launch joint action with Soviets to force Afghan government to expel Axis diplomats from Kabul.	
14 June	Bose arrives in Tokyo.	
1 August	Japan gives puppet regime in Burma 'independence'.	
1 September		Silver arrives in Kabul for his ninth visit.
3 September	Allied invasion of Italy	

8 September	Italy surrenders.	Rasmuss introduces Silver to Inouye, Japanese attaché in Kabul.
Sometime in September		Witzel and Doh are expelled from Kabul after Silver tells the British about them.
23 September		Silver leaves Kabul for India at end of his ninth visit.
29 September		Silver arrives back in India.
1 October		Silver reaches Delhi to meet Peter Fleming.
2 October		High powered meeting at MI6 HQ in London *re.* Silver.
14 October	Japan gives puppet regime in Philippines 'independence'.	
21 October	Bose proclaims Provisional Free India Government in Singapore.	
29 October	Germany, Japan and a total of nine countries, including Thailand and Croatia, recognise Azad Hind Government.	
Throughout the year	Three and a half million Bengalis die of starvation as Churchill's war-time cabinet refuse to divert shipping to feed the starving Bengalis.	
1944	4 February	The Japanese offensive from north western Burma in Arakan opens.

	Sometime in February		Rasmuss leaves Kabul.
	15 March	Japanese offensive in Assam	
	13 April		Silver leaves Delhi for Kabul for his tenth trip.
	Beginning of May		Silver arrives in Kabul.
	25 May		Silver leaves Kabul.
	6 June	D Day.	
	7 June	Japanese retreat from Imphal and Kohima.	
	9 June		Silver returns to Delhi.
	18 July	Tojo's Cabinet resigns.	Silver leaves Delhi for Kabul for his eleventh trip.
	20 July	Bomb plot against Hitler.	
	3 August		Silver reaches Kabul.
	5 September		Silver leaves Kabul at the end of his eleventh visit.
	24 September		Silver reaches Delhi.
1945	1 January	Allied offensive in Burma opens.	
	5 March		Silver leaves Delhi for twelfth and last visit to Kabul.
	26 March		Silver arrives in Kabul.
	27 April		Silver leaves Kabul for India having failed to see the Russians.

	30 April	Hitler commits suicide.	
	3 May	Rangoon abandoned by Japanese.	
	6 May		NKVD tell Hill in Moscow that Silver is no longer welcome.
	7 May	Unconditional surrender of Germany. War ends in Europe.	
	17 May		Silver returns to Delhi from Kabul for the last time.
	6 August	Atomic bomb dropped on Hiroshima. Soviet Union declares war on Japan.	
	9 August	Atomic bomb dropped on Nagasaki.	
	14 August	Unconditional surrender of Japan. End of war in the Pacific.	
	18 August	Bose dies in air crash.	
	End August		Silver is paid unspecified amount by the British and returns to Ghalla Dher for work in the tribal areas.
1947	15 August	India becomes an independent country. Pakistan is created as a homeland for Muslims of the subcontinent.	
1948	31 January	Gandhi is assassinated by a Hindu extremist.	

26 February	Silver arrives in India from Ghalla Dher having decided that with his province now part of Pakistan and his family already in India he must join them.
Sometime in 1983	Silver dies.

Money given to Silver by the Axis powers

Date	Paid by whom	Amount in today's money	Notes
May 1941	Italians	£19,443	
June 1941	Italians	£77,669	Silver gave the British a lower figure of £34,946. The figures I have quoted are based on Quaroni's telegram to Rome
July–August 1941	Italians	£75,953	
September–October 1941	Germans	£1,521,750	
November–December 1941	Germans	£145,335	
January–April 1942	Germans	£195,108	
October 1942	Germans	£106,500	
15 July 1943	Germans	£85,933	Money paid to Silver's courier
September 1943	Germans	£221,761	
September 1944	Japanese	£63,212	
Total		£2,512,664	

The money was paid in various currencies:

      Indian Rupees

      Afghani Rupees

      Gold sovereigns

      Pounds sterling (notes)

      US dollars

Afghani rupees were introduced in 1935 and 3.95 Afghanis were worth 1 Indian rupee, a fixed rate. Source: *Statesman's Yearbook* 1941. At the time 13 Indian rupees = £1.

Historical inflation rates have been obtained from http://inflation.stephenmorley.org/

The worth of gold sovereigns, £213 in today's money, was obtained from http://goldsovereignexpert.com/info/much-gold-sovereign-worth

The US dollar / pound sterling exchange rate in the 1940s was £1 = $ US 4.03. Source: History of the stock exchange.

For clarity the amounts in this table are shown in today's equivalent value only. The amount paid at the time, whatever the original currency, or gold sovereigns, is shown in the text of the book.

The dates given are the periods when Silver was in Kabul, always receiving the money at the end of his stay.

In March 1941 Subhas Chandra Bose and his brother Sarat paid Silver a total of £3,089.

During the war the Germans held £20.3 million, in today's money, in their safe in the Kabul embassy. This was in a mixture of pounds, dollars and gold sovereigns.

From 1943 the British provided Talwar with accommodation in Delhi including domestic help and a security guard, paid for his holidays to hill stations and other places and, almost certainly, some money. In 1945, after the end of the war, the British, according to E. W. Wace a British police officer, paid Silver "a lump sum of money for his services." The amount is not known as the British, before they left India, destroyed the files that probably contained this information. Of the five countries that Silver worked for, the Russians were the only ones who did not pay him, but took a fair amount of the money that the Nazis gave him. The only Russian payment in this entire Silver story was to Cheena, an communist associate of Silver. He was paid £1,161 in July 1941 for financing his return to India from the Soviet Union.

The Faqir of Ipi—During the war the Axis paid the Faqir a total of £1,993,428 in two payments. The Italians paid £233,058 in 1941 and the Germans paid £1,760,370 in 1942. In March 1941 the Faqir demanded £3,787,500 to be paid every other month should he succeed in provoking a revolt against the British along the entire front between British India and Afghanistan.

British Guide to Good Mullahs

Agency/district/tribal area	Total number of Mullahs	Hostile/ Most Hostile	Unfriendly	Not friendly/Not Satisfactory	not openly hostile/not well disposed	neutral /not hostile/indifferent	uncertain/doubtful	well disposed/satisfactory/calm	friendly	good	Unrated
Khyber Agency	14	1		9	3 including leading Mullah Abdul Baqi	1					
Kohat district and tribal area	4		1			2		1			
Kurram agency	7	1 Abdul Rahman - one of the two leading mullahs			2	1	3				
Bannu district and tribal area	16	4 - including leading mullah, Lutfuallah	1	2	1 - Fakir Mubarak Shah, a leading Sufi with 2000 followers	1		4	1	1	1

Settled south west of North-West frontier province	17	1		1	1		1		1	6	6 - including Qazi Muhammad Hassan, one of the leading mullahs influential among the Japs	
North Waziristan agency	11	5		1	1	3			1			
South Waziristan agency	18	6 - including Sher Ali			5 - including Fazal Din	3	3		1			
Totals	**87**	**18**	**2**	**13**	**13**	**11**	**7**	**6**	**9**	**7**		**1**

Main Characters

Surname	First name	Notes
Silver		Real name Bhagat Ram Talwar. During the war he also had other names: Rahmat Khan, Harbans Lal, Kishan Chand, Rom. The Russians also called him Bhagat Ram Gurudashal and Bhagat Ram Gumassat.
Allakhverdov	Michel Andrevevich	Code name 'Zaman', head of NKVD in Kabul.
Amanullah		King of Afghanistan 1919–1929, tried to modernise the country but was forced into exile in Italy, dying in Switzerland in 1960.
Amery	Leo	Churchill's fellow Harrovian, who was Secretary of State for India in Churchill's war cabinet. His son John joined the Nazis and was hanged for treason after the war.
Anzilotti	Enrico	Secretary of the Italian legation in Kabul and the only European to visit the Faqir of Ipi during the war.
Auchinleck	Claude	Commander in Chief of the British Army in India from 1943–1947.
Bakshi	Satya Ranjan	A Bengali revolutionary and devoted follower of Subhas Bose.

Bose	Sarat	Subhas Bose's older brother, his financier, political collaborator and a major politician in his own right.
Bose	Subhas	A charismatic Indian revolutionary who sought Axis help to free India and who Silver escorted to Kabul in 1941.
Brinckman	Kurt	A member of the SS *Sicherheitsdienst*. He arrived in Kabul in 1940 to open a dental surgery as a cover for intelligence operations.
Cheena	Achhar Singh	A prominent member of Kirti, the Punjab communist party.
Chichaev	Colonel Ivan	NKVD's man in London during the war.
Connor-Green	W. R.	First secretary, British Embassy in Kabul and SOE's man in the Afghan capital.
Doh	Wilhelm	An Abwehr agent who arrived in Kabul in July 1941 as additional wireless operator and had the codename 'Giessen'.
Engert	Cornelius van	An Austrian by birth, he was the first American minister plenipotentiary to be posted to Kabul 1942–43.
Fitin	Pavel Mikhailovich	A Siberian by birth, he headed the NKVD foreign intelligence during the wartime intelligence collaboration between the British and the Soviets.
Fleming	Peter	Author, adventurer who headed D (for deception) Division in Delhi during the war and was Silver's British spy master.
Fraser-Tytler	Sir William Kerr	British minister in Kabul (1935–1941).
Ganguli	Santimoy	A young Bengali revolutionary follower of Bose, who accompanied Silver to Kabul and was taught sabotage tricks by Quaroni.
Graur	Colonel Andrei Grigorevich	Head of NKVD's Anglo-American desk in Moscow from 1944.

Hashim	Khan	Prime Minister of Afghanistan from 1929 to 1946.
Hill	Colonel George	Head of SOE mission in Moscow during the war who liaised with the Russians over Silver.
Inouye		Japanese attaché in Kabul.
Ipi	Faqir of	A tribal guerrilla leader and fierce enemy of the British.
Khan	Abad	A Peshawar transport contractor and left wing activist who worked with Silver
Khan	Abdul Ghaffar	Known as 'frontier' Gandhi, his Red Shirt movement preached non-violence amongst the Pathans Silver was an active member of the movement.
Khan	Sahib	Older brother of Ghaffar Khan, and chief minister of Congress ministries in NWFP 1937–39 and 1945–47.
Khan	Shah Nawaz	A captain in the 1/14th Punjab Regiment of the British-Indian Army. He was a Japanese prisoner of war who joined Bose's INA and after the War was put on trial by the British.
Kishan	Ram	Silver's political mentor who was left to die in a Russian sanatorium by Cheena.
Korotkow	Alexander Mikhailovich	A prominent NKVD official operating under the name of Colonel Mikhailov tried in October 1943 to blackmail Rasmuss into becoming a double agent.
Liddell	Guy	MI5's director of counter-espionage during the Second World War.
Linlithgow	Lord	Known as 'Hopie', he was Viceroy of India 1936–43.
Magan	William	Part of Fleming's D Division in Delhi who worked with Silver to transmit false military information to the Germans.

Malhotra	Uttam Chand	Generally known as Uttam Chand. An Indian shopkeeper in Kabul, he sheltered Silver, and was effectively his sub-agent in the Afghan capital.
Menzies	Sir Stewart	Known as 'C', headed MI6 from 1939–1952.
Mountbatten	Louis	Supreme Allied Commander South-East Asia 1943–46.
Muhammad	Ali	Minister for Foreign Affairs for Afghanistan 1939–1952.
Mutaguchi	Lt General Renya	Commander of the Japanese 15th Army who tried and failed to capture Imphal in 1944.
Ossipov	Alexander	His real name was Gaik Badalovich Ovakimyan. The NKVD official who liaised with Hill over Silver he was the best known Soviet intelligence official in the west.
Otroshchenko	Andrei M	Sasha was his cover name, also used the name of Captain Raitsev, and conducted a long interrogation of Silver in April 1942.
Philby	Kim	A high-ranking member of British intelligence who spied for the Russians and defected to the Soviet Union in 1963.
Pilditch	Sir Denys	Director of the Intelligence Bureau (DIB), the British intelligence agency in India, during the war.
Pilger	Dr Hans	Head of the German mission in Kabul 1937–1945.
Quaroni	Pietro	Head of the Italian mission in Kabul 1936–1943 and the man who recruited Silver as a spy.
Rasmuss	Karl	German commercial attaché in Kabul May 1941–February 1944 and the man who lavished Nazi money on Silver.
Sainsra	Gurcharan Singh	Silver's communist colleague and fiction writer who helped concoct reports to fool the Nazis.

Shah	Mian Akbar	Politically active in the North West Frontier Province, he had been to the Soviet Union, and was often jailed by the British.
Shamir	Pir	A mysterious holy man from Syria who might have been a British agent used to destabilise Afghanistan.
Singh	Bhagat	An Indian revolutionary executed by the British and condemned by Gandhi for his use of violence to free India. He was one of Silver's great heroes
Slim	Field Marshall William	Commander of the 14th Army that defeated the Japanese at Imphal and later became Commander-in-Chief, Allied Land Forces South East Asia in 1945.
Sodhi	Harmindar Singh	Treasurer of the Kirti Party, who accompanied Silver to Kabul. He was later arrested by the British and made a full confession.
Squire	Sir Giles Frederick	British minister in Kabul 1943–1948.
Swatantra	Teja Singh	A high official of the Kirti party who Silver consulted frequently and took advice from while he worked for the British during the war.
Talwar	Gurudasmal	Father of Silver and a rich landowner.
Talwar	Hari Kishan	Brother of Silver who was executed by the British for killing a policeman during a botched attempt to assassinate the Governor of Punjab.
Talwar	Jamuna Das	Silver's eldest brother, a member of the Congress party who Silver helped get elected to the NWPF Assembly.
Talwar	Ram Kaur	Silver's wife.
Talwar	Mathura Devi	Silver's mother.
von Trott	Adam	A prominent anti-Nazi who worked with Subhas Bose in Germany during the war and was executed following the failed bomb plot against Hitler.

Witzel	Lieut. Dietrich	Head of the Abwehr in Kabul May 1941–September 1943.
Wylie	Sir Francis	British minister in Kabul (1941–1943).
Zugenbühler		Abwehr agent who arrived in Kabul in July 1941 as additional wireless operator and had the codename 'Rashad'.

Codes used in the Silver Operation by the British

First name	Surname/Place/ others including religion, nationality, organisations	Code	Narrative
Bhagat	Ram (Silver)	A	Also known as Talwar
Rakhmat	Khan	AB	
Pudshotan	Das	AC	
Sayyid	Mortas	AD	
	Almazov	AE	
	Wylie	AF	
Uttam	Chand	AX	
	Rasmuss	B	
	Anzilotti	BA	
	Pilger	C	
	Witzel	D	
	Mary (name for radio links with Germans)	DB	
	Tom (name for radio links with Germans)	DC	
Subhas	Chandra Bose	E	
	Delhi	GP	
	Kabul	I	
	Afghanistan	K	
	Kassim	LJ	
	India	M	

	Peshawar	MA
	Khyber	MG
	Iran	MM
	Iraq	MN
	North West Frontier Provinces	MP
	Rupee	MX
	Mahommedan	MZ
	Hindu	NA
	Tehran	NC
	Pathan	PC
General	Wavell	TB
	Gandhi	U
	Congress	UA
	British	VA
	American	VC
	Soviet	VD
	Germans	VE
	Allies	VP
	Viceroy	VH
	Italian	VI
	Russia	VJ
	Communists	VK
	'Bengal Volunteer'	VX
	Should not be used	YT
	Japanese	ZA
	Axis	ZD
	Rome	ZM
	Tokyo	ZQ
	Moscow	ZR
	Inouye	ZS

Endnotes

Introduction

See my biography of *Subhas Bose, The Lost Hero*, revised edition 2014.—All
references refer to this edition unless otherwise stated.

2. WO 208/773, National Archives Kew.
3. Yasmin Khan, *The Raj at War*, p. 20.
4. WO 208/773, *op. cit.*
5. War Cabinet minutes GT1252, Cab 24/17. Balfour's Memo 7 August 1917, GT1696 Cabinet Papers 24/22.
6. Patrick French, *Liberty or Death*, p. 100.
7. Mansergh and Lumby (edited), *The Transfer of Power 1942–1947*, vol. II, p. 853-4.
8. Richard Aldrich, *Intelligence and the War Against Japan*, p. 133.
9. Madhusree Mukerjee, *Churchill's Secret War*, p. 66.
10. *Ibid.* p. 205.
11. Guy Liddell, *Diaries*, Vol. II, p. 103.
12. George Orwell, *Collected Essays*, Vol. I, p. 437.
13. E. H. Carr, *The Twenty Years' Crisis*, p. 163.
14. Philip Mason, *A Matter of Honour*, p. 347.
15. WO 106/3796; *Churchill's Secret War*, *op. cit.*, p. 71.
16. Colin Smith, *Singapore Burning*, p. 86.
17. Michael Howard, *Strategic Deception in the Second World War*, vol. 5 p. 208-209.
18. Guy Liddell *op. cit.*, p. 103.
19. Thaddeus Holt, *The Deceivers*, p. 308.

Chapter 1

1. David Gilmour, *The Long Recessional*, p. 57.
2. John Colville, *The Fringes of Power*, p. 534.
3. Gabriel Gorodetsky (edited), *The Maisky Diaries*, p. 421.
4. Winston Churchill, *Frontiers and Wars* p. 118.
5. *Ibid.* p. 134.
6. Beatrice and Sydney Webb, *Indian Diary*, p. 129-130.
7. Olaf Caroe, *The Pathans*, p. 433.
8. Duff Hart-Davis, *Peter Fleming*, p. 41.
9. Webb & Webb, *op. cit.* p. 127.

10   Talwar, *The Talwars of Pathan Land and Subhas Chandra's Great Escape, op. cit.*, p. 4, p. 5.
11   *Ibid.*, p. 6.
12   *Ibid.*, p. 7.
13   *Ibid.*, p. 41.
14   *Ibid.*, p. 9.
15   *Ibid.*, p. 23.
16   Nigel Collett, *The Butcher of Amritsar*, p. 282.
17   Webb & Webb, *op. cit.*, p. 131.
18   Talwar, *op. cit.*, p. 43.
19   *Ibid.*, p. 42.
20   C. Majumdar, *History of the Freedom Movement in India*, p. 425.
21   Talwar, *op. cit.*, p. 42.
22   *Ibid.*, p. 43.

Chapter 2

1   Rajmohan Gandhi, *Ghaffar Khan*, p. 44.
2   Ghaffar Khan, *My Life and Struggle*, p. 14.
3   Antol Lieven, *Pakistan a Hard Country*, p. 390.
4   Penderel Moon (ed.), *Wavell, the Viceroy's Journal* p. 259, p. 495.
5   Talwar, *op. cit.* p. 43-44.
6   *Ibid.*, p. 13.
7   Mihir Bose, *op. cit.* p. 130.
8   Talwar, *op. cit.* p. 15.
9   *Ibid.*, p. 44.
10   *Ibid.*, p. 19.
11   *Ibid.*, p. 22.
12   *Ibid.*, p. 45.
13   *Ibid.*, p. 45-46.
14   *Ibid.*, p. 46.
15   *Ibid.*, p. 46.
16   *Ibid.*, p. 34.
17   *Ibid.*, p. 47.
18   *Ibid.*, p. 47-48.

Chapter 3

1   Talwar, *op. cit.*, p. 50.
2   *Ibid.* p. 51.
3   Charles Chenevix Trench, *Viceroy's Agent*, p. 261-262.
4   Sayad Wiqar Ali Shah, *The Ghalla Dher Movement, Studies in People's History*, p. 213, 214. I have used his article for much of the details on peasant problems in this chapter.
5   Talwar, *op. cit.*, p. 51.
6   Mihir Bose, op. cit., p. 69, 114 & 215-240

Chapter 4

1   Material on Sodhi and Cheena from their confessions to the police in the Bose Conspiracy file L/P&J/12/218 IOR.
2   William Magan, *Middle Eastern Approaches*, p. 13.

3 Talwar, *op. cit.*, p. 56.
4 *Ibid.*, p. 56
5 Cheena's confession, *op. cit.*
6 Talwar, *op. cit.*, p. 57.
7 Abad Khan's confession, File 44/25/44 Poll(I) National Archives, New Delhi.
8 *Ibid.*
9 Bhagat Ram story, WO 208/773, National Archives, Kew.

Chapter 5

1 Abad Khan's confession, *op. cit.*
2 Robert Byron, *The Road to Oxiana*, p. 283-284.
3 Mihir Bose, *op. cit.*, p. 261.
4 Talwar, *op. cit.*, p. 70.
5 *Ibid.*, p. 70.
6 *Ibid.*, p. 70.
7 *Ibid.*, p. 78.
8 *Ibid.*, p. 81.

Chapter 6

1 All references from Mihir Bose, *op. cit.*, p. 255-272 unless otherwise indicated.
2 Talwar, *op. cit.*, p. 84.
3 Bose saw much in common between communism and fascism on the basis that 'both believed in the supremacy of the state over the individual. Both denounced parliamentarian democracy, both believed in party rule. Both believed in the dictatorship of the party and in the ruthless suppression of dissenting minorities. Both believed in a planned industrial reorganisation of the country'. No democrat, he amazingly even suggested that India could work out a 'synthesis' between these two dictatorial ideologies. See Mihir Bose, *op. cit.*, p. 169.
4 Talwar, *op. cit.*, p. 91.
5 *Ibid.*, p. 93.
6 *Ibid.*, p. 96.

Chapter 7

1 Henderson (Berlin) to Foreign Office, 6 July 1937, British Library, IOR; L/PS/12/1878. Cited in Eunan O'Halpin, *Ireland and Afghanistan compared: Britain's neutral neighbours in the Second World War.*
2 Quaroni interrogation L/P&S/12/1805 IOR.
3 *Ibid.*
4 *Ibid.*
5 Talwar, *op. cit.*, p. 114.
6 Pietro Quaroni, *Diplomatic Bags*, p. 1.
7 Talwar, *op. cit.*, p. 114.
8 Robert Byron, *op. cit.*, p. 282.
9 Pietro Quaroni, *op. cit.*, for this and other references p. 110-115.
10 *Ibid.*
11 *Ibid.*
12 These and following Quaroni references, Azad Hind p. 34-37 cited in Mihir Bose, *op. cit.*, p. 267-269, p. 271-272.

13 Political Archives of the Foreign Office of Germany, cited in Sisir Bose (ed), *Netaji and India's Freedom*, p. 241.
14 FOLDER: 'Secret telegrams, Afghanistan 1941' 26 March 1941, Italian Diplomatic Archives at Farnesina, Rome.
15 L/P&S/12/1805 IOR.
16 Farnesina, *op. cit.*
17 Bhagat Ram story, WO 208/773.
18 Talwar, *op. cit.*, p. 120.
19 Mihir Bose, *op. cit.*, p. 269.
20 Talwar, *op. cit.* p. 122.

Chapter 8

1 Milan Hauner, *op. cit.*, p. 208.
2 Winston Churchill, War Memoirs, Vol. III, *The Grand Alliance*, p. 236.
3 Milan Hauner, *op. cit.*, p. 159.
4 Adolf Hitler, *Table Talk* 17-18/9/1941.
5 Anthony Eden, *Facing the Dictators*, p. 516; Ivone Kirkpatrick, *The Inner Circle* p. 97.
6 Mihir Bose, *op. cit.*, p. 332.
7 Milan Hauner, *op. cit.*, p. 25.
8 *Ibid.*, p. 435-436.
9 *Ibid.*, p. 31.
10 Mihir Bose, *op. cit.*, p. 287-290.
11 Quoted on back cover of Giles MacDonogh, *A Good German*.
12 Milan Hauner *op. cit.*, p.231-232.
13 L/P&S/12-1805, *op. cit.*
14 *Ibid.*, p. 161.
15 Milan Hauner, *One Man against the Empire*.
16 *Ibid.*
17 *Ibid.*
18 Winston Churchill, *op. cit.*, p. 134.
19 *Ibid.*
20 Jawaharlal Nehru, *A Bunch of Old Letters*, p. 252.
21 Milan Hauner, *One Man against the Empire*, *op. cit.*
22 *Ibid.* cites MSS. Eur. D.670 IOR.
23 *Ibid.*
24 Milan Hauner, *op. cit.*, p. 228.
25 Telegram 2 February 1944 from [Norweb] to Foreign, WO 208/773.

Chapter 9

1 Abad Khan's confession *op. cit.*
2 Sodhi's confession, *op. cit.*, p. 38.
3 *Ibid.*, p. 39.
4 Talwar, *op. cit.*, p. 126.
5 Sisir Bose *op. cit.*, p. 145.
6 Talwar, *op. cit.*, p. 133-135.
7 *Ibid.*, p. 134.
8 Robert Byron, *op. cit.*, p. 282.
9 Telegram 3 June 1941, *op. cit.*
10 Telegram 5/6/1941, No 267—268, *op. cit.*

11　Telegram 6/6/1941, *op. cit.*
12　Telegram 5/6/1941, *op. cit.*
13　Telegram 6 June 1941, *op. cit.*
14　The Bhagat Ram story, *op. cit.*
15　Talwar, *op. cit.* p. 137
16　Mihir Bose, *op. cit.*, Ganguli interviews May, August 1977, February 1978.
17　There is a discrepancy about when the pair left Kabul, Uttam Chand has one date, Talwar two, one in his memoir (p. 137) another in his confession. I have taken the latter, the Bhagat Ram story.
19　Talwar, *op. cit.*, p. 138.

Chapter 10

1　See File No. F44/32, Home Poll, NAI. This also has the 'jail document' of the Indian communists. John Callaghan, Rajani Palme Dutt p. 199.
2　Sodhi's confession, *op. cit.*
3　*Ibid.*, p. 41.
4　Cheena's confession, *op. cit.*
5　*Ibid.*
6　Note to Silver 17-12-1941, Bose Conspiracy Files, *op. cit.*
7　Bhagat Ram story, *op. cit.*
8　Abad Khan's confession, *op. cit.*
9　Bhagat Ram story, *op. cit.*
10　L/P&S 12/1805 IOR. See also Milan Hauner, *One Man Against the Empire.*
11　Milan Hauner, *One Man Against the Empire op. cit.*
12　20 July 1941, *op. cit.* Farnesina.
13　Bhagat Ram story *op. cit.*
14　Mihir Bose, *op. cit.* p. 346; Essays p. 343, p. 346 cited in O'Sullivan p. 170.
15　WO 106/3767 cited in Hauner, *op. cit.*, p. 313.
16　Talwar, *op. cit.* p. 140-141.
17　Bhagat Ram story *op. cit.*
18　*Ibid.*
19　There are again discrepancies in dates with Uttam Chand giving a date in September and Silver a date in August. Here I have followed Uttam Chand's dates as they seem more credible for, as we shall see, Silver clearly lied about the number of visits he made to Kabul. Uttam Chand confession *op. cit.*

Chapter 11

1　gold sovereign is worth £213 in today's money (2016). http://goldsovereignexpert.com.
2　My interview with Uttam Chand in New Delhi 20 October 1977.
3　*Ibid.*
4　Bhagat Ram story *op. cit.*
5　Essays on the history of Russian foreign intelligence, p. 346, cited in Donal O'Sullivan, *op cit.*, p. 170.
6　*Ibid.*, p. 38, p. 170
7　Uttam Chand told the British that in fact Silver did not give the Russians a report at all but told them the report he had been bringing with him for Rasmuss had been lost, because the Mohmand guide who was carrying it and some survey maps had been searched and the papers confiscated. He considered it much more likely that Silver made over the papers to Rasmuss.

This charge was made after Uttam Chand had been arrested and wanted to curry favour with the British and throw doubt on Silver's credibility. While we cannot be sure in this instance it seems unlikely that Silver lied. Uttam Chand's confession *op. cit.*

8   Bhagat Ram story *op. cit.*
9   Uttam Chand's confession, *op. cit.*
10   Sodhi's confession *op. cit.*
11   Milan Hauner, *op. cit.* p. 269, p. 271; Joan Beaumont, *Great Britain and the Rights of Neutral Countries: The Case of Iran, 1941.*
12   Winston Churchill, Vol. III, *op. cit.*, p. 420.
13   Milan Hauner, *op. cit.*, p. 271.
14   Intelligence Summary No. 32 dated 12 August 1941 File WO 208/773.
15   Uttam Chand's confession *op. cit.*
16   Interview with Uttam Chand *op. cit.*
17   2.10.43 L/P&S/12/1805.
18   Uttam Chand's confession *op. cit.*
19   Talwar *op. cit.*, p. 148.
20   Abad Khan's confession, *op. cit.*
21   Uttam Chand's confession *op. cit.*
22   Quaroni telegrams, *op. cit.*
23   As if to cover this up in his memoirs he made this a 20 day visit giving false dates of arrival and departure and claiming that he returned from Kabul an ill man suffering from fever and liver trouble and spent the next ten weeks in India under medical care.

Chapter 12

1   Uttam Chand *op. cit.*
2   *Ibid.*
3   Milan Hauner email to author of interview with Witzel 26 September 2008.
4   Talwar, *op. cit.* p. 150.
5   Quaroni, *op. cit* L/P&S/12 1805. Milan Hauner, *op. cit.* p. 511, p. 512.
6   *Bhagat Ram story op cit.* WO 208/773 for this and following accounts of meetings with Germans.
7   Mihir Bose, *op. cit.* p. 354, p. 355,p 356. WO 208/3812.
8   Milan Hauner, *op. cit.* p. 511.
9   Talwar, *op. cit.*
10   Uttam Chand confession, *op. cit.*
11   Milan Hauner, *op. cit.* p. 514.
12   Donal O'Sullivan, *op. cit.* p. 172, p. 173.
13   Talwar, *op. cit.* p. 150, p. 151.
14   IPI File. The Bose Conspiracy L/P&J/216-218 IOR *op. cit.* Lost Hero *op. cit.* p. 359.
15   Talwar, *op. cit.* p. 121.
16   *Ibid.*

Chapter 13

1   Milan Hauner, *op. cit.*, p. 107.
2   Quoted in Yasmin Khan, *op. cit.*, p. 107.
3   *Transfer of Power*, Vol. 1, Document No. 23, cited in Mihir Bose, *op. cit.*, p. 320.

4   Foundation of India Mission, 1 December 1945 HS1/203 PRO.

5   Communist Party in India, Mackenzie 26 August 1942, HS1/212 PRO.

6   *Ibid.*

7   Richard Aldrich, *op. cit.*, p. 161.

8   Mihir Bose, *The Lost Hero*, First Edition, p. 179. [This and following note are only two references to this edition]

9   *Ibid.* p. 179-180

10   This estimate was made by Lt-Commander Edmond Taylor of the American Office of Strategic Services Mission in India. Richard Aldrich, *op. cit.*, p. 156.

11   The Bose Conspiracy, *op. cit.*

12   Silver Case *op. cit.*, Mss Eur F161/180 IOR.

13   Milan Hauner, *op. cit.*, p. 513.

14   Telegram No. 175 *op. cit.*, Farnesina.

15   Abad Khan's confession, *op. cit.*

16   Uttam Chand confession *op. cit.*

17   Bhagat Ram Story, *op. cit.*

18   Telegram from Hill 27.6.42 HS 1/190 for this and following references to the offer.

19   *Ibid.*

20   *Ibid.*

21   In recent years Russian scholars have put forward different dates for when this contact was made between the British and Russians and where. Was it Moscow? Was it London? And there has also been an extraordinary suggestion that Bose was a British agent. This is so ridiculous as to require little refutation. See in particular *The Lost Hero* about British request to the Russians to try and capture Bose just before Ossipov made the offer to Hill *op. cit.*, p. 362–p. 364.

22   The Bose Conspiracy, *op. cit.* cited in *Lost Hero*, p. 365.

23   Talwar, *op. cit.*, p. 159.

24   *Ibid.*, p. 161.

25   *Ibid.*

26   Information on Afghanistan received from NKVD, HS1/190 *op. cit.*, for correspondence with Faqir.

27   *Ibid.*

28   *Ibid.*

29   *Ibid.*

30   HS1/190, *op. cit.*

31   *Ibid.*

32   Talwar, *op. cit.* p. 162.

33   Richard Aldrich, *op. cit.* p. 138.

34   Mihir Bose, *op. cit.*, p. 342.

35   Talwar, *op. cit.*, p. 163.

36   Mihir Bose, *op. cit.*, p. 366.

37   Bhagat Ram story *op. cit.*

Chapter 14

1   See *Dealing with the Devil* by Donal O'Sullivan whose chapter on Bhagat Ram uses material from my biography of Subhas Bose. In this chapter I have found his book very useful and relied on it.

2   Ben Pimlott, *Hugh Dalton*, p. 295, p. 296.

3   Patrick French, *op. cit.*, p. 170.

4   Philip Knightley, *The Second Oldest Profession*, p. 121-122.
5   Donal O'Sullivan *op. cit.*, p. 52-68.
6   Bruce Lockhart, *British Agent*, p. 320.
7   Martin Kitchen, *SOE's Man in Moscow*, Intelligence and National Security.
8   Kim Philby, *My Silent War*, p. 17.
9   HS 7/278, National Archives.
10   M. R. D. Foot, *SOE*, p. 209.
11   Donal O'Sullivan, *op. cit.*, p. 40-43.
12   G. A. Hill, *Reminiscences of Four Years with NKVD*, p. 33.
13   John R. Deane, *The Strange Alliance*, p. 50-51, cited in O'Sullivan *op. cit.*, p. 43.
14   5 October 1943, Guy Liddell, *Diaries* Vol. 2, p. 122-123.
15   Telegram 11 December 1942, HS 1/190.

Chapter 15

1   Bhagat Ram story, *op. cit.*
2   *Ibid.*
3   *Ibid.*, See Cross-examination of Silver.
4   *Ibid.*
5   *Ibid.*
6   *Ibid.*
7   *Ibid.*
8   *Ibid.*
9   HS1/191, *op. cit.*
10   Cross-examination, Bhagat Ram story, *op. cit.*
11   *Ibid.*
12   *Ibid.*
13   HS1/190, *op. cit.*
14   *Ibid.*
15   *Ibid.*
16   According to German records, or at least as conveyed by Pilger to Berlin, Silver said he had been released on bail the next day. This would suggest that in disclosing his arrest he told two lies, one to the Germans about how he secured his freedom and he then spun a different story to the British. Milan Hauner, *op. cit.*, p. 554.
17   Mihir Bose, *op. cit.*, p. 367.
18   Talwar, *op. cit.*, p. 172.
19   *Ibid.*, p. 178.
20   HS1/191, *op. cit.*
21   Talwar, *op. cit.* p. 180.
22   Hill Telegram 22.4.43 HS1 1/191: Afghanistan, Politics, Bhagat Ram Affair 1943-1945.
23   Mihir Bose, *op. cit.*, p. 370-371.
24   *Ibid.* This document from the Soviet archives was kindly supplied to me by Milan Hauner.
25   *Ibid.*, p. 371.

Chapter 16

1   Talwar, *op. cit.*, p. 184.
2   Duff Hart-Davis, *op. cit.*, p. 258.
3   Victoria Schofield, *Wavell* p. 213.

4   Duff Hart-Davis, *op. cit.*, p. 261.
5   *Ibid.*, p. 303.
6   *The Spectator* 23 August 1946.
7   Duff Hart-Davis, *op. cit.*, p. 301.
8   *Ibid.*, p. 265.
9   *Ibid.*, p. 269.
10   *Ibid.*, p. 277.
11   Hugh Trevor Roper, *The Wartime Journals*, p. 198, p. 199.
12   14 August 1942, Fleming Archives.
13   Talwar, *op. cit.*, p. 184.
14   *Ibid.*
15   *Ibid.*

Chapter 17

1   While the British stressed the situation in Kabul they were also worried by
     the rebellion of the fierce Hur sect, led by their spiritual leader, the Pir of
     Pagaro which Rasmuss and company reported wrongly as the Pir acting in
     concert with Bose's organization and the Faqir. The Pir had nothing to do
     with the Faqir, and acted quite independently. The only thing linking them
     was that both of them were part of the century old problem of British coping
     with tribes who valued their own freedom and their historic ways. The Pir
     of Pagaro's actions saw a series of terrorist attacks on railways. Combined
     with the impact of floods in Sind and Baluchistan, they seriously hampered
     rail traffic between Karachi and the North West. The British used draconian
     measures to supress the rebellion, with many laws passed including the 'Hur
     Suppression Act' in May 1942 and Martial Law imposed from June 1942 to
     the end of May 1943. During the martial law officers could shoot to death
     on sight any person suspected of being a disciple of Pir Pagaro. The Pir was
     not finally dealt with until the spring of 1943 when he was captured and
     executed. His teenage son was kept a virtual state prisoner at a school in
     Middlesex, just outside London. It turned him into an ardent cricket fan and
     after Pakistan's independence he became the first living saint to play first-class
     cricket. See Peter Oborne, *Wounded Tiger*, p. 91-92.
2   7 May 1943 HS1/191 Bhagat Ram Affair, *op. cit.*
3   *Ibid.*, 10 May, 1943.
4   *Ibid.*
5   *Ibid.*
6   *Ibid.*
7   My Uttam Chand interview, *op. cit.*
8   7 May 1943 HS1/191 Bhagat Ram Affair, *op. cit.*
9   *Ibid.*
10   *Ibid.*
11   *Ibid.*
12   *Ibid.*, Hill telegram 1 June 1943.
13   *Ibid.*, 3 June 1943.
14   *Ibid.*
15   *Ibid.*
16   William Magan, *op. cit.*, p. 18.
17   The story Magan tells in his book [*Middle Eastern Approaches* p. 16, p. 17]
     is that in January 1942 Pilditch asked him to come to his home for a chat
     and told him: 'a promising double agent case, known as the Silver case, had

been initiated by the Intelligence Bureau, who were using it to send false information to the German legation in Kabul. He would like me to study the possibility of having a link of the case to Berlin through the Middle East, to which end I was to liaise with those working DA (double agent) cases from Persia and the Middle East'. Long after the war Magan, despite all the evidence to the contrary, kept insisting that Russians telling the British about Silver was simply 'not true. We arrested and recruited him ... and the Russians were not given a chance to see him' although DIB instructed Silver 'to give Russians copies of his reports to the German legation' [Magan interview with Eunan O'Halpin 11 September 2000]. The problem with the story are the dates. In January 1942 Silver was not in British custody. Then, as we have seen, apart from those who had read the Cheena confession, and it had had a very limited circulation, none of the British even knew about Silver. January did see Sodhi arrested but since Magan does not tell us when in January he went to Pilditch's house it is impossible to know whether he met Pilditch after Sodhi had made his confession. This had all the details about Silver. If Magan's conversation with Pilditch came after Sodhi's arrest, and Pilditch had read the confession, he could not have told Magan the British had recruited Silver. If he did he was deliberately misleading Magan. And certainly the British police in India did not believe this story as the brief note, entitled the Silver Case prepared by E. W. Wace of the Punjab police, shows: 'Shortly after Hitler's invasion of Russia ... [date inked in in red: 29 November 1942] the arrest in Lahore of a Communist absconder led to important results in the world of espionage ... interrogation of the absconder ... showed that he was a double agent, working for the Russians in Kabul while posing as a German agent in the German Kabul Embassy. Eventually he agreed to work for us now that Russia was in the war'. And Pilditch himself told a high powered meeting of all the British intelligence organisation in London in October 1943, that Silver had defected to the Russians when he discovered that Bose was not going to Moscow but to Berlin. 'He was so angry' he went to the Russians as he 'has a fanatical hatred of the Germans'. Magan's book had a fulsome dedication 'to members of the Security Service (MI5)' and half the royalties were given to the Security Service Benevolent Fund. MI5 also 'agreed to the book's publication' so this may be the version MI5 wanted to put out. And it is worth noting that after the war IPI was subsumed into MI5 and this distortion of the truth could be old India hands wanting to get credit for Silver.

18   William Magan, *op. cit.*, p. 18
19   Guy Liddell, *Diaries*, Vol. 11, *op. cit.*, p. 103.
20   *Ibid.*
21   He was not named, the information being redacted when this SOE file was lodged with the National Archives in Kew. What Vivian and the others wanted to know was how they could solve this problem of handling Silver. The unnamed MI5 officer: 'read several recent telegrams which he had received with regard to the Bhagat Ram [Silver] affair and explained the difficulties which IPI had in obtaining rapid answers to the NKVD queries. The whole problem in the exchange of information in respect of this affair was the time lag caused by the lack of direct communication between Moscow and Kabul or Delhi. Owing to NKVD insistence that this information should only go through SOE it was impossible to avoid the present channels, which are SOE Moscow to SOE London, Broadway, IPI, Delhi, Kabul and all the way back again. It was obvious that this was the

most unsatisfactory arrangement, and the DIB enquired whether it was not possible to set up a more direct means of communication [meeting with DIB 5.10.43]'. HS1/191 *op. cit.*

22 *Ibid.*
23 *Ibid.*
24 *Ibid.*, Hill telegram 28 May 1943.
25 *Ibid.*, 8 October 1943.
26 *Ibid.*
27 *Ibid.*, Hill telegram 1 September 1943.
28 *The Times* 22 June 1943.
29 14 July 1943, L/P&J/216-218, *op. cit.*, IOR.

Chapter 18

1 WO 208/30. Further details of this conspiracy and how it is developed is from this file. See also Milan Hauner, p. 334-335 and Eunan O'Halpin, *Ireland and Afghanistan compared: Britain's neutral neighbours in the Second World War.*
2 L/P&S/12/1805 *op. cit.*
3 Cypher telegram 26 April 1943 *op. cit.*, WO 208/30.
4 *Ibid.*
5 *Ibid.*, Cypher telegram SS Foreign Affairs India Office to Secretary of State for India (Wylie), 12 May 1943.
6 *Ibid.*, Letter from Wylie to Pilditch, 10 March 1943.
7 *Ibid.*
8 *Ibid.*, Cypher telegram Wylie to GOI External Affairs Dept., 1 May 1943.
9 *Ibid.*
10 *Ibid.*
11 *Ibid.*, Outward telegram Foreign Office to Moscow, 12 May 1943.
12 *Ibid.*
13 *Ibid.*, Telegram from Sir A. Clark Kerr, Moscow to Foreign Office, no. 407, 21 May 1943.
14 *Ibid.*, Cypher telegram from His Majesty's Minister Kabul to SS Foreign Affairs no. 139, Kabul 27 May 1943.
15 *Ibid.*, Cypher telegram from His Majesty's Minister Kabul to SS Foreign Affairs, Kabul 30 May 1943.
16 *Ibid.*, Cypher telegram, Inward From HM Minister Kabul to SS Foreign Affairs India Office, 3 June 1943.
17 *Ibid.*
18 *Ibid.*, Cypher telegram, Inward From HM Minister Kabul to SS Foreign Affairs India Office, 8 June 1943.
19 *Ibid.*, Cypher telegram, Inward From HM Minister Kabul to SS Foreign Affairs India Office, 9 June 1943.
20 *Ibid.*, Letter from W. J. Gallman, US Ambassador to London to R. M. A. Hankey, Foreign Office London.
21 *Ibid.*, E 3432/1757/G, Foreign Office 11 June 1943.
22 *Ibid.*
23 *Ibid.*, Cypher telegram, Outward From SS Foreign Affairs India Office to HM Minister Kabul to, 15 June 1943.
24 *Ibid.*
25 *Ibid.*
26 *Ibid.*

Chapter 19

1   Duff Hart-Davis, *op. cit.*, p. 283.
2   Letter to Hugh Toye, 6 May 1982.
3   Fleming Archives, *op. cit.*
4   Note to Mr Silver of IPI 3.9.42, L/P&J/216-218, *op. cit.*
5   Mihir Bose, *op. cit.*, p. 385.
6   *Ibid.* p. 399.
7   L/P&S/12/1805, *op. cit.*
8   Talwar, *op. cit.*, p. 187
9   Weightman to Squire 18 October 1943, L/P&S/12/1805, *op. cit.*
10 Talwar, *op. cit.*, p. 190-191.
11 Interview with Uttam Chand Delhi 20 October 1977.
12 *Ibid.*
13 Hill telegram *op. cit.*, HS1/191.
14 Telegram from London to Hill, 25 October 1943, *op. cit.*
15 Tikhomirov, p. 244 and p. 263, cited in O'Sullivan, *op. cit.*, p. 187.
16 Milan Hauner, *op. cit.*, p. 558.
17 L/P&S/12/1805, *op. cit.*
18 *Ibid.*
19 HS 1/191, *op. cit.*
20 *Ibid.* Telegram from Hill to London, 22 December 1943.
21 HS1/1910, *op. cit.*
22 *Ibid.* 17 April 1944.
23 *Ibid.* Telegram London to Hill 13 March 1944.

Chapter 20

1   This comment is in the original document and clearly inserted by a British official.
2   HS 1/191, *op. cit.*, 12 May 1944.
3   *Ibid.*
4   *Ibid.*
5   *Ibid.* 18 May 1944.
6   Talwar, *op. cit.*, p. 193.
7   *Ibid.*, p. 193-194.
8   *Ibid.*, p. 194-195.
9   *Ibid.*, p. 195.
10 Guy Liddell, *Diaries*, Vol. II, p. 213 *op. cit.*
11 Talwar, p. 196, *op. cit.*
12 *Ibid.*
13 *Ibid.* p. 197.
14 *Ibid.* p. 196.
15 The three cartoons appeared in the communist organ, *People's War*, on 19.07.42, 13.09.42 and 26.09.43 (see pages 44, 46, 53). Adhikari was editor of *People's War* for some of this period.
16 Sisir Bose (ed.), *A Beacon Across Asia*, p. 203.
17 Mihir Bose, *op. cit.*, p. 414.
18 Terence O'Brien, *The Moonlight War*, p. 88.
19 Talwar, *op. cit.*, p. 210.
20 *Ibid.*
21 *Ibid.*

22 *Ibid.*
23 *Ibid.*, p. 209.
24 Hill, Telegram 25 November 1944.
25 Bhagat Ram Affair HS1 1/191, *op. cit.*,
26 Telegram from London to Hill in Moscow, 21 January 1945.
27 Telegram London to Hill, 7 March 1945.
28 Telegram Hill to London 15 March 1945.
29 HS 1/191, *op. cit.*
30 Talwar, *op. cit.*, p. 223.
31 *Ibid.*
32 Terence O'Brien, *op. cit.*, p. 219.
33 The Silver case, *op. cit.*, MSS Eur F161/180.
34 Mihir Bose, *op. cit.*, p. 455-462 for this and following paragraphs.
35 *Ibid.* p. 459.
36 *Ibid.*, p. 460.
37 Nirad Chaudhuri, *Thy Hand Great Anarch!*, p. 795.
38 Email from Dr Shah to me 8 June 2016.
39 Talwar, *op cit.*, p. 224.
40 Silver Case, Mss Eur F161/180, *op. cit.*

Epilogue

1   My interview with Milan Hauner, London 27 April 2016.
2   My interviews with Ganguli, Calcutta, May, August 1977 and February 1978.
3   Hauner interview, *op. cit.*
4   *Ibid.*
5   *Ibid.*
6   *Ibid.*
7   *Indian Express*, 23 January 1975.
8   Mihir Bose, *op. cit.*, p. XXVI.
9   My Uttam Chand interview *op. cit.*
10 Talwar, *op. cit.*, p. viii.
11 *Ibid.*, p. 180.
12 *Ibid.*, p. 142-143.
13 *Ibid.*, p. 256-257.

Bibliography

This book is based on research in the archives kept at various libraries and government record offices around the world, supplemented by personal interviews with various individuals. In addition I have consulted the various government records which have been published in book form and also other books and articles relevant to my book.

Archival Material

India Office Library and Records, British Library London
Indian Political Intelligence

In consequence of the development of Indian anarchist activities in England in 1909, the India Office suggested (after consultation with Scotland Yard and the Government of India) that an officer of the Indian Police should be placed on deputation in England. The organisation was first called the India Political Intelligence Office but the name finally decided for this organisation in 1921 was Indian Political Intelligence or IPI. This was the Raj's MI5. The IPI's documents were opened to the public in the late 1990s. They cover the period 1913 to 1947. There are five files on the Bose Conspiracy: L/P&J/12/214-218

L P&S 12 1572—Afghanistan Annual Reports 1939–1947

L P&S 12 1805—Afghanistan, Italian Legation, Axis Intrigues, Information supplied by the Italian legation (Quaroni)

P&J 1812 L/P&J/7/792

The National Archives, Kew, London

WO 208/773—North West Frontier Politicals and Incidents

WO 208/30—February 1943–February 1944. Axis conspiracies in Afghanistan

HS1/190 vol. 1 June to December 1942—Afghanistan—Politics—SOE / Soviet/ NKVD/Relations in Afghanistan. Bhagat Ram Affair & Connected Symbols Lists

HS/191 vol. II 1943–1945—Afghanistan—Politics—SOE / Soviet/ NKVD/ Relations in Afghanistan. Bhagat Ram Affair & Connected Symbols Lists

HS1/203 and HS1/212 Far East—India—General

University of Reading, the Special Collections Service at the Museum of English Rural Life
Peter Fleming Papers

Government of Japan
Records in the keeping of the Chief of the Reference Room, Diplomatic Record Office.

Italian diplomatic archives—Farnesina, Rome
Pietro Quaroni's Secret Telegrams from Kabul 1941 and 1942 and Political reports, 1942 and 1943

Hoover Institution Archives, USA
Hill, G. A., Reminiscences of Four Years with NKVD

US Army War College Library, Ridgway Hall, Carlisle, PA
The Thaddeus Holt Collection

National Archives of India, New Delhi
Home Department Files in the political series in particular,
F44/32 for Material on Indian communism
F 44/25/44 for Abad Khan Confession

Interviews

Bhagat Ram Talwar(correspondence only), Uttam Chand Malhotra, New Delhi 20 October 1977, Ganguli, a series of interviews in Calcutta with between May and August 1977 and in February 1978, Adhikari, New Delhi 28 June 1978, Satya Ranjan Bakshi, Calcutta June 1978, Soli Batlivala, Bombay, June 1978

Official Documents

Documents on German Foreign Policy 1918–45, Series D. vols 12–13 (1
    February 1941 to 11 December 1941, English series)
Akten zur Deutschen Auswartiges Politik 1918–45 Series E, vols 1–4 (German
    Language Series)

Confidential Publications of the British Raj

During British rule the intelligence reports that the Raj's officials had gathered
    were periodically published in book form-rarely more than a hundred
    copies and with the circulation limited to top officials. Since India became
    free these have been published by Indian publishers. The relevant ones are:
Political Trouble in India 1907–17 (compiled 1917) by James Campbell Ker
Communism in India 1919–24 (compiled 1926) by Cecil Kaye
Communism in India 1924–27(compiled 1933) by David Petrie
Terrorism in India 1917–36 (compiled 1937) by H. W. Hale

Other Books and Articles

A list of all the books relevant to this topic would require a bibliography
    almost as big as this book. What follows is fairly selective:

Adamec, Ludwig W., *Historical dictionary of Afghanistan*, London, 1991
Adhikari, G., (ed.), *Documents of the History of the Communist Party of
    India:* vol. I 1917–1922; vol. II 1923–1925, vol. III A, 1926; B, 1927; C,
    1928, New Delhi, 1971–82.
Aldrich, Richard J., *Intelligence and the war against Japan,* Cambridge, 2000
Alexander, Martin, *Knowing Your Friends*, Intelligence and National Security,
    vol. 13, Spring 1998
Allen, Louis, *Sittang: The Last Battle,* London, 1973;
———,———, *The End of the War in Asia,* London, 1976
Barker, A. J., *The March on Delhi, London,* 1963
Beaumont, Joan, 'Great Britain and the Rights of Neutral Countries: The Case
    of Iran', *Journal of Contemporary History*, 1981
Bhargava, Moti Lal and Americk, Singh Gill., *Indian National Army—Secret
    Service,* New Delhi, 1988
Booth, Nicholas, *Zig-Zag*, London, 2007
Bose (ed.), Sisir, *A Beacon Across Asia; Netaji and India's Freedom,* Calcutta
    1973

Bose, Sisir K. (ed.), *Netaji and India's Freedom,* Calcutta, 1975

Byron, Robert, *The Road to Oxiana,* London, 1950

Callaghan, John, *Rajani Palme Dutt,* London, 1993

Caroe, Olaf, *The Pathans,* London, 1958

Carr, E. H., *The Twenty Years' Crisis,* London, 1948

Chand, Uttam, *When Bose Was Ziauddin,* Delhi, 1946

Chaudhuri, Nirad, *Thy Hand, Great Anarch!,* London, 1987

Chenevix Trench, Charles, *Viceroy's Agent,* London, 1987

Churchill, Winston, *Frontiers and Wars,* London, 1972

———, ———, *The Second World War,* London, 1959

Collett, Nigel, *The Butcher of Amritsar,* London, 2005

Colville, John, *The Fringes of Power,* London, 1985

Cruickshank, Charles, *SOE in the Far East,* Oxford, 1983

Draper, Alfred, *Amritsar, The massacre that ended the Raj,* London, 1981

———, ———, *Dawns Like Thunder, The Retreat from Burma 1942,* London, 1987

Eden, Anthony, *Facing the Dictators,* London, 1962

Edwardes, Michael, *The Last Years of British Rule,* London, 1963

Elphick, Peter, *Singapore the Pregnable,* Fortress, London 1995

———, ———, *Far Eastern File, the Intelligence War in the Far East,* 1930–1945, London, 1997

Farago Ladislas, *The Game of the Foxes,* London 1972

Foot, M. R. D., *SOE 1940–1946,* London 1984

French, Patrick, *Liberty or Death,* London 1997

Fujiwara Iwaichi, *F. Kikan,* Hong Kong, 1983

Gandhi, Rajmohan, *Ghaffar Khan,* New Delhi, 2008

Gilbert, Martin, *Winston S. Churchill,* vol. VII, London, 1986

Gilmour David, *The Long Recessional, the Imperial Life of Rudyard Kipling,* London 2002

Glendevon, Lord, *The Viceroy at Bay,* London, 1971

Goel Sita Ram, *Netaji and the C.P.I.,* Calcutta, 1955

Gopal, Ram, *Indian Muslims, A Political History (1858–1947),* Bombay 1959.

Gopal Sarvepalli, *Radhakrishnan, A Biography,* London, 1989

Gorodetsky (ed.), Gabriel, *The Maisky Diaries,* London, 2015

Haithcox, John Patrick, *Communism and Nationalism in India: M. N. Roy and Comintern Policy 1920–39,* Princeton, 1971

Hart-Davis, Duff, *Peter Fleming,* London 1974

Hastings, Max, *The Secret War,* London, 2015

Hauner Milan, *India in Axis Strategy,* Stuttgart, 1981

———, ———, 'One Man Against Empire', *Journal of Contemporary History,* vol. 16, no. 1, January 1981

Hitler, Adolf, *Table Talk 1941–44*, edited by Hugh Trevor-Roper London, 1953

Hill, G., *Go Spy the Land*, London, 1932

———, ———, *Dreaded Hour* , London, 1968

Holt, Thaddeus, *The Deceivers*, London, 2005

Howard Michael, *British Intelligence in The Second World War, vol.Five*, London, 1990

Ienaga, Saburo, *The Pacific War*, New York, 1978

James, Lawrence, *Raj, The Making and Unmaking of British India*, London, 1997

Khan, Shah Nawaz, *My Memories of the I.N.A. and Its Netaji*, New Delhi 1946;

———, ———, *The I.N.A. Heroes*, Lahore, 1947

———, ———, *Netaji Inquiry Committee Report*, New Delhi, 1956

Khan, Yasmin, *The Raj at War*, London, 2015

Kirby, David Gordon, *Operation Blunderhead*, Stroud, 2015

Kirkpatrick, Ivonne, *The Inner Circle: Memoirs*, London, 1959

Kitchen, Martin, *SOE's Man in Moscow* http://www.tandfonline.com/doi/abs/10.1080/02684529708432432

Knightley, Philip, *The Second Oldest Profession*, London, 1980

———, ———, *Philby, KGB Masterspy*, London 1988

Lewin, Ronald, *The American Magic*, New York, 1982

———, ———, *Slim: The Standard-Bearer*, London, 1976

Liddell, Guy, *Diaries,* vols I & II (ed. Nigel West), London, 2005

Lieven, Antol, *Pakistan a Hard Country*, London, 2011

Lockhart, Bruce, *Memoirs of a British Agent*, London, 1933

Lyett, Andrew, *Ian Fleming*, London, 1995

MacDonogh, Giles, *A Good German Adam von Trott zu Solz*, London 1989

Macintyre, Ben, *Double Cross*, London, 2012

Mackenzie, William, *The Secret History of SOE*, London, 2000

MacMunn G. F., *The Armies of India* (first published 1911) reprinted New Delhi, 2002

Magan, William, *Middle Eastern Approaches*, Wilby, 2001

Majumdar, R. C., *History of the Freedom Movement in India* (3 vols), Calcutta, 1962, 1963

Mansergh & Lumby (ed.), *The Transfer of Power 1942–1947,* volumes I–XI, London, 1970–1980

Marston, Daniel, *The Indian Army and the End of the Raj*, Cambridge, 2015

Mason, Philip., *A Matter of Honour: An Account of the Indian Army, its Officers and Men*, London, 1974

Moon (ed.), Penderel, *Wavell, the Viceroy's Journal*, Oxford, 1973

Mukerjee, Madhusree, *Churchill's Secret War*, New York, 2005

Nayer, Kuldip, *Without Fear, The Life and Trial of Bhagat Singh,* Noida, 2007

Nehru, Jawaharlal, *A Bunch of Old Letters,* Bombay, 1958

Oborne, Peter, *Wounded Tiger,* London, 2014

O'Brien, Terence, *The Moonlight War,* London, 1987

O'Connor, Bernard, *Churchill and Stalin's Secret Agents, Operation Pickaxe at RAF Tempsford*, Stroud, 2012

O'Halpin, Eunan, *Ireland and Afghanistan compared: Britain's Neutral Neighbours in the*
——,——, *Second World War,* IIIS, discussion paper no. 196, December 2006

Orwell, George, *Collected Essays,* London, 1970

O'Sullivan, Dónal, *Dealing with the Devil,* New York, 2010

Page, Bruce and Leitch, David and Knightley, Phillip, *Philby, The Spy who Betrayed a Generation,* London, 1977

Philby, Kim, *My Silent War,* London, 1968

Pimlott, Ben, *Hugh Dalton,* London, 1985

Quaroni, Pietro, *Diplomatic Bags,* London, 1966

Raghavan, Srinath, *India's War,* London, 2016

Schneer, Jonathan, *Ministers at War, Winston Churchill and his War Cabinet,* London, 2015

Schofield, Victoria, *Wavell,* London, 2006

Shah, Sayad Wiqar Ali, *Ethnicity, Islam and Nationalism,* Islamabad, 2015;
——,——, *The Ghaller Dher Movement, Studies in People's History,* Islamabad, 2015

Siddique, Abubakar, *The Pashtun Question,* London, 2014

Simmons, Mark, *Agent Cicero, Hitler's most Successful Spy,* Stroud, 2014

Singer Andre, *Lords of the Khyber* London, 1984

Singh, Mohan, *Leaves from my Diary,* Lahore, 1946
——,——, *Soldiers' Contributions to Indian Independence,* New Delhi, 1975

Sisman, Adam, *Hugh Trevor-Roper, the Biography*, London, 2010

Smith, Colin, *Singapore Burning,* London, 2005

Talwar, Bhagat Ram, *The Talwars of Pathan Land and Subhas Chandra's Great Escape,* New Delhi, 1976

Toye, Hugh, *The Springing Tiger: A Study of a Revolutionary* (reprint), Bombay, 1974

Trevor Roper, Hugh, *The Wartime Journals,* London 2012
——,——, *The Secret War*, London 2014

Van der Bijl, Nicholas, *To Complete the Jigsaw, British Military Intelligence in the First World War,* Stroud, 2015

Wavell, Lord., *The Viceroy's Journal,* London, 1973

Webb, Sydney & Beatrice, *Indian Diary,* Oxford, 1990

Webster, Jason, *The Spy with 29 Names*, London, 2014

Weinberg Gerhard L., *A World at Arms, A Global History of World War II*, Cambridge 1994

Wheatley, Dennis, *The Deception Planners*, London, 1980

Young, Peter, *World War 1939–1945*, Aylesbury, 1966